Legal Guide to Life Assurance Companies

Legal Guide to Life Assurance Companies

Kay Strang MA, LLB
Solicitor, Semple Fraser WS, Edinburgh

Butterworths
London, Dublin, Edinburgh
2000

United Kingdom	Butterworths, a Division of Reed Elsevier (UK) Ltd, Halsbury House, 35 Chancery Lane, LONDON WC2A 1EL and 4 Hill Street, EDINBURGH EH2 3JZ
Australia	Butterworths, a Division of Reed International Books Australia Pty Ltd, CHATSWOOD, New South Wales
Canada	Butterworths Canada Ltd, MARKHAM, Ontario
Hong Kong	Butterworths Asia (Hong Kong), HONG KONG
India	Butterworths India, NEW DELHI
Ireland	Butterworth (Ireland) Ltd, DUBLIN
Malaysia	Malayan Law Journal Sdn Bhd, KUALA LUMPUR
New Zealand	Butterworths of New Zealand Ltd, WELLINGTON
Singapore	Butterworths Asia, SINGAPORE
South Africa	Butterworths Publishers (Pty) Ltd, DURBAN
USA	Lexis Law Publishing, CHARLOTTESVILLE, Virginia

A CIP Catalogue record for this book is available from the British Library.

ISBN 0 406 92363 9

Typeset by Doyle & Co, Colchester
Printed by Redwood Books, Trowbridge, Wilts

Visit us at our website: http://www.butterworths.co.uk

Preface

When I worked in the insurance and investment industries, I always wished a book like this existed. Now it does, and I have to thank Michael Kerr and Tom McKean, both Fellows of the Faculty of Actuaries at Alba Life, for sharing their understanding of those areas where the law merges with the actuarial and technical. I am also indebted to Robert Surridge, solicitor, at Axa Sun Life for his review and comments on the text. Lastly, I fully appreciate the support of Semple Fraser WS over the last year, not least in providing me with access to materials and the assistance of their first-rate librarian, Isabel Hood. The law is stated as at May 2000.

K. S.

Contents

Table of Statutes

Table of Statutory Instruments

Table of European Legislation

Table of Cases

List of Abbreviations

AA	appointed actuary
ABI	Association of British Insurers
ACT	Advance Corporation Tax
AR	appointed representative
AVR	Asset Valuation Regulations
CA 1985	Companies Act 1985
DBS	defined benefits scheme
DPA 1984	Data Protection Act 1984
DTI	Department of Trade and Industry
EEA	European Economic Area
EFTA	European Free Trade Association
EMU	European Monetary Union
FA 1998	Finance Act 1998
FPS	final pensionable salary
FRS	Financial Reporting Statement
FSA 1986	Financial Services Act 1986
GAD	Government Actuary Department
GAR	guaranteed annuity rate
GMP	guaranteed minimum pension
GN	Guidance Notes
GPP	group personal pension scheme
IC(A)R	Insurance Companies (Amendment) Regulations
IC(CI)R 1990	Insurance Companies (Credit Insurance) Regulations 1990
IC(TID)R 1994	Insurance Companies (Third Insurance Directive) Regulations 1994
ICA 1982	Insurance Companies Act 1982
ICR	Insurance Companies Regulations
IOB	Insurance Ombudsman Bureau
ISA	Individual Savings Account
LAPR	life assurance premium relief
LAUTRO	Life Assurance and Unit Trust Regulatory Organisation
MFR	minimum funding requirement
OFT	Office of Fair Trading
OPS	occupational pension scheme
OPS(MFR)R 1996	Occupational Pension Scheme (Minimum Funding Requirement and Actuarial Valuations) Regulations 1996

OTC	over the counter
PEP	Personal Equity Plan
PGN	Prudential Guidance Notes
PIA	Personal Investment Authority
PP	personal pension
PPA 1975	Policyholders Protection Act 1975
PR	protected rights
PRE	policyholders' reasonable expectations
PSA 1993	Pensions Schemes Act 1993
PSA	pension scheme actuary
PSO	Pension Schemes Office
PT	pensioner trustee
RBS(RDA)(SSAS)R	Retirement Benefits Scheme (Restrictions on Discretion to Approval) (Small Self-administered Schemes) Regulations 1991
SERPS	State Earnings Related Pension Scheme
SIB	Securities and Investments Board
SORP	Statement of Recommended Practice
SSAS	small self-administered scheme
TA	tied agency
TV	transfer value
UT	unit trust
WRPA 1999	Welfare Reform and Pensions Act 1999

Chapter 1
Introduction

1. HISTORY

A. Regulation of life assurance

[1.1]
Most older life assurance companies originated in widows and orphan funds to protect the families of working men in a particular industry. Policies would be written for accident or death and underwriting decisions taken on the amount of premium. These companies would be owned by the policyholders and were often established by a private act or royal charter. The concept of 'mutuality' which is topical at the moment, describes, in relation to insurance, a company owned by those investing in its with profits funds (as opposed to for example unit linked funds) and who would share in the profits of the company. A company owned by shareholders is described as 'proprietary' and profits are divided among the shareholders and those investing in the with profit funds, usually 10% going to shareholders and 90% to policyholders.

[1.2]
As indemnity insurance in the shipping industry against loss or damage to ships had preceded life insurance, much of the early statutory and case law covering matters such as insurable interest, uberrimae fidei and other underwriting principles are part of maritime law. The early statutes on life assurance include the Life Assurance Act 1774, which prohibited wagers on human life which it distinguished from insurance by the absence of insurable interest, and the Life Assurance Companies Act 1870, which introduced deposit requirements for insurers engaged in life business following the collapse of a number of life assurance companies. There then followed piecemeal legislation which covered, inter alia, fit and proper tests for the officers of insurance companies and restrictions on the uses to which premiums could be put. These were eventually consolidated in the Insurance Companies Act 1974. Sweeping changes to the marketing and selling of life assurance were introduced by the Financial Services Act 1986 and to the operational, investment and prudential rules on the introduction of the three Life Directives[1] into UK law.

1 79/267/EEC, 90/619/EEC and 92/96/EEC. Directives are European legislation which all member states are obliged to implement via national legislation within specified time limits (usually three years). In some circumstances directives can have 'direct effect', which means that, notwithstanding the lack of implementing national legislation, the provisions of the directive can be relied upon.

B. Single market in financial services

[1.3]
The UK joined the EC[1] in 1972. The basic principles of the EC are freedom of movement of goods, services, people and capital among member states (see EC Treaty,[2] art 53 and following). In order to accomplish this, the EC set out, amongst other things, to establish a single market in financial services. Financial services can be broken down into the following four major categories:

1. Deposit taking.
2. General insurance.
3. Life insurance.
4. Investments (in stocks and shares either directly or through some pooled arrangement such as unit trusts or investment trusts).

Traditionally these services have been provided by banks and building societies, insurance companies and investment management or stock broking firms respectively.

1 The EEC changed to the EC (European Community) by virtue of the Single European Act 1987 and then to the EU (European Union) by virtue of the Maastricht Treaty 1992.
2 Previously the Treaty of Rome (which was renamed and renumbered by the Treaty of Amsterdam) which came into force on 1 May 1999 and was incorporated into UK law by the European Communities (Amendment) Act 1998.

[1.4]
Within the EC there was much variation in the provision of these services and the prudential rules governing these organisations: for example, in Germany there were very tight controls over policy conditions and the emphasis was on consumer protection, whereas in the UK the view was that regulatory control over policy conditions would stifle innovation. It was argued that in order for a single market to exist and for companies to compete on an equal footing, there had to be a level playing field throughout the EC.

[1.5]
Beginning in the 1970s the European Commission drafted a series of directives for banking, insurance (life and non-life) and investment. These directives broadly set out the minimum financial provisions within which organisations had to operate and a common regime for the remaining operational matters. It was left open to member states to adopt stricter regimes in some areas. The provisions were primarily concerned with the capital structure of these organisations, demarcating the limits of their activities, setting standards of probity for their officers, conditions of entering into contracts with customers, provision for compensation to customers and generally setting out the conditions for authorisation and subsequent supervision by the relevant government department.

[1.6]
Meeting this criteria would allow an organisation established in one member state to provide financial services in another without having to go through a further set of authorisation procedures: this is referred to as

the 'single passport'. In addition to creating a level playing field so that national organisations would not have a competitive advantage over organisations from other EC states, the prerequisite of a single market in financial services was that the public or any regulatory department from another member state dealing with these organisations would know they met certain minimum but critical criteria and that money invested with such an organisation would be safe (of course there have been a number of spectacular failures despite the regulatory controls, eg BCCI and Barings).

[1.7]

The insurance directives were brought into UK law by the Insurance Companies Act 1982 (ICA 1982) and numerous sets of regulations discussed at **[1.15]** below. The regulatory authority in the UK was the Department of Trade and Industry (DTI), is now the Treasury, and will be the Financial Services Authority once the Financial Services and Markets Bill becomes law. Equivalent legislation in the other areas of financial services are the Banking Act 1987, the Building Societies Act 1986, the Investment Services Regulations 1995, SI 1995/3275. The respective supervisory or regulatory authorities were the Bank of England, the Building Societies Commission and the Securities and Investments Board (SIB) for investment. These regulatory authorities and the regulatory regime relate primarily to the prudential supervision of these organisations, ie that they are run in accordance with the sound financial and organisational criteria in the above Acts and regulations made under them.

C. First Life Directive 79/267/EEC

[1.8]

In order to create a single market in insurance it was imperative to create a 'level playing field' for insurance companies throughout the EC. The First Life Directive 79/267/EEC therefore set out minimum standards covering authorisation, solvency margins, technical or mathematical reserves and minimum guarantee funds[1] to allow EC insurers to set up branches in other member states on an equal footing with the resident insurance companies. It also divided insurance into two categories namely 'general business' and 'long-term business' and set out the different classes of such business. It also banned the formation of any new composite insurers (ie companies which conducted both categories of business), which is discussed at Chapter 2 below. This directive was brought into force in the UK by ICA 1982. The classes of long-term business are set out at ICA 1982, Sch 1 see Appendix 3:[2]

1 See definitions at **[1.54–1.58]** below.

2 Class V 'Tontines' was defined in the First Life Directive 79/267/EEC as where 'associations of subscribers are set up with a view to jointly capitalising their contributions and subsequently distributing the assets thus accumulated among the survivors or among the beneficiaries of the deceased'; Class VI 'Capital Redemption' was defined in the First Life Directive as 'operations based on actuarial calculation whereby, in return for single or periodic payments agreed in advance, commitments of specific duration and amount are undertaken'; Classes VIII and IX were introduced by regulations following the Third Life Directive 92/96/EEC and relate to a type of group welfare assurance peculiar to France and life assurance prescribed by social insurance legislation respectively and have no application to the UK.

D. Second Life Directive 90/619/EEC

[1.9]
This directive introduced transitional arrangements relating to cross-border selling which were largely superseded by the Third Life Directive 92/96/EEC when it was introduced into UK law on 1 July 1994. It was implemented in the UK by two sets of regulations which amended ICA 1982. The regulations took effect from 20 May 1993. As ICA 1982 had already been amended by regulations following the Second Non-Life Directive 88/357/EEC (ie for general insurance), the first set of regulations (Insurance Companies (Amendment) Regulations 1993, SI 1993/174) implementing the Second Life Directive 90/619/EEC simply extended the amendments to include life business. Insurance companies authorised in one member state (ie 'home' member state) were allowed to 'actively' or 'passively' sell long-term business (except class VII business which relates to pension fund management), in another member state (ie 'host' member state). The insurance company could only sell in host states the classes of insurance it was already authorised to sell in its home state.

[1.10]
Active selling is where the insurance company advertises or markets its services in the host state and the policyholder purchases as a result of these activities. Passive selling or 'own initiative business' is where the policyholder approaches the insurance company in another member state either directly or through an IFA. Both methods of selling required home state authorisation but member states had the option to insist on host state authorisation in addition for active selling. Host states could stipulate the information to be given for authorisation and had six months from the date of application to authorise.

[1.11]
There were two other options available to member states in implementing the Second Life Directive 90/916/EEC, namely: (i) the option in art 27.1 to limit the writing of group assurance contracts on a services basis to the active regime; and (ii) the option in art 27.2 to prohibit the use of local intermediaries for own initiative business.

[1.12]
The second set of regulations, the Insurance Companies (Cancellation No 2) Regulations 1993, SI 1993/1092 dealt with policyholders cancellation rights. Member states were allowed to impose cooling-off periods of between 14 and 30 days. These regulations have now been revoked. The current regulations covering cancellation rights in respect of life policies which are also investments are the Financial Services (Cancellation) Rules 1994 which took effect from 1 January 1995. For life policies which are not investments, provisions in the ICA 1982 apply.

[1.13]
The overall effect of the Second Life Directive 90/916/EEC was rather nugatory, as most of the restrictions and distinctions were swept aside by the Third Life Directive 92/96/EEC the following year.

E. Third Life Directive 92/96/EEC

[1.14]
The following gives a brief overview of the main features of the new regime for life insurance introduced by the Third Life Directive 92/96/EEC, which has since been amended and will be explored in more detail in subsequent chapters.

(i) Legislative changes

[1.15]
The adoption of the Third Life Directive 92/96/EEC and Non-Life Directive 92/49/EEC completed the single market in insurance. They were implemented by the UK on 1 July 1994. The implementing regulations were:

1. The Insurance Companies (Third Insurance Directives) Regulations 1994 (IC(TID)R 1994), SI 1994/1696, which amended:
   - The Insurance Companies Act 1982 (ICA 1982).
   - The Insurance Companies (Credit Insurance) Regulations 1990 (IC(CI)R 1990), SI 1990/1181.
   - The Insurance Companies (Amendment) Regulations 1992 (IC(A)R 1992), SI 1992/2890.
   - The Financial Services Act 1986 (FSA 1986).
   - The Data Protection Act 1984 (DPA 1984).
   - The Policyholders Protection Act 1975 (PPA 1975).
2. The Insurance Companies Regulations 1994 (ICR 1994), SI 1994/1516, which completely replaced the Insurance Companies Regulations 1981, SI 1981/1654 (note: these were amended again in 1995 and 1996 by the Insurance Companies (Amendment) Regulations 1995 (IC(A)R 1995), SI 1995/3248 and the Insurance Companies (Amendment) Regulations 1996 (IC(A)R 1996), SI 1996/942, mainly to take account of a change in attitude to derivative controls and counterparty risk).
3. The Insurance Companies Accounts and Statement (Amendment) Regulations 1993, SI 1993/1993 amended the Insurance Companies (Accounts and Statements) Regulations 1983, SI 1983/1811 (these have since been replaced by the Insurance Companies (Accounts and Statements) Regulations 1996, SI 1996/943).

(ii) Scope of the single market in insurance

[1.16]
The central feature of the single market for insurance introduced by the Third Life Directive 92/96/EEC was the 'single passport'. This passport enables, for example, a UK company authorised in the UK, to carry on insurance business anywhere within the EC subject to a notification procedure. Consequently, compliance with financial supervisory rules for those companies carrying on insurance business in other member states will be simplified because only one set of regulatory returns will need to be filed annually. An equivalent single passport was also introduced for banks and for investment organisations.

[1.17]
If a UK company sells insurance in another EC state (whether on a services or branch[1] ('establishment') basis) the host state, although it has no power to intervene unilaterally in the financial supervision of the UK company, does retain powers under the directives to prevent persons entering into contracts and to prohibit advertising if it is considered to be in conflict with 'the general good'.[2] It can also enforce its own legal requirements other than those relating to insurance supervision.

1 'Branch' is defined in the Third Life Directive 92/96/EEC as 'an agency or branch of an assurance undertaking' and this is subject to the Second Life Directive 90/619/EEC, art 3, which states: '. . . any permanent presence of an undertaking . . . shall be treated in the same way as an agency or branch, even if that presence does not take the form of a branch or agency but consists merely of an office managed by the undertaking's own staff or by a person who is independent but has permanent authority to act for the undertaking as an agency would.'

2 Commission Interpretative Communication 'Freedom to Provide Services and the General Good in the Insurance Sector' 97/C 365/04, see Appendix 2.

[1.18]
This would mean that, in respect of a branch of a European company selling insurance in the UK while ICA 1982 and associated regulations would not apply to the branch, operations would have to be carried out within the UK legal framework which would include, inter alia, FSA 1986, which covers the selling and marketing of insurance products which fall within the definition of 'investment business'.

[1.19]
It is recognised for the single market to work supervisory authorities in each member state would have to co-operate and methods established for communicating and exchanging information. The directive does put some limit on the exchange of confidential information (see Third Life Directive 92/96/EEC, art 15 and ICA 1982, Sch 2B).

[1.20]
Certain institutions fall outwith the scope of the directive (see Third Life Directive 92/96/EEC, art 2 and First Life Directive 79/267/EEC, arts 2, 3 and 4).

(iii) Authorisation

[1.21]
UK insurers who were already authorised under ICA 1982 were automatically authorised to do the same classes of business under the amended Act. This authorisation can be extended to cover the carrying out of business in other member states but subject to the requirement of notification to the regulators in the other states.

(iv) Sound and prudent management

[1.22]
The criteria for sound and prudent management was listed in a new Sch 2A to the ICA 1982. It was intended that this will not only provide

criteria for authorisation but also a ground for supervisory intervention. The one completely new element in the list of criteria involved a collective test of the fitness and properness of the board of directors: the terms of this are identical to those contained in the legislation for friendly societies and are also similar to banking legislation. The criteria covers the following:

1. The business is carried on with integrity, due care and professional skills and the business is run by fit and proper directors, controllers, managers and main agents.
2. The business is run by a sufficient number of fit and proper persons.
3. The business is conducted in a sound and prudent manner: there are a number of tests which must be met to satisfy the supervisory authorities that the business is being conducted along those lines. Some of the criteria are a bit circular but the main points are: adequate accounting and other records and adequate systems of control; supervision of subsidiaries; having due regard to the interests of present and future policyholders and compliance with the terms of ICA 1982.

(v) Prior approval of policy conditions

[1.23]
The Third Life Directive 92/96/EEC, art 29 abolished 'prior approval or systematic notification of general and special policy conditions, scales of premiums, technical bases used in particular for calculating scales of premiums and technical provisions, forms and other printed documents which an undertaking intends to use in its dealings with policyholders'.

[1.24]
ICR 1994, SI 1994/1516, reg 4 and Sch 1 covers the information an insurance company must submit as part of its application for authorisation. The following points should be noted:

1. The DTI exercised an option (Third Life Directive 92/96/EEC, art 29) to retain prior notification of proposed (a) technical bases used for the calculation of premiums and (b) technical provision for life assurance (ICR 1994, Sch 1, para 13).
2. By virtue of Third Life Directive 92/96/EEC, art 39 the DTI could insist on non-systematic notification of policy conditions and printed documentation to insure compliance with legislation or for monitoring purposes or provision of statistical information (ICA 1982, s 44 and ICR 1994, Pt XI).
3. The IR still require systematic notification of policy conditions for tax approval but this is to be dispensed with at some future date.

(vi) Composites

[1.25]
New composites were banned. However, existing composites could continue to carry on business and operate within the single market provided they

managed their life and non-life businesses separately. Further, new 'healthcare' composite companies could be created: UK and European companies which are authorised, or are seeking authorisation to carry on long-term business are able to apply for authorisation to carry on accident and or sickness insurance business (Classes 1 and 2 in ICA 1982, Sch 2, Pt I); similarly a general insurance company authorised solely for either or both of those classes will be able to apply for authorisation to carry on all or any class of long-term business. The DTI allowed these new composites to be created in the UK (ICA 1982, s 6(c)).

(vii) Conduct of business rules

Disclosure

[1.26]
The information to be supplied to a policyholder before entering into the contract was increased (Third Life Directive 92/96/EEC, art 31 and Annex II) and had to cover information on the company and the insurance policy. The details are set out in ICA 1982, Sch 2E. The information which must be given in writing should be supplied in English unless the policyholder requests that it should be supplied in another language where that language is an official language of a member state.

[1.27]
It is an offence under FSA 1986, s 133 to make misleading statements about insurance policies which may effect a person's decision regarding a policy of insurance.

[1.28]
During the term of the insurance contract, insurance companies are under an obligation to provide information as set out in ICA 1982, Sch 2E.

Advertising and intermediaries

[1.29]
The Third Life Directive 92/96/EEC, art 41 allows freedom to advertise through any medium subject to the general good requirements.

[1.30]
The form and content of advertisements are contained in ICR 1994, SI 1994/1516, Pt VII, regs 35 and 36.

[1.31]
Any person advertising insurance who is connected with the insurance company has to disclose information about his connection (see ICA 1982, s 74).

Cancellation

[1.32]
This had already been dealt with under the Second Life Directive 90/916/EEC, art 15 and is implemented by ICA 1982, s 76.

1 Where there is an overlap with conduct of business provisions in FSA 1986, it is the FSA which is to apply instead of ICA 1982 (see Chapter 7).

(viii) New DTI (now HM Treasury) powers

[1.33]

> 'Every member state shall take all steps necessary to ensure that the competent authorities have the powers and means necessary for the supervision of assurance undertakings with head offices within their territories . . .' (The First Life Directive 79/267/EEC, art 23(3) as substituted by Third Life Directive 92/96/EEC, art 10.)

[1.34]
The powers of the DTI (now HM Treasury) were extended as follows:

1. To veto managers and shareholders who are not 'fit and proper'. (Note: the criteria for fit and proper, although based on the obligations that already existed in ICA 1982, a new collective test was introduced (see **[1.23]** above)).
2. Powers to freeze the assets of an insurer were widened.
3. Information gathering and investigative powers were also extended to include, amongst other things, power to requisition an independent report and to obtain information on a company's premises without a court order.
4. To enable the Secretary of State to suspend a UK company's authorisation immediately. (Note: it was considered that suspension of authorisation protects the policyholder more than the complete withdrawal of authorisation.)

These powers can be exercised where for example an insurance company fails to meet the criteria of sound and prudent management.

(ix) Financial

[1.35]
The main changes included:

1. The appointed actuary has to certify that premiums for contracts of long-term business are adequate together with income derived from them and other resources of the company to meet, on reasonable actuarial assumptions, all the commitments under them. The certificate relates to premiums for business in the previous year.
2. Amendments to the regulations covering the calculation of long-term liabilities and valuation of assets for solvency purposes.
3. The inclusion of derivatives as admissible assets and as permitted links.
4. Investment principles were set out for assets covering non-linked liabilities: linked liabilities had to be matched as closely as possible by the underlying units.

(See the Third Life Directive 92/96/EEC, arts 17–25 and Chapter 3 below.)

(x) Benefits of single market

[1.36]
The principal perceived benefits to insurance companies as a result of the implementation of the directive were:

1. Insurers would have greater freedom to design and sell new products (ie as a result of the abolition of prior notification of policy terms and conditions and rates). This would be balanced by the requirement of insurers to disclose information to prospective policyholders about themselves and the products they are offering. This factor really had a greater effect on some member states such as Germany rather than the UK, which had always operated a more liberal regime in this respect.
2. The single passport removes a significant layer of bureaucracy where insurers have branches in other member states.
3. Insurance companies would be allowed greater access to new financial instruments: in the UK insurers would be allowed a wider use of derivatives to cover technical provisions and permitted links and to raise hybrid capital (which covers various forms of subordinated debt[1]) which could count towards the required margin of solvency.

1 An issue or debt ranking below other debts in right of payment in a liquidation or for interest: holders will obtain higher interest for higher risk.

[1.37]
The perceived benefits to consumers were:

1. they would have a wider choice of products and at the same time know more about the insurance company they were purchasing from; and
2. the cooling-off period and disclosure requirements would provide better protection. (Note: the disclosure requirements for Life Assurance were already broadly covered by rules under FSA 1986. However, similar disclosure requirements were extended to contracts which were not within the scope of FSA 1986, and to any changes in the information relating to all life contracts during the term of the contract.)

A number of factors still hamper the creation of a true single market in financial services, most notably the differences in taxation treatment of long-term business.

2. OVERLAP BETWEEN ICA 1982 AND FSA 1986

A. Selling, marketing and prudential regimes

[1.38]
The Insurance division of the DTI, now HM Treasury, ensure that the life company continues to meet the capital, financial and organisational requirements set out in the legislation in order to reduce the risk of insolvency or losses for investors. These requirements are set out in ICA 1982 and subsequent regulations. This is distinct from the regime introduced by FSA 1986, which regulates and supervises the marketing and selling of life assurance products which are investments. The chief

regulatory body under FSA was the SIB and the specific Self Regulatory Organisation (SRO) to which insurance companies take membership is the Personal Investment Authority (PIA) (formerly LAUTRO).

[1.39]
The interaction of the two Acts is complicated because not all insurance business is investment business as defined in FSA 1986. So there are two selling and marketing regimes for insurance business. The matter is discussed more fully in Chapter 7.

[1.40]
The matter is complicated further in that FSA 1986, through two SROs, namely IMRO and SFA, also regulates investment firms and stockbrokers in relation to their capital and other prudential requirements. FSA 1986, Sch 10 effectively carves out the areas of the Act which apply to insurance companies. Further, an insurance company which manages its own investments in-house will not need to be authorised or supervised by IMRO but if it is managed by a subsidiary company then membership of IMRO by the subsidiary is necessary.

[1.41]
Yet a further complication was that membership of the SIB could be sought directly rather than through a SRO, although SIB generally discouraged this.

[1.42]
Both prudential and Financial Services Act supervision for all the above types of financial services organisations will fall to the Financial Services Authority, which was established in October 1997. The Bank of England Act 1998 transferred the responsibility for banking supervision to the Financial Services Authority and the powers of this single regulatory body and the new regime are set out in the Financial Services and Markets Bill due to come into force by autumn 2000 (see Chapter 10).

B. Regulatory failure

(i) Selling and prudential supervision

[1.43]
In the 1980s and early 1990s as the Thatcher government advocated the notion of self-sufficiency and a nation of shareholders, investment in endowments, personal pensions, Tessas and PEPs became popular. However, whereas Tessas and PEPs sold by banks, building societies and unit trust companies were a success story, the mis-selling of personal pensions (and possibly of endowments) by insurance companies damaged the reputation and the capital reserves of many life assurance companies and has still not been wholly resolved. In addition, there have been failures in the prudential supervision generally, most notably in Barings, where the systems of control appeared to be inadequate.

(ii) Consolidation

[1.44]
The above failures coincided with a great deal of corporate movement, as building societies and banks joined forces with insurance companies or set up their own subsidiary insurance company from scratch in order to exploit the potential for the cross-selling of financial products. Companies grouped in this way are sometimes referred to as 'bancassurance' or as 'financial conglomerates'. It is recognised by the EU that whereas the supervision of one specialised financial entity is difficult in itself, to supervise a group of financial services organisations requires special regulations.

(iii) Reasons for failure

[1.45]
It is almost certain that some regulatory failures can be partly blamed on the mis-match of an industry attempting to integrate its activities and a regulatory regime that remained specialised. This is an area that the new Financial Services Authority is hoping to address.

[1.46]
It is yet to be seen whether the new regime will fare better than the previous one. If the overriding reason for mis-selling is the difference in complexity between insurance/pension products and products sold by banks and building societies then a possible solution would be to simplify these products. Some of the complexity is cosmetic but a great deal of the complexity arises from the long-term nature of the products and the interaction with different tax regimes (see Chapter 5 for full discussion).

3. OVERVIEW OF A LIFE ASSURANCE COMPANY

A. Establishment

[1.47]
The life company can either be a mutual or proprietary company incorporated under the Companies Acts and is authorised to conduct long-term business under ICA 1982, which in turn gives it an automatic right to conduct investment business in terms of FSA 1986. As so much of the business requires actuarial input, it is a requirement of ICA 1982 that the company have an 'appointed actuary' whose primary role is to safeguard the interests of the policyholders: the directors of a life company have duties to both the policyholders and, where relevant, the shareholders in the case of a proprietary company. The role of the appointed actuary and other actuaries within the life company are discussed at Chapter 4 and the duties of directors especially in financial services groups of companies is discussed at Chapter 2.

B. Activities

[1.48]
A life company can only carry on the classes of long-term business it has been authorised to carry on and any activities connected with that business

(see ICA 1982, s 16 and Chapter 2 for further discussion). The different types of products sold by a life company are discussed at Chapter 5. The types of reassurance arrangements a life company can enter into and the purposes of reassurance is covered at Chapter 6. Again, because of its specialised nature there are important differences in the accountancy and tax regimes applicable to life companies, which are discussed at Chapter 8. Special rules have evolved for any changes in the corporate structure of life companies. The steps to be taken to (1) demutualise, (2) transfer/merge, and (3) wind up life companies are explained at Chapter 9.

C. Capital and investment

[1.49]
The linchpin of the prudential regime is that the life company maintains a certain amount of capital over and above the amount necessary to meet its liabilities at any time: this is referred to as a 'margin of solvency'. The calculation is complex and requires much actuarial input. In valuing assets and liabilities, the actuary has to make assumptions about a number of economic criteria and also about the nature of the different classes of long-term business conducted by the company. In addition to the capital requirements, there are restrictions and rules governing the structure of the internal funds and the types of investment in which the assets of a life company can be placed and the limits on these investment (see Chapter 3).

D. Investor protection

[1.50]
The prudential regime and the marketing and selling regime under FSA 1986 is designed to give investors protection. Should these fail, then the PPA 1975 and the PIA Ombudsman Scheme provide some financial security for investors and a method of seeking redress. These are discussed in Chapter 7.

E. Future developments

[1.51]
The supervision of financial services industry is set to change when the Financial Services and Markets Bill becomes law, Chapter 10 covers the changes proposed by the Bill and some other developments affecting life assurance.

4. LEGISLATION AND NON-STATUTORY MATERIALS

[1.52]
In addition to the insurance statutes and regulations, there are a number of Prudential Guidance Notes (PGN) and Dear Director letters issued by the DTI which seek to clarify some of the statutory provisions and shed light on how the DTI will interpret these provisions. The Faculty and Institute of Actuaries also publish Guidance Notes (GN) and Dear

Appointed Actuary letters for members of the profession involved in the insurance industry. The Association of British Insurers also publish Statements and Codes of Practice. These can be found in *Butterworths Insurance Law Handbook* (6th edn, 2000).

5. DEFINITIONS

A. Introduction

[1.53]
In understanding insurance company legislation it is necessary to understand the meaning of a number of key terms. This section provides the statutory definitions for insurance business, terms relating to the capital requirements and EU terms.

B. Insurance Business

[1.54]
This is defined at ICA 1982, s 95 and is classified at ICA, Schs 1 and 2. There have also been a number of cases on the point, which are discussed at Chapter 2.

C. Capital requirements – terms

(i) Mathematical or technical reserves

[1.55]
The provision made by an insurer to cover liabilities (excluding liabilities which have fallen due and liabilities arising from deposit back arrangements) arising under or in connection with contracts for long-term business (ICR 1994, SI 1994/1516, reg 2).

(ii) Margin of solvency

[1.56]
The margin of solvency of an insurance company is the excess value of its assets over the amount of its liabilities, that value and amount being determined in accordance with the valuation regulations (ICA 1982, s 32(5)). Under ICR 1994, SI 1994/1516, regs 17–21 there are broadly two calculations used in determining the margin of solvency required for each class of long-term business: (1) the first calculation is a multiple of a percentage of the mathematical reserves, and (2) the second calculation is a multiple of a percentage of the 'capital at risk'.[1]

1 'Capital at risk' is defined at ICR 1994, reg 18(7): '(a) in any case in which the amount is payable in consequence of death other than a case falling within sub-paragraph (b) below, the amount payable on death, and (b) in any case in which the benefit under the contract in question consists of the making of an annuity, payment of a sum by instalments or any other kind of periodic payment, the present value of the benefit, less in either case the mathematical reserves in respect of the relevant contracts.' 'Margin of solvency' is further broken down into 'UK, margin of solvency' which relates

to assets and liabilities in the UK and 'EEA margin of solvency' which relates to assets and liabilities in the EEA. These margins of solvency apply only to insurers with head offices outside the EEA (ICA 1982, ss 96 and 32).

(iii) Guarantee fund and minimum guarantee fund

[1.57]
The guarantee fund is one third of the margin of solvency but in any event shall not be less than the minimum guarantee fund which is 600,000 ECU for mutual insurers and 800,000 ECU for all others (ICR 1994, SI 1994/1516, reg 22 and Sch 5).

D. European terms

(i) EU, EEA and EFTA

[1.58]
1. The EU comprises the following member states:
   France, Germany, Luxembourg, Belgium, Netherlands, Italy, UK, Spain, Ireland, Greece, Portugal, Austria, Denmark, Sweden, Finland.
2. The EEA in addition includes:
   Iceland, Liechtenstein and Norway.
3. The EFTA countries include in addition to the member states at 1 above:
   Iceland, Liechtenstein, Norway and Switzerland.

(ii) EC company

[1.59]
An 'EC company' means 'an insurance company:

'(a) which is incorporated in or formed under the law of a member State other than the UK;
(b) whose head office is in that member State; and
(c) which is authorised in accordance with Article 6 of the First General Insurance Directive [73/329/EEC] or Article 6 of the First Long Term Insurance Directive [79/267/EEC].'

[1.60]
Further, 'In relation to any time before it becomes a member State, each of the following namely Iceland, Liechtenstein and Norway, shall be treated as if it were a member State for all the purposes of this Act' (ICA 1982, s 2(6) and (7)).

(iii) EFTA company

[1.61]
This is defined at ICA 1982, s 72B(7) as an insurance company whose head office is in an EFTA country and which is authorised in accordance with art 6 of either the First General Insurance Directive 73/329 or the First Long Term Insurance Directive 79/267/EEC and whose business in the UK is not limited to reinsurance business. (Note: Switzerland has a special insurance agreement with the EC.)

6. SUMMARY

[1.62]

1. A life assurance company is a special type of company governed not only by the Companies Acts and FSA 1986 but by ICA 1982.
2. Its internal investment, financial and organisational structure make it necessary for special legal rules to be applied in relation to corporate changes, accountancy and tax.
3. This underlying structure is necessary because of the long-term nature of the products/services sold by the life company to the public and an understanding of the product/services is difficult without an understanding of the underlying structure.
4. Investment, financial and operational restrictions all go some way to protecting the consumer.

Chapter 2
Corporate and fund structures

1. INTRODUCTION

[2.1]
This chapter looks at the establishment of life companies and how they may divide up their operations, become part of a financial group; the inter-group agreements which may need to be put in place; some of the risks associated with financial groups; and the broad characteristics of the different types of funds within life companies.

2. ESTABLISHMENT OF LIFE COMPANIES

A. Introduction

[2.2]
In terms of ICA 1982, s 2, in order to carry on life insurance business in the UK authorisation under ICA 1982, ss 3 or 4 is required. The exceptions to this are EC companies authorised in another member state, insurance business (other than industrial insurance business) carried on by Lloyd's, or by Friendly Societies registered under the Friendly Societies Act 1992 or certain forms of trade union insurance. Carrying on insurance business without authorisation is an offence and is discussed at Chapter 7 below.

[2.3]
The procedure is that an application must be made in terms of ICA 1982, s 5. The information to be provided is detailed at ICR 1994, SI 1994/1516, Sch 1. The information and the criteria for authorisation varies depending on the location of the head office of the applicant.

B. UK applicants

[2.4]
For applicants with their head office in the UK the following three conditions must be met in terms of ICA 1982, s 7:

1. the applicant must be either (i) a company incorporated under the Companies Acts or NI Order 1986 or (ii) a registered society or (iii) established by Act of Parliament or Royal Charter and already authorised under ICA 1982, s 3 or s 4 and wants to extend authorisation to cover further classes of business;
2. the share capital must be fully paid up; and

3. the directors and controllers, managers and main agents (see definitions at **[2.7, 2.8 and 2.9]** below) need to pass the fit and proper test.

C. EEA applicants

[2.5]
In addition to point 3 at **[2.5]** above, ICA 1982, ss 8 and 10 require that EC companies[1] (already authorised in a member state other than the UK) must have a general representative, who can be an individual or a company, based in the UK to receive notices and act as the insurer's agent. The general representative must also pass the fit and proper test.

1 EC and EFTA companies authorised in another member state will be able carry on insurance business in the UK as a result of the passporting provisions of the Third Life Directive 92/96/EEC subject to the notification procedure set out at ICA 1982, Sch 2F. Host states can only refuse to allow insurers authorised in another member state (home state) from carrying on insurance business if it would be contrary to the 'general good': the Commission have attempted to define this concept in Draft Commission Interpretative Communication 'Freedom to Provide Services and the General Good in the Insurance Sector' 97/C 365/04, see Appendix 1.

D. Non-EEA applicants

[2.6]
The Treasury must be satisfied that the applicant is entitled under the law of the place where its head office is situated to carry on insurance business. In addition to point 3 at **[2.4]** above and the requirement to have a general representative, insurance companies based outside the EU may have to pay a deposit in terms of ICA 1982, s 9 and ICR 1994, SI 994/1516, regs 7–15 and have assets equal to the solvency margin in the EEA, a proportion of which (at least the greater of the minimum guarantee fund and the appropriate guarantee fund) should be in the UK (ICR, reg 33).

E. Definitions of controller, manager and main agents

[2.7]
'Controller' is defined at ICA 1982, s 96C and covers the managing director, chief executive or a de facto director of the company or parent company. In the case of a UK company, it also covers a 10% or more shareholder or someone with 10% or more of the voting rights or is generally in a position of 'significant influence' by virtue of a shareholding or voting rights in the company or its parent.

[2.8]
'Manager'[1] is defined at ICA 1982, s 96D and covers for UK companies both (a) sub-contractors (note: this would include an investment management company and appointed representatives) and (b) employees who report directly to the managing director or chief executive and exercise managerial functions or are responsible for maintaining accounts or other company records. For non-UK companies, only (b) applies.

1 Reference to 'manager' in ICA 1982, s 56, which deals with insurance companies in liquidation, has a separate meaning.

[2.9]

'Main Agent' is defined at CA 1982, s 96E and covers agents in respect of general insurance business only.

F. Information for authorisation

[2.10]

This is contained at ICR 1994, SI 1994/1516, Sch 1 and is divided into four parts, depending on the location of the head office of the company: companies with head office in the UK; non-EC companies whose head office is in a EEA state other than the UK; companies whose head office is not in an EEA state and the fourth dealing with reinsurance business of companies not located in the UK. (Note: EC and EFTA companies based in EEA are only subject to the notification requirements set out at ICA 1982, Sch 2F.)

[2.11]

Part 1: this section covers the information required by a UK company which is:

1. Company details: date and place of incorporation, registered number, summary of objects of company (ie copy of memorandum of association), the financial year end, auditors and principal banker's details.
2. Directors details: ICR 1994, SI 1994/1516, Sch 6 sets out the information to be supplied by directors, controllers or managers which includes details of:
   (a) qualifications;
   (b) all employment over the previous ten years;
   (c) current and previous directorships;
   (d) all companies in which the person holds 10% or more of the voting rights;
   (e) all other authorisations, refusals or withdrawals of applications for authorisation, convictions, any financial failures, dismissal from office, refusal of membership of any professional body, disqualification as director, action by any regulatory body all within ten years prior to the notification;
   (f) any other relevant details; and
   (g) in addition details of any existing or proposed association between the controllers and directors and insurance brokers, agents, loss adjusters or reinsurers.
3. Financial details: a financial statement on assets and liabilities at the date of authorisation, a scheme of operations and projections for the first three financial years.
4. Other information: the classes of business intended to be covered, the type of investment representing the insurance funds, copies or drafts of reinsurance treaties, standard broker or agency agreements, outsourcing agreements and an actuarial certificate from the person to be appointed actuary agreeing with the financial information provided.

G. Practicalities of application

[2.12]
Prudential Guidance Note (PGN) 1994/4 recommends that the application is made in draft initially and that if necessary a meeting can be held with the regulatory authority prior to submitting the application to discuss outline proposals. PGN 1994/4 outlines the form the application should take. The application process is likely to take between six and nine months.

H. Memorandum and articles

[2.13]
The memorandum and articles should be much like those of other companies except that in the memorandum the objects of the company are limited to carrying on insurance business and activities connected with that business and the articles provision should be made for the division of profit or surplus and the voting and participation rights of policyholders or/and shareholders.
For example:

> '1. The surplus of the assets over liabilities of the Company shall be ascertained by an actuarial investigation at such intervals, not being less than once in every twelve months, as the Directors may deem expedient in the interests of the Company.
>
> 2. Subject to any law, enactment, regulation or rule, the Directors shall set aside out of the surplus ascertained pursuant to Article 1 above for allocation to the policyholders of the Company entitled to participate in the profits of the Company such amount (hereinafter called 'the policyholders' divisible surplus') as may be determined by the Directors on the advice of the actuary employed by them.
>
> 3. The Directors may, out of the surplus remaining after making such allocation and after appropriating or reserving such sums as the Directors shall deem fit or reserved for such purposes as they consider necessary in the interests of the long-term business (within the meaning of the Insurance Companies Act 1982 or any statutory modification amendment or re-enactment thereof) transfer to profit and loss account such sums not exceeding in the aggregate one ninth of the policyholders' divisible surplus as they think proper.'

(Note: the example is based on the Articles of Britannia Life Ltd.)

I. Carrying on insurance business and criminal sanctions

[2.14]
In terms of ICA 1982, s 2, '. . . no person shall carry on any insurance business in the United Kingdom unless authorised to do so under section 3 or 4 . . .' ICA, s 14 makes it a criminal offence to carry on insurance business without authorisation. The courts have held that the words

'carrying on insurance business' should be construed narrowly because breach of ICA, s 2 carries with it penal sanctions and that only the business of providing insurance cover needs to be authorised: *Secretary of State for Trade and Industry v Great Western Assurance Co* [1997] 2 BCLC 685, CA.

[2.15]
It has also been held that soliciting insurance business fell within the meaning of 'carrying on insurance business': *R v Wilson* [1997] 1 All E R 119 (see Chapter 7 for position of investor and status of contract where it is entered into in contravention of ICA 1982, s 2).

3. FINANCIAL GROUPS

A. Introduction

[2.16]
The functions within a life company can be categorised as follows:

1. Board, Secretariat and Appointed Actuary.
2. Administration (Life and Pension Products).
3. Actuarial.
4. Finance (incorporating Accounting and Treasury).
5. Investment Management.
6. Corporate Services (Legal, Compliance, Facilities Management, Human Resources, Payroll).
7. IT Support and Development.
8. Marketing (including product development); Sales and Public Relations.

Although all of these functions can be found within the one company, technically any function apart from 1 could be separated and assumed by a parent, subsidiary or sister company or in some cases out-sourced outwith the group. ICA 1982, s 3(2) looks at some of the more typical corporate structures and the reasons why companies have chosen to adopt these in preference to operating divisions or departments within a single company.

B. Possible corporate structures

(i) Investment management

[2.17]
A life company may have huge funds running into billions which have to be invested. External fund managers will levy charges on the fund and it is often more economic to retain this function in house. However, life companies also link many of their products to unit trusts. It may be more economic to set up their own unit trusts which have to be established and managed by a separate authorised company, which can attract not only insurance fund investment but also direct investment from the public (ie purchasing units or PEPs or now ISAs). The sums used to purchase the

units also have to be invested in assets which underpin the value of the units and investment managers are needed for this function. If the investment management function is simply a department within the life company, it can manage the life company's funds and invest in external unit trust funds but cannot manage funds invested in unit trusts by third parties by virtue of ICA 1982, s 16(1):[1]

> 'An Insurance company . . . shall not carry on any activities, in the United Kingdom or elsewhere, otherwise than in connection with or for the purposes of its insurance business.'

There are therefore obvious synergies in establishing as part of the group an investment management company to deal with both insurance funds and unit trust funds. The additional advantage is that, once established, the investment management company can also market itself to and attract funds from third parties outwith the group and so increase its revenue.

1 It is possible for the insurance company to ask HM Treasury for an order under ICA 1982, s 68 to dispense with or modify the requirements of, inter alia, ICA, s 16.

[2.18]
The separate company, if it is a subsidiary of the life company, is owned by the policyholder fund or, in the case of a proprietary company, it could also be held in the shareholder fund. It could also be held directly by a parent company (if the life company is itself a subsidiary) either directly or via a holding company. Irrespective of whether the investment management function is internal or external, the life company has a responsibility for setting the investment parameters that the fund has to follow (see **[2.32]** below).

(ii) Administration etc

[2.19]
If the life company goes down the route of setting up other companies in the group, it may want to provide a central administration, finance/accounting, corporate services, marketing or IT function rather than replicating each function in each company in the group. If this is to be achieved then a separate services company may need to be set up (again by virtue of ICA 1982, s 16(1)) together with inter-company agreements between all the companies in the group using the services, and the service company. It is important to note that if, for example, administration is being provided by the life company to the fund management company which is solely and directly referable to its own funds under management then this should not constitute a breach of ICA, s 16. If, however, administration services are provided to the fund management company in respect of third party funds, then this would constitute a breach of ICA, s 16.

(iii) Sales

[2.20]
There are a number of different arrangements for selling life products:

(a) a direct sales force employed by the life company;
(b) distance selling, ie via a call centre or over the Internet;
(c) a tied sales force of individuals, partnerships or companies who enter into appointed representative or tied agency agreements with the life company; and
(d) selling through independent financial advisers (IFAs).

The type and level of advice to the public depends on the distribution outlet used. All the arrangements are regulated currently by PIA. One of the fundamental rules is that advice is *either* independent *or* limited to the products sold by one company or a marketing group of companies. This is referred to as 'polarisation'.

Polarisation[1]

[2.21]
Under the SIB Core Conduct of Business rules, advisors who give advice to customers on the sale of investment products must either be IFAs or appointed representatives/tied agents of a particular life company. That is, they must either give advice across the whole range of products available by different companies or advice relating exclusively to the products of one company or marketing group of companies:

> '4(1) A firm which advises a private customer on packaged products must either:
> (a) be a product company or its marketing group associate; or
> (b) do so as an independent intermediary.
> 4(2) A firm which is a product company or its marketing group associate must not advise private customers to buy packaged products which are not those of the marketing group.
> 4(3) A firm which acts as an independent intermediary in advising a private customer on packaged products must act as an independent intermediary whenever it advises private customers on packaged products in the course of regulated business.'

1 Polarisation does not apply to investment managers advising a private client on packaged products.

Marketing groups

[2.22]
The PIA rules continue by insisting that a life assurance company which sells via IFAs and tied agents must make the same products available through each distribution channel.

> 'Where a company representative is authorised to sell any category of investment contract offered for sale by a Member –
>
> (a) the Member shall ensure that the company representative is authorised to sell each category of investment contract offered for sale by the Member; and

(b) where that Member is a member of a marketing group which is also a member of PIA shall ensure that each of their company representatives is authorised to sell each category of investment contract offered for sale by the members of the group, whether or not they are also Members of PIA.' (*PIA Rule Book*, 1994, L3 2(1).)

Typically, a life company will have products which range from the comparatively simple to the extremely complex. The complex products are usually designed mainly for distribution through the IFA channel and the simpler through the appointed representative/tied agent route. However, under the rules the appointed representatives/tied agents must be capable of giving advice on all products and this involves training time and costs and also a greater risk of mis-selling. To avoid this, some companies set up two life companies, each specialising in products suitable for each of the two distribution channels. But the rules go further and it is necessary, under (b) above, that the two companies are not part of the same marketing group or the onerous training standards have to be met. The company has to decide which route is commercially more attractive.

Review of polarisation rules

[2.23]
The Office of Fair Trading (OFT) (which has responsibility for ensuring that the rules under FSA 1986 do not distort competition) has recently carried out a review of the rules and has recommended that, for certain products such as unit trusts and shares in open-ended investment companies (OEICs), the rules are abandoned, but retained for life and pensions products. The effect of this would be to allow an IFA to tie to a number of companies for the sale of units and shares in OEICs. The rationale is that the life and pensions products are more complex and consumers still require the protection of polarisation, whereas the former products are more straightforward and are, in any event, being sold directly to the public without advice (although some life and pensions products are also sold on an execution only basis). Secondly, competition would be increased without sacrificing consumer protection. The recommendations have been criticised as confusing and it is maintained that independent advice is still needed across the range of financial products.

Authorisation and responsibility for advice

[2.24]
Whereas IFAs must be authorised directly by a self-regulating organisation (SRO) under FSA 1986 and are responsible for the advice they give to customers, no separate authorisation is needed for appointed representatives/tied agents, and it is the life company which is ultimately responsible for the advice given by their appointed representatives/tied agents. The life company must therefore ensure that the tied agents or appointed representatives are trained and competent to give advice across their product range. FSA 1986, s 44 covers the relationship between the life company and the appointed representative/tied agent:

'44(1) An appointed representative is an exempted person as respects investment business carried on by him as such a representative.

44(2) For the purposes of this Act an appointed representative is a person

(a) who is employed by an authorised person (his 'principal') under a contract for services which –

(i) requires or permits him to carry on investment business to which this section applies; and

(ii) complies with subsections (4) and (5) below; and

(b) for whose activities in carrying on the whole or part of that investment business his principal has accepted responsibility in writing.'

[2.25]
FSA 1986, s 44(4) and (5) deal with the power of the principal to restrict the activities of the appointed representative to giving advice or procuring or endeavouring to procure persons to enter into investment agreements soley with the principal. The agreement must make provision for this and the restriction can only be relaxed in expressly agreed and limited circumstances.

(iv) Out-sourcing

[2.26]
As employment rights become more onerous and as office space is usually at a premium, a life company may consider it more economic to out-source a number of activities to external consultants. This is most frequently chosen as an option in IT, where the needs of the company can fluctuate quite dramatically. For example, the Year 2000 problem and the possibility of joining the European Monetary Union (EMU) have systems implications and most companies would find it necessary to increase their IT staff to deal with these issues. Also, if a company is launching a new product, systems have to be created or redesigned to cover new functions and this too can be a drain on the company's own resources. It can apply equally to all the functions listed above apart from Board, Secretariat and Appointed Actuary.

(v) Other types of financial services

[2.27]
A life company may want to diversify and look for partners in the banking or building society or the general insurance industries. This type of consolidation among different sectors of financial services was prompted by the idea of having a kind of financial services supermarket, where customers could pick up a range of products from mortgage and house insurance to unit trusts, ISAs, deposit accounts, endowment policies and pension plans. Rather ironically, it is now supermarkets which are setting up financial services companies and marketing a range of financial products.

C. Tax

[2.28]
The structure of a group of financial services companies can have tax and VAT implications (see Chapter 8).

4. INTER-GROUP AGREEMENTS

A. Introduction

[2.29]
If a life company forms part of a group of companies, a number of inter group agreements should be put in place for investment management, administration or support services, and tied agency. These should all be arm's-length agreements and they should all make clear the services to be provided and the cost and comply with regulatory and legislative[1] requirements. They are discussed in more detail below.

1 For the tax treatment of transactions between associated companies see ICTA 1988, s 770 and 770A, which introduces the transfer pricing rules at ICTA, Sch 28AA.

B. Investment management agreement

(i) IMRO requirements

[2.30]
The investment managers appointed will almost certainly be regulated by IMRO. The IMRO rules require agreements to be entered into between the investment managers and their customers. Customers are divided into private and non-private customers. In the case of the former, a full customer agreement[1] is normally required and an abbreviated agreement for non-private customers. But the rules on customer agreements do not extend to non-private customers which are also authorised (see IMRO Conduct of Business Rules).

1 An industry standard agreement for pension fund management is at Appendix 6 produced by the Institute of Pension Fund Management and covers the IMRO requirements for a full customer agreement.

[2.31]
As a life company is classified as a non-private authorised customer IMRO rules do not apply unless the investment managers also provides custodial services. IMRO Rules Ch 11 2.3.

(ii) HMT requirements

[2.32]
The prudential regulator (currently HM Treasury) issues Prudential Guidance Notes on a number of statutory provisions. The recommendations contained in them are not mandatory but a company would have to justify any departure from the recommendations to the regulator. PGN 1994/6

on 'Systems of Control over the Investments (and Counterparty Exposure) of Insurance Companies with particular reference to the use of Derivatives' discusses at Annex B the controls to be placed on Investment Managers:

> 'Where investment management is contracted out to a third party, the directors of the insurance company must nevertheless satisfy themselves that the appropriate controls are in place and are effective . . . In determining what are appropriate and effective controls we would normally expect the insurance company, as a minimum, to focus on the following areas –
>
> (a) There should be a clear contract which sets out the parameters in which the investment manager may operate. It is unlikely that the managers' 'standard' contract (even if it is approved by their own regulators) will be sufficient for this purpose. We would expect tailoring to be made to reflect the legislative constraints (eg admissibility limits and permitted links), any investment limits set by the insurer and more generally, the insurer's specific circumstances. For example 'to invest in whatever the manager considers appropriate' is not good enough. Apart from any specific limits, the parameters need to strike an appropriate balance between risk and reward, taking due account of the nature of the company's insurance liabilities and as appropriate, the interests or reasonable expectations of its policyholders.
>
> (b) The extent of reporting by the managers should be sufficient to enable the insurance company to assess whether or not actual operations are in line with the company's strategy, and in particular meets the risk/reward criteria set. Reporting should also provide sufficient information for the insurer to check how close it is to relevant asset admissibility limits (or to its own limits if lower).
>
> (c) Additional more detailed monitoring of the managers' operations may be necessary in certain circumstances. However, where the manager is subject to its own regulatory regime (eg IMRO), there is unlikely to be any need for the insurer to carry out its own 'audits' of the managers' operating controls. This does not mean that the insurer can absolve itself from all responsibility of ensuring that the managers' systems and controls are adequate, merely that credit can be taken for certain areas, such as operation of client money rules, which are subject to audit by other parties.
>
> (d) If the investment manager is to hold funds on behalf of the insurance company or to be a counterparty to certain investment transactions then the extent of capitalisation and form of regulation of the manager will need to be taken into account. These considerations will need to be regularly reassessed; eg manager A may be suitable if placing £10m of business but not for £100m. Similar considerations will also apply where the insurance company alters its investment strategy and moves into newer forms of investment activity for which the existing investment manager has little or no experience.'

(iii) Investment management agreement

[2.33]
The following matters should be addressed in order to comply with the PGN:

1. The description of the investment parameters will usually be quite extensive and drafted or overseen by the appointed actuary, who will ensure they are within relevant statutory investment restrictions (see Chapter 3). It can be included as a schedule to the agreement and the various parameters and restrictions can be dealt with on a fund by fund basis. Each fund should be separately managed within the restrictions and parameters and attention paid to ICA 1982, ss 28, 29 and 31A, which prohibit unfairness in the treatment between funds, but other than that the fund managers usually have investment discretion.
2. There should also be limits on the number of counterparties and on exposures to counterparties (see Chapter 3 below).
3. The fund managers may have an obligation to publish unit prices of any unit linked funds in compliance with the relevant statutory or regulatory requirements.
4. The life company have to supply the fund managers with relevant information, eg where net new money has to be allocated; the fund managers must prepare regular reports in a format determined by the life company, which should include regular valuations of the funds usually against set performance measures.
5. The appointment of a custodian and bank and the payment of their fees.
6. Remuneration is usually a percentage of the funds under management.
7. As there is a large element of delectus personae the clauses on assignability and delegation should be drafted quite narrowly (ie these can be allowed but not in relation to discretionary investment powers).
8. Dealing restrictions and warnings, voting and lending and borrowing powers.
9. General clauses on the initial value and composition of the funds and the term of the agreement.
10. General clauses on termination, indemnity, notice, force majeure, amendments, etc.

There should be formal procedures in place within the life company for overseeing the operation of and amending the agreement and schedule: for example an investment committee established to do this and report regularly to the Board of the life company.

C. Tied agency agreement

[2.34]
A checklist for a tied agency (TA) agreement is at Appendix 10 and should include the following special terms, namely:

1. The status, authority and remit of the tied agent/appointed representative (TA/AR).
2. An undertaking that the TA/AR will comply with the PIA rules.

3. Prohibitions under FSA 1986, s 44(4) and (5) (ie to only give advice, etc on the life company's products).
4. An undertaking from the life company to be responsible for the authorisation and the acts of the TA/AR in terms of FSA 1986, s 44(2) and 44(6), but with the limitation at FSA 1986, s 44(8) (ie the knowledge or intention of the TA/AR will not necessarily be attributable to the life company in determining whether an offence has been committed).
5. Compliance with money laundering provisions.

D. Services agreement

[2.35]
A checklist is at Appendix 7. It is relatively straightforward and should include a description of the services, who is to provide them, standards of service and how the cost of the services is to be calculated and paid.

5. RISKS

A. Introduction

[2.36]
The corporate governance regime (the 'Combined Code' which applies to listed companies and can be adapted by unlisted companies is designed to encourage best management practices within companies and so reduce risk. Following the *Turnbull Report* in September 1999, companies are required to state in their annual report how they have complied with financial, operational, compliance and risk management provisions in the Combined Code. Insurance Companies have had to work within a prudential regime which includes mandatory requirements on adequate systems of control for a number of years. This section, however, deals with risks associated with groups of financial services companies. Life companies can, by a process of evolution or design, form part of a group of companies, some of which may have parallel interests to the life company and others which may have other responsibilities: for example, a company managing unit trusts to which some of long-term fund is linked may also have responsibilities to third party unit trust holders. A bank which is a tied agent of an insurance company will have duties to the life company but also to its own depositors and shareholders. Where the group is a mixture of financial companies and companies from other sectors, the difficulties in mapping out the respective rights and obligations increase. Generally, the policyholders of a life company are in a similar position to a company's creditors whose interests should take precedence over the shareholders.

[2.37]
A study was carried out by the OECD in 1993 on financial conglomerates, and a joint report was produced by Mr Koguchi of the OECD Financial Affairs Division and Professor Forestieri of Universita Bocconi, Milan. Amongst other matters is a discussion of the risks associated with financial conglomerates. It is important for those managers running a life company

to be able to identify and manage areas of potential risk. The following is a brief outline of the main risks associated with the consolidation of the financial services industry identified in the report.

B. Conflict of interest

[2.38]
Although conflicts of interest can occur in a single company, there is more scope for this type of problem in groups of companies. Although it can be useful to have some directors (usually those on the parent company board) sitting on the boards of all the companies in the group, it can increase the areas of potential conflicts.[1] A balance has to be struck between the group's interest and those of individual companies and between different classes of customer. There are also more risks of self-dealing, excessive risk taking by non-regulated associated companies (or those companies in a less disciplined regulatory environment) and more scope for manipulation of intercompany transactions.

1 The director of a subsidiary company must act in the interests of the subsidiary company rather in the interests of the group: *Charterbridge Corpn v Lloyds Bank Ltd* [1969] 2 All ER 1185.

C. Spread of financial problems[1]

[2.39]
Financial solvency or a build-up of risks in one company can either have a domino effect on other companies in the group or change public perception of the group as a whole, leading to a loss of confidence in the group's ability to perform. Financial problems may be hidden from regulators by 'double gearing', which involves using the same capital to support margins of solvency or other capital requirements in more than one company. An additional risk is that the problem may become systemic and affect different areas of the market. The more complex the corporate structure the more difficult it is to assess these risks.

1 It has been recognised for some time that the best way of controlling the spread of risks is for supervisory authorities to work together more closely and this is one of the matters the Financial Services and Markets Bill is hoping to address.

D. Anti-competitive

[2.40]
It is also recognised that, if there is a fragmentary approach to supervision and standards vary from one regime to another, regulatory arbitrage becomes a problem and its effects may distort the market.

6. FUND STRUCTURES

A. The distinction between general and long-term business

[2.41]
The different categories of insurance business are listed at ICA 1982, Sch 1. There is a major division between general and long-term business, and

within each of these categories is a list of particular policies which fall under these respective heads. The reason for the distinction is explained below. Secondly, ICA introduced a prohibition on any one insurance company conducting both types of business but this has been relaxed to a limited extent.

(i) Indemnity premium risk

[2.42]
General insurance business indemnifies people against accidents, crime, natural disasters, professional negligence which results in financial loss or damage to their property, their mental and physical health or the health of someone close to them. The most common examples are home building and contents insurance and car insurance. The main point to note is that the policies covering these types of risk are normally renewed annually. This means that, in addition to any initial underwriting, any claims made against the policy can be taken into account when setting the next year's premium. So the insurance company has control over the level of premium and can make annual adjustments to premiums to reflect the previous year's experience. Long-term insurance business, on the other hand, covers people against death from whatever cause (suicide is usually not covered for the first year of the policy) and/or illness (not all illnesses will be covered) over periods of typically ten years or more. There is less scope as in general insurance to alter the premium (although some contracts do make provision for the premium to be increased). So when, for example, a devastating illness such as AIDS flared up in the 1980s, there was no opportunity to return to policies already set up and take a tougher underwriting decision. The insurance company funds bore the loss. For future policies, more stringent questions could be asked and premium levels for new policies could be increased to help offset any losses on previous business, but this may in turn make the business less competitive.

(ii) Indemnity payment risk

[2.43]
In traditional (rather than unit linked) long-term business, however, the amount to be eventually paid out in traditional policies in the event of death or illness is certain: if someone insures their life for £50,000 then £50,000,[1] together with any relevant bonuses, is the sum paid to their estate. In contrast, a general insurance company, although limits are set, these limits in many policies run into millions. So, if the same person who has insured their life with the life assurance company in the above example, dies as a result of an accident at work for which the employer is responsible and covered by insurance, then the loss will be open ended and depend on the quantification of damages due to his family.

1 In unit linked business the risk is passed to the policyholder in that the unit price may fluctuate: eg a premium of £10,000 is paid into a unit linked bond. The stockmarket crashes and the assured then dies. His estate is paid 101% of the bid value of the units which is less than £10,000.

(iii) Investment

[2.44]
The remaining difference between the two types of insurance business is that long-term business includes in many policies an investment element as well as a protection element.

(iv) The incompatibility of the two types of insurance business/the prohibition on composites

[2.45]
It was considered prudent to separate the two types of business because of the danger of, for example, the general insurance fund running into heavy losses and being bailed out by a raid on the life or pensions funds:

> 'Whereas the Member States have different regulations and practices as to the simultaneous carrying on of life assurance and non-life assurance; whereas newly formed undertakings should no longer be authorised to carry on these two activities simultaneously; whereas Member States should be allowed to permit existing undertakings which carry on these activities simultaneously to continue to do so provided that separate management is adopted for each of their activities, in order that the respective interests of life policy holders and non-life policyholders are safeguarded and the minimum financial obligations in respect of one of the activities are not borne by the other activity . . .' (First Life Directive 79/267/EEC.)

This is part of the philosophy that different types of risk have to be managed and regulated in an appropriate way.

[2.46]
New composites, therefore, cannot be created. Existing composites can continue to carry on business and operate provided they manage their life and non-life businesses separately (First Life Directive 79/267/EEC, art 14). The Third Life Directive 92/96/EEC allowed a relaxation of the position by allowing new 'healthcare' composite companies to be created: UK and European companies which are authorised, or are seeking authorisation, to carry on long-term business are able to apply for authorisation to carry on accident and or health insurance business (ICA 1986, Sch 1, Pt I, Gp 1); similarly, a general insurance company authorised solely for those classes will be able to apply for authorisation to carry on all or any class of long-term business (ICA, s 6).

B. Internal funds

[2.47]
Internal funds will develop according to the number of classes of business being carried out and the variety of contracts entered into within these classes. Internal systems and procedures have to be developed in tandem to administer these. The following provides a description of the main subdivisions of internal long-term funds.

(i) Pooled and segregated funds

[2.48]
When policyholders' premiums are invested in a pooled or segregated fund, the policyholder has a contractual right to sums on the occurrence of certain events, but has no right to any of the assets in the fund. In pooled funds, the policyholder may be able to choose from a variety of investment funds with differing investment philosophies, but has no say in how the fund is invested. In contrast, the policyholder in a segregated fund may have a right to choose how the assets are invested and either make investment decisions or appoint someone (formally it is the life company who appoints the third party) to manage the investment of his fund. Many segregated funds relate to pensions business, where, on either an individual or company/partnership basis, the policyholders want to have more control over the management of their pensions portfolio. The assets purchased in a segregated fund must still comply with insurance legislation on investments (see Chapter 3).

(ii) With-profit and non-profit

[2.49]
Policyholders investing in with-profit funds are entitled to share in the company's profits. Each year, on the recommendations of the appointed actuary, the company will declare annual and reversionary/terminal bonuses rates, which are then applied to the value of each investment. Once declared, these bonuses are added to the investment/sum assured and are guaranteed, provided premiums continue to be paid. Future bonuses are frequently calculated by reference to the total sum assured and declared guaranteed bonuses. In addition, if the past profits of the life company are sufficient, when a policy reaches its maturity date a terminal bonus may be added to top up the sum assured and previously declared bonuses. In non-profit business, all the stated benefits are guaranteed, but if the company does well no share in the profits are included. The profit split between shareholders and policyholders will depend on the company's articles.

[2.50]
Annual bonus rates have declined over the last few years, mainly because of the lower rate of inflation and interest rates. This trend is expected to continue. Some companies have tried to sustain a balance by declaring a low annual bonus rate, which means that fewer assets have to be tied up in low yield government stock (ie low risk investments are used to match or underpin guaranteed sums). This in turn allows the life company to invest to a larger extent in equities, which, although riskier, tend to produce higher returns (in the long term) which can then be reflected in terminal bonuses. In contrast, in unit linked funds the investment value may fluctuate depending on the performance of the underlying assets. The life company must publish a document setting out its policy on bonuses.

(iii) Property linked and index linked and non-linked funds

[2.51]
A property linked fund is where the benefits are determined by the value of units in an internal unitised fund or a unit trust.[1] Index linked is where benefits are determined by the value of an index such as the FTSE 100. It should be noted that not all indices are eligible to be used in index linked contracts. ICR 1994, SI 1994/1516 stipulates that the index must be frequently published (eg the FT 30 cannot be used because it is only priced once a day) and the underlying asset must be admissible (eg a gold index is not allowed as gold is not an admissible asset). The critical difference for policyholders is that the risk of counterparty failure in the case of property linked contracts is borne by the policyholder; the life company bears the risk in index linked contracts. Non-linked funds are those where assets cover the liabilities of the insurance company under the contracts.

1 It is also possible to set up a linked fund known as a 'broker fund', where a broker would actively market and sell units in a fund administered by the life company and where an external fund manager is appointed – the assets belong to the life company and the life company has to take responsibility for the acts and omissions of the broker involved.

(iv) Pensions and life funds

[2.52]
The main difference between pensions and life funds is the different tax treatment. Life funds are taxed on income less expenses, whereas pension funds are exempt from tax provided they are comprised of sums from exempt approved pension schemes. However, recent changes introduced by the Finance Act 1998 (FA 1998) means that from 5 April 1999, pension funds effectively receive equity dividend income net of tax, and these funds can no longer reclaim advanced corporation tax (ACT). This makes the funds less tax efficient. For an overview of the mechanics of ACT see *Butterworths UK Tax Guide 1998/99*, para 23.01. The life company is taxed on any profits from pension business (see Chapter 8).

(v) Shareholder and policyholder long-term funds

[2.53]
Proprietary companies will have both a shareholder and policyholder fund, whereas mutuals will have only a policyholder fund. When a distribution of profits is made to policyholders (ie bonuses) and/or shareholders, a full actuarial valuation is required in terms of ICA 1982, s 18. Where both the policyholders and the shareholders share in the surplus of a fund, the share given to policyholders cannot reduce from one year to the next by more than 0.5% (see ICA 1982, s 30). So, for example, if in 1998 the total surplus is £10,000 and £9,000 is distributed to policyholders and £1,000 to shareholders, then in 1999 if the total surplus remains at £10,000, the minimum amount that can be distributed to policyholders is £8,950. It is usual for shareholders' profits from the with-profit funds to be expressed as a fraction (frequently one-ninth) of the bonus given to policyholders. In

this way, it is in the shareholders' interests to maximise returns to policyholders.

7. SUMMARY

[2.54]

1 Life companies require authorisation under ICA 1982 before they can commence long-term insurance business and this is the only business they can conduct.

2. Life companies may hive off a number of their functions into separate corporate entities which can allow greater freedom and economies but increases the number of inter-company agreements which need to be put in place and monitored and it may also have tax implications.

3. The order of risk increases when a life company is part of a financial services group.

4. General and long-term business must be conducted by separate companies, apart from healthcare composites.

5. Funds within a life company with different characteristics are managed separately.

Chapter 3
Capital requirements and investment restrictions

I. INTRODUCTION

A. Capital requirements

[3.1]

Insurance companies must operate within a margin of solvency (First Life Directive 79/267/EEC, s 32) 'in order to provide against business fluctuations' (preamble to First Life Directive). The margin of solvency of an insurance company is the regulatory determined amount of its assets over the amount of its liabilities, the value of the assets being determined in accordance with the Asset Valuation Regulations (AVR) at ICR 1994, Pt VIII, SI 1994/1516 (as amended by IC(A)R 1995, SI 1995/3248 and 1996, SI 1996/942). (ICA 1982, s 32(5)(a).) The liabilities of insurers under their long-term contracts are determined in accordance with ICR 1994, Pt IX. For example, if a company has assets valued at £2,000 and liabilities (ie mathematical reserves – see **[3.2]** below) of £1,500, then there is surplus assets of £5,000. If the calculation of the solvency margin (see **[3.2]** below) is £200 then the company has sufficient excess assets to cover the solvency margin.

[3.2]

Under ICR 1994, SI 1994/1516, regs 18–21, the calculation of the margin of solvency depends on the class of business covered. For classes I, II and IX (traditional or non linked business – see **[3.7]** below) the aggregate of the following two calculations is used in determining the margin of solvency:

(i) the first calculation is a multiple of a percentage of the mathematical reserves;[1] and
(ii) the second calculation is a multiple of a percentage of the 'capital at risk'.[2]

The percentage varies depending on the precise nature of the contract. For classes III, VII and VIII (linked business) the first calculation applies if the insurance company bears an investment risk, and if not, but other conditions are satisfied then the first calculation applies in a slightly modified form. For classes IV and VI (permanent health and capital redemption) the first calculation applies. For class V (tontines) the margin of solvency is 1% of the assets of the tontine.

1 Mathematical or technical reserves is the provision made by an insurer to cover liabilities (excluding liabilities which have fallen due and liabilities arising from deposit back arrangements) arising under or in connection with contracts for long-term business (ICR 1994, reg 2). (A deposit back arrangement is where under a contract of reassurance an amount is deposited by the reassurer with the reassured (see ICR 1994, reg 2).)

2 Capital at risk is defined at ICR 1994, reg 18(7): '(a) in any case in which an amount is payable in consequence of death other than a case falling within sub-paragraph (b) below, the amount payable on death, and (b) in any case in which the benefit under the contract in question consists of the making in consequence of death, the payment of an annuity, payment of a sum by instalments or any other kind of periodic payment, the present value of the benefit, less in either case the mathematical reserves in respect of the relevant contracts.'

[3.3]
'Margin of solvency' is further broken down at ICA 1982, s 32 into 'UK margin of solvency', which relate to assets and liabilities in the UK and 'EEA margin of solvency', which relate to assets and liabilities in the EEA. These margins of solvency apply only to insurers with head offices outside the EEA carrying on insurance business in the UK or EEA respectively.

[3.4]
Failure to maintain a minimum margin of solvency can result in withdrawal of authorisation although there is provision for the company to provide a short-term financial scheme to HM Treasury outlining how they propose to remedy the situation (ICA 1982, s 33).

[3.5]
In addition, an insurance company must maintain a guarantee fund. The guarantee fund is one sixth of the margin of solvency, but in any event is not to be less than the minimum guarantee fund, which is 600,000 ECU for mutual insurers and 800,000 ECU for all others (ICR 1994, SI 1994/1516, reg 22 and Sch 5, para 7).

B. Investment restrictions

[3.6]
It follows that in requiring insurers to hold assets to match their liabilities and cover a minimum solvency margin, these assets should be invested in a sound and prudent manner. It is critical that insurers do not concentrate all their funds in predominately high risk investments (eg unlisted securities) or invest with only one counterparty because, as a strategy, it is not considered sound nor particularly prudent. ICR 1994, SI 1994/1516, Schs 10 and 12 detail the restrictions to be placed on the investments of long-term funds.

[3.7]
These restrictions depend on whether the contract or policy is 'linked' (ie the benefits under the contract depend on the performance of the underlying investment), in which case the underlying investment must be a 'permitted link' (ICR 1994, SI 1994/1516, Sch 10); if not (ie with or without profits business), then assets covering the benefits must fall under the list

of assets at ICR, Sch 12 which can be invested in up to the regulation limits, if they are to be counted when calculating the margin of solvency. There are further restrictions at ICR, Sch 12 on the limits of exposure to counterparties. The restrictions do not apply to free assets (ie assets over and above those necessary to cover the margin of solvency).

[3.8]
There are also general obligations on reducing investment risks at ICA 1982, ss 28–36.

[3.9]
The DTI also produced Prudential Guidance Notes (PGN) in 1994 when the Third Life Directive was introduced, and in 1996, following amending regulations (PGN 1994/6 on 'Systems of Control over Investments (and counterparty exposure) of insurance companies with particular reference to the use of derivatives' and PGN1996/2 on linked contracts which replaced the previous note PGN 1994/9). The DTI also issued PGN 1995/1 on the Asset Valuation Regulations (AVR) and PGN 1995/3 on the use of derivatives.

[3.10]
The detailed requirements are part of the whole prudential regime affecting the conduct of insurance companies and summed up in the overriding principle of 'sound and prudent' management (ICA 1982, Sch 2A, para 5).

2. GENERAL OBLIGATIONS

[3.11]
The following is a brief outline of ICA 1982, ss 28–36:

1. Separation of assets and liabilities
   An insurance company must be able to identify and separate the assets and liabilities attributable to its long-term business and keep proper accounting records for that business (ICA 1982, s 28).
2. Application of assets
   There is prohibition on the use of assets covering long-term business to be used for any other purpose than that business (ICA 1982, s 29). The main exception is where there is an allocation of surplus after an actuarial investigation, in the form of bonus to policyholders or distribution to shareholders.
3. Allocation to policyholders
   If there is a surplus then the policyholders must recover the 'relevant minimum' in the form of bonuses. The relevant minimum of surplus allocated must not be more than 5% less than the previous years allocation (see ICA 1982, s 30). Shareholders normally take a distribution which represents a percentage of the policyholders' allocation. There are no regulations covering this point, but it is a practice which has grown over the years and is embodied in the companies' articles. The benefit of this form of distribution is that the interests of policyholder and shareholder are aligned as both benefit from higher bonuses.

4. Restrictions on transactions with connected persons
   The term 'connected persons' is defined in terms of control of the insurance company. The term 'control' is defined as:
   '(a) a person in accordance with whose directions or instructions the directors of the insurance company or of a body corporate of which it is a subsidiary are accustomed to act; or
   (b) a person who either alone or with any associate or associates is entitled to exercise, or control the exercise of, 15% or more of the voting power at any general meeting of the insurance company or of a body corporate of which it is a subsidiary'. (ICA 1982, s 31(5A).)

   The meaning of 'associate' is defined at ICA 1982, s 96C(4) and, where the person is an individual, includes immediate family, trustees of a settlement where the person has a life interest, any company of which that person is a director, employee or partner: if the person is a company, then directors, employees and subsidiaries of the company and anyone with whom an arrangement exists to deal in the shares or votes of that company.
5. Fairness in treatment of funds
   There must be no unfairness in the way investments are allocated as between different funds (ICA 1982, s 31A).
6. Solvency margin
   All insurance companies must operate within the solvency margin (ICA 1982, s 32). Failure to do so will result in the intervention of HMT, who will insist on a scheme being drawn up to detail the steps necessary for remedying the situation. The ultimate sanction is withdrawal of authorisation.
7. Form and situation of assets
   The rule is that if liabilities under policies are in a particular currency and exceed 5% of the company's total liabilities then the company must hold sufficient assets in that currency to cover at least 80% of the company's liability in that currency (ICA 1982, s 35 and ICR 1994, SI 1994/1516, reg 27). This does not apply to linked business, but it is obviously important that a company match its linked liabilities to appropriate assets and currencies. Liabilities in sterling can be held anywhere in any member state and liabilities in other currencies are to be held in any member state or the country of that currency (ICR 1994, reg 31).
8. Adequacy of assets
   ICA 1982, s 35(A) provides the foundation for the detailed regulations at ICR 1994, Schs 10 and 12. The criteria for adequacy depend on whether the benefits are linked or not. Linked benefits are defined as those which are:

   > 'determined by reference to the value of or the income from property of any description . . . or by reference to fluctuations in, or in an index of, the value of property of any description.' (ICA 1982, s 35A(4).)

   If the benefits are linked to an internal fund or collective investment scheme, the liabilities must be covered by the units or assets of the internal fund or collective investment scheme. If benefits are linked to a share index then they must be covered by units representing the index or by assets of appropriate safety, yield and marketability which correspond as closely as possible to the assets on which the index is based. Lastly, linked assets must also comply with regulations under ICA 1982, s 78 (ie ICR 1994, Sch 10).

If the benefits are not linked benefits, the underlying assets must have the appropriate safety, yield and marketability for the class of business they relate to. In addition, they must be appropriately diversified and spread with no excessive reliance or concentration on any particular type of investment. Nor must there be a concentration on a few counterparties (ICA 1982, s 35A(1)(a) and (b)).

9. Adequacy of premiums
   Before entering into new contracts, the company must be satisfied that on reasonable actuarial assumptions the premiums and income from them together with other resources will be sufficient to meet all liabilities under the contract (ICA 1982, s 35(B)).
10. Avoidance of contracts for unlimited amounts
    There is an outright prohibition at ICA 1982, s 36 on entering into contracts of uncertain or unlimited amounts, but this section is not yet in force.

3. PERMITTED LINKS

A. Introduction

[3.12]

Linked benefits can only be determined by reference to the permitted links at ICR 1994, SI 1994/1516, Sch 10. These are divided into property linked and index linked. Property linked is where benefits are determined by the value of units in an internally linked fund or unit trust; index linked is where benefits are determined by the value of an index. The main criteria for establishing to which category benefits are linked is that if the insurer bears the whole risk of counterparty default, the assets are index linked (ie the policyholders benefits are determined wholly by reference to the index); if the benefits reduce to reflect part or all of the reduction in the value of the linked assets resulting from counterparty default, the benefits are property linked. For example:

(a) Property linked: A US equity fund has two assets; stock A worth £100 and stock B worth £200 and 300 units are in force giving a unit price of £1. If a policy is invested in the US equity fund and has 10 units in that fund valued at £1 each, the value of the policy is £10 and this is the sum which would be paid on a claim. If the life company's custodian defaulted and title to stock B was lost, or if the stock was on deposit with a bank that fails, the value of stock B is nil. The unit price would then be calculated as (100 + 0)/300 = £0.333 and the value of the policy is now 10 x 0.333 = £3.33 (ie down from £10). The policyholder suffers the loss.
(b) Index linked: A policyholder invests £1,000 in a policy which guarantees a return of premium increased by any increase in the FTSE

100 index. If the FTSE 100 index was 6,000 at the commencement of the policy and rose to 12,000 at maturity, the policyholder would be entitled to receive 1,000 x 12,000/6000 = £2,000. To finance the guarantee, the life company buys matching derivatives with a bank. If the bank defaulted, the company would have no assets, but would nevertheless have to pay the policyholder the £2,000. The life company suffers the loss.

B. Close matching test

[3.13]
By virtue of ICA 1982, s 35A(2) and (3), an insurance company must hold assets whose value matches their unit liability as closely as possible. The 'close matching' test applies to property and index linked contracts, whether entered into before 1994 or not.

[3.14]
The DTI have offered the following guidance at para 2.2 of the PGN 1996/2:

> 'As a general rule, where benefits are linked to the value of certain assets, a company is not permitted to hold different assets and cover the mismatching risk by means of a reserve. However, in certain circumstances, it is permissible for the insurer to hold assets other than any which determine the unit liability provided that they are "assets of appropriate safety and marketability" whose value matches those of the unit liability "as nearly as may be".'

They point out that this is likely to happen in relation to index linked contracts and where the unit liability is wholly or partly reinsured.

[3.15]
Further, the 'close matching' test does not prevent surplus assets being held within a linked fund, although having sums in excess of net current liabilities to policyholders does not necessarily mean there is a surplus (eg where sums are due to brokers in respect of linked assets but which have not yet been paid. Nor does it prevent small shortfalls provided there is a satisfactory mismatching reserve.

C. Classes of business covered

[3.16]
All class III business and some class VII business are covered; classes I, IV and VI may also offer linked benefits. The regulations on permitted links (apart from rules on permitted derivatives) do not apply to linked contracts under class VII(a), ie pension fund management, ICA 1982, s 35A(5)[1] (see ICR 1994, SI 1994/1516, reg 43 for other exclusions). Both investment and protection policies can be unit linked.

1 Linked business is insurance business, ie how much is paid on a claim and when it is paid depends on whether a person is alive or dead; class VII(a) business does not require this dependence on human life.

D. Property which can be a permitted link

[3.17]
The following property can be a permitted link in terms of ICR 1994, SI 1994/1516. reg 43C and Sch 10:

1. listed securities which are readily realisable not falling in any of the undernoted categories;
2. unlisted securities which are readily realisable not falling in any of the undernoted categories;
3. land in an EEA state, Australia, Canada, Channel Islands, Gibraltar, Hong Kong, the Isle of Man, New Zealand, the Republic of South Africa, Singapore and the US;
4. loans fully secured on land in the countries at 3 above, not used for domestic purposes and with terms and conditions covering rates of interest and due dates for payment of interest and capital;
5. units or other beneficial interests in a scheme falling under the UCITS Directive, or a collective investment fund where the fund holds property which can be a permitted link, the units are readily realisable at a price representing the net value per unit of the assets and liabilities of the fund and the price of units is published regularly;
6. approved securities (basically gilts);
7. loans or credit with an approved credit or financial institution or investment firm;
8. income due from any of the property above;
9. permitted derivative contracts;
10. cash; and
11. internal funds managed by the insurance company or by someone for whose acts and omissions the insurer is responsible (eg Broker funds, where an external broker appointed by the insurer manages an internal fund, and for whose acts and omissions in managing the fund the insurer is responsible).

E. Indices to which benefits can be linked

[3.18]
Benefits can only be linked to an 'approved index'. This is defined at ICR 1994, SI 1994/1516, Sch 10, Pt II as either:

(a) an index which is:
   1. calculated independently;
   2. published at least once per week;
   3. based on property within permitted property links except permitted derivative contracts and internal funds;
   4. calculated on a basis made available to the public which includes certain rules of calculation;

   (ie this will cover the main indices of major stock markets),

or

(b) a national index of retail prices in states belonging to Zone A;[1]

(ie this means that annuities which are linked in this way are categorised as Class III business),

or

(c) an index which is:
   1. based on permitted property links listed above except derivatives and internal funds; and
   2. in respect of which a derivative contract is listed.

   (ie this will cover equity indices on the basis of which index options or futures are traded on a regulated market DTI PGN 1996/2, at para 6.3).

1 See ICR 1994, reg 45 which uses same definition as in Directive 89/647/EEC on solvency ratios for credit institutions: Zone A includes all EEA states and Australia, Canada, Czech Republic, Japan, Mexico, New Zealand, Saudi Arabia, South Korea, Switzerland, Turkey and US.

F. Diversification

[3.19]
The rule on diversification of assets does not generally apply to linked funds, but there are exceptions:

> 'Securities which are unlisted may not account in aggregate for more than 10% of the linked benefits under a contract. A similar percentage limit applies to holdings in collective investment schemes other than –
>
> (a) those qualified to be UCITS; or
> (b) those which have been marketed to the policyholder in accordance with the marketing rules which apply to the collective investment scheme in question.'
>
> (PGN 1996/2, para 9.1.)

[3.20]
There may also be implicit diversification requirements contained in marketing materials, which HMT would consider when assessing any possible breach of policyholders' reasonable expectations (see Chapter 4). The example given in the PGN is where a company offers a linked contract designed to deliver income of 7% pa[1] net and the marketing material states:

> 'The fund will be invested in assets offered by major financial institutions. In the unlikely event that one of these institutions defaults on its obligations, you may receive less than promised above.'

1 The DTI may mean 'growth' rather than 'income'.

[3.21]
The DTI's view is that:

> '. . . such wording, in particular the use of the phrase 'major financial institutions' conveys an expectation of a reasonable level of diversification. One counterparty would be completely unacceptable in this case. It would be even less acceptable if that counterparty turned

out to be a connected company of the insurance company, however major a financial institution that connected company happened to be.'

[3.22]
Lastly there may be implicit requirements for the diversification of counterparty exposure arising from the use of derivatives.

G. Non-permitted links

[3.23]
The regulations are absolute: if, however, a non-permitted link gets into the fund by accident, the insurance company must take all reasonable steps to remedy the situation.

[3.24]
If, in taking steps to remedy the breach a loss is sustained, the insurance company must make good the loss. The company should also inform HM Treasury and the auditors of the breach and the remedial action to be taken. HM Treasury have indicated that they do not need to be informed when the following three factors are all present, namely:

1. the financial effect is minimal;
2. the breach is a one off and is unlikely to recur; and
3. it does not cast doubt on the integrity of the company's control systems at the time of the breach.

(PGN 1996/2, para 10.)

4. ASSET ADMISSIBILITY AND EXPOSURE

A. Assets and limits

[3.25]
ICR 1994, SI 1994/1516, Sch 12 set out at Pt II the assets which are admissible in covering non linked benefits and the percentage of the long-term fund which can invest in them.

[3.26]
The asset admissibility rules will not allow a company to invest all its assets in, for example, one immovable property because (a) it is not readily sellable and (b) income from rents may depend on only one tenant and if the tenant defaults, there is no income from the investment and its market value may fall: however, a company could invest all its funds in gilts because they are (a) readily realisable and (b) there is little risk of default because, in the last resort, the government could print more money. So there are limits on investment in property of 5% but none on gilts.

[3.27]
Further, PGN 1995/1 on the valuation of assets regulations makes it clear that ICR 1994, SI 1994/1516, Sch 12 has to be read along with the general

principle of adequate diversification and of appropriate safety, yield and marketability at ICA 1982, s 35A:

> '. . . compliance with the admissibility limits does not necessarily mean automatic compliance with s 35A.'

B. Valuation for calculation of solvency margin

[3.28]
Once a company has classified its assets in accordance with ICR 1994, SI 1994/1516, Sch 12, it applies the Asset Valuation Rules (AVR) at ICR, Pt VIII (ICR, regs 44–57) and finally returns to the admissibility limits to ascertain how much of the value can be taken into account for solvency margin, or other regulatory purposes.

[3.29]
Companies can hold assets not included in ICR 1994, SI 1994/1516, Sch 12 or over the limits, but they are simply given a nil value or disregarded when calculating assets covering liabilities.

C. Breach of admissibility limits and AVR

[3.30]
It is important for insurance companies to set investment limits for fund managers somewhere below the regulation limit to allow for market movements which may take the fund over the limits and result in a breach:

> 'Notwithstanding the admissibility limits in [ICR 1994, SI 1994/1516] Schedule 12, appropriate procedures should be in place for setting prudent limits to the company's aggregate exposure to certain categories of asset. Such limits should take account of s 35A(1) of the Act [ICA 1982] concerning the suitability of assets to cover insurance liabilities. They may take account of the level of the company's free assets, bearing in mind the possibility that such assets might in future be needed to cover insurance liabilities or the prescribed minimum margin of solvency.' (PGN 1994/6 on systems of control over investments.)

[3.31]
The regulators have conceded that strict compliance with the AVR rules can produce an unintentionally harsh result and may offer companies an ICA 1982, s 68[1] concession:

> 'There is no guarantee that such a concession will be granted and it is likely to be given only on a temporary basis and with conditions attached. Where the AVR derive directly from the detailed requirements of the EC Third Directives [92/49/EEC and 92/96/EEC], the Department is unable to grant a concession except "in exceptional circumstances . . . temporarily and under a proper reasoned decision".' (PGN1995/1.)

1 Concessions can be granted in relation to ICA 1982, ss 16–22, 23(1), 25–34 and 35–36 and the provisions and regulations made under these sections and any valuation regulations: ICA 1982, s 68(4).

D. Counterparty exposure

[3.32]
In terms of ICR 1994, SI 1994/1516, Sch 12, para 4, the counterparty exposure limit is:

'(a) where the counterparty is an individual or an unincorporated body of persons, 5% of the business amount;[1]
(b) where the counterparty is a [government body, public body, local authority or nationalised industry], 5% of the business amount;
(c) where the counterparty is a body corporate or group, each of
  (i) 20% of the business amount;
  (ii) 10% of the business amount . . . where the exposure arises other than by reason that debts are due or to become due as a result of short term deposits made with an approved credit institution;
  (iii) 5% of the business amount where the exposure is other than to bodies which are approved counterparties.'

1 The term 'business amount' is defined at ICR 1994, Sch 12, para 2 and is broadly the long-term liabilities of the company 'less any reinsurance ceded and excluding property linked liabilities, together with (a) the amount of the required margin of solvency (or the minimum guarantee fund if greater) . . . and (b) the amount of any deposit back in connection with a contract of reinsurance . . .'

[3.33]
The percentages for counterparty exposure and for asset admissibility are of the business amount defined at **[3.32]** above.

[3.34]
Insurers should also check the creditworthiness of their counterparties.

5. SYSTEMS OF CONTROL

A. Introduction

[3.35]
ICA 1982, Sch 2A outlines the criteria of sound and prudent management. Part of that criteria is to have adequate systems of control. Guidance on systems of control for monitoring compliance with investment regulations is given in PGN 1994/6. It is divided into three parts, dealing with aggregate exposure to counterparties, investment managers and derivatives.

B. Monitoring aggregate counterparty exposure

[3.36]
1. It is first emphasised that the limits represent maximum amounts which can be valued for solvency purposes. This means that limits for

solvency purposes should be set below the maximum and, provided the insurance company has the minimum solvency margin, assets over and above that margin do not need to comply with the detailed restrictions on investment.

2. Secondly, exposure needs to be accumulated across the spectrum of investments as there may be many different types of investment dealing going on with the same counterparty.
3. The corporate structure of counterparties has to be monitored to ensure an amalgamation does not push the insurance company over the limits:

   > 'For example, the limits would apply to combined dealings with Bank XYZ or with the derivatives trading subsidiary of that bank, together with the stockbroker balances with the broker owned by Bank XYZ's parent company.' (PGN 1994/6.)

4. The exposure is based on what is actually owed to the insurer and margining can help reduce this (ie where, for example, the value of any collateral given to the insurer is balanced against the amount due from the counterparty, and if one value is greater than the other the difference or margin, payment is made to the party holding the asset with the lower value).
5. Subsidiary operations of the insurance company are to be taken into account when setting and monitoring exposure, but parents and sister companies can be ignored. Good group management, however, should ensure that the basic principles apply across the group.
6. Although reinsurance is not covered by the rules, it is nevertheless prudent to limit exposure to any one reassurer. If there is a large amount of liabilities reassured to one reassurer, it would be usual to arrange a deposit back from the reassurer: a corresponding loan to the reassurer is made; the interest on the deposit back and the loan are identical sums. The advantage is that if the reassurer fails, the company has possession of the deposit.

C. Monitoring investment managers

[3.37]

Although IMRO rules require investment managers to monitor and audit the funds under management, this does not absolve the insurance company from ultimate responsibility. To satisfy the requirement of adequate systems of control, the DTI recommended the following minimum standards:

1. There should be a tailor-made investment contract[1] in place which sets out the limits within which the investment managers can operate. The balance between risk and reward has to be judged and made clear (usually within the limits the investment managers have discretionary investment powers).
2. The reporting requirements imposed on the investment managers should be sufficient to allow the insurance company to judge whether or not the investment operations are compliant.
3. The capital adequacy rules for investment managers also have to be monitored if the manager is a counterparty to some of the investment transactions.

4. If the investment manager is a company, the 'fit and proper' tests under ICA 1982 apply.

1 See Chapter 2.

D. Controls over derivatives

(i) Admissible derivatives

[3.38]
Guidance is given on the use of derivatives[1] subject to the asset valuation rules in insurance funds at PGN 1995/3. It also applies to the use of derivatives in property linked funds.

1 ICR 1994, SI 1994/1516 applies to over the counter (OTC) and exchange-traded derivatives.

[3.39]
It is important that both management in the life company and investment managers are aware of the seven criteria which derivatives must meet in order to be given an admissible value, namely that they:

(a) are for the purposes of reduction of investment risk or efficient portfolio management;
(b) satisfy the 'in connection with' test:

> 'As a general rule, free-standing derivatives are inadmissible. The usual requirement is that a derivative must be used in connection with an asset of a different type for the purposes of efficient portfolio management or reduction of investment risks. However under [ICR 1994, SI 1994/1516] regulations 55(2) and (3), free standing derivatives or combinations thereof can be admissible provided that they satisfy certain conditions. We refer to the alternative tests jointly as the "in connection with" test. An analogous test applies in linked funds.' (PGN 1995/3, para 4.11.)

(c) are covered;
(d) are listed on a regulated market or transacted with an approved counterparty;
(e) are capable of being readily closed out;
(f) are based on underlying assets which are themselves admissible, an index of such assets or an official index of retail prices; and
(g) have a prescribed pricing basis.

(ICR 1994, SI 1994/1516, reg 55 and PGN 1995/3, para 2.1–2.3: the PGN also gives practical examples of the criteria.)

(ii) Directors and management responsibilities

[3.40]
PGN 1994/6 on controls stresses that directors of an insurance company collectively will need to have sufficient expertise to understand the issues arising out of the use of derivatives, and that management fully understand and comply with the following issues:

1. Investment managers are suitably qualified to transact in derivatives.
2. The company's policy on the use and monitoring of derivatives is clearly drafted and monitoring should include compliance audits.
3. Systems should be put in place to ensure that the company's solvency position and policyholders' reasonable expectations (PRE) are never in danger. Systems should be triggered on adverse market movements to hedge or close out a position. Particular attention needs to be paid to uncovered transactions (ie only allowed in relation to assets not matching the technical provision).
4. Those monitoring the use of derivatives are sufficiently independent from those transacting in derivatives.
5. Management is capable of analysing the risk of the transactions on a single or aggregate basis.
6. Adequate accounting and other systems are in force to cope with the volumes and volatility of the transactions.
7. Management have regular statistical information and regular reports on all off-balance sheet transactions.
8. Sufficient controls to check positions and prices and authorisation where dealing limits exceeded, etc.
9. Valuation models are tested, especially against the robustness of the portfolio to stress in changing investment conditions.

6. SUMMARY

[3.41]

1. Insurance companies must operate within a minimum margin of solvency. The type and amount of assets which can be used to cover the margin of solvency are restricted. The investment restrictions are to ensure that the insurance company's investment philosophy follows the principle of sound and prudent management, which is the cornerstone of continuing authorisation under ICA 1982.
2. Investments in long-term funds are divided into investments which qualify as permitted links (property and indices) (ICR 1994, SI 1994/1516, Sch 10); and for non-linked business the limits on exposure to assets and counterparties apply as set out in ICR, Sch 12.
3. The calculation of liabilities are determined by reference to ICR 1994, Pt IX.
4. Adequate systems of control must be in place to monitor compliance with the regulations and particular attention must be given to the use of derivatives.

Chapter 4
The roles of the actuary

1. INTRODUCTION

[4.1]
It is essential to a proper understanding of the operations of a life assurance company to grasp the extent of the roles of the actuaries within the company. The appointed actuary, the reporting actuary and the pensions scheme actuary are creatures of legislation and although ICA 1982, the Pension Schemes Act 1993 (PSA 1993) and secondary legislation under these Acts provide an outline of their respective roles, much of the detail is left to professional guidance notes (GN) issued by the Faculty of Actuaries (Scotland) and the Institute of Actuaries (England).

2. THE APPOINTED ACTUARY

A. Introduction

[4.2]
The appointed actuary has a central role in the overall running and supervision of a life assurance company. In terms of ICA 1982, s 19(1):

> 'Every insurance company . . . shall within one month of beginning to carry on long term business appoint an actuary as actuary to the company; and whenever an appointment . . . comes to an end the company shall as soon as practicable make a fresh appointment.'

[4.3]
The appointed actuary must be a Fellow of either the Institute or the Faculty of Actuaries and be at least 30 years old (Insurance Companies (Accounts and Statements) Regulations 1996, SI 1996/943 (IC(AS)R), reg 30). Both of these bodies insist on onerous criteria being met before issuing a certificate. Essentially, the applicant needs several years of relevant experience and up-to-date compliance with continuing professional development. In addition, on appointment the appointed actuary will have to satisfy the Government Actuary that he is in a position to fulfil all his statutory obligations and the profession's standards of practice: this usually involves an invitation to the proposed appointed actuary to attend an informal discussion at the Government Actuary Department (GAD) on his or her responsibilities.

B. Statutory responsibilities

(i) Annual valuation and determination of surplus

[4.4]
It is the statutory duty of the appointed actuary to conduct an annual investigation into the insurance business of the company and its financial position (ICA 1982, s 18). In particular, he has to investigate and report on the valuation of assets and liabilities in respect of long-term business. If, as is usual, the different classes of business are held in separate funds (which in turn may have subdivisions corresponding to product variations), each fund has to be valued separately and any excess or shortfall of assets over liabilities established.

[4.5]
The investigation will determine:

(a) whether a statutory certificate under IC(AS)R 1996, SI 1996/943, reg 28(b) can be given;
(b) the margin of solvency (ICA 1982, s 32);
(c) whether there is a surplus (ICA 1982, s 30);
(d) what rights any group of policyholders have to share in that surplus ICA 1982, s 29(2); and
(e) whether a dividend may be declared (ICA 1982, s 29(7)).

[4.6]
The valuation of assets and liabilities is to be carried out in accordance with the regulations contained in ICR 1994, SI 1994/1516: valuation of assets is dealt with at Pt VIII at regs 44–57 and determination of liabilities at Pt IX, regs 58–75. The appointed actuary must be aware of the method of valuing assets, but the ultimate responsibility for this rests with the directors.

[4.7]
When the investigation is complete, or if a similar exercise is carried out at any other time, for example if the company is restructuring; or with a view to distributing profits or if the Treasury call for an investigation into the financial status of the company under ICA 1982, s 42, an abstract of the actuary's report is to be made available to the public. The format of the abstract is set out at IC(AS)R 1996, SI 1996/943, Sch 4.

[4.8]
The annual abstract is included in the HM Treasury returns of the company (ICA 1982, s 18(1)(b)) together with documents under ICA, ss 17 (profit and loss account, revenue account, balance sheet plus notes, statements, reports and certificates) and 21(auditors' report) and IC(AS)R 1996, SI 1996/943, , Schs 1, 3, 4 and 6. These documents are referred to collectively as the annual DTI (now HMT) or Supervisory Returns. The remaining documents to be provided by the appointed actuary are discussed below and those required from the directors and auditors are covered at Chapter 8.

Valuation of assets

[4.9]
The DTI produced a PGN 1995/1 on the asset valuation regulations (ICR 1994, SI 1994/1516, Pt VIII – AVR). The AVR interact with the rules on the admissibility of assets (see Chapter 3). The DTI recommend the following steps in determining the value of assets:

1. the asset has to be categorised correctly under the regulations;
2. rules are then applied based on prudent valuation methods which approximate to the value which would be achieved in an orderly run-off; and
3. the admissibility rules should then be applied to determine how much of the value can be attributed to the solvency margin calculation.

[4.10]
If there is no valuation rule for a particular asset (eg gold), it must be given a nil value. There is also an overriding rule for all valuations, namely that if the value arrived at under the rules is unlikely to be realised then a lesser value must be given.

Determination of liabilities

[4.11]
ICR 1994, SI 1994/1516, reg 61 states:

> 'An insurance company which has or may have . . . an obligation . . . to deliver assets or make payment shall –
>
> (a) at all times identify the assets held by it which it considers most suitable to cover such obligation; and
> (b) make prudent provision for the effect on the amount of its excess assets of adverse variations between the value of the assets identified and the value of the assets which it is or may be obliged to deliver or the amount of the payment which it is or may be obliged to make.'

[4.12]
ICR 1994, SI 1994/1516, reg 64 states:

> 'The determination of the amount of long term liabilities . . . shall be made on actuarial principles which have due regard to the reasonable expectations of policy holders and shall make proper provision for all liabilities on prudent assumptions that shall include appropriate margins for adverse deviation of the relevant factors.'

[4.13]
The approach generally adopted is that the valuation method and basis (assumptions) must have appropriate margins for prudence. It is also important to test the resilience of surplus to sudden changes in assets. The appointed actuary can determine his own test, but most follow the tests suggested by GAD, namely:

	Equity values	*Property values*	*Fixed interest yields*
(a)	-25%	-20%	-10% (eg 5%–4.5%)
(b)	-20%	-10%	-20% (eg 5%–4%)
(c)	-25%	-20%	+3% absolute (eg 5%–8%)

[4.14]
ICR 1994, SI 1994/1516, reg 64 also states that the determination of the liabilities is to be carried out in conformity with ICR, regs 65–75. GN 8 points out that ICR, regs 65–75 only provide minimum criteria and require professional interpretation in their application and regard to PRE. The guidance is that in determining liabilities:

> 'the valuation basis should be sufficiently strong to enable an appropriate level of reversionary bonus to emerge . . . but not as requiring implicit or explicit provision for any element of terminal bonus.'

[4.15]
GN 8, para 3 provides guidance on each of the above regulations.

[4.16]
Some changes have been proposed to ICR 1994, SI 1994/14516, regs 58–75 and are expected to be implemented by the end of this year.[1]

1 Insurance Companies (Amendment) Regulations, SI 2000/1231 effective from 29 May 2000.

Margin of solvency

[4.17]
ICA 1982, s 32 states that: 'every insurance company . . . shall maintain a margin of solvency of such amount as may be prescribed by or determined in accordance with regulations . . .'

[4.18]
A calculation in respect of each class of business to determine the solvency margin as set out at ICR 1994, SI 1994/1516, regs 16–26 has to be carried out and a statement in respect of each fund made on what the required minimum margin is.

[4.19]
The appointed actuary has to assess the amounts of mathematical reserves and capital at risk to be used in the calculation of the margin of solvency. In addition, the appointed actuary has to advise the company on how to maintain the margin of solvency: it is a professional requirement that in addition to the annual valuation, the appointed actuary at any time should be satisfied that the company is in a sound financial position and that the prudential rules are being met. In order to achieve this, systems have to

be put in place to allow the appointed actuary to monitor and measure key operations within the company. This would include information on:

1. volumes of business;
2. premium rates;
3. surrender values, maturity values and paid-up values and claims;
4. investment performance and strategy;
5. exposures to derivatives;
6. expense levels;
7. tax and legislation; and
8. reassurance arrangements. (See GN 1, s 4.2 for more details.)

[4.20]
This information should enable the appointed actuary to judge the financial position of the company especially compliance with the minimum solvency margin requirement throughout the year.

Determination and distribution of surplus

[4.21]
If the result of the ICA 1982, s 18 investigation is to establish an excess of assets over liabilities then the restriction at ICA, s 29(1) that assets of an insurance company which represent its long-term business can only be used for the purposes of that business is waived in respect of assets representing the excess and so allowing distributions to be made to policyholders and shareholders (ICA, s 29(2)).

[4.22]
In reaching a decision on the distribution of any surplus, the appointed actuary should take into account the information detailed at **[4.19]** above.

[4.23]
GN 1, para 8.2 states that:

> 'If the Appointed Actuary has reason to believe that the company plans to announce or otherwise undertake to make a specific allocation of profits to policyholders and/or shareholders in anticipation of the results of a [ICA 1982] s 18 investigation (notwithstanding that, to comply with [ICA 1982] s 29(2), confirmation that the investigation shows a sufficient excess of assets over liabilities must precede an actual transfer of assets out of the long-term fund), the appointed actuary must take all reasonable steps to ensure that the directors will be in a position to consider a suitable written actuarial report on the subject before the announcement is due to be made or the undertaking given.'

[4.24]
The appointed actuary should also ensure that the statutory provisions for distributing a surplus are also repeated in the company's articles.

(ii) Formalities of supervisory returns

[4.25]
Documents included in the Supervisory Returns must be signed in accordance with IC(AS)R 1996, SI 1996/943, reg 27. Guidance on completion of the returns is also given in PGN 1998/1.

[4.26]
In terms of ICA 1982, s 22, the abstract, along with the accounts and auditors statement (if any), must be deposited with the Treasury within six months[1] of the end date of the accounts together with five printed copies or, alternatively, one printed copy and one copy in a form approved by the Treasury and signed. The six-month period can be extended by up to three months at the Treasury's discretion, but they are reluctant to exercise it in practice.

1 The FSA has announced its intention to shorten the timescale for submission of the returns to three months.

[4.27]
Under ICA 1982, s 23, shareholders and policyholders have a right to receive copies of the abstract of the report and the other documents submitted annually to the Treasury. The Treasury can exempt the company from complying with this if they consider disclosure of the information would be harmful to the insurer's business.

[4.28]
Regulators can also require returns on a more frequent basis (ICA 1982, s 42). This is only done where either the company is new or in difficulties and usually the regulator will only ask for certain forms rather than a full set of returns.

[4.29]
If there is a surplus it is excluded from the requirements of ICA 1982, s 29 and if it is to be allocated to policyholders then ICA 1982, s 30 applies. If there is a shortfall, HM Treasury can intervene in the running of the company, for example by insisting on closing to new business (ICA 1982, ss 41 and 45). In practice, a company in serious financial difficulties is likely to be bought over by a larger and stronger office.

[4.30]
The appointed actuary must be satisfied at all times that the company is solvent, not just once a year (GN 1, para 4.1).

(iii) IC(AS)R 1996

[4.31]
These set out the information to be included in the annual returns to the supervisory body by the directors, auditors and appointed actuary. IC(AS)R, SI 1996/943, Sch 4 prescribes the format of the abstract of the

actuary's valuation report and IC(AS)R, Sch 6, Pt I covers the matters to be certified by the directors: IC(AS)R, Sch 6, Pt II prescribes the additional certification required to be made by the appointed actuary and IC(AS)R, Sch 6, Pt III covers the auditors' report.[1] The actuarial certificate includes the following:

1. Annual certification of data adequacy
   The appointed actuary must certify whether in his opinion proper records have been kept by the company adequate for the purpose of the valuation of the liabilities of its long-term business.
2. Certification of mathematical reserves
   IC(AS)R 1996, Sch 6, Pt II 8(a)(ii) requires the appointed actuary to certify that the mathematical reserves shown in the returns constitute proper provision for all of the long-term liabilities.
3. Compliance with valuation and liabilities regulations
   The appointed actuary must state that ICR 1994, SI 1994/1516, Pts VIII and IX (ie the valuation regulations and assessment of liabilities regulations) have been complied with.
4. Compliance with Professional Guidance Notes
   The appointed actuary must state in the form of a list all the Professional Guidance Notes which have been complied with. Usually, the appointed actuary will specify GN 1 and GN 8 as the relevant Guidance Notes.
5. Annual certificate of premium adequacy
   The appointed actuary must certify whether the premiums for business during the financial year, together with any income earned from these, are sufficient, on reasonable actuarial assumptions, and taking into account the other financial resources of the company that are available for the purpose, to enable the company to meet its commitments in respect of these contracts and in particular to establish adequate mathematical reserves.
6. Annual certification of solvency margin
   The appointed actuary must state the amount of the required minimum solvency margin including any amounts resulting from an increase in liabilities due to a distribution of surplus.

1 The certificates required by the directors and auditors are dealt with in Chapter 8.

C. Professional standards of practice

(i) Guidance Notes 1, 2 and 8[1]

[4.32]
In 1975, a joint Guidance Note was issued by the Faculty and Institute of Actuaries (GN 1) which set out the role of the appointed actuary in more detail. This note stresses the importance of access to the board of the company and, in particular, that the actuary should report to the board on the result of the annual valuation of assets and liabilities, the policyholders' reasonable expectations (PRE) and recommendations on the distribution of surplus before any bonuses or dividends are declared.

1 See Appendix 5.

[4.33]
GN 8 provides additional guidance which covers the annual actuarial investigation. It is updated regularly and provides amplification of the statutory requirements.

[4.34]
GN 2 'Financial Conditions Reports' recommends that in addition to the report to HMT the appointed actuary also report in more depth to the Board of the company. GN 2 sets out a possible format for such a report.

(ii) Status of GN 1 and 8 and whistle-blowing requirements

[4.35]
Both Guidance Notes are considered mandatory by the profession. GN 1, para 3 describes the appointed actuary's responsibilities to both company and regulator. There is scope for conflicts to arise for example if the appointed actuary is part of a company incentive scheme to increase new business levels he must be careful to balance this with his regulatory responsibilities to ensure the adequacy of premium rates:

> 'Circumstances may arise such that the Appointed Actuary considers that there is a material risk that the long-term fund will be insufficient to cover its liabilities or that the company will fail to meet its obligations under [ICA 1982] . . . In these circumstances the Appointed Actuary must inform the company accordingly. If the company fails to take action to remedy the position and does not advise the DTI *(now HMT)* of the situation then it is the Appointed Actuary's duty to advise the Department after so informing the company.' (GN 1, para 3.2.)

1 In addition to issuing Guidance Notes they also issue 'Dear Actuary' letters which are usually more informal.

(iii) Future financial soundness (GN 2)

[4.36]
The appointed actuary should also report to the Board on the future financial soundness of the company. In practice, this involves setting up a model (on computer) with a range of variables and assumptions and possible outcomes. Strategies have to be developed for avoiding or dealing with possible adverse outcomes which the model highlights. This requirement is consistent with good corporate governance principles, which are concerned with the control and management of risks.

(iv) Policyholders' reasonable expectations (PRE)

INTRODUCTION

[4.37]
It is the *overall* duty of the appointed actuary to safeguard the reasonable expectations of the policyholders. This puts the appointed actuary in a

different position from other officers of the company, who may have to balance the interests of policyholders with the interests of shareholders and other creditors. The priority of interests is that the reasonable expectations of the policyholders are satisfied before any decision is made on distribution of profits to shareholders. Of course, mutuals do not need to prioritise as the policyholders are in effect the shareholders.

Equitable Life Assurance Society v Hyman

[4.38]
The concept of PRE was discussed in *Equitable Life Assurance Society Ltd v Hyman* [2000] 2 All ER 331, CA, where the High Court noted that there was no statutory definition of the term, but that it did appear originally in ICA 1973, ss 12 and 21 and subsequently in ICA 1982, ss 37 and 45. The court quoted from a Report prepared in June 1993 for the Institute of Actuaries, and accepted the following conclusions of the Report which were that:

> 'The holders [of policies with a discretionary element] may reasonably expect life offices will behave fairly and responsibly in exercising the discretion available to them. They may also expect a reasonable degree of continuity in an office's approach to determining variable charges or benefits.'

and that:

> 'in the normal day to day actuarial management of a life policy, PRE is synonymous with equity and the almost universal method for measuring it is asset share calculation.'

[4.39]
The asset share is made up of a 'guaranteed value', which is the value of the premiums paid (less initial charges), the guaranteed investments returns (ie Equitable Life had a table of guaranteed investment returns which were applicable to the policies under discussion) and the allocated annual bonuses. It was accepted that the guaranteed value may be less than the asset share for the following reasons *Equitable Life Assurance Society Ltd v Hyman*:

> 'First , the guaranteed investment return . . . may be less than the actual rate of investment earned by the Society's with-profits fund. Second, unless the policy matures on the very day an annual bonus is declared, there will be a period after the declaration of the bonus and before the maturity date during which the with-profits fund will have continued to earn an investment return. This return, too, may exceed the guaranteed investment return. Third, the policy of the Society, in recent years at least, has tended to depress annual bonuses relatively to final bonuses. The reason for this policy is that once annual bonuses have been declared and allotted to individual policies, they become reversionary contractual liabilities of the Society and appropriate

provision must be made in the Society's accounts. They need to be funded from reserves represented by fixed interest securities.[1] Fourth, there will in any event be some part of the surplus that will not be allocated as a bonus but will be carried forward as a reserve.'

1 The implications are that if the annual bonus is kept low, the life company can invest in equities which can give a higher rate of return than fixed interest securities and so increase the amount available for terminal bonuses.

[4.40]
The court also accepted that the factors which might shape PRE would include:

'(a) the terms of the contract between policyholders and the Society (ie Equitable Life);
(b) statements made to the policyholders by the Society;
(c) past practice of the Society; and
(d) practice in the industry.'

[4.41]
The High Court found in favour of Equitable Life but this was reversed by the Court of Appeal (Lord Morritt dissenting). Lord Justice Woolf held the Society had exercised its discretion regarding bonuses in an impermissible way by reducing the PRE (ie policyholders would have expected to receive their asset share irrespective of how rights were exercised under the policy); and the policy adopted by the Society had a collateral purpose designed to negative a benefit to which the policyholder was otherwise entitled. Lord Waller held that it was the terms of the policy which prevented the exercise of any discretion and any allotment of a final bonus which was conditional on the choice of the policyholder: he did not accept that the expression 'annuity increased by the related bonuses' could be different depending on whether it was being taken as an annuity or used as a basis for calculating the 'Policy Annuity Value'. The result of the further appeal to the House of Lords is due shortly.

Practical measures of PRE

[4.42]
Equitable Life Assurance Society Ltd v Hyman case discussed PRE in relation to with-profits policies only. In practice, PRE applies to all long-term policies and the 'reasonable expectations' varies with each type of contract, broadly:

(a) non-profit contracts – PRE is met when the company pays out the guaranteed benefits when due;
(b) with-profit contracts – meeting PRE, as well as including (a) above, also requires that the final maturity value will give a reasonable return after taking into account inflation and the cost of risk as compared to deposits and other forms of saving vehicles; and
(c) unit linked contracts – PRE is met if the performance of the chosen linked fund is consistent with the performance of the underlying assets

– eg if the policy holder has chosen a Japanese Fund, its performance should be consistent with the performance of the Japanese stock market.

Development of PRE

[4.43]
It may be that the concept of PRE will be transformed into a legislative requirement in the new Financial Services and Markets Bill as 'the interests of customers', which would include not just investment performance and policy pricing, but also the marketing and selling of products. There is a debate over whether the appointed actuary's role should also be extended to ensure the interests of customers is being met in the marketing and selling of products. It is argued that if the actuary's role is so extended, mis-selling of products would be less likely.

[4.44]
The present position is that policyholders can request a copy of the company's 'With Profit Guide', which is largely written by the appointed actuary and describes how the company manages its with profit business, especially its bonus policy. In addition, quotations of future benefits in marketing material and on statements to policyholders requires input from the appointed actuary (see GN 22).

D. Auditors and directors

[4.45]
The supervisory returns are not subject to audit and an auditor can rely on the appointed actuary's certificate. The directors, although relying on the appointed actuary for calculations, are ultimately responsible for the supervisory returns.

E. DTI/HM Treasury Prudential Guidance Notes

[4.46]
Responsibility for supervising life assurance companies has moved from the DTI to HM Treasury. Eventually, the Financial Services Authority will have overall control of both prudential and marketing/selling supervision. In their role as prudential supervisors, these organisations are assisted by the GAD.

[4.47]
Copies of PGNs are included in *Butterworths Insurance Law Handbook* (5th edn, 1998).

F. Possible changes in Financial Services and Markets Bill

[4.48]
Discussions are taking place on the role of the appointed actuary becoming more involved in compliance with the regulations, but many in the actuarial profession think that this detracts from their central role in helping to run the life company.

3. THE REPORTING ACTUARY

A. Introduction

[4.49]
The Companies Act 1985 (CA 1985), Sch 9A created a new role for actuaries, namely the reporting actuary to be responsible for the calculation of the mathematical reserves/technical provisions for long-term business which have to be included in the annual financial statements of the company:

> 'The computation shall be made annually by a Fellow of the Institute or Faculty of Actuaries on the basis of recognised actuarial methods and with due regard to the actuarial principles laid down in the Council Directive 92/96/EEC.'[1] (CA 1985, Sch 9A, para 46(3).)

1 The Third Life Directive.

[4.50]
These calculations, unlike those of the appointed actuary in the Supervisory Returns, are subject to audit. Also, the directors can outline the approach they wish the reporting actuary to adopt in preparing the calculations, whereas it is considered improper for them to influence the calculations prepared for the Supervisory Returns, even though the directors are ultimately legally responsible for them. The reporting actuary must bear in mind that the calculations appearing in the financial statements may be relied on by third parties. The reporting actuary may, but need not, be the same person as the appointed actuary.

B. Duties of reporting actuary

[4.51]
The reporting actuary needs to understand accounting principles and be familiar with SSAP2 (produced by the Accounting Standards Board) and the relevant sections of the Statement of Recommended Practice (SORP) produced by the ABI (see Chapter 8). The reporting actuary will prepare a report for the Board setting out the approach adopted in calculating the long-term business provision and the methods and assumptions used. The report should also cover any disclosure required by the Companies Act (Insurance Companies Accounts) Regulations 1993, SI 1993/3246. If the reporting actuary uses the same basis for his calculations as the appointed actuary has used in the Supervisory Returns, it is nevertheless the reporting actuary who remains responsible for the calculations as they appear in the financial statements. The reporting actuary can arrive at different conclusions from the appointed actuary but should however defer to the appointed actuary on questions relating to PRE. A full description of the role of reporting actuary can be found in GN 7.[1]

1 See Appendix 5.

4. THE PENSIONS ACTUARY

A. Introduction

[4.52]
Under the Pensions Act 1995 (PA), s 47(1)(b), it is the duty of the trustees of an occupational pension scheme (OPS) to appoint, inter alia, a scheme actuary.[1] This section took effect in April 1997. If a company with an OPS has sufficient resources, it can establish, administer and invest the pension fund in-house. In addition to trustees, the company may want to employ: a lawyer to draft the trust deed and scheme rules and other documents and advise on compliance with legislation; pension administrators to collect contributions, send out benefit statements, arrange for payments of benefits; investment managers to make investment decisions, unless the trustees feel confident taking those decisions themselves (in which case, if they are managing investments as defined in FSA 1986, they will need to be authorised: FSA, s 191); an auditor to produce annual audited accounts; and an actuary to value the scheme, set minimum funding levels and calculate benefits. This is a costly exercise and many companies prefer to set up a fully insured pension scheme.

1 Prior to the Pensions Act 1995 a defined benefit scheme still needed an actuary to perform a triennial valuation. However, apart from that the trustees did not have to seek actuarial advice on, for example, transfer value calculations etc.

[4.53]
In a fully insured scheme, the insurance company provides all the expertise to manage an OPS from inception to winding up. It may be that no member trustees need to be appointed under the Occupational Persion Schemes (Member-nominated Trustees and Directors) Regulations 1996, SI 1996/1216. (In a Small Self Administered Scheme (SSAS) the insurance company (or a subsidiary) would also be appointed as pensioner trustee.) The insurance company's investment department or associated investment management company would invest the sums which would form part of the long-term fund. The insurance company provides the services of a scheme actuary. The current obligations of the pension scheme actuary are discussed below.

B. Obligations of pension scheme actuary (PSA)

[4.54]
As in the case of the appointed actuary, the obligations of the pension scheme actuary are set out in a mixture of legislation and professional guidance notes. The duties of the PSA are more onerous in relation to OPS which are defined benefit schemes rather than defined contribution schemes.[1] The PSA also needs to hold a current practising certificate from either the Faculty or Institute of Actuaries. In general, the PSA is accountable to the trustees of the scheme.

1 See Chapter 5 below.

(i) Actuarial valuation reports, minimum funding requirement (MFR) and scheme contributions

[4.55]
A full MFR actuarial valuation (for defined benefit schemes) has to be carried out at intervals of three to four years (PA 1995, ss 56–61 and the Occupational Pension Scheme (Minimum Funding Requirement and Actuarial Valuations) Regulations 1996, SI 1996/1536), reg 10) (OPS(MFR)R 1996). The point of the MFR valuations is to ensure the scheme is adequately funded. Once an MFR has been completed, the PSA will draw up a recommended schedule of contributions (to be agreed by the trustees and the employer and which must then be certified by the PSA as being accurate), which may need to be amended and re-certified in the light of the results of annual checks.[1] The valuations have to be carried out in accordance with the OPS(MFR)R 1996 as amended and Actuarial Guidance Notes GN 9 and GN 27. Essentially, the test is whether the scheme has sufficient funds to pay cash equivalents (see below) of accrued early leaver benefits for all current members and for those with preserved benefits and a corresponding concept for current pensioners and other beneficiaries. The test is considered to be weaker than that originally contemplated in the Goode Report.[2]

1 Ongoing valuations have to be carried out to ensure the contribution rate is adequate: PA 1995, s 41 and OPS(MFR)R, reg 30.

2 Professor Roy Goode was appointed as Chairman to the Pensions Law Review Committee to report on pensions law following the Maxwell pension scandal. It was recommended in the report that MFR be based on the scheme's ability to fund annuity contracts for members.

[4.56]
In terms of PA 1995, s 41 and the Occupational Pension Schemes (Disclosure of Information) Regulations 1996, SI 1996/1655, the trustees must make the actuarial reports available to members of the scheme and recognised trade unions.

(ii) Certification of tax-free limits

[4.57]
Compliance with FA 1986, which introduced a limit on the amount of assets which could be held tax free in a non-insured exempt approved scheme, is also the responsibility of the PSA. The PSA must certify that tax free assets do not exceed 105% of liabilities (ICTA 1988, Sch 22, para 2(3)). This also involves carrying out a valuation and applies to both defined benefit and defined contribution schemes.

(iii) State Earnings Related Pension Scheme (SERPS) and contracted-out schemes

[4.58]
Defined benefit schemes which have contracted out of SERPS had to provide a guaranteed minimum pension (GMP) which mirrored the member's entitlement had he or she remained in SERPS up until 5 April 1997. GMP was introduced in April 1978 by the Social Security Pensions

Act 1975. Under the original legislation, an actuary had to certify (Certificate A) that the scheme was able to provide a GMP for each of its members. GMP no longer accrues within schemes. For members of a contracted out scheme post 5 April 1997, benefits have to be at least broadly equal to those set out in a 'reference scheme'.[1] Again, the PSA has to certify that this is the case for at least 90% of members and their spouses. The relevant professional guidance note is 'Retirement Benefit Schemes – Adequacy of Benefits for Contracting-out on or after 6 April' (GN 28).

1 Details of the reference scheme are set out at PSA 1993, Sch 12B and Occupational Pension Schemes (Contracting-Out) Regulations 1996, SI 1996/1172, regs 25 and 26.

(iv) Certification on transfer

[4.59]
The PSA is also responsible for the calculation of cash equivalents (ie a sum which represents preserved pension rights) for individual transfers. The relevant legislation is PSA 1993, ss 94–97 and the Occupational Pensions Schemes (Transfer Values) Regulations 1996 (SI 1996/1847): The relevant guidance note is GN 11 'Retirement Benefit Schemes – Transfer Values'. For bulk transfers, PSA 1993, s 73 and the Occupational Pension Schemes (Preservation of Benefits) Regulations 1991 (SI 1991/167) provide that if the trustees want to dispense with the consent of all the members to the transfer, the PSA must certify, inter alia, that the benefits in the new scheme are at least comparable to the benefits in the old scheme. GN 16 provides full details.

(v) Certification on winding up

[4.60]
If a defined benefit scheme is winding up, the PSA must determine the liabilities of the scheme and any deficit or surplus. PA 1995, ss 73–77 and the Occupational Pension Schemes (Deficiency on Winding Up etc) Regulations 1996, SI 1996/3128 and GN 19 deal with the winding up of a scheme. If there is a deficiency, measured as the difference between the assets and the sum of the cash equivalents, it is treated as a debt on the employer.

(vi) Changes to trust deed

[4.61]
If the trustees wish to amend the scheme documentation in an OPS without obtaining all the scheme members' consent, the PSA must be able to certify that the proposed amendments will not have an adverse effect on members' accrued rights. The relevant legislation is PA 1995, s 67 and Occupational Pension Schemes (Modification of Schemes) Regulations 1996, SI 1996/2517.

(vii) Supervisory body and duty to 'whistle blow'

[4.62]
The Occupational Pensions Regulatory Authority (OPRA) is the supervisory authority for OPS. Under PA 1995, s 48, the PSA of an OPS

has a duty to 'whistle-blow' to OPRA if there has been a breach of the regulations which could be of 'material significance'. This extends the traditional role of the actuary, which is usually limited to purely financial matters. There is no duty for the PSA to seek out breaches, only to report them when they occur. Other professional advisers have a right to whistle blow, but are not required to do so. It is thought that the PSA and other professional advisers are consequently immune from civil action from employers if they do fulfil their duty or exercise their rights.

5. OTHER NON-STATUTORY ACTUARIAL ROLES

[4.63]
In addition to their statutory roles, actuaries are frequently managing directors of life companies, and their other roles within a life company may also include product development, quotations and liaising with the Compliance Officer on matters under FSA 1986.

6. RELATIONSHIP BETWEEN STATUTORY ACTUARIAL ROLES AND DIRECTORS AND AUDITORS

A. Directors

[4.64]

> 'The directors of an insurer writing long-term insurance business . . . are responsible for all the statements made and amounts shown in financial statements prepared under the Companies Act. To the extent that these statements contain amounts calculated by an actuary, the directors will be placing reliance on the professional expertise of the actuary to calculate the amounts. Nonetheless the directors remain legally responsible for the preparation of the financial statements and ensuring that they give a true and fair view of the state of affairs, and results of the company.' (GN 7, see Chapter 8.)

B. Auditors

[4.65]
The supervisory returns are not subject to audit, and the auditor can place reliance on the certificates issued by the appointed actuary. CA 1985, Sch 9A requires that the technical provisions are included in the financial returns and they are subject to audit (see GN 7 and Chapter 8).

7. SUMMARY

[4.66]
1. Every insurance company must appoint an actuary whose role is to produce, inter alia, the annual supervisory returns for which the

directors are ultimately responsible and to ensure the company operates within its solvency margin at all times.

2. The overall duty of the appointed actuary is to safeguard the policyholders' reasonable expectations.
3. The reporting actuary is responsible for the calculation of the technical/mathematical reserves/provisions in the financial returns, which are subject to audit.
4. The pensions actuary is responsible for carrying out MFR and other valuations for occupational pension schemes.
5. Actuaries can play many other non-statutory roles in a life company.

Chapter 5
Long-term contracts

1. INTRODUCTION

[5.1]
The classes of contracts a life company can enter into are listed at ICA 1982, Sch 1 based largely on the First Long-Term Insurance Directive, art 1. The Schedule and the Article are at Appendix 1. In practice, they broadly fall into four categories, namely:

1. life policies which may or may not have an investment factor;
2. policies relating to health;
3. pensions; and
4. life or pensions annuities.

[5.2]
A typical life insurance contract is provided for ten years or over because there are certain tax advantages afforded to such contracts. To qualify for the tax advantages, a contract has to meet the conditions set out at ICTA 1988, Sch 15. Policies which meet the conditions are referred to as 'qualifying policies', and the conditions as the 'qualifying rules'. Failure to continue paying premiums or early cancellation of the contract may result in a charge to tax (see **[5.12]–[5.15]** below). Again, pension contracts, to benefit from certain tax advantages have to meet the conditions set out at ICTA 1988, Ch XIV, in particular, benefits under pensions contracts must not be paid (except in specific circumstances, eg early retirement due to ill-health) until the person receiving the benefits has reached 'normal retirement age'. This is usually somewhere between 50 and 75 years, and the benefits for the most part are paid in the form of pension annuity contract covering the remainder of the persons life.

2. LIFE POLICIES

A. Introduction

[5.3]
Life policies can be taken out to cover the life of the policyholder or another person, where insurable interest exists, or on a joint life basis. Funds may be invested on a with- or without-profits basis, or on a unit linked basis or on a unitised with-profit basis. Premiums are quoted to cover the mortality risk (ie tables covering age/sex/health are usually used by underwriters and any difficult medical information is passed to the chief medical officer (CMO) of the life company for comments); commission and expenses[1] and

investment, if any. Policies are either for protection only or have a mixture of protection and investment; some unit linked policies have minimal protection (see *Fuji Finance v Aetna Life Assurance Co Ltd* [1996] 4 All ER 608, CA). Policies can be taken out by paying regular premiums or single premiums. If the policies comply with the tax requirements, they are 'qualifying'; non-qualifying policies can also be sold.

1 Expenses are usually loaded so that the administration costs and commission are recouped over the first one to two years of a traditional (ie with-/without-profits) policy. Unit linked policies usually include a bid/offer spread, annual management expenses of about 1%, an annual policy fee and some initial charge for setting up the policy.

B. Term insurance

[5.4]
This is probably the most simple of the contracts and consists of a premium being paid for a term of 10–25 years, which will provide life cover for the term. It can be set up for a shorter period without affecting the tax position (see **[5.12]–[5.15]** below). On the death of the life assured within the term, the life company will pay the trustees (if any) or executors or joint policyholder the sum assured plus any bonuses. If the policyholder survives the term then nothing is paid and the policy lapses. Term assurance contracts can be structured as follows:

1. Level term – where the sum assured remains the same throughout the term.
2. Decreasing term – where the sum assured decreases over the term: this is used to cover outstanding repayment mortgages where the capital outstanding decreases and is often cheaper than level term insurance.
3. Convertible term – where the policyholder has the right at some point during the term to convert the policy (usually without further underwriting) to an endowment or whole of life policy.
4. Renewable term – where the policyholder has the right to renew the policy for a further term (again without further underwriting).

(Note: the rights mentioned at 3 and 4 above can only be exercised where ten years of the term remain, otherwise the policy may cease to qualify for tax purposes (see **[5.12]–[5.15]**).)

C. Whole of life

[5.5]
This primarily provides protection for the whole of a person's life: payment of the sum assured is made whenever death occurs. It also acquires a surrender value, normally after one to two years.

D. Guaranteed whole of life

[5.6]
On payment of a single premium, a guaranteed return (usually linked to the FTSE) can be made to the policyholder after, typically, five years. The

policyholder can, at the end of the five years, leave the sum invested or withdraw part or all of the sum. These types of policies are non-qualifying and the guarantee is usually underpinned by some derivative contract.

E. Endowment assurance

[5.7]

This provides the life cover on the same level term basis as **[5.4]** above, but a proportion of the premium charged will cover the risk and expenses and the remainder will be invested, so that at the end of the term (if the life assured has not died) the policy will mature and the sum assured together with any investment return (whether by way of bonuses or the increase in the value of units) will be paid to the policy holder.

F. ISAs

[5.8]

These were introduced on 6 April 1999 and were intended to replace PEPs (existing PEPs can continue, but with no further contributions). They come in two forms, namely 'maxi' or 'mini'. The maxi ISA involves investing in a mixture of cash, equities (either directly or through a unit trust or other collective investment scheme) and insurance; a mini ISA involves an investment in one of these types of investment. There is an initial limit of £7,000 for 1999/2000 and thereafter an annual limit of £5,000.[1] The limits are split as follows: the full £7,000 can be placed in equities in the first year and thereafter the limit is reduced to £3,000; no more than £1,000 in cash (£3,000 for 1999/2000); £1,000 for insurance in the first and subsequent years. The cash from a maturing Tessa can be transferred to a Tessa only ISA without affecting these limits. If funds are withdrawn, reinvestment is only possible within the original limits.

1 The £7,000 limit has been retained for 2000/01.

[5.9]

The proceeds of ISAs, like PEPs, are free of income tax and capital gains tax. They also obtain a 10% tax credit paid on UK dividends and unit trust distributions until 5 April 2005. This applies to UK dividends and UT distributions in an insurance ISA. An insurance company has to apply to the Inland Revenue to become an ISA manager, but can only manage an insurance mini ISA. If the insurance element is to be combined with the other elements, an authorised person under the Financial Services Authority can apply to be manager. Insurers can, in these circumstances, make use of a subsidiary.

[5.10]

The government has introduced CAT standards (ie low charges, easy access and fair terms). The CAT standard is not a guarantee of investment performance, and individuals still need to decide whether the particular product is suitable to meet their financial needs.

[5.11]
There are different CAT standards for each type of investment. The relevant legislation is Individual Savings Account Regulations 1998, SI 1998/1870. as amended.

G. Taxation of life policies

[5.12]
ICTA 1988, Sch 15 (see Appendix 4) covers the taxation of life policies. Tax relief is given if the policy is a 'qualifying policy': endowment or whole of life policies[1] must satisfy a number of conditions, which in broad terms are as follows:

1. the policy must be taken out for a period of ten years or more;
2. premiums must be paid regularly and kept up to date;
3. the total premiums in any 12-month period must not be greater than twice the amount paid in any other similar period, or one eighth of the total premiums paid over the whole term;
4. the policy must guarantee that the sum paid on death is at least 75% of the premiums which would be payable if the policy ran its term, but there is a statutory concession on this (A 45);
5. partial or total surrender is possible without the policy ceasing to qualify; and
6. options and variations of policy conditions can have the effect of making the policy non-qualifying (see IR Press Release, 27 January 1988, on the IR's view of what constitutes a variation).

1 The qualifying rules are not usually a problem for term assurance contracts. Non-qualifying policies typically pay tax on the difference between maturity or surrender value and the premiums paid. On death, the surrender value rather than the actual death benefit is used. As term assurance contracts have no maturity or surrender value, no tax is payable. It is not uncommon to have term assurance contracts, therefore, for a term of less than ten years, but they must be for at least a term of 12 months: ICTA 1988, Sch 15, para 10(1).

[5.13]
If these conditions are met, the lump sum paid out at maturity is free of tax.[1] If not, a higher rate tax payer may have a charge to tax on the occurrence of a chargeable event, namely:

1. on death;
2. on the maturity of the policy;
3. on the total or partial surrender of the rights under the policy including bonus; or
4. the partial or total assignment of the rights for money or money's worth;
5. withdrawals in excess of 5% pa;
6. change of life/lives assured.

1 Pre-14 March 1984, tax relief was also given on premiums paid to qualifying policies – life assurance premium relief (LAPR) – and this still exists for policies taken out prior to that date.

[5.14]
The method of calculating the charge to tax for higher rate tax payers is referred to as 'top-slicing'. Essentially, a policyholder is allowed to take

5% of the sum assured each year and not incur a tax charge until the policy matures (eg when the policyholder may expect to be a lower rate tax payer, eg after retirement). At maturity, tax is due on the excess of maturity value over premiums paid, where the maturity value includes the 5% pa annual withdrawals taken previously. If there is a gain, basic rate tax is assumed to have been paid already, so only higher rate tax payers at the date of maturity have to pay tax.

[5.15]
The law on policyholder taxation is currently under review as it is considered too complex, and also difficult for life offices to administer. For a full treatment of the subject see *Butterworths' UK Tax Guide 1999/2000*.

3. HEALTH CONTRACTS

A. Critical illness

[5.16]
This contract provides cover if the policyholder is diagnosed as suffering from a list of diseases. It is usually underwritten to exclude any illness the policy holder has suffered from in the past. It can be offered with or without an investment element.

B. Income replacement

[5.17]
This contract provides cover if the policy holder has to take time off work as a result of accident or injury, and suffers a loss of income as a result. Maximum cover limits apply, so that usually the combined benefit from the policy and the state represents less than 75% of previous earnings. This provides an incentive to return to work. The definition of 'incapacity' is important, especially if it relates to incapacity to do 'any occupation' rather than the one the policyholder is qualified to do. Payment ceases on retirement.

4. PENSIONS

A. Introduction

[5.18]
There are roughly nine different types of exempt approved pension arrangement in the UK. For a pension to benefit from the tax advantages, the Pensions Schemes Office (PSO) of the Inland Revenue must approve its structure. Although there is scope for automatic approval for occupational pension scheme (OPS) arrangements which meet all the conditions in ICTA 1988, Ch 1, Pt XIV, s 590 (see Appendix 4), the usual route is to ask the IR for approval under ICTA, s 591. Under this section, approval is discretionary. The PSO have issued Practice Notes (IR 12) 1997

on how they exercise their discretion, and this is supplemented by Joint Office Memoranda of the PSO and the Occupational Pensions Board. The key criteria for approval is that scheme rules must not permit contribution levels and maximum benefits to exceed the Revenue limits.

[5.19]
In addition, the scheme must be 'exempt' if it is to obtain the full range of tax advantages (ICTA, s 592). Broadly, OPS have to be set up under irrevocable trust (note: personal pensions can be set up by special resolution of the life company or by deed poll).

[5.20]
There are a number of different types of unapproved arrangements, mainly designed to fund benefits in excess of Revenue limits, which can also be sold by life companies.

[5.21]
Some of the arrangements can be set up to be contracted out of SERPS.[1] If it is contracted out, the scheme must provide benefits which are equivalent to the benefits the member would have received from SERPS. The advantage of contracting out is that reduced NI contributions are paid by both employee and employer, but, to balance this, the scheme must provide benefits to at least equal the SERPS type benefit. Contributions to pensions schemes from both employer and employee are tax deductible whereas NI contributions are paid after tax.

1 See **[4.58]** on changes relating to SERPS.

[5.22]
Some arrangements can be set up to be fully insured, which means that a life company invests the fund and provides all the administration, or it can be self invested, which means the trustees of the scheme can either on their own or through an appointed fund manager invest the fund. Under FSA 1986, s 191, trustees of an OPS would be considered to be carrying on investment business and so need authorisation, unless the day-to-day management is passed to an authorised firm, eg IMRO regulated fund managers. Lastly, a life company can also provide pension fund management without the administration, or the administration on its own and allow the trustees or personal pension holder to manage the investment.

[5.23]
The remaining distinctions are covered below.

B. Occupational pensions schemes (OPS)

(i) Introduction

[5.24]
OPS are where employers set up a scheme for all or part of the workforce. This is contrasted with individual arrangements like personal pensions,

where the individual is responsible for his/her own arrangements, although employers can contribute to some individual arrangements. OPS can be contributory or non-contributory (ie the employer alone funds the scheme). There are no direct limits on employer contribution but if the scheme becomes over funded a refund can be made to the employer in terms of PA 1995, s 37 and ICTA 1988, Sch 22: tax under, Sch D, case VI has to be deducted from the repayment in terms of ICTA 1988, s 602. The position on underfunding is discussed below. The limit on employee contributions is 15% of the employee's remuneration in that year. Benefits can include tax free cash (TFC) pension, spouses pension, children's pension, death benefits: Revenue limits apply to each of these. There are three sets of limits depending on when a member joined a scheme. The current limits are:

1. for a member's pension, two-thirds of final pensionable salary (FPS);
2. for the TFC, 150% of FPS;
3. a spouse or dependent's pension of two-thirds of the member's allowable pension on death after retirement; and
4. death in service benefit of up to four times salary and a spouse or dependent's death in service benefit of two-thirds of the member's maximum pension.

[5.25]
These limits are subject to an overall earnings cap which increases periodically.

[5.26]
Benefits must accrue at a given rate: a maximum of 1/60th of FPS per year of pensionable service to a maximum of 40 years for the pension (although it can also accrue at 1/30th for 20 years) and 3/80ths for the tax free lump sum. Benefits must be taken at retirement and normal retirement age is between 60 and 75. There must be no discrimination in retirement ages or benefits between men and women in respect of service post-17 May 1990 (*Barber v Guardian Royal Exchange Assurance Group* ECJ (C-262/88) [1990] 2 All ER 660, ECJ and PA 1995, ss 62–66). Pension benefits are not assignable.[1]

1 Personal pensions can be used by lenders as security for mortgage purposes: the lenders do not take an assignment, but leave it up to the borrower to decide how best to repay the mortgage at the end of the term.

[5.27]
Special rules apply to 20% directors (ie controlling directors who own at least 20% of the ordinary share capital of the company in the last ten years).

(ii) Defined benefit schemes

[5.28]
These are sometimes referred to as final salary schemes, and are probably the most complex arrangements because of the funding requirements. These schemes offer their members a pension usually expressed as 1/60 x final pensionable salary (FPS) x years of service. Revenue maximum rules

put a limit on this as 40/60 x FPS. Thus, retirement provision can be at two-thirds of FPS and part of this can be taken as tax free cash (TFC). There are specific rules on what can be included as FPS. The pensions actuary has to calculate the level of contributions required by employer and employee to fund the future benefit. PA 1995 introduced the 'minimum funding requirement' (MFR), which is the amount necessary to cover the cash equivalents of members benefits. If the scheme is under funded then the employer has to make good the shortfall within a stated period (PA 1995, s 60). If over-funded, any contributions returned to the employer may be taxed at 40% (see ICTA 1988, ss 601–603 and Sch 22).

[5.29]
If the scheme is contracted out, the SERPS equivalent benefit, referred to as a guaranteed minimum pension (GMP), must be paid although this is being phased out (see **[4.58]**).

(iii) Defined contribution schemes

[5.30]
These are sometimes referred to as money purchase schemes because the scheme simply sets contributions at a certain level for the employer and or employee (within Revenue limits) and at retirement each member will have a fund which will provide tax free cash and the purchase of an annuity. The fund cannot provide benefits above the Revenue maximum. If this type of arrangement is contracted out of SERPS, the equivalent benefit is referred to as 'protected rights' (PR).

(iv) Hybrid schemes

[5.31]
It is also possible to have an arrangement which provides a mixture of guaranteed and money purchase benefits.

(v) Additional voluntary contributions (AVC)

[5.32]
If a member of an OPS is not contributing up to the Revenue maximum in the OPS, he or she can take out a top up policy called an AVC. The terms of the OPS must allow employees this option. Only pension benefits are available (ie no lump sums). At retirement, the benefits under the OPS and the AVC have to be taken at the same time and the combined effect should not breach Revenue maximum limits. Contributions must cease on leaving the OPS.

(vi) Free standing additional voluntary contribution (FSAVC)

[5.33]
These are much the same as AVCs, but are not connected to the OPS and on a change of employment they can continue.

(vii) Buy out policy (BOP)

[5.34]
This is an arrangement which the trustees may consider if they are winding up the scheme or an employee is leaving. With the consent of the member, the trustees buy out or secures the benefits under the OPS using these individual policies. They cannot take further contributions and must reflect the benefits available in the main OPS.

(viii) Executive pension schemes

[5.35]
These are designed for directors, executives and key employees and are provided and established by employers.

(ix) Small self-administered schemes (SSAS)

[5.36]
These are schemes set up for 12 or fewer directors of a company. The relevant legislation is the Retirement Benefits Schemes (Restrictions on Discretion to Approve) (Small Self-Administered Schemes) Regulations 1991 (SI 1991/1614) RBS(RDA)(SSAS)R 1991 and IR 12 (1991) and PSO Memorandum 109. The regulations affecting these schemes are generally less rigorous than for the OPS because the scheme is in effect run by the members. For example, investment in the employing company is allowed to a greater extent in SSAS (50% after two years) as opposed to a limit of 5% self investment in an OPS. However, although this may present a few problems in relation to security of benefits it does provide more scope on the tax front. For this reason, it is a condition of approval that a pensioner trustee (PT) be appointed. In order to be considered for this role, the requirements set out at SSASR 1991, reg 9 have to be met, namely that the individual or body must:

(a) be widely concerned with OPS;
(b) have dealings with the PSO over a period of time; and
(c) give an undertaking to the PSO to refuse to consent to any termination of the scheme otherwise than in accordance with the approved terms of the winding up rule (IR 12 (1991), PN 20.4).

[5.37]
A life company will usually have a trustee company which will take up this role and, in practice, it involves overseeing the running of the scheme to ensure compliance with RBS(RDA)(SSAS)R 1991, SI 1991/1614. Appointments and resignation of PT are covered at PN 20.9. A PT must not be connected with a member, other trustee or employer of the scheme (PN 20.8).

(x) Pension fund management

[5.38]
Policies can also be designed to manage the funds of a self administered, as opposed to a fully insured, OPS. The policy must meet the

'correspondence' provisions at ICTA 1988, s 431B(2)(b), which states that 'pension business' includes 'any contract (including a contract of insurance) entered into for the purposes of, and made with the persons having the management of, an exempt approved scheme as defined in Chapter 1 Part XIV, being a contract so framed that the liabilities undertaken by the insurance company correspond with liabilities against which the contract is intended to secure the scheme'.

C. Personal arrangements

(i) Personal pension (PP)

[5.39]
These can be set up by a number of institutions as well as life companies (ie banks, investment firms and building societies). The institution becomes administrator of the scheme and there need not be trustees. The regime for PPs is set out at ICTA 1988, Pt XIV, Ch IV. The IR provide practice notes at IR 76, which set out in more detail conditions for approval. The PP can be taken out by anyone with relevant earnings who is not a member of an OPS.[1] It is a money purchase arrangement and members' IR maximum contribution levels (expressed as a percentage of relevant earnings) increase with age, subject to an overall earnings cap. Employers can also make contributions to the PP, but both employer and employee contributions are taken in combination when applying the IR limits. The advantage of the PP is that it is 'portable', which means that the member can retain the same PP while changing jobs or moving from employed to self employed status. On leaving an OPS, benefits can be left or transferred to a new OPS or PP or APP (an appropriate personal pension which could be used for contracting out of SERPS). This involves the calculation of a Transfer Value (TV). The pensions mis-selling scandal arose largely as a result of employees being advised to leave their final salary schemes and transfer to a PP or to join a PP where they had a choice to join a defined benefit schemes (DBS). On transfer, the TV was reduced by sales costs before being invested in the PP. Also, whereas the pension is guaranteed in DBSs, as in all money purchase arrangements, the risk is with the policyholder as the value of the fund (if invested in unit linked policies rather than a with-profit policy) could be reduced by a stock market crash.

1 It is not possible to belong to an OPS and a PP in respect of the same relevant earnings: if a member of an OPS has another source of income then a PP could be obtained.

[5.40]
Investment choices for PP have increased (see Memorandum 101). On retirement, an annuity must be purchased with an insurance company unless the drawdown arrangements which were introduced on 1 May 1995 are utilised, see **[5.54]** below. PP became available on 1 July 1988.

[5.41]
It is also possible for an employer to arrange a group personal pension scheme (GPP), usually set up with one pension provider and where the employer and employees agree to a certain levels of contribution.

(ii) Retirement annuity contracts (RAC)

[5.42]
These were the forerunner to the PP, but were narrower in scope, in that: (i) only the self-employed and employees not eligible to join an OPS could take them out (prior to the introduction of PP, employees could be compelled to become members of their employer sponsored scheme); (ii) employers could not contribute to them and they could not be used to contract out of SERPS; and (iii) an annuity could commence between 60 and 75 years.

(iii) Taxation of pensions

[5.43]
Contributions by employees up to Revenue maximum obtain tax relief at the highest rate paid by the employee; employers' contributions are expenses and are tax deductible. The pension fund is run on a tax free basis, ie no tax is levied on investment income or gains; the withdrawal of advance corporation tax (ACT) is expected to have an effect on the fund's performance as ACT charged on UK dividend income cannot be reclaimed by the fund.

[5.44]
The lump sum and death benefits are free of CGT and normally free of IHT. The annuity is subject to income tax at the rate payable by the pensioner.

5. STAKEHOLDER PENSIONS

A. Introduction

[5.45]
The non-tax aspects of stakeholder pensions is contained in the Welfare Reform and Pensions Act 1999 (WRPA 1999), Pt I and The Stakeholder Pension Schemes Regulations 2000, SI 2000/1403. The tax aspects of the regime are contained in the draft Finance Bill 2000 and draft regulations will be issued shortly. The current timetable is to allow schemes to begin registering with OPRA and IR from October 2000 and begin operating from 6 April 2001.

B. WRPA 1999, Pt I

(i) The conditions of registration

[5.46]
WRPA 1999, Pt I, ss 1–8 deals with stakeholder pensions.
WRPA 1999, s 1 sets out the conditions which must be met in order to register a scheme as a stakeholder scheme under WRPA 1999, s 2. The conditions include:

1. that it is set up under trust or in some other way prescribed by regulations (see **[5.49]**);
2. that the documentation complies with the regulations;

3. that the benefits are money purchase benefits;
4. that charges against contributions, benefits and value of rights under the scheme comply with the regulations;
5. the scheme complies with the disclosure regulations under PSA 1993, s 113;
6. that subject to minimum contribution levels and other restrictions, members can contribute what they like;
7. subject to maintaining tax approval, the scheme must accept transfer payments from a number of arrangements; and
8. the scheme has tax exemption or approval.

(ii) Employers' duties

[5.47]

1. That at all times there is at least one scheme designated and registered as a stakeholder scheme and offers membership to all relevant employees – before designating a scheme the employer has a duty to consult employees and any representative organisations.
2. Supply the name and address of the designated scheme and any other information under the regulations.
3. Allow representatives of the designated scheme reasonable access to the relevant employees.
4. If requested to do so by an employee who is a member of a qualifying scheme, deduct contributions from his salary and pay to the trustees or manager of the scheme.
5. If the scheme ceases to be registered under WRPA 1999, s 2 to withdraw his designation of the scheme (the employer can also withdraw designation of scheme in other circumstances).

Failure to comply with the above requirements will attract a civil fine.

(iii) OPRA

[5.48]

OPRA will keep a register of stakeholder schemes and have powers of inspection to ensure compliance with WRPA 1999.

C. Stakeholder Pensions Schemes Regulations 2000

[5.49]

The Stakeholder Pensions Schemes Regulations, SI 2000/1043 broadly cover the following:

- The scheme can be set up under trust or contractually with a Financial Services Authority authorised scheme manager. Both arrangements must provide a default investment option and be wound up on loss of registration. Trust-based schemes must have independent trustees, but can restrict membership. Contract-based schemes must be open to all and produce a statement of investment principles which includes need for diversification.
- The 1% charge is the only charge that can be levied and there are regulations on how it is to be calculated. Additional charges for advice and other services must be made in a separate contract.

- Information on contributions, fund growth and charges must be provided to members at least once per year.
- Exemptions for employers who have under five employees, who arrange a GPP and contribute at least 3% of basic pay and have payroll deduction facilities, or if an OPS offered within 12 months of commencing work (and may exclude under those 18 years old and those within five years of retirement).

D. Draft Finance Bill clauses

[5.50]
The draft Bill provides an integrated tax regime for all defined contribution schemes and covers the following:

- contributions of £3,600 pa, irrespective of earnings;
- limits on contribution levels increased and can continue for five years after earnings stop;
- contributions paid net of tax and provider making claim from Revenue;
- Occupational money purchase schemes can opt into new regime;
- carry back/carry forward rules replaced by simpler rules;
- 10% of contributions can pay for life cover (at present only 5%);
- tax relief for waiver of contribution insurance simplified and to apply to more than ill-health (eg unemployment);
- shares from approved employee share scheme can be transferred to scheme;
- UK residency a requirement unless abroad on 'Crown duties';
- cannot be member of defined benefit scheme or defined contribution scheme which is not part of this regime and contribute under this regime;
- phased vesting of benefits;
- electronic applications.

6. ANNUITIES

A. Life annuities

[5.51]
If a regular income from capital is wanted, either for a term or for life, then an annuity can be purchased. The amount paid for the annuity will depend on interest rate levels, the age and, if 'impaired life' annuity is applied for, the state of health of the policy holder and whether any additional feature is added, such as index linking.

B. Pension annuities

(i) Compulsory purchase annuities

[5.52]
It is an important feature of the tax exempt approved pension regime that although some of the benefits can be taken as tax free cash, the majority of the sum invested purchases an annuity on retirement. So, when

retirement age is reached and benefits have not been secured by any other method, an annuity must be purchased – hence the name.

(ii) Deferred annuity

[5.53]
When a member leaves an occupational pension scheme – eg on change of employment – before normal retirement age, the pensions actuary can work out, on a number of assumptions, what the pension will be on retirement and may recommend to the trustees to secure the future liabilities of the scheme by purchasing a deferred annuity.

(iii) Drawdown arrangements

[5.54]
Normally, the annuity has to be purchased on retirement, but because of current low annuity rates, the IR allowed life companies to offer an 'income drawdown' arrangement. They were designed to allow policyholders who had retired to put off purchasing an annuity by drawing down capital from their pension fund to meet their income needs, and purchase an annuity when rates are favourable (FA 1995, Sch 11). An example of how the arrangement can work is that the policy could be divided into, for example, 1,000 arrangements. The capital drawn down (or encashment of a number of the arrangements) each year would be used partly to purchase an annuity and partly to provide income. Each year, a lesser amount of capital to provide purely income would be needed as annuity income built up. They are currently under scrutiny by the regulators.

(iv) Open market options

[5.55]
This is an option given to money purchase arrangements to shop around and purchase an annuity on the open market. Some life companies offer enhanced rates to impaired lives (eg smokers). The current low level of annuity rates is a result of annuitants continuing to live longer and the yields on gilts being at historically low levels.

C. Guaranteed annuity rates

[5.56]
A number of life companies sold products with guaranteed annuity rates (GAR). This was financially reasonable while interest rates were high. However, the drop in interest rates over the past few years has meant that returns on gilts (ie the securities used to back annuities) have been insufficient to meet the guaranteed amounts, and so insurers have had to use their reserves. As reserves are reduced mutual insurers become vulnerable to takeover because there are very limited methods whereby a mutual can raise new capital (see Chapter 6). Some actively seek this as a means to boost their capital, for example, the recent takeover by Lloyds TSB

of Scottish Widows. The Equitable Life Assurance Society (EL) decided that if it was to meet the guaranteed amounts, it would not in addition pay terminal bonuses to these policyholders. One of the policyholders challenged this and took EL to court. The following is a summary of the judgment.

(i) Equitable Life Assurance Society Ltd v Hyman [2000] 2 All ER 331, CA

FACTS

[5.57]
EL issued pension policies with GAR and also an option to take benefits in fund form to purchase an annuity with some other life company.

[5.58]
EL articles stated that the directors had an absolute discretion in declaring bonuses and apportioning bonuses among policyholders and their decision is final and conclusive.

[5.59]
As current annuity rates dropped below the guaranteed annuity rates, EL changed its final bonus policy to allow those with GAR policies to opt for either a GAR and no final bonus or a reduced final bonus or to take the fund option with the final bonus.

ARGUMENTS FOR EL

[5.60]
EL argued that each with-profits policyholder was entitled to a 'notional asset share' of the with-profits fund. This was represented partly by the 'contractual entitlement', which was the sum of the premiums paid (less initial charges), guaranteed investment returns and annual allocated bonuses. Any difference between the asset share and the contractual entitlement is made up by allocating terminal bonuses. Those with GAR were obtaining more than their asset share and EL, in fairness to the reasonable expectations of all policyholders, reduced the final bonus of those who took the GAR accordingly.

ARGUMENTS FOR POLICYHOLDERS

[5.61]
Three main arguments were put forward on behalf of the policyholders:

1. Policyholders in exercising their contractual right to take GAR should not prejudice the amount of bonus allocated to them.
2. The directors in taking into account the form in which the policyholders chose to take benefits when allocating bonuses were exercising their discretion improperly.
3. That the directors had failed to take into account the contractual rights of the policyholders in allocating final bonuses and deprived policyholders of their asset share.

COURT'S DECISION

[5.62]
The court held that:

1. The contract between EL and the policyholders did not prohibit an allocation of final bonus from being conditional. The definition in the policy of 'related bonuses' refers to 'such amounts as under the rules and regulations of the Society have been allotted' and art 65 of the Society's Articles permits the directors to apportion the total declared bonus among the participating policyholders 'on such principles and by such methods as they may from time to time determine'.
2. The communications to the policyholders by EL and the previous practice (which was to give GAR and final bonus) did not create a reasonable expectation that the fund option would equal the value at current rates of the GAR based annuity, nor that the same rate of final bonus would be applied to all policyholders. That the directors did take into account the PRE of all policyholders and the exercise of their discretion was not improper.
3. The policyholders were not deprived of their asset share.

APPEAL

[5.63]
The appeal by the policyholder against the High Court judgment was heard by three judges, who found in favour of the appellant (Lord Morritt dissenting). Equitable Life has been given leave to appeal to the House of Lords. The leading judgment given by Lord Woolf was that the Society had exercised its discretion in an impermissible way by reducing the PRE (ie policyholders would have expected to receive their asset share irrespective of how rights were exercised under the policy); and the policy adopted by the Society had a collateral purpose designed to negative a benefit to which the policyholder was otherwise entitled. Lord Waller held that it was the terms of the policy which prevented the exercise of any discretion and any allotment of a final bonus which was conditional on the choice of the policyholder: he did not accept that the expression 'annuity increased by the related bonuses' could be different depending on whether it was being taken as an annuity or used as a basis for calculating the 'Policy Annuity Value'.

7. UNDERLYING INVESTMENT FOR PRODUCTS

[5.64]
Investment policy will be determined depending on the type of fund the product is invested in:

1. Unit linked
   For unit linked products, there are a range of investment options which the policyholder is free to choose: eg UK small companies funds; Japanese funds; European Growth funds, etc. The marketing literature

will describe the investment philosophy of each fund in terms of market sector, type of investment, whether the fund is designed to maximise capital.

2. Non-profit
   Non-profit funds are usually invested in fixed interest or cash, and the term of the assets would normally tie in with the policy term.
3. With-profit
   With-profit funds will invest in a mixture of equities, properties and fixed interest investments.
4. Guaranteed products
   These are usually backed by derivatives. For example, if growth in the FTSE 100 is guaranteed over a period, then the sums paid (single premiums) to the company will normally be invested in a way that covers the guaranteed amount ie using over the counter (OTC) derivatives or a combination of these and financial reassurance.

8. SUMMARY

[5.65]

1. The products offered by life companies are complex, partly because of their long-term nature, but also because of the interaction with different legal and tax regimes.
2. They are also difficult to administer as systems have to be developed for dealing with each product and all the legal and other variations to it.
3. Different investment strategies have to be formed to suit different types of products.

Chapter 6
Reassurance

1. INTRODUCTION

A. Risk

[6.1]
Why do life companies reassure large sections of their business? The answer to this question has become more complex as increasing varieties of financial arrangements are classified as 'reassurance'. The traditional answer is reasonably straightforward, namely to spread the risk. The concepts of 'risk' and 'insurable interest' have traditionally been the critical factors in determining whether to classify contracts as insurance and reassurance contracts. The concept of 'insurable interest' is designed to differentiate insurance from a wager, or a bet, on a person's life, which was prohibited under the Life Assurance Act 1774. The concept of 'risk' is designed to differentiate insurance from mere deposit taking activities carried on by banks and building societies. Increasingly, these distinctions are becoming blurred, or disappearing altogether, as the financial arrangements entered into by life companies and their reassurers take on the characteristics normally associated with deposit taking and lending.

B. Traditional and financial reassurance

[6.2]
In this chapter, the traditional reassurance arrangements and the more complex financial reassurance arrangements will be analysed to show the purpose of entering into these arrangements, and also to highlight the drift away from the core concepts of insurable interest and risk. Prior to doing so, the financial mechanics of different types of life assurance business has to be understood and the following section deals with this.

2. FINANCIAL MECHANICS OF LIFE ASSURANCE BUSINESS

A. Traditional with-profits and non-profits business

[6.3]
The valuation of assets and liabilities and the maintenance of the statutory solvency margin is critical to the continued operation of the life company. In traditional business this is a more acute problem than for unit-linked business, for reasons which are explained below. Traditional life policies can be sold with or without participation in the profits of the life company.

The appointed actuary will value the assets and liabilities of the life fund annually and, if there is a surplus, all or most (ie usually 90%) of it can be allocated to policyholders. Bonus notices may be issued giving policyholders a share of the surplus on a pro-rata basis, depending on the amount assured. Policies under discussion include whole of life, term assurance, endowments, deferred pensions and permanent health insurance. In this type of business, if the life company has accepted the risk, then, as soon as the first premium is paid the, life company has an immediate liability for the sum assured. For example, a monthly premium of £50 is paid to provide life cover of £5,000. On the business being written, the life office has assets of £50 (less commission and other expenses) and has liabilities of £5,000 (plus any declared bonuses). The life office is therefore undercapitalised and the problem prior to selling new traditional business is how to find the capital of £4,950. It is, of course, not as straightforward as this, as it is obvious that the chances or risk of the policyholder dying immediately the business is written (provided the underwriting has been carried out prudently) is low.

[6.4]
Secondly, as the policyholder and the policy become older, while the risk of paying out increases, the risk to the capital of the life office decreases. So, after five years, although the policyholder is older and the mortality risk is greater, the life office has received £3,000 in premiums (less expenses plus growth) against a liability of £5,000 (plus any declared bonuses). If the life office has performed well in its choice of investments and fund management and kept costs low, the dent to capital if the sum assured becomes payable on death after five years is reduced. The situation is not so pronounced where payments are made to the policyholder on early surrender as penalties are applied: on surrendering the policy earlier than its term, the life office will want to recoup expenses which are incurred; the bulk of expenses are incurred over the first two years of the policy, and that is why policies of under two years normally have a surrender value which is less than the premiums paid. If the policy runs to its term (eg a ten-year endowment), then at the end of ten years the life office will have received £6,000 (less expenses plus growth) and pay out £5,000 together with any declared bonus and terminal bonus. Ideally, the actuary will have set bonuses at a rate which is less than the growth less expenses so that the life office can make a profit. The profit on the contract can be used to increase bonus rates in the future, pay shareholders or support further new business. (See Chapter 4 for a discussion of the roles of the actuaries in valuation, determining bonuses, setting premium levels and calculating surrender values.)

B. Annuities business

[6.5]
Traditional annuities business is virtually a mirror image of the life business discussed above: the capital sum is paid by the policyholder to the life office at the outset and the life office pays the annuitant a periodic

sum (monthly or annual) for a fixed period, or until death. The cost of an annuity will generally fluctuate with interest rates. So, when interest rates are low, annuity rates will also be low and so the cost of buying a set annuity amount will increase (ie the annuity amount = premium/1000 x annuity rate).

[6.6]
When setting annuity rates, the life company has to decide:

(a) the interest it will earn;
(b) how long the annuitant will live; and
(c) what expenses it will incur.

The life company will make a profit or loss if these assumptions turn out to be better or worse than the actual experience.

C. Traditional pensions business

[6.7]
Pensions can be analysed into a package of investment, annuities and term assurance, together with one or two important additional features. Exempt approved pension schemes (ie those approved by the Revenue and benefiting from favourable tax treatment which are discussed more fully in Chapter 5) provide a lump sum on death during employment, tax free cash and an annuity/ pension on retirement. Within pension business, there are (for present purposes) two types of arrangements, namely defined contribution and defined benefit arrangements. In the former, the contribution level is agreed and paid by the employee and employer and in this way a fund is built up. The life company can offer a sum assured to cover death benefits, but it is also possible simply to return the fund on death; on retirement, the fund is used to provide tax free cash and purchase an annuity. In a defined benefit arrangement, the lump sum death benefits are usually expressed as a multiple of salary and the pension a fraction of final pensionable salary multiplied by the number of years in service. Periodically, these arrangements have to be evaluated by the pensions actuary to ensure they are properly funded. In essence, defined benefit schemes have the same problems as a life company namely, to maintain sufficient capital over a long period to meet long-term financial commitments. In so far as the life company offers life cover and annuities, there will be a corresponding mortality and capital risk, but the remaining funding requirements are assumed by either the employee or the employer. The trustees of the pension scheme are responsible for ensuring the appropriate contributions are made.

D. Unit linked business

[6.8]
Unit linked business does not altogether share the problems of risk associated with traditional business. In most unit linked products, the policyholder takes the risk: the premiums invested buy units in a pooled fund, which is regularly valued, and the policyholder is entitled to the total

value of his or her units at any time during the contract. The value can fluctuate depending on the performance of the underlying assets, which are usually unit linked insurance funds. On death, the policyholder will normally receive 101% of the value of his or her units, so there is a minor mortality and capital risk to the company. However, in many linked contracts (eg whole of life and low cost endowment mortgages) there can be significant additional death benefits: the sum at risk would then be the difference between the death benefits and the unit value. The life company can cover its expenses by taking initial charges, annual charges and operating a bid offer spread in the purchase or sale of units[1] (although movement towards a single pricing system is now a favoured approach).

1 Policies can be constructed with an allocation percentage which is less or more than 100%. For example:
allocation % = 90%
bid offer spread = 95%
if the policyholder pays a premium of £100 then £90 would be invested in the unit fund and after applying the bid offer spread, the value of the unit holding would be £90 x (1-5%) = £85.50.

[6.9]
The question has been raised whether certain unit-linked contracts are genuine insurance arrangements. In *Fuji Finance Inc v Aetna Life Assurance Co Ltd* [1996] 4 All ER 608, CA it was initially held that a contract which offered virtually the same amount on death as on survival was not a contract of insurance under the Life Assurance Act 1774, s 1 and the life office was in breach of ICA 1982, s 16, which only allows authorised insurers to conduct *insurance* business. The facts were that Fuji took out a unit linked life policy with Tyndall Assurance on the life of one of their managers, Mr Tait. In terms of the policy, a sum calculated on the basis of the price of units allocated to the policy was payable on surrender or death. If the policy was surrendered within five years, additional charges would be levied. The policyholder then utilised the switch option on the policy and exploited the time delay between the valuation of the fund and the price being published. By doing this, Fuji was able to increase the surrender value from £50,000 to £1,000,000 in six years. Tyndall was taken over by Aetna Life Assurance, and this company reviewed and changed the switching process. Fuji claimed this was a breach of contract and surrendered the policy and sued for damages.

[6.10]
Two preliminary points were put to the court:

1. Was the policy void by virtue of having no insurable interest?
2. If the policy was not a policy of insurance was it unenforceable in terms of ICA 1982, s 16?

[6.11]
The Vice-Chancellor, who heard the case at first instance, held that:

1. To qualify as a policy of insurance on the life of a person, the sum paid must be contingent on an uncertain event relating to human life. In this case, the same sum was payable on surrender as on death and

the policy was therefore not a policy of life assurance and so could not be void under the Life Assurance Act 1774, s 1.

2. Since it was not a policy of insurance, it contravened ICA 1982, s 16, but, having been issued in good faith, it was not automatically unenforceable.

[6.12]
This decision was appealed to the Court of Appeal, which reversed the decision and held that the policy was a contract of life assurance: they argued that it did not matter that the sum payable on death equalled the sum on surrender and that the contingency related to the time of payment, which was uncertain, and the policy was a contract of life assurance.

[6.13]
They did not need to fully answer the second point (although the three judges offered different opinions), which was on the status of the policy if not a policy of life assurance (ie under ICA 1982, s 16, an insurance company can only transact insurance business or business connected with insurance business). The case was then appealed to the House of Lords and was due to be heard in July 1998. However, parties settled out of court and the Court of Appeal decision stands. Insurers have to be careful to ensure that policy wordings on benefits payable are sufficiently linked to contingencies on human life. This decision has a knock on effect in respect of any reassurance of this type of business.

3. CAPITAL

A. New business strain

[6.14]
At **[6.3]** and **[6.4]** it was explained how mortality and capital risk emerged from the sale of one policy. However, when dealing with several thousand policies, certain adjustments have to be made. Firstly, the actuary has to take a view about the cost of mortality risks across a class of business. Obviously, when the business is new the mortality risk will be low and over time will increase. Technically, therefore, premiums should start off low and increase over time. However, life companies considered this too difficult to administer and operate a system whereby the excess proportion of the premium in the early years of a policy is put to one side and a fund is built up and invested, which should cover any sum paid at maturity or death. This fund is known as a reserve under a policy and, overall, is part of the life company's reserves.

[6.15]
Generally, life expectancy has improved over the years, but any individual life company may experience adverse mortality risk. If this happens, the difference between the amount of any claim and the amount of reserve under the policy is referred to as 'the sum at risk'. Funding this difference

is referred to as the 'new business' strain. Reassurance is a method of stabilising fluctuating mortality experience. A life office will set limits on the amounts of business it will retain and reassure the rest in order to balance capital requirements and new business.

[6.16]
For example, in year 1 of a policy:

Premium received – £1000
Expenses incurred – £200
Commission paid – £900
Increase in reserves – £500
Statutory profit (loss) – £600

This 'loss' will be recouped out of future premiums but, if the company writes a great deal of new business in a year, it could generate substantial statutory losses, which reduces available capital.

[6.17]
This only applies to with- and without-profits contracts: for linked business, it is usual for a monthly charge to be applied which varies with age to cover mortality risk.

B. Additional capital

[6.18]
The life company may also wish to raise or hold capital over and above the statutory amount necessary for other reasons. These reasons can include: (a) showing how financially strong the company is, which can help from a marketing point of view; (b) in order to pursue more flexible investment strategies; and (c) to invest in, for example, distribution outlets in order to expand the business.

C. Raising capital

[6.19]
The options for raising capital include the following:

(i) capital can be built up slowly over a long period by writing profitable business;
(ii) if the life office is a mutual, it could demutualise and raise capital from its sale or flotation;
(iii) if the life office is a private proprietary company and part of a group of financial services companies, it can raise capital from its parent company;
(iv) if the life office is a plc, it can issue new shares or offer other forms of stock;
(v) capital can be raised by borrowing from a bank or some other organisation; and
(vi) all or part of the business can be reassured.

D. Cost of capital

[6.20]
The appointed actuary then has to consider the cost of raising the capital. In this respect, reassurance may have an advantage over loans and other forms of capital in the way it is treated for tax purposes. Detailed commentary is contained in Macleod and Levitt *Taxation of Insurance Business* (4th edn, 1999). There are two types of reassurance, traditional and financial, and they are discussed in the following two sections.

4. TRADITIONAL REASSURANCE

A. History of reassurance

[6.21]
It is thought that the first reassurance agreement was between two Scottish life offices in the mid-nineteenth century. By 1900, 48 life offices, which were members of the life offices Association, developed a standard contract to cover all reassurance arrangements between life offices. This contract is known as the Reassurance Agreement 1900 and is still used today. A checklist of clauses for a traditional reassurance agreement is at Appendix 8. The relationship between life office and reassurer is similar to the relationship between life office and policyholder: the principles of uberrima fides and insurable interest are both present. The policyholder has no contractual relationship with the reassurer, and his policy with the life office remains unaffected by the reassurance arrangements. In the twentieth century, specialist reassurers emerged and these offices do not deal directly with the public, but only with life offices. It is now more common to reassure through the specialist reassurers and, usually, reassurance through a life office is limited to inter-group reassurances (ie where one life office is owned by another).

B. Types of reassurance arrangements

[6.22]
There are basically two types of traditional reassurance arrangement and two types of basis on which they can be provided: the two arrangements are (i) facultative and (ii) treaty; the two bases are (i) original terms and (ii) risk premium basis.

(i) Facultative reassurance

[6.23]
This is carried out on an individual policy basis, and the life company cannot accept the proposal for life assurance until the reassurer has agreed to reassure the policy. Acceptance by the reassurer is usually by way of exchange of certificate, or an endorsement is placed on a copy of the original policy. The reassurer may, however, decline to accept, and the reasons may be that the reassurer's limit of retention has been reached, the premium is

too low or the underwriting is unacceptable. As this method of reassurance is administratively time consuming and costly, it is more appropriate for very large risks, and the treaty method below is preferred in most other cases.

(ii) Treaty reassurance

[6.24]
Under a treaty, the life company negotiates with the reassurer to provide automatic cover within defined parameters, which will usually include the class of insurance to be covered, age of the life assured and sum assured. This gives the life office scope to accept proposals quickly and more efficiently.

[6.25]
There are four different types of treaty:

1. First surplus treaty – whereby the life company can commit the reassurer to cover the balance exceeding the life company's retention limit up to an agreed limit (ie the first surplus).
2. Second surplus treaty – as its name suggests, this really is an addition to (1) and provides for further automatic cover if the first surplus is exceeded.
3. Quota share treaty – whereby the life company reassures a fixed percentage of every contract written for a specific class of business.
4. Facultative/obligatory treaty – whereby the life company has an option to reassure individual risks with the reassurer or elsewhere, but if it does so, the reassurer is obliged to accept within agreed limits.

[6.26]

> 'Rather than make special arrangements for each case it is simpler to conclude a reassurance treaty with a reassuring office. Under the treaty the reassurer agrees to accept a share of the risk on all the policies the ceding company underwrites, and where the sum assured exceeds the ceding company's retention; the amount that the reassurer will accept automatically is limited to, say, up to ten times the retention of the ceding company and, of course, is not more than the reassurer's own retention. The ceding company thus obtains automatic cover for a considerable amount and is free to accept immediately any case presented to it, within the agreed limits, without having to obtain reassurance cover facultatively for each case; this last may be very difficult when the nearest possible reassurer is some thousand miles away, rather than across the square in Edinburgh.' (AD Wilkie MA, FFA, FIA, FSS 'Reassurance' (1963) *Actuarial Students' Magazine*, 25 February.)

(iii) Original terms basis

[6.27]
If the reassurance of a proportion of risk is on identical terms to the original policy in terms of premiums, bonus rates and commission, it is said to be on 'original terms'. The reassurer will share in any interest, surrender and

profits, including mortality profits. Further, it is common for the reassurer to pay higher commission to assist the life company with initial expenses (ie the reassurer does not incur any sales or marketing costs).

(iv) Risk premium basis

[6.28]
On this basis, the reassurer does not pay surrender values or maturity values, as the life office can pay these from the reserves mentioned at **[6.14]** above, but pays only death claims. The liability of the reassurer each year will be the difference between the nominal sums assured and the reserves[1] under the policies. The premium paid to the reassurer will vary over the term of the policy, eg in the case of a ten-year endowment policy, the premium will initially be large and then reduce. If the investment performance of life office funds are good, it is usually more beneficial to have reassurance on this basis.

1 The ceding company will accumulate the reserves for the whole policy and the difference between the sum assured and the reserves is the amount at risk.

5. FINANCIAL REASSURANCE

A. Introduction

[6.29]
Financial reassurance has been particularly popular in the life assurance industry, not only as a method of easing the capital strain on new business and spreading risk but also as a means of raising capital in a tax efficient way.[1]

1 Craig Thornton 'Alternative sources of capital for life offices' (1999) *The Actuary*, April.

B. Structure of financial reassurance

[6.30]
There are two aspects to financial reassurance:

1. the traditional reassurance of the mortality risk of the reassured business; and
2. a cash advance from the reassurer, which, together with interest, is repaid in the form of a reassurance premium.[1] The cash advance, in fact, represents the expected future profits from the reassured business and the premium is the actual profits realised. The interest on the advance will usually be at LIBOR plus a margin to reflect, mainly, the risk of profits failing to emerge. The life company will invest the cash advance in deposits or some other safe assets. More could be earned in equities, but the market could fall just prior to a payment becoming due.

1 (See Appendix 9 for sample wording.)

C. Financing products

[6.31]
Financial reassurance can be combined with derivatives to underpin guaranteed products.

D. Accountancy treatment of financial reassurance

[6.32]
The reassurance premium is only paid if profits are realised. As future profits cannot be included in the accounts as assets, liabilities secured against future profits have no statutory value. The cash advance can therefore be used as statutory capital.

[6.33]
The life company is effectively mortgaging future profits to achieve an immediate statutory profit. However, developments in Financial Reporting Standards (FRS 5) may mean that the substance of the transaction has to be dealt with, rather than its legal or financial form.

[6.34]

> 'Adequate disclosure of a transaction is important to an understanding of its commercial effect. For most transactions, the disclosures currently required will be sufficient for this purpose. However, where the nature of any recognised asset or liability differs from that of items usually found under the relevant balance sheet heading, the differences should be explained. Furthermore, to the extent that a transaction has not resulted in the recognition of assets or liabilities, disclosure may nevertheless be required in order to give an understanding of its commercial effect.' (FRS 5, p 7.)

[6.35]
If there is a change in the treatment of financial reassurance, it could affect the capital position of some companies.

E. Tax treatment of financial reassurance

[6.36]
The Inland Revenue has always had the power to examine the substance of a transaction. As there are tax advantages to be had from setting up the above reassurance rather than structure the transaction as a loan, the Revenue may wish to examine matters in more detail. There are two possible challenges to the above types of arrangements, namely (1) that there is only minimal insurable interest or the premium paid is incommensurate with the risk assumed, and (2) that the transactions are circular and self cancelling and do not have a legitimate commercial purpose, but are designed solely to obtain a fiscal advantage.

[6.37]

In relation to (1), the position is that the principles which apply to life assurance must also apply to reassurance, and that includes the existence of insurable interest: *Lower Rhine and Würtemburg Insurance Association v Sedgwick* [1899] 1 QB 179, CA. It is, therefore, important in financial reassurance to include the element of pure reassurance which covers some element of the risk under the policies reassured, so that the overall transaction is not categorised as a loan for accounting or regulatory purposes.

[6.38]

In relation to (2), the fundamental rule is that a tax payer is entitled to organise his affairs in a way which is tax efficient:

> 'Every man is entitled if he can to arrange his affairs so that the tax attaching under the appropriate Acts is less than it otherwise would be. If he succeeds in ordering them so as to secure that result, then, however unappreciative the Commissioners of Inland Revenue or his fellow tax payers may be of his ingenuity, he cannot be compelled to pay an increased tax.' (*IRC v Duke of Westminster* [1936] AC 1, HL, per Lord Tornlin.)

[6.39]

Balancing this approach is the principle that a court is entitled to look through any sham transactions and give a correct legal characterisation to the arrangements. This second approach was favoured in *W T Ramsay Ltd v IRC* [1981] 1 All ER 865, HL. The facts in this case were as follows.

[6.40]

A tax-avoidance scheme was devised so that the tax-payer who had made a capital gain could cancel it by making an equivalent loss. Basically, the scheme involved the creation of two assets – Loan 1 and Loan 2, each for £218,750.[1] They were made by the tax-payer to one of the Scheme companies, C Ltd. The terms of the loan were that Loan 1 was to be repaid after 30 years, at market value, and Loan 2 after 31 years. C Ltd could make early repayment, or had to repay if it went into liquidation. The interest payable on each loan was 11% pa: the tax-payer had a right to vary the interest once only on each loan. A few days after the loans were made, the tax-payer exercised his right and reduced the interest on one loan to zero and increased the interest on the other to 22%. The same day, the tax-payer sold Loan 2 (which had increased in value) for £391,481. This produced a gain of £172,731, which the tax-payer contended was not a chargeable gain (ie as the asset sold was a debt within the meaning of FA 1965, Sch 7, para 11). Loan 2 was then transferred to a wholly-owned subsidiary of C Ltd, and was extinguished by the liquidation of that subsidiary. C Ltd then went into liquidation, whereupon Loan 1 was repaid to the tax-payer. The shares in C Ltd, for which the tax-payer had originally paid £185,034, became of little value and he sold them to an outside company for £9,387, so the tax-payer made a loss of £175,647.

1 The money to enable the tax-payer to make the loans was provided by a finance house in terms which ensured it would be repaid out of the loans when discharged.

[6.41]
The appeal by the tax-payer was dismissed for the following reasons:

1. It was the task of the Revenue and the court to ascertain the legal nature of any transaction to which it was sought to attach a tax or tax consequence, and if the legal nature was that which emerged from a series or combination of transactions which were intended to operate as such, it was the scheme or combination or transactions rather than the individual transaction to which regard was to be had.
2. Accordingly, where a tax-payer used a scheme comprising a number of separate transactions with the object of avoiding tax, the Revenue and the court were not limited to considering the genuineness or otherwise of each individual step or transaction in the scheme, but could consider the scheme as whole, and if it was found that the composite transaction produced neither a gain nor loss, it could treat it as a nullity for tax purpose.
3. Applying that principle, the only conclusion consistent with the intentions of the parties, and with the documents taken as a whole, was that there was an integrated and inter-dependent series of transactions which had produced neither gain nor loss and in those circumstances, it would be wrong and a faulty analysis to pick out and segregate for tax purposes the one transaction that produced the loss. Accordingly, the scheme was to be treated as a nullity for tax purposes.

[6.42]
There is a defence under ICTA 1988, s 703, if it can be shown that 'the transaction or transactions were carried out either for bona fide commercial reasons or in the ordinary course of making or managing investments, and that none of them had as their main object, or one of their main objects, to enable tax advantages to be obtained'.

[6.43]
It has been held that the Revenue is not allowed to strike at a transaction simply because it may have a tax avoidance motive (see *Furniss v Dawson* [1984] 1 All ER 530, HL).

[6.44]
For a full discussion of the powers of the Revenue to look behind the form of a transaction and the current state of the law, see *Butterworths' Tax Guide* (17th edn, 1999/2000).

6. SUMMARY

[6.45]
Reassurance is a useful tool in the life assurance industry in:

- spreading mortality risks;
- raising capital;
- meeting capital requirements; and
- designing products.

[6.46]
The more elaborate and artificial the arrangement, however, the more scope the Revenue has for challenging it, and this is always a consideration when advising on the legal aspects of reassurance arrangements.

Chapter 7
Investor protection

1. INTRODUCTION

[7.1]
Chapters 2, 3 and 4 have dealt with among other things the prudential regime as it applies to the management of funds once contracts have been entered into and premiums paid to the insurance company. This chapter deals with the conduct of business regime as it relates to acquiring new business, together with the regime for overseeing those who manage life companies and also the powers and sanctions available to the supervisory authorities to enforce both regimes.

[7.2]
The main purpose of the prudential regime is to safeguard the interests of policyholders and to promote the UK as a safe financial centre for investment business. Further protection is given to policyholders by provisions of ICA 1982, FSA 1986 and PPA 1975.

2. CONDUCT OF BUSINESS

A. Introduction

[7.3]
The provisions of ICA 1982 cover conduct of business as it relates to non-investment insurance contracts (ie protection only policies) and insurance contracts which are classified as investments under FSA 1986, Sch 1, para 10. However, insurance business which is also investment business is also dealt with by FSA 1986. FSA rules take precedence. FSA 1986, Sch 10 modifies the provisions of the main body of that Act in its application to insurance business which is also investment business in a number of respects; partially in recognition of the supervisory role and prudential regime already in place under ICA 1982; and partially, in the case of the conduct of business rules, in recognition of the split between investment and non-investment business. Insurance companies may find that the cost of compliance with two separate regimes for conduct of business is too high, and simply comply with FSA 1986 across the range of its contracts (and checking that compliance with ICA 1982 would follow from this) as FSA 1986 has the more demanding policing regime.

B. Provisions in ICA 1982

[7.4]
The fundamental rule is that the policyholder is to be given accurate information about the policy, the insurer and the intermediary (if any), on which to base a decision, and also have the right to cool off or cancel the contract within a set time limit if, on reflection, the policy is not suitable. The conduct of business rules are at ICA 1982, Pt III, ss 72–81 and cover:

- advertisements;
- the information to be supplied to policyholders;
- insurance intermediaries; and
- statutory notices on the policyholders right to cancel.

[7.5]
The detail is contained at ICA 1982, Sch 2E and ICR 1994, SI 1994/1516, regs 35–43 and Schs 7, 8 and 9.

[7.6]
ICA 1982, s 81 sets out criminal sanctions for breach of ICA 1982, ss 72 (on advertisements) and 74 (on insurance intermediaries).[1]

1 It is possibly a drafting error that ICA 1982, s 75 on statutory notices is not included as ICA 1982, s 75(4) makes contravention of the section an offence.

(i) Insurance advertisements

[7.7]
This is covered by ICA 1982, s 72 and ICR 1994, SI 1994/1516, regs 35, 36 and 37. 'Insurance advertisement' is defined at ICA 1982, s 72(5) and 'advertisement' at ICA 1982, s 72(6) as an advertisement in any medium (publication, TV or radio) which invites people (directly or indirectly) to enter into contracts of insurance and 'advertisement' includes 'every form of advertising'. It is likely that this catch-all expression covers advertisements on the Internet.

[7.8]
ICA 1982, s 72(3) makes it an offence to contravene regulations made under ICA 1982, s 72 (ie advertisement regulations). ICA 1982, s 72(4) provides a defence to anyone who issues an advertisement which contravenes the regulations on the direction of someone else, provided he was not instrumental in preparing the contents of the advertisement. There are two presumptions at ICA 1982, s 72(7):

(a) that an advertisement issued on behalf of a person is issued by that person; and
(b) if a person is specified in the advertisement as being the person inviting or offering to enter into contracts, then the advertisement is issued by that person.

[7.9]
ICR 1994, SI 1994/1516, reg 35 relates to overseas (non-UK and non-EEA) insurance companies and provides that their advertisements carry a statement to the effect that they are based overseas and are not supervised by the UK authorities and policyholders do not have the protection of PPA 1975.

[7.10]
ICR 1994, SI 1994/1516, reg 36 provides for UK and EC companies to state the amount of subscribed and paid up capital if it states the amount of authorised capital in an advertisement.

[7.11]
ICR 1994, SI 1994/1516, reg 37 provides for these statements to be made prominently, clearly and legibly. ICR 1994, reg 37, sub-s 4 provides that ICR 1994, regs 35 and 36 do not apply to contracts which cover large risks only, or are investment advertisements approved by an authorised person under FSA 1986, s 57. FSA 1986, Sch 10, para 5(1) mirrors this latter provision by dis-applying ICA 1982, s 72 in relation to insurance policies which are investments as they are covered by FSA 1986 regime.

(ii) Information to policyholders

[7.12]
ICA 1982, s 72A provides for and ICA 1982, Sch 2E sets out the information to be supplied to policyholders before they enter into a contract and during the contract:

1. Information to policyholders before entering into a contract of insurance
   - (a) a definition of each benefit and option;
   - (b) the term of the contract and the means by which it may be terminated;
   - (c) the method of paying premiums and the duration of the payments;
   - (d) the method of calculating and distributing bonuses;
   - (e) an indication of surrender and paid up values and the extent to which such values are guaranteed;
   - (f) an indication of the premiums for each benefit, whether it is a main or supplementary benefit;
   - (g) for unit linked policies, a definition of the units to which benefits are linked and an indication of the nature of the underlying assets;
   - (h) information on the following:
     - (i) the arrangements with respect to the period within which the policyholder may cancel the contract;
     - (ii) the tax arrangements;
     - (iii) complaints arrangements; and
     - (iv) any compensation or guarantee arrangements if the insurer is unable to meet its liabilities under the contract.
   - (i) choice of law.

In addition, details of the name and legal form of the company, the company's home state or the state of the branch through which the contract is effected, the address of the head office and, if relevant, the address of any branch through which the contract is to be entered into.

2. Information to policyholders during the contract
   (a) if there has been any change to any of the information required under 1 above, the insurer must inform the policyholder in writing of the change; and
   (b) if the contract provides for payment of bonuses, the insurer shall at least once every calendar year, except the first, inform the policyholder in writing of the amount of any bonus payable under the contract and of which the policyholder has not been previously informed: it is sufficient for the insurer to give information which would allow the policyholder to calculate the bonus.
3. Information to policyholders of EFTA companies
   This is covered by ICA 1982, s 72B and requires the insurer to issue, along with or shortly after the proposal or policy, a statement of the address of the establishment which is covering the risk or commitment.

[7.13]
The above provisions do not apply to investment business carried on by an authorised insurer (ICA 1982, Sch 2E, para 1(2)). There is no corresponding carve out in FSA 1986, Sch 10. FSA 1986 and PIA rules prescribe the information to be sent to policyholders for investment business. The information is described as the 'key features' document.

(iii) Insurance intermediaries

[7.14]
ICA 1982, s 74 and ICR 1994, SI 1994/1516, regs 38, 39 and 40: the regulations provide mainly that intermediaries inviting people to enter into insurance contracts make it clear to prospective policyholders how they are connected to the insurance company, eg whether tied as opposed to being an independent financial adviser or otherwise connected in terms of the definition at ICR 1994, reg 38. ICR 1994, reg 38 defines for the purposes of ICR 1994, reg 39 that a person is connected to an insurance company where:

(a) a person or anyone connected to him (ie partner, director, controller[1] or manager) is a partner, director, controller or manager of the insurance company or its controller;
(b) the insurance company or anyone connected with it (ie partner, director, controller or manager) is a partner, director, controller or manager of the person or its controller;
(c) the person or its holding company has a 10% or more interest in the shares of the insurance company or its controller;
(d) the insurance company or its controller has a 10% or more interest in the person or its controller; or

(e) where the person has entered into a contract with the insurance company or associated company other than an employment contract and undertakes not to perform any services relating to insurance business for any other insurance company.

1 The definition of controller for insurance companies is at ICA 1982, s 96C and is noted at **[7.45]** below: the definition of controller for non-insurance companies is a holding company.

[7.15]
There are exceptions for renewal business and arranging amendments of the original contract and where the circumstances of the policyholder have not changed (ICR 1994, SI 1994/1516, reg 40).

[7.16]
ICA 1982, s 74(3) makes it an offence to breach the regulations.

[7.17]
Again, the provisions do not apply in relation to insurance contracts which constitute investment business (FSA 1986, Sch 10, s 5(2) and (3)).[1]

1 There are no complimentary carve-out provisions in ICA 1982.

(iv) Statutory notices

[7.18]
ICA 1982, ss 75–77 and ICR 1994, SI 1994/1516, regs 41 and 42 and Schs 7, 8 and 9 set out that notices are to be sent to policyholders or prospective policyholders intimating their right to cancel the contract within 14 days[1] after the contract has become binding. The provisions refer to an 'EC contract', which is defined at ICA 1982, s 75(5B) as one where:

> '(a) the Insurer is a UK, EC or EFTA company or a member of Lloyd's; and (b) the other party is habitually resident in the United Kingdom.'

1 Ten days for non-EC contract.

[7.19]
The ICR 1994, SI 1994/1516, Schedules set out the format of these notices:

- ICR 1994, Sch 7 sets out the form of notice for non-investment contracts;
- ICR 1994, Sch 8 relates to investment contracts; and
- ICR 1994, Sch 9 is the notice of cancellation which the policyholder has the right to return to the insurer.

[7.20]
The legal effects of the exercise of the right to cancel are spelled out at ICA1982, s 76(4), namely:

> 'Where a person serves a notice of cancellation, then
> (a) if at the time when the notice is served the contract has been entered into, the notice shall operate so as to rescind the contract; and

(b) in any other case, the service of the notice shall operate as a withdrawal of any offer to enter into the contract which is contained in, or implied by, any proposal made to the insurer by the person serving the notice of cancellation and as notice to the insurer that any such offer is withdrawn.'

[7.21]
ICA 1982, s 76(5) goes on to provide that any sum paid to the insurer is recoverable and so too is any sum paid by the insurer. The section is silent on whether any investment or gains or losses are added to or subtracted from the sum paid. Problems have arisen in practice in the interaction of the cancellation rules and the IMRO rules on ensuring the customer's funds are invested promptly (ie 'timely execution' rules). If the fund manager invests the customer's funds immediately and then 14 days later the customer cancels the contract and there has been an investment gain, the insurance company simply takes the gain and the original sum invested is returned to the customer. If there has been a loss, the investor suffers on the basis that there is no risk free period only a right to cancel.

[7.22]
ICA 1982, s 75(4) makes it an offence to fail to follow the statutory notice requirements but such failure does not invalidate the contract.

[7.23]
FSA 1986, Sch 10, para 5(3) disapplies ICA 1982, ss 75–77 in so far as they relate to investment contracts. There is no corresponding carve-out in ICA and the position of ICR 1994, SI 1994/1516, Sch 8 is slightly anomalous.

C. Conduct of investment business provisions in FSA 1986

(i) Authorisation

[7.24]
FSA 1986, s 22 gives automatic authorisation under FSA 1986 to insurers authorised under ICA 1982. FSA 1986, s 31 gives authorisation to persons authorised in another member state to carry on investment business.

(ii) Conduct of investment business

[7.25]
FSA 1986, Ch V, ss 47–63 deals with the conduct of investment business. The sections are mostly enabling sections under which rules or statements of principles have been made. They cover the following:

1. Misleading Statements and Practices (FSA 1986, s 47).
2. Statements of Principle (FSA 1986, s 47A).
3. Conduct of Business Rules (FSA 1986, s 48).
4. Financial Resources Rules (FSA 1986, s 49).
5. Power to modify Rules under FSA 1986, ss 48 and 49 (FSA 1986, s 50).

6. Cancellation Rules (FSA 1986, s 51).
7. Notification Regulations (FSA 1986, s 52).
8. Indemnity Rules (FSA 1986, s 53).
9. Compensation Fund (FSA 1986, s 54).
10. Clients' Money (FSA 1986, s 55).
11. Unsolicited Calls (FSA 1986, s 56).
12. Restrictions on Advertising (FSA 1986, s 57).
13. Exceptions to FSA 1986, s 57 (FSA, s 58).
14. Employment of Prohibited Persons (FSA 1986, s 59).
15. Public Statement as to Person's Misconduct (FSA 1986, s 60).
16. Injunctions and Restitution Orders (FSA 1986, s 61).
17. Actions for Damages (FSA 1986, s 62).
18. Restriction of Right of Action (FSA 1986, s 62A).
19. Application of Rules and Regulations to Members of SRO (FSA 1986, s 63A).
20. Modification of Rules and Regulations (FSA 1986, s 63B).
21. Codes of Practice (FSA 1986, s 63C).

(iii) Application to insurance companies

[7.26]
FSA 1986, Sch 10 generally carves out the areas of activity of authorised insurers which are governed by FSA 1986. FSA 1986, para 4(2) modifies the application of the conduct of business rules of FSA 1986 as applied to insurance companies. The rules under FSA 1986, s 48 only apply to insurance companies in relation to:

> '(a) procuring proposals for policies the rights under which constitute investment business for the purposes of this Act and advising persons on such policies and the exercise of the rights conferred by them;
> (b) managing the investments of pension funds, procuring persons to enter into contracts for the management of such investments and advising persons on such contracts and the exercise of the rights conferred by them; and
> (c) matters incidental to those mentioned in paragraph (a) and (b) above.'

[7.27]
Statements of principle under FSA 1986, s 47A and Codes of practice under FSA 1986, s 63A covering the above three matters and falling under the rule making power of FSA 1986, s 48 also apply to insurance companies.

[7.28]
Further modifications include:

1. Rules under FSA 1986, s 49 do not apply to insurers authorised in a member state other than the UK (FSA 1986, Sch 10, para 4(3)).
2. FSA 1986, ss 53 and 54 relating to the Indemnity Rules and the Compensation Fund do not apply to insurance business. The PPA 1975

effectively covers compensation for policyholders (PPA 1975, Sch 10, para 4(4), see **[7.51]** below).

3. FSA 1986, s 59 on the employment of prohibited persons does not apply to insurers unless the employment relates to any activity in sub-para 4(2) quoted above or any investment business connected with these matters (FSA 1986, Sch 10, para 4(5)).
4. Rules made by any Self Regulating Authority to which an insurance company is a member under any of the provisions of FSA 1986, Ch V must take account of ICA 1982, Pt II. The same applies to rules and regulations made by the Secretary of State under FSA 1986, Pt V (FSA 1986, Sch 10, paras 3(1) and 4(6).

(iv) Non-application of provisions of ICA 1982

[7.29]
At FSA 1986, Sch 10, para 5 are the provisions which carve out or restrict the scope of ICA 1982, ss 72–77 to non-investment insurance business.[1]

1 It does not seem to cover ICA 1982, s 72B.

(v) Sanctions under FSA 1986

[7.30]
A range of sanctions are available under FSA 1986, ss 60–62 against persons who have contravened any of the regulations made under FSA 1986, Ch V and specified sections of the chapter, namely:

1. The Secretary of State can publish a statement detailing any misconduct of an authorised person – a notice must be sent to the person first stating the reasons for the decision to publish and the person has a right to refer the matter to a tribunal (ie set up under FSA 1986).
2. The Secretary of State can apply for an injunction (England) or interdict (Scotland) if there has been a contravention and the contravention is likely to continue or recur and the authorised person is unwilling to remedy matters and can also apply for a restitution order if the authorised person has profited from the contravention.
3. A 'private investor' (ie an individual who is not acting in the course of carrying on investment business or a small business investor – Financial Services Core Glossary 1991) can sue for damages for any loss sustained as a result of any contravention by an authorised person.

D. Conclusions

[7.31]
For activities narrated at FSA 1986, Sch 10, para 4(2), insurers have to comply with the provisions of FSA 1986 and regulations and rules made under it, although the rules have to take into account ICA 1982, Pt II. ICA 1982, Pt III, ss 72–77 are expressly limited in scope in both or either of ICA 1982 and FSA 1986. So, for the contents of advertisements, the

information to be supplied to policyholders, the obligations of intermediaries and cancellation or cooling off rights, it is FSA 1986 which applies to long-term business which is also investment business.

3. SUPERVISORY POWERS

A. Introduction

[7.32]
Again, there is an overlap of powers between the two regulatory regimes, but it is balanced in favour of the Treasury because they have ultimate responsibility for regulating the prudential regime of insurance companies. Modifications are therefore made under FSA 1986, Sch 10 to the enforcement and intervention powers and the power to withdraw authorisation under FSA 1986. Basically, FSA 1986 is restricted to certain areas, and in those areas the SRO has to obtain the agreement of the Treasury before any exercise of their powers under FSA 1986 have effect. FSA 1986, Ch XV, Pt II deals with the interaction of the SIB and SROs with other regulatory authorities (the Treasury for insurers), some of which has been incorporated into ICA 1982.

B. Provisions in ICA 1982

[7.33]
ICA 1982, ss 38–48 sets out the powers of intervention of the Treasury in an insurance company's business; ICA 1982, s 37 sets out the grounds on which the Treasury can exercise the powers. ICA 1982, ss 11 and 12A give the Treasury the power to withdraw or suspend authorisation.

(i) Powers of intervention

[7.34]
The powers include the following:

1. Investments
   In relation to investments which cover the liabilities of the company, the Treasury can prohibit investments of a certain type or to insist on disposal of investments of a certain type (ICA 1982, s 38).
2. Maintenance of assets in UK
   The Treasury can require, in the case of non-UK companies, that the assets matching UK liabilities be situated in the UK. They can also require UK companies to situate assets matching EC liabilities in the EC (ICA 1982, s 39).
3. Custody of assets
   If a requirement has been imposed under ICA 1982, s 39, the Treasury can also require that the assets are held in custody by a person approved by the Treasury. The assets once held in custody cannot be released without the consent of the Treasury (ICA 1982, s 40).
4. Prohibition on disposal of assets

The Treasury can obtain an injunction in the High Court in England, or interdict in the Court of Session in Scotland, preventing a company dealing or disposing of any of its assets covering its EC liabilities. The grounds for obtaining the injunction or interdict are any of the grounds set out at ICA 1982, s 37(3) – see **[7.35]** below (ICA, s 40A).

These powers are also exercisable in relation to an EC company at the request of the supervisory authority of the home state of the EC company under ICA 1982, Sch 2F. In *Secretary of State for Trade and Industry v Prevision Sanitaria Nacional PSN Mutua de Seguros y Resseguros a Prima Fija (PSN)* [1998] CLY 3369, the Secretary of State, at the request of the Spanish regulatory authority, applied ex parte for an order under ICA 1982, s 40A and Sch 2F, para 12 to prevent a Spanish insurance company from disposing of assets held in a London bank. The company argued that the provision in the Schedule only gave a power to apply for an injunction and not to grant one. The court upheld the application on the basis that Council Directives 79/267 and 90/619 (ie First and Second Life Directives) obliged the home state to ensure that insurance companies had sufficient technical and mathematical provision and the UK was obliged to comply with a request to enforce them.

5. Limitation of premium income
   The Treasury can require a company to ensure that total premiums do not exceed a stated amount in a given period (ICA 1982, s 41). This is because new business can create capital problems.
6. Actuarial investigations
   The Treasury can require the appointed actuary to make an actuarial investigation into the whole or part of the financial condition of the company at a given date (ICA 1982, s 42).
7. Acceleration of information under accounting provisions
   The Treasury can require statements under ICA 1982, ss 22 and 25 (ie audited accounts and descriptions of business carried out) to be deposited with them (ICA 1982, s 43 and Chapter 8).
8. General investigations
   The Treasury can appoint a competent person to investigate whether the criteria of sound and prudent management are being fulfilled for UK or non-EC companies. The Treasury can also make the appointment on notification that someone intends to become a controller under ICA 1982, ss 60 or 61. When a company is under investigation, it is a duty of anyone who was or is a director, manager, controller, actuary, auditor or solicitor of the company to co-operate with the person appointed. ICA 1982, s 47B restricts the power by making it subject to the evidential rules on privilege (ICA 1982, s 43).
9. Power to obtain information and production of documents
   Documents include information in any form. ICA 1982, s 44 extends the powers under ICA 1982, s 43 to include employees and agents and subsidiary and parent and sister companies. It also allows someone authorised by HMT to search the premises of a company on which a requirement under this section has been imposed. The same restrictions regarding privilege applies (ICA 1982, s 44).

10. Entry and search of premises
    A justice of the peace in England or a sheriff in Scotland can grant a warrant for the entry, search and recovery of documents if (a) an order has been made under ICA 1982, s 44 and there are reasonable grounds for supposing the documents requested are on the premises but will not be produced; or (b) there are reasonable grounds for believing an offence has been committed which on indictment would carry a two-year plus term of imprisonment and there are documents on the premises relating to that offence and if requested would be destroyed or tampered with etc. The warrant is granted on information on oath by the Treasury or someone authorised by them under ICA 1982, s 44. Any documents recovered can be kept for three months or if proceedings are commenced within three months to the conclusion of any criminal trial (ICA 1982, s 44A).
11. General
    The Treasury also has a widely drafted power to take what action appears to be appropriate for the protection of policyholders (ICA 1982, s 45). Notice must be given if powers are to be exercised on the basis of the unfitness of certain persons (ICA 1982, s 46). The Treasury can also rescind, vary and publish in the register of companies any of the requirements they make (ICA 1982, s 47). HMT can also bring Civil Proceedings on behalf of the insurer (ICA 1982, s 48).

(ii) Grounds on which powers exercisable

[7.35]
The grounds are set out at ICA 1982, s 37. They broadly include the following:

1. Powers under ICA 1982, ss 38 and 41–45 can be exercised if:
   (a) there is a risk the company may not be able to meet PRE;
   (b) the criteria of sound and prudent management is not being met;
   (c) the company or a subsidiary or subordinate company (see ICA 1982, s 31 for definition) has failed to satisfy an obligation under ICA 1982 or previous insurance legislation;
   (d) that the company has furnished misleading or inaccurate information;
   (e) that inadequate reassurance is in place;
   (f) there exists a ground which would prohibit authorisation being granted if it were applied for; or
   (g) there has been a substantial departure from any forecast or proposal under ICA 1982, s 5.
2. Powers under ICA 1982, ss 39, 40 and 40A can be exercised on the following limited grounds:
   (a) The Treasury have withdrawn or suspended the authorisation of the insurer under ICA 1982, ss 11 or 12A;
   (b) the company has failed to maintain a minimum solvency margin or failed to comply with the localisation of assets rules and currency matching rules; or
   (c) breach of the valuation of assets rules.

3. The power under ICA 1982, s 44 (2) to (4) can also be exercised if the Treasury think it would be in the interests of present and future policyholders to do so.
4. The powers under ICA 1982, ss 43A and 44 can also be exercised by the Treasury in performing their functions under the Act.
5. The powers under ICA 1982, ss 38, 41, 42, 44(1) or 45 can, whether or not any of the grounds above exist or not, also be exercised in relation to a company which has been issued an authorisation, a company in which a person has become a controller as defined in ICA 1982, s 96 or acquired a notifiable holding (ICA 1982, s 61A(1)). This looks as though it means that the powers are exercisable on any of these events occurring. The power must be exercised within five years of the event and any requirement imposed will not extend beyond ten years from the date of the event.
6. Powers under ICA 1982, s 45 can not be exercised if the Treasury can achieve the desired result by exercising powers under ICA, ss 38–44.
7. In exercising their powers, the Treasury must state the grounds on which they are doing so.

(Note: The Treasury have supervisory powers over UK insurance companies and non-EC insurance companies operating in the UK: EC insurance companies are supervised by their home state. The supervisory powers of the Treasury will be transferred to the FSA – see Chapter 10)

C. Withdrawal and suspension of authorisation

[7.36]
ICA 1982, s 11 gives the Treasury power either on grounds of:

1. failure meet an obligation under ICA 1982 or FSA 1986 (or rules of relevant SRO);
2. failure to meet a law of another EEA state which implements the long-term directives;
3. failure to comply with sound and prudent management criteria;
4. that were it to apply for authorisation it would fail;
5. withdrawal of authorisation in member state where it has its head office; or
6. at the request of the company

to withdraw authorisation to effect all or certain classes of insurance business.

[7.37]
Notice must be given under ICA 1982, s 12. The Treasury, under ICA 1982, s 12A, can, if it appears to the Treasury that the grounds above are made out and that authorisation should be suspended as a matter of urgency, withdraw authorisation immediately. The direction under this section does not prohibit a company effecting a contract of insurance on the basis of an obligation in an existing contract. Notice is still required and time limits apply to the direction and the company has a chance (within one month) to make representations (written or oral) to the Treasury against the direction.

[7.38]
Final withdrawal of authorisation really applies to companies which have been authorised but have either ceased to carry on insurance business or not carried out any insurance business for a period of 12 months from the date of authorisation under ICA 1982, s 3 or if authorised under ICA 1982, s 4 from the date of the Act (ICA 1982, s 13).

D. Provisions in FSA 1986

[7.39]
FSA 1986, Sch 10, paras 6 and 7 set out how the enforcement provisions in FSA 1986, Ch VI, ss 64–71 interact with those in ICA 1982. The provisions in FSA 1986 are broadly similar to those in ICA 1982. FSA 1986, Sch 10, para 6 disapplies some of FSA 1986, Ch VI and provides that prior to exercising the remaining powers notice must be given to the Secretary of State. FSA 1986, Sch 10, para 7 amends ICA 1982 by introducing breach of FSA 1986 as a ground for withdrawal of authorisation (see **[7.36]** above).

E. Lack of authorisation

(i) ICA 1982, provisions

[7.40]
ICA 1982, s 14 makes it an offence to carry on insurance business without authorisation. It is also an offence to obtain authorisation by issuing false information. The sanction is a maximum of two years' imprisonment or a fine or both and, if directors, chief executive, manager, secretary or other officer connived in the offence, they too will be guilty of that offence (ICA 1982, s 91). Regulators have found difficulties in practice in determining what acts count as 'carrying on insurance business'. In *Secretary of State for Trade and Industry v Great Western Assurance Co* [1997] 2 BCLC 685, CA brokers of insurance companies based in Belgium and Barbados were operating in the UK. Their activities included advising on likely premium rates and settling claims. The Court of Appeal held, inter alia, that insurance business was not limited to providing cover under contracts of insurance but also to the effecting and carrying out of these contracts and the brokers were carrying on insurance business in the UK on behalf of the insurance companies and the insurance companies were therefore in breach of ICA 1982 for failing to obtain authorisation.

(ii) FSA 1986 provisions

[7.41]
Contracts entered into with unauthorised persons are unenforceable under FSA 1986, s 132 and sums paid under it are recoverable together with any losses sustained. The court can hold the contract enforceable and money paid or property under it can be retained if it is satisfied:

> '(3)(a) that the person carrying on insurance business reasonably believed that his entering into the contract did not constitute a contravention of section 2' of ICA 1982; and

'(b) that it is just and equitable for the contract to be enforced or, as the case may be, for the money or property paid or transferred under it to be retained.'

[7.42]
It is also provided that the unenforceability of the contract will not effect the validity of any re-insurance contract in respect of it. FSA 1986, s 133 also makes it an offence to make misleading statements in relation to insurance contracts.

4. DIRECTORS, CONTROLLERS AND NOTIFIABLE HOLDINGS

A. Introduction

[7.43]
Prudential Guidance Note (PGN) 1995/5 covers guidance on notifiable persons and holdings and includes a useful flowchart on the notices required on appointment or changes to notifiable persons or holdings. The following is a summary of the main provisions of ICA 1982. Those dealing with insurance companies, eg in joint venture arrangements, must be careful they do not inadvertently become a controller of an insurance company.

B. Managing director and chief executive

[7.44]
An insurance company must serve notice on the Treasury when appointing a managing director or chief executive. The proposed appointee must sign the notice to the effect that it is sent with his or her knowledge or consent. The Treasury can object on the grounds that the person is not 'fit and proper' or that were he or she appointed, the criteria of sound and prudent management would not be satisfied. A preliminary notice of objection by the Treasury can be responded to by the company within one month and the Treasury must take the representations into account before issuing a notice of objection. The Treasury do not have to disclose the details of grounds of objection. If three months elapse with no written objection from the Treasury the appointment can be made (ICA 1982, s 60).

C. Controllers

[7.45]
'Controller' is defined at ICA 1982, s 96C and covers the managing director, chief executive or a de facto director of the company or parent company. In the case of a UK company, it covers someone who on his own or with associates[1] has a 10% or more shareholding or 10% or more of the voting rights or is generally in a position of 'significant influence' by virtue of a shareholding or voting rights in the company or its parent. For non-UK companies the percentage is 15% (ICA 1982, s 96C(1)(e)).

1 'Associate' is defined at ICA 1982, s 96C(4) and includes where the person is an individual: (a) wife, husband, minor son or daughter; (b) the trustees of any trust with

a life interest in possession, or in Scotland, a life interest; (c) any company in which directorship held; or (d) any employee or partner.
and where the person is a company: (e) any director, subsidiary undertaking or employee or director in the subsidiary.
and where there has been some agreement on shares or exercising voting rights with another person: (f) the other person. (The definition of 'subsidiary undertaking' is at CA 1985, s 258: PGN 1995/5.)

[7.46]
A similar procedure to that applying to the appointment of a managing director or chief executive at ICA 1982, s 60 applies to persons becoming controllers. There is an overlap as the definition of 'controller' includes inter alia managing director and chief executive. ICA 1982, s 61 deals with controllers who are not managing directors or chief executives.

D. Notifiable holdings

[7.47]
The definition of 'notifiable holding' is given at ICA 1982, s 96 as 'voting rights or shares which, if acquired by any person, will result in his becoming' a 10, 20, 33 or 50% shareholder controller or a majority shareholder controller. So any increase in shareholding which takes the shareholder into a higher band is notifiable prior to any increase.

[7.48]
Again, a similar notification procedure to that at ICA 1982, s 60 applies (ICA 1982, s 61A).[1] Details of shareholder controllers are included in the authorisation process (ICR 1994, Sch 1).

1 The procedures at ICA 1982, ss 60–61A are supplemented by provisions under ICA 1982, Sch 2D and ICR 1994, Sch 6.

E. Changes of director controller or manager

[7.49]
Notification to the Treasury of any changes to directors, controllers and managers must also be made (ICA 1982, SI 1994/1516, s 62).

[7.50]
'Manager' is defined at ICA 1982, s 96D and covers for UK companies both (a) sub-contractors[1] and (b) employees who report directly to the managing director or chief executive and exercise managerial functions or are responsible for maintaining accounts or other company records. For non-UK companies only (b) applies.

1 This would include an investment management company and appointed representatives.

5. PPA 1975

[7.51]
PPA 1975 has been amended by the 1997 Act of similar title, but many of the amendments are not yet in force. The obligations under the Act are

administered by the Policyholders Protection Board. The Act provides protection for policyholders where the insurance company is in liquidation or in financial difficulties: if a company is in liquidation, the Board undertake to pay at least 90% of the liabilities of the insurer. In practice, another insurance company may take over some or all of the liabilities and the Board may help achieve this. The funds to meet this commitment are levied from insurance companies and based on their previous year's net premium income. After a case[1] was successfully brought by an American company to obtain funds under the Act a new PPA 1975, s 4 was added which made it clear that the Act only gave protection to UK policies which are 'protected risks or commitments'.[2]

1 *Scher v Policyholders Protection Board (Nos 1 and 2)* [1994] 2 All ER 37n, HL, where partners in a law and accountancy firm based in the US and Canada brought actions against the Board for payment under PPA 1975 on policies taken out by the partnership. The court held that because some of the partners operated as corporations, they were not 'private policyholders' in terms of PPA 1975, s 6(7) and the Board need not indemnify them. On the second point, whether they were holders of UK policies in terms of PPA 1975, s 4(2), the court held that the policy was a UK policy if performance under the contract would have formed part of an insurance business which the insurer was authorised to carry on in the UK, regardless of the actual place of performance.

2 'Protected commitments' is defined as: 1. policies issued by a company authorised under ICA 1982, s 3 or s 4 through an establishment situated in: (i) the UK; (ii) another EEA state; or (iii) the Isle of Man or Channel Islands *and* the risk or commitment is situated in the case of: (i) an EEA state, the Channel Islands or Isle of Man; (ii) in the UK; or (iii) the UK, Channel Islands or Isle of Man; or 2. a policy issued by an EEA company through an establishment in an EEA state and where the risk or commitment is situated in the UK (ICA 1982, s 4).

6. PIA OMBUDSMAN

[7.52]

This ombudsman scheme replaced the Insurance Ombudsman Bureau (IOB) for dealing with the complaints of customers of life assurance companies. It is designed to provide an informal and cheap method of redress. Insurers have to pay an annual fee to cover costs and a fixed sum for every case referred to the ombudsman. Unlike the IOB, it is a statutory creation and is subject to judicial review. Also, the PIA rules insist on companies having a formal complaints procedure in place. The current ombudsman regime for life assurance (being one of numerous schemes for redress by consumers of financial services) is to be replaced by a single ombudsman scheme under the Financial Services and Markets Bill.

7. SUMMARY

[7.53]

1. Ensuring that: (a) insurance companies comply with rules on maintenance of capital and conduct of business; (b) senior management, controllers and shareholders of insurance companies are monitored; and (c) providing the Treasury and the Financial Services Authority with powers of intervention and ultimately withdrawal of authorisation gives the policyholder a reasonably robust system of protection.

2. Carrying on insurance business without authorisation under ICA 1982 is a criminal offence and, under FSA 1986, s 132, a policyholder can recover any sums paid plus any losses sustained in entering into a contract of insurance with an unauthorised person.
3. In addition, if the above system fails and the company cannot meet its liabilities, PPA 1975 provides further cover. Alternatively, the PIA ombudsman can award compensation to customers for other failures of the insurer.

Chapter 8
Accounts and tax

1. INTRODUCTION

[8.1]
This chapter is designed to provide an overview of the legal background to accounts and tax and enable the non-accountant to achieve a basic understanding of insurance company accounts and the tax position.

2. ACCOUNTS

A. Introduction

[8.2]

> 'Every insurance company . . . shall, with respect to each financial year . . . prepare a revenue account for the year, a balance sheet as at the end of the year and a profit and loss account for the year.' (ICA1982, s 17(1).)

[8.3]
Essentially, an insurance company has to account for its income and expenditure, the balance of its assets and liabilities and its investment gains and losses.

[8.4]
Because of its specialised nature, there are special rules for determining each of these and for their treatment in the accounts. These are set out at CA 1985, Sch 9A and discussed below. Much explanatory material can be found in the Statement of Recommended Practice (SORP) prepared by the Association of British Insurers (the ABI). The following is a brief explanation of the background to insurance company accounts.

(i) The profit and loss account

[8.5]
This is divided into a technical and non-technical account. Income and expenditure in the technical profit and loss account will include:

1. Premiums and the cost of acquiring these premiums (ie direct costs, such as commission, and indirect costs, such as advertising costs and the administrative expenses connected with the processing of proposals

and issuing policies). Acquisition costs can be deferred if it is expected they will be recouped from future margins built into the policies after taking account of contractual liability.

2. Payment of claims, the expenses associated with administrating claims and reassurance premiums.
3. Investment income and investment expenses and investment losses (and unrealised investment gains and losses). It is argued in SORP that as investments are part of the operations of the insurance company, it would be inappropriate to classify them as fixed assets and they should go into the profit and loss account. It is further argued that unrealised gains and losses, having little relevance in the context of readily marketable investments, should also be included in the profit and loss account. It is recommended that, as it is the long-term performance of investments which are of importance to insurers, this should be included alongside the actual investment returns.
4. Tax attributable to the long-term fund.
5. It should also include movements to or from the fund for future appropriations (the FFA), which is a fund holding assets which have not been allocated to either the shareholder fund or the policyholder fund at the year end.

[8.6]
The non-technical account takes the balance of the technical account as its starting point and is prepared at a higher level of detail.

(ii) The balance sheet

[8.7]
The principal items include the following.

Technical provisions

[8.8]
These are subdivided and include:

(a) The long-term business provision can be calculated on the same basis as the supervisory returns under ICA 1982, but excluding certain contingency reserves. Reserves meant to cover adverse contingencies relating to investment performance, resilience and closing the fund to new business are not considered to be assets and are therefore excluded. In addition, a summary of the main assumptions used in the calculation of reserves must be added to the accounts, covering interest rates, mortality and morbidity, allowance for future bonuses and expenses.
(b) The linked liability provision is an easier calculation because the liabilities under the contracts should equal the value of the net assets underpinning them. If there is a mis-match, it must be disclosed.
(c) Claims outstanding is the amount required to cover the total costs of settling claims arising out of events which have been notified by the end of the accounting period, less any amounts already paid.

Reserves

[8.9]
These have to be considered to see whether they should be included or not, and have to be signed off by the reporting actuary.

Present value of in-force business

[8.10]
The acquisition of a portfolio of long-term business should, according to Financial Reporting Statement (FRS) 6 and 7, be classified as an asset.

Long-term reassurance contracts

[8.11]
If they relate to a transfer of risk relating to mortality, morbidity, investment, persistency (ie the risk of loss from early termination of the contract), expenses (ie that the margins in the contract are insufficient to cover future expenses), they should appear in the technical account and also in the balance sheet. It is recommended that financial reassurance (ie one which does not cover, or only partially covers, these risks) should be accounted for so that the substance of the transaction is properly recorded.

B. Legal background

[8.12]
CA 1985, s 255 and Sch 9A set out the requirements for insurance company accounts. These provisions were brought into force by the Companies Act 1985 (Insurance Company Accounts) Regulations 1993, SI 1993/3246, which in turn implemented the Insurance Accounts Directive. For insurance undertakings not established under CA 1985, the Insurance Accounts Directive (Miscellaneous Insurance Undertakings) Regulations 1993, SI 1993/3245 apply. The previous CA 1985, Sch 9A was optional and allowed a number of exemptions to the rules on disclosure for insurance companies. CA 1985, Sch 9A is now mandatory and the exemptions have been withdrawn. The financial statements of insurance companies have to show a 'true and fair' view and auditors have to state in their report that this requirement has been fulfilled.

[8.13]
The provisions apply to financial years commencing on or after 23 December 1994.

[8.14]
CA 1985, Sch 9A is supplemented by the SORP produced by the ABI which recommends a modified statutory solvency basis (MSSB) for insurance company accounts. This means that the supervisory returns prepared under ICA 1982, ss 28 and 29 are modified to comply with the financial reporting requirements under CA 1985, Sch 9A.

[8.15]
In terms of ICA 1982, ss 28 and 29:

1. Insurance companies must maintain a separate long-term business fund.
2. Adequate records must be kept to enable assets and liabilities of the long-term fund to be identified separately.
3. The assets in the fund must only be used for that business.
4. Transfers from the fund other than reimbursements can only be made from surplus after an actuarial investigation.

[8.16]
The reporting under these sections is referred to as the 'statutory solvency basis'; in order to comply with CA 1985, two modifications are necessary, namely:

1. Reserves are excluded from technical provisions and moved to a section headed 'capital reserves' along with retained surplus.
2. Acquisition costs (ie for insurance policies) which are expected to be recouped in the future are to be deferred.

[8.17]
It is the opinion of the ABI that compliance with the MSSB, together with the Financial Reporting Standards (FRP) and Standard Statements of Accounting Practice (SSAP) and Urgent Issues Task Force (UITF), 'abstracts' issued by the Accounting Standards Board is capable of providing a true and fair view of both mutual and proprietary insurance company accounts.

C. Summary of CA 1985, Sch 9A

[8.18]
This Schedule is divided into two parts: part one relates to single insurance companies and is divided into four chapters and part two relates to insurance groups:

(i) Part I

CHAPTER I

[8.19]
Section A sets out general rules for the format of financial statements. Certain items may be merged in the accounts if separate disclosure is made in the notes. However, no-set off of assets and liabilities is permitted. Section B sets out the actual format of the balance sheet and the profit and loss account. The profit and loss account is split into technical and non-technical and examples prepared by the ABI are noted at **[8.25]** below. The notes to these describe the items featured in the accounts and how they are to be treated. On the balance sheet, format note 17 covers the accounting treatment of deferred acquisition costs (DAC); note 19 defines

the FFA; note 21 defines the long-term business provision and note 26 the technical provision for linked liabilities. The notes to the profit and loss format defines acquisition and administrative expenses (notes 6 and 7); the treatment of investment income, expenses and charges and unrealised gains and losses on investment; note 10 allows investment gains to move between the technical and non-technical accounts.

Chapter II

[8.20]
Section A sets out three broad accounting principles:

1. That it is presumed the companies are carrying on business as a going concern.
2. That accounting policies must be applied consistently within the same accounts and from one year to the next.
3. The amount of any item shall be determined on a prudential basis.

Section B sets out current value accounting rules for assets.
Section C sets out historic cost accounting rules.
Section D sets out rules for determining provisions. The amount of technical provisions must at all times be sufficient to cover any liabilities arising out of insurance contracts as far as can be reasonably foreseen.

[8.21]
Derogation from these principles is possible if the directors consider there are special reasons for doing so and state the reasons in the notes to the accounts.

Chapter III

[8.22]
This lists the notes to accompany the accounts.

Chapter IV

[8.23]
This covers the definitions of some of the terms used in CA 1985, Sch 9A.

(ii) Part II

[8.24]
This covers insurance groups and allows CA 1985, Sch 4A (Form and Content of Group Accounts) to apply with certain modifications. Insurance group accounts must comply with CA 1985, Sch 9A, Pt I in so far as it is practical to treat the group as if it were a single company. CA 1985, s 255A defines an insurance group as one where the parent company is an insurance company or where:

'(a) the parent company's principal subsidiary undertakings are wholly or mainly insurance companies, and

(b) the parent company does not itself carry on any material business apart from the acquisition, management and disposal of interests in subsidiary undertakings.'

D. Examples of technical/non-technical accounts, investment returns

[8.25]
The following example is extracted from the 'Statement of Recommended Practice on Accounting for Insurance Business' published by the Association of British Insurers, and is reproduced here with their permission.

STATEMENT OF RECOMMENDED PRACTICE
on Accounting for Insurance Business

APPENDIX

Illustrative example of the presentation and disclosure requirements of the SORP

This example is provided as an aid to understanding and does not form part of the Statement of Recommended Practice.

The purpose of this example is to illustrate some of the disclosure requirements of the SORP. It does not represent a complete set of financial statements for an insurer complying with all legal and accounting requirements. In particular, while references to notes to the financial statements are shown in the example profit and loss and balance sheet formats, not all these notes are included in this example. The example does not cover all the options permitted by the SORP, including those for investment accounting. In addition, it should not be assumed to reflect any materiality considerations which insurers will need to take into account in providing the relevant disclosures.

ABC INSURANCE GROUP PLC

Consolidated profit and loss account: technical account - general business
for the year ended 31 December 19X8

		19X8		19X7	
	Note	**£000**	**£000**	£000	£000
Earned premiums, net of reinsurance:					
Gross premiums written	*4*	**129,077**		117,351	
Outward reinsurance premiums		**(15,974)**		(16,562)	
			113,103		100,789
Change in the gross provision for unearned premiums		**(4,778)**		8,188	
Change in the provision for unearned premiums, reinsurers' share		**285**		(314)	
			(4,493)		7,874
			108,610		108,663
Allocated investment return transferred from the non-technical account[1]			**44,260**		41,740
Other technical income, net of reinsurance			**262**		482
Claims incurred, net of reinsurance:					
Claims paid:					
Gross amount		**(114,134)**		(107,006)	
Reinsurers' share		**15,944**		12,719	
		(98,190)		(94,287)	
Change in the provision for claims:					
Gross amount		**(9,198)**		(10,370)	
Reinsurers' share		**766**		1,414	
		(8,432)		(8,956)	
			(106,622)		(103,243)
Changes in other technical provisions, net of reinsurance			**(1,415)**		(213)
Net operating expenses	*8*		**(28,221)**		(27,529)
Other technical charges	*11*		**(500)**		(550)
Change in equalisation provision	*29(d)*		**(4,250)**		(3,750)
Sub-total (balance on the technical account for general business)			**12,124**		15,600

1 The allocation may be based on the longer term rate, or the actual rate of return on investments supporting general business technical provisions and associated shareholders' funds.

ABC INSURANCE GROUP PLC

Consolidated profit and loss account: technical account - long term business
for the year ended 31 December 19X8

	Note	19X8		19X7	
		£000	**£000**	£000	£000
Earned premiums, net of reinsurance:					
Gross premiums written	*4*	**375,298**		272,194	
Outward reinsurance premiums		**(7,890)**		(7,035)	
			367,408		265,159
Investment income	*6*	**208,693**		199,701	
Unrealised gains on investments		**64,213**		5,923	
			272,906		205,624
Claims incurred, net of reinsurance					
Claims paid:					
Gross amount		**(181,847)**		(157,277)	
Reinsurers' share		**15,559**		8,917	
			(166,288)		(148,360)
Change in the provision for claims:	*29(a)*				
Gross amount		**108**		(652)	
Reinsurers' share		**120**		247	
			228		(405)
			(166,060)		(148,765)
Change in other technical provisions, net of reinsurance					
Long term business provision, net of reinsurance:					
Gross amount		**(46,833)**		(43,814)	
Reinsurers' share		**26**		706	
		(46,807)		(43,108)	
Other technical provisions, net of reinsurance		**(234,408)**		(135,786)	
			(281,215)		(178,894)
Net operating expenses	*8*	**(108,658)**		(88,937)	
Investment expenses and charges	*9*	**(12,763)**		(11,614)	
Other technical charges	*11*	**(175)**		(160)	
Tax attributable to the long term business	*16*	**(20,809)**		(3,824)	
Allocated investment return transferred to the non-technical account[2]		**(1,025)**		750	
Transfers to the fund for future appropriations		**(37,578)**		(32,147)	
			(181,008)		(135,932)
Sub-total (balance on the technical account for long term business)			**12,031**		7,192

2 Where the longer term rate basis of allocating investment return is adopted, it should be applied to both general and long term business if applicable. Where an allocation based on the actual level of investment return on investments supporting general business technical provisions and associated shareholders' funds is made from the non-technical account to the technical account for general business, no allocation should be made from the technical account for long term business to the non-technical account.

ABC INSURANCE GROUP PLC

Consolidated profit and loss account: non-technical account
for the year ended 31 December 19X8

	Note	19X8 £000	19X8 £000	19X7 £000	19X7 £000
Balance on the general business technical account			**12,124**		15,600
Balance on the long term business technical account		**12,031**		7,192	
Tax attributable to shareholders' profits on long term business	*16*	**4,519**		3,252	
Pre-tax profit arising on long term business			**16,550**		10,444
Investment income	*6*	**40,673**		46,189	
Unrealised gains on investments		**2,391**		2,736	
Allocated investment return transferred from the long term business technical account[3]		**1,025**		(750)	
Investment expenses and charges	*9*	**(1,041)**		(500)	
		43,048		47,675	
Allocated investment return transferred to the general business technical account[3]		**(44,260)**		(41,740)	
			(1,212)		5,935
Other income			**63**		34
Other charges	*12*		**(909)**		(678)
Operating profit based on longer term investment return	*10*	**32,078**		29,150	
Share of operating profit of associated undertaking accounted for on the equity basis[4]		**252**		225	
Operating profit based on longer term investment return: group and share of profits of associate		**32,330**		29,375	
Short term fluctuations in investment return		**(1,464)**		5,710	
Change in equalisation provision		**(4,250)**		(3,750)	
Profit on ordinary activities before tax	*13*		**26,616**		31,335
Tax on profit on ordinary activities	*16*		**(8,638)**		(11,741)
Profit for the financial year after tax			**17,978**		19,594
Dividends proposed			**(4,000)**		(700)
Retained profit for the financial year transferred to reserves	*27*		**13,978**		18,894

All income and expenditure relates to continuing operations.

3 Allocations of investment return between the technical and non-technical accounts are based on the longer term rate of investment return.

4 This does not include income from associated undertakings which are held as part of the investment portfolio.

ABC INSURANCE GROUP PLC

Consolidated statement of total recognised gains and losses
for the year ended 31 December 19X8

	Note	19X8 £000	19X7 £000
Profit for the financial year		**17,978**	19,594
Currency translation differences on foreign currency net investments:	27		
Group		**400**	(120)
Share of associates		**13**	(3)
Total recognised gains and losses relating to the financial year		**18,391**	19,471

Statement of historical cost profits and losses
for the year ended 31 December 19X8

There is no material difference between the results for the current year and the previous year as described in the profit and loss account and the results on an unmodified historical cost basis. Accordingly, a note of the historical cost profits and losses for the year is not given.

Reconciliations of movements in shareholders' funds
for the year ended 31 December 19X8

		Group		Company[5]	
	Note	19X8 £000	19X7 £000	19X8 £000	19X7 £000
Profit for the financial year		**17,978**	19,594	**4,102**	790
Dividends		**(4,000)**	(700)	**(4,000)**	(700)
Retained profit for the financial year		**13,978**	18,894	**102**	90
Other gains and losses relating to the year (net)	27	**413**	(123)	**-**	-
Net addition to shareholders' funds		**14,391**	18,771	**102**	90
Opening shareholders' funds		**235,445**	216,674	**148,362**	148,272
Closing shareholders' funds		**249,836**	235,445	**148,464**	148,362

5 There is no specific requirement to provide this reconciliation for the parent company, but it is considered good practice to do so.

ABC INSURANCE GROUP PLC

Consolidated Balance Sheet
as at 31 December 19X8

	Note	**19X8**		19X7	
		£000	**£000**	£000	£000
ASSETS					
Intangible assets	*17*		**9,300**		10,000
Investments					
Land and buildings	*18*	**192,226**		182,824	
Investments in group undertakings and participating interests	*19*	**15,914**		15,346	
Other financial investments	*20*	**1,580,905**		1,497,692	
Deposits with ceding undertakings		**4,611**		3,552	
			1,793,656		1,699,414
Assets held to cover linked liabilities	*21*		**747,873**		502,911
Reinsurers' share of technical provisions					
Provision for unearned premiums	*29(b)*	**3,817**		3,532	
Long term business provision	*29(a)*	**4,159**		4,133	
Claims outstanding	*29(c)*	**34,217**		33,331	
Other technical provisions	*29(b)*	**315**		401	
			42,508		41,397
Debtors					
Debtors arising out of direct insurance operations	*22*	**16,078**		14,077	
Debtors arising out of reinsurance operations		**8,008**		7,817	
Other debtors	*23*	**24,858**		20,364	
			48,944		42,258
Other assets					
Tangible assets	*24*	**2,724**		2,576	
Cash at bank and in hand	*25*	**12,230**		8,697	
Other - present value of acquired in force business[6]		**2,825**		3,000	
			17,779		14,273
Prepayments and accrued income					
Accrued interest and rent		**7,905**		9,281	
Deferred acquisition costs	*29(e)*	**72,930**		55,719	
Other prepayments and accrued income		**8,635**		5,803	
			89,470		70,803
Total assets			**2,749,530**		2,381,056

6 No guidance is given in the SORP on where acquired or self-generated PVIF should be shown in the balance sheet.

ABC INSURANCE GROUP PLC

Consolidated Balance Sheet ***(continued)***
as at 31 December 19X8

LIABILITIES	*Note*	19X8 £000	19X8 £000	19X7 £000	19X7 £000
Capital and reserves					
Called up share capital	*26*	**100,000**		100,000	
Share premium account	27	**40,000**		40,000	
Profit and loss account	27	**109,836**		95,445	
Shareholders' funds attributable to equity interests			**249,836**		235,445
Subordinated liabilities	*28*		**388**		-
Fund for future appropriations			**217,889**		180,311
Technical provisions					
Provision for unearned premiums	*29(b)*	**54,307**		49,529	
Long term business provision	*29(a)*	**1,119,592**		1,072,759	
Claims outstanding	*29(c)*	**289,516**		280,426	
Equalisation provision	*29(d)*	**8,000**		3,750	
Other technical provisions	*29(b)*	**5,771**		4,442	
			1,477,186		1,410,906
Technical provisions for linked liabilities	*29(a)*		**718,181**		483,773
Provisions for other risks and charges	*31*		**24,155**		18,296
Deposits received from reinsurers	*32*	**14,910**		16,274	
Future margins	*32*	**(10,000)**		(12,000)	
			4,910		4,274
Creditors					
Creditors arising out of direct insurance operations		**20,537**		19,181	
Creditors arising out of reinsurance operations		**6,210**		6,794	
Amounts owed to credit institutions	*33*	**90**		100	
Other creditors including taxation and social security	*34*	**5,376**		6,517	
Accruals and deferred income			**32,213**		32,592
Deferred reinsurance commissions	*29(e)*	**947**		880	
Other accruals and deferred income		**23,825**		14,579	
			24,772		15,459
Total liabilities			**2,749,530**		2,381,056

ABC INSURANCE GROUP PLC

Parent Company Balance Sheet
as at 31 December 19X8

		19X8		19X7	
	Note	**£000**	**£000**	£000	£000
Fixed assets					
Investments	*19*		**137,026**		137,026
Current assets					
Debtors	*23*	**4,938**		1,536	
Cash		**10,500**		10,500	
		15,438		12,036	
Creditors: amount falling due within one year	*34*	**(4,000)**		(700)	
Net current assets			**11,438**		11,336
Net assets			**148,464**		148,362
Capital and reserves					
Called up share capital	*26*		**100,000**		100,000
Share premium account	*27*		**40,000**		40,000
Profit and loss account	*27*		**8,464**		8,362
Shareholders' funds attributable to equity interests			**148,464**		148,362

These financial statements were approved by the board of directors on 31 March 19X9 and were signed on its behalf by:

D Smith
Director

ABC Insurance Group PLC

Notes to the Accounts (extracts)

1 Basis of preparation and consolidation

The group financial statements, which consolidate the financial statements of the company and its wholly owned subsidiary undertakings, have been prepared in accordance with the provisions of Section 255 of, and Schedule 9A to, the Companies Act 1985 except as noted below under depreciation. The balance sheet of the parent company is prepared in accordance with the provisions of Section 226 of, and Schedule 4 to, the Companies Act 1985. The financial statements have also been prepared in accordance with applicable accounting standards and under the historical cost accounting rules, modified to include the revaluation of investments, and comply with the revised Statement of Recommended Practice issued by the Association of British Insurers.

The results of all subsidiary undertakings are included in the consolidated accounts. The results of subsidiary undertakings acquired during the year are brought into the accounts from the date of purchase.

As permitted by Section 230 of the Companies Act 1985, no profit and loss account of the parent company is presented.

2 Accounting policies (extracts)

The following accounting policies have been applied consistently in dealing with items which are considered material to the group's financial statements.

2(a) Basis of accounting for general insurance business

All classes of general business except marine, aviation and transport are accounted for on an annual basis.

Marine, aviation and transport business is accounted for on the non-annual basis because the directors consider that the information on premiums receivable and claims payable is insufficient for reliable estimates to be made at the end of the underwriting year in which the business incepts. The excess of premiums written over claims and expenses paid in respect of business commencing in an underwriting year is carried forward as a technical provision within outstanding claims. No profit is recognised until the end of the second year following the end of the underwriting year when the technical provision is replaced by a provision for claims outstanding. Where appropriate, provision for losses is made in respect of open underwriting years where ultimate claims and expenses are expected to exceed ultimate premiums and relevant investment return for classes of business which are managed together.

2(b) Basis of accounting for long term insurance business

The group has adopted the modified statutory solvency basis of accounting for long term insurance business.

Where long term reassurance contracts are structured to provide financing as well as transfer of risk, they are accounted for as insurance contracts. A linked presentation is adopted in the balance sheet to reflect the liability due to the reinsurer which is contingent upon the emergence of future margins required to finance the repayment of the liability.

2(c) Premiums

General business written premiums comprise the premiums on contracts entered into during the year, due in the accounting period, irrespective of whether they relate in whole or in part to a later accounting period. Premiums are disclosed gross of commission payable to intermediaries and exclude taxes and levies based on premiums.

Premiums written include adjustments to premiums written in prior accounting periods and estimates for "pipeline" premiums. An estimate is made at the balance sheet date to recognise retrospective adjustments to premiums or commissions. Outward reinsurance premiums are accounted for in the same accounting period as the premiums for the related direct insurance or inwards reinsurance business.

For general business accounted for on the annual basis, the provision for unearned premiums comprises the proportion of gross premiums written which is estimated to be earned in the following or subsequent financial years, computed separately for each insurance contract using the daily pro rata method, adjusted if necessary to reflect any variation in the incidence of risk during the period covered by the contract.

In respect of long term business, premiums are accounted for on a receivable basis, or in the case of unit-linked business when the liability is recognised, and exclude any taxes or duties based on premiums. Outward reinsurance premiums are accounted for on a payable basis.

ABC INSURANCE GROUP PLC

Notes to the Accounts *(continued)*

2(d) ***Acquisition Costs***

Acquisition costs comprise all direct and indirect costs arising from the conclusion of insurance contracts.

For general business, deferred acquisition costs represent the proportion of acquisition costs incurred which corresponds to the unearned premiums provision.

For long term business, an explicit deferred acquisition costs asset has been established in the balance sheet. Deferred acquisition costs are amortised at a rate based on the pattern of anticipated margins in respect of the related policies. Acquisition costs are are not deferred to the extent that available future margins are not expected to cover them.

2(e) ***Claims***

Claims incurred in respect of general business consist of claims and claims handling expenses paid during the financial year together with the movement in the provision for outstanding claims.

Claims outstanding comprise provisions for the estimated cost of settling all claims incurred but unpaid at the balance sheet date whether reported or not, and related internal and external claims handling expenses. Anticipated reinsurance recoveries, and estimates of salvage and subrogation recoveries, are disclosed separately as assets. Claims provisions relating to Accident and Health and Motor (Third party liability) business are discounted.

Long term business claims reflect the cost of all claims arising during the year, including policyholder bonuses allocated in anticipation of a bonus declaration.

2(f) ***Unexpired risks***

Provision is made for unexpired risks arising from general business where the expected value of claims and expenses attributable to the unexpired periods of policies in force at the balance sheet date exceeds the unearned premiums provision in relation to such policies after the deduction of any acquisition costs deferred. The provision for unexpired risks is calculated separately by reference to classes of business which are managed together, after taking into account relevant investment return.[7]

2(g) ***Equalisation provision***

An equalisation provision has been established and calculated in accordance with the requirements of the Insurance Companies (Reserves) Act 1995 to mitigate exceptional high loss ratios for classes of business displaying a high degree of claims volatility.

2(h) ***Long term business provision***

The long term business provision has been computed having due regard to the principles laid down in Council Directive 92/96/EEC. In particular, a prospective net premium valuation method has been adopted for all major classes of business, with the exception of linked contracts where the provisions are based on the market value of the related assets. Within the long term business provision, an explicit provision is made for vested bonuses, including those vesting following the current valuation. No provision is made for future reversionary or terminal bonuses.

2(i) ***Fund for future appropriations***

The fund for future appropriations comprises amounts arising in relation to participating policies and other non-linked policies, the allocation of which to policyholders or to shareholders has not been determined at the balance sheet date. When the allocation of funds is determined, appropriate transfers are made out of this fund.

2(j) ***Investments***

Group

Investments held to cover linked long term insurance liabilities are stated at current value. Other investments are also stated at current value, with the exception of redeemable fixed interest securities held as part of a portfolio of such securities intended to be held on an ongoing basis in the activities of the insurance undertaking which are stated at amortised cost, and certain interests in associates.

Land and buildings, other than those occupied by the group for its own purposes, are treated as investment properties and valued at open market value. Valuations are carried out by independent professionally qualified valuers every three years. In the intervening years, these valuations are reviewed by the directors on the basis of independent professional advice, and any decreases in values accounted for as value adjustments. Land and buildings occupied by the group for its own activities are stated at market value, less accumulated depreciation of buildings.

---

7 It is optional to take account of relevant investment return when determining the provision for unexpired risks.

ABC INSURANCE GROUP PLC

Notes to the Accounts *(continued)*

Listed investments are stated at mid-market value on the balance sheet date, or on the last stock exchange trading day before the balance sheet date.

Unlisted investments, for which a market exists, are valued at the average price at which they were traded on the balance sheet date, or on the last trading day before that date. Other unlisted investments are valued by the directors on a prudent basis having regard to their likely realisable value.

Where investments in group undertakings are held by the long term fund, they are reflected at current value in the consolidated balance sheet. The difference between the current value and the consolidated net assets is accounted for as a separate asset or liability in the group financial statements.

Interests in associates attributable to the long term business and which affect or establish policyholder rights, or otherwise held as part of the group's investment portfolio, are accounted for as investments in the group financial statements. Other investments in associates are accounted for in the group financial statements on the equity basis.

Where investments have been sold after the balance sheet date, or are to be sold in the short term, the market value is reduced by the actual estimated realisation costs.

Company

Investments in group undertakings and associates are stated at cost less provisions for permanent diminution in value.

2(k) ***Investment return***

Interest receivable is accounted for on an accruals basis. Dividend income, grossed up where appropriate by the imputed tax credit, is recognised on the date on which the related investment is marked "ex-dividend".

Realised gains or losses represent the difference between net sales proceeds and purchase price or, in the case of investments valued at amortised cost, the latest carrying value.

Unrealised gains and losses on investments represent the difference between the current value of investments at the balance sheet date and their purchase price. The movement in unrealised investment gains/losses includes an adjustment for previously recognised unrealised gains/losses on investments disposed of in the accounting period.

Investment return (including realised and the movement in unrealised investment gains and losses) on investments attributable to the long term business and associated shareholders' funds is reported in the technical account for long term business. Other investment return is reported in the non-technical account.

2(l) ***Allocation of investment return***

An allocation is made from the non-technical account to the general business technical account of the longer term investment return on investments supporting the general insurance technical provisions and related shareholders' funds. For long term business, an allocation is made from the long term business technical account to the non-technical account of the difference between the longer term investment return and the actual return on investments of the long term business which are directly attributable to shareholders. The longer term investment return is an estimate of the long term trend investment return for the relevant category of investments having regard to past performance, current trends and future expectations.[8]

2(m) ***Goodwill***

Goodwill arising on acquisitions, being the difference between the fair value of the purchase consideration and the fair value of the net assets acquired, is capitalised in the balance sheet and amortised on a straight line basis over 15 years.

General business claims provisions on acquisitions are disclosed on an undiscounted basis. The difference between this and fair value is included as a separate component of goodwill and amortised over the expected run-off period of the claims in the portfolio of business acquired.

For long term insurance business, the present value of in-force business (PVIF) arising on acquisition is recognised in the balance sheet as an asset. To the extent that the acquired PVIF will be recognised as profit over the remaining lifetime of the related in-force policies, it is amortised on a systematic basis, and the discount unwound, over the anticipated lives of the related contracts in the portfolio. The carrying value of the asset is tested annually for impairment.

2(n) ***Foreign currencies***

Assets and liabilities denominated mainly in a foreign currency are translated using the closing rate method. Exchange differences on opening net assets are taken to the fund for future appropriations in respect of long term insurance business and otherwise to reserves. Other exchange differences are dealt with in the profit and loss account through either the non-technical account or, in the case of long term insurance business, the long term business technical account.

---

[8] There is no requirement to allocate investment return between the technical and non-technical accounts. Listed companies are however "strongly encouraged" to disclose technical results which reflect the longer term rate of investment return.

ABC INSURANCE GROUP PLC

Notes to the Accounts *(continued)*

3 Segmental analysis

3(a) Class of business

	19X8 £000	19X7 £000
Gross Premiums written		
General business	**129,077**	117,351
Long term business	**375,298**	272,194
	504,375	389,545

	19X8 £000	19X7 £000
Profit on ordinary activities before tax		
General business	**12,376**	15,825
Long term business	**16,550**	10,444
Other income and charges	**(846)**	(644)
Short term fluctuations in investment return	**(1,464)**	5,710
	26,616	31,335
Segmental net assets		
General business	**175,632**	164,009
Long term business	**74,204**	71,436
	249,836	235,445

3(b) Geographical analysis

	19X8 £000	19X7 £000
Gross Premiums written		
United Kingdom	**472,525**	361,297
Germany	**19,337**	14,123
USA	**12,513**	14,125
	504,375	389,545
Profit on ordinary activities before tax		
United Kingdom	**23,875**	20,755
Germany	**2,607**	2,098
USA	**1,598**	2,772
Short term fluctuation in investment return	**(1,464)**	5,710
	26,616	31,335
Segmental net assets		
United Kingdom	**182,036**	171,944
Germany	**35,030**	32,921
USA	**32,770**	30,580
	249,836	235,445

ABC INSURANCE GROUP PLC

Notes to the Accounts *(continued)*

5 **Prior years' claims provisions for general business**

Material (under) or over provisions, before adjustment for discounting, for general business claims provisions at the beginning of the year compared with payments and provisions at the end of the year in respect of prior years' claims were as follows:

	19X8	19X7
	£000	£000
Class of business:		
Motor (third party liability)	**5,575**	-
Marine, aviation and transport	**(6,187)**	(4,809)
Fire and other damage to property	**(6,004)**	(5,928)
Reinsurance	**(8,507)**	(2,005)
	(15,123)	(12,742)

7 **Bonuses - long term business**

The total bonuses attributable to the financial year amounted to £40.6 million (19X7: £34.1 million).

10 **(a) Longer term investment return**[9]

The longer term return is based on historical real rates of return and current inflation expectations adjusted for consensus economic and investment forecasts. In respect of equity and property investments, the return is calculated by grossing up actual income earned, after adjustment for special factors, by a multiple representing the longer term rate of investment return divided by the estimated long term dividend yield. For redeemable fixed income securities the amortised cost basis is adopted to determine the longer term rate of return and for irredeemable securities and other short term assets the interest income received has been used for this purpose.

The principal assumptions underlying the calculation of longer term investment return are:[10]

	Equities				Property			
	Longer term return		**Dividend Yield**		**Long term return**		**Rental yield**	
	19X8	19X7	**19X8**	19X7	**19X8**	19X7	**19X8**	19X7
	%	%	%	%	%	%		
UK	**9.0**	9.5	**3.5**	3.5	**8**	8	**5**	5
USA	**8.5**	8.5	**2.5**	2.5	**n/a**	n/a	**n/a**	n/a
Germany	**7.0**	7.0	**2.0**	2.0	**n/a**	n/a	**n/a**	n/a

9 Where allocations of investment return between the technical and non-technical accounts reflect the longer term rate of investment return.

10 Assumptions for fixed interest have not been disclosed as returns have been calculated on an amortised cost basis.

ABC INSURANCE GROUP PLC

Notes to the Accounts *(continued)*

(b) Comparison of longer term investment return with actual returns

The actual return on investments attributable to general business and long term business is set out below.

	19X3 - 19X8 £000	19X2 - 19X7 £000
Actual return attributable to shareholders:		
- general insurance business	**230,150**	224,411
- long term insurance business	**67,400**	64,350
	297,550	288,761
Longer term return credited to operating results:		
- general insurance business	**216,400**	210,475
- long term business	**62,750**	61,550
	279,150	272,025
Excess of actual returns over longer term returns	**18,400**	16,736

11 Other technical charges

	General business 19X8 £000	General business 19X7 £000	Long term business 19X8 £000	Long term business 19X7 £000
Amortisation of goodwill in acquired claims provisions	**500**	550		
Amortisation of acquired present value of in force contracts ("PVIF")			**175**	160

12 Other charges

	Non-technical account 19X8 £000	Non-technical account 19X7 £000
Amortisation of goodwill	**200**	200
Other corporate expenses	**709**	478
	909	678

ABC INSURANCE GROUP PLC

Notes to the Accounts *(continued)*

17 Intangible assets

Group

	Goodwill	Goodwill in acquired claims provisions	Total
	£000	£000	£000
At beginning of year	5,550	4,450	10,000
Amortisation	(500)	(200)	(700)
At end of the year	5,050	4,250	9,300

19 Investments in group undertakings and participating interests

	Group Current value		Company Cost	
	19X8 £000	19X7 £000	**19X8 £000**	19X7 £000
Shares in group undertakings				
Excess of current value over net asset	**-**	-	**137,026**	137,026
value consolidated	**15,000**	14,500	**-**	-
Interest in associated undertaking				
at equity valuation	**914**	846	**-**	-
	15,914	15,346	**137,026**	137,026

Under paragraph 3 (1A) of Schedule 4A to Companies Act 1985, it is not permitted to make consolidation adjustments to assets changes in the values of which affect or establish policyholder rights. In relation to group companies held by the long term fund, the difference between the current value and the net assets consolidated has been included in the consolidated balance sheet as an additional asset.

Investments in group undertakings, which are all wholly owned, are as follows:

Name	Country of incorporation	Class of shares held	Principal activity	Held directly or indirectly
Example Life Assurance Limited	Great Britain	Ordinary	Life assurance	Directly
Example General Insurance Limited	Great Britain	Ordinary	General insurance	Directly
Example Life Assurance Subsidiary Limited	Germany	Ordinary	Life assurance	Indirectly

Interests in associated undertakings represent the investments in 300,000 ordinary shares of Example General Associate Limited and 300,000 ordinary shares of Example Life Associate Limited, constituting 30% investments in the nominal share capital of each of these companies. The interest in Example Life Associate Limited is held by the long term fund as part of the investment portfolio and is included within other financial investments. The interest in Example General Associate Limited is a strategic investment and has been accounted for using the equity basis. No additional disclosures are made regarding the associate companies due to their immateriality relative to the group.

ABC INSURANCE GROUP PLC

Notes to the Accounts *(continued)*

29(d) Equalisation provision

An equalisation provision has been established in accordance with the requirements of the Insurance Companies (Reserves) Act 1995. This is not a liability because it is in addition to the provisions required to meet the anticipated ultimate cost of settlement of outstanding claims at the balance sheet date. Notwithstanding this, it is required by schedule 9A to the Companies Act 1985 to be included within technical provisions in the balance sheet. This has had the effect of reducing shareholders' funds by £5.5 million (19X7: - £2.6 million). The movement in the equalisation provision during the year resulted in a decrease in the general business technical result and the profit before taxation of £4.3 million (19X7: £3.7 million).

30 Discounting of provision for outstanding claims

(a) Claims on certain classes of business are discounted as follows:

Class	Rate	Mean term to settlement
Accident and Health	3%	5 years
Motor (Third party liability)	3%	6 years

The mean term to settlement is estimated on the basis of past experience.

(b) The effect of discounting these claims is to reduce net outstanding claims from £44.9 million (19X7: £42.7 million) to £38.7 million (19X7: £37.3 million) and to increase the profit on ordinary activities before tax by £0.8 million (19X7: £1.5 million).

32 Reinsurance transactions

Long term business

On 1 January 19X6 the company entered into a reassurance arrangement to assist in the financing of the acquisition costs of new long term business. The net amount of the financing outstanding under the reassurance arrangement at 31 December 19X8 amounting to £10 million (19X7: £12 million) is included within 'Deposits received from reinsurers.' Linked presentation has been adopted whereby the corresponding asset to recognise that part of the future margins arising on the reassured block of policies out of which the reassurance liability will be repaid is deducted from the deposit liability. The company is under no obligation under the terms of the reassurance contract, and has no intention, to repay the liability to the reinsurer in the event that the actual level of margins is insufficient.

The components of net profit for the year arising from this reassurance contract were:

	19X8 **£000**	19X7 £000
Reassurance premiums payable	(2,000)	(1,000)
Interest payable	(840)	(910)
Emergence of attributable margins	2,840	1,910
	-	-

E. Life companies as subsidiary

[8.26]
Companies that own life companies show their value as 'embedded value', which represents the present value of future shareholder profits. The change in embedded value is the profit for the year.

F. Form of accounts

[8.27]
The annual accounts, accompanying notes, forms and certificates and auditors report must be set out in accordance with the IC(AS)R 1996, SI 1996/943. The contents of certificates required under IC(AS)R, reg 28 by directors and actuary and report required under IC(AS)R, reg 29 by the auditors are set out at IC(AS)R, Sch 6. The obligations of the appointed actuary are dealt with at Chapter 4 above. The directors broadly have to certify:

(i) that the return has been prepared in accordance with the IC(AS)R 1996;
(ii) that proper accounting records have been maintained and adequate information has been obtained by the company;
(iii) that adequate systems of control have been established and maintained by the company over its transactions and records;
(iv) that reasonable enquiries have been made into connected person status;
(v) that ICR 1994, SI 1994/1516 on location and matching have been complied with;
(vi) that the statement under IC(AS)R 1996, reg 31 (ie information on the financial interests of the appointed actuary in the company) is based on information obtained in compliance with that regulation;
(vii) that ICA 1982, ss 28–31A have been complied with;
(viii) statements on guarantees, linked funds, and agreements between insurance companies; and
(ix) that the directors are satisfied that systems of control and the return comply with published guidance (note: a list of the guidance is to be included in the return).

[8.28]
The statements are to be omitted if, in the opinion of those signing the certificates, the statements cannot be truthfully made. If statements are omitted, a note to this effect has to accompany the certificate.

[8.29]
The auditor's report, in addition to statements required under CA 1985, shall state that the returns under IC(AS)R 1996, SI 1996/943, including the directors' certificate, have been prepared in accordance with these regulations. They also have to state that it was reasonable for the directors to have made the statements and they must add any explanations or qualifications to this if they cannot give an unqualified statement to this

effect. The auditors must also state to what extent they have relied on the appointed actuary's certificate and whether any uncertainty on any matter expressed by them in the return is material in calculating the available assets over the minimum margin of solvency.

G Role of auditor

[8.30]
IC(AS)R 1996, SI 1996/943, reg 32 states that auditors qualified to audit insurance company accounts must meet the criteria at CA 1989, Pt II.[1]

1 Eligibility under CA 1989, s 34(1) does not meet the eligibility requirements under IC(AS)R 1996, reg 32.

[8.31]
ICA 1982, s 21A places a duty on the auditor to 'whistle blow' to HMT or the Secretary of State. Failure to do so may result in disqualification. There is no contravention of duty to the client by the auditor in complying with this duty.

3. TAX

A. Introduction

[8.32]
The taxation of life companies is extremely complex and what follows is no more than a very brief summary. A more specialist text is Macleod and Levitt *Taxation of Insurance Business* (4th edn 1999).

[8.33]
A life assurance company must, for tax purposes, separate its life business from any other category of insurance business that it carries on (ICTA 1988, s 432). This is because special rules (described below) apply in respect of the taxation of life assurance business, whilst other insurance business is taxed as trading profit.

B. The two methods

[8.34]
The IR may choose to tax life assurance business under the 'I – E' (income minus expenses) method or as a trade under, Sch D, Case I. The IR usually prefer the I – E method as this generally results in a higher tax charge. The profits of mutual insurance companies are always taxed under the I – E method as their profits are not liable to tax under Sch D, Case I.

(i) Sch D, Case I

[8.35]
Under Sch D, Case I, normally expenses are deducted from income and gains, and tax levied on any resultant profit. The special nature of life

contracts, however, has resulted in modifications to the general rules. The two main features of life business, which make it difficult to tax under the ordinary rules, are: first, that liabilities crystallise over a long period; and, secondly, the other party to the contract has obligations to pay premiums which the life company invests and returns on maturity, death or surrender. The tax rules have been modified as follows:

1. The liability of the life company to the policyholders can be deducted in computing profits under Sch D, Case I.
2. Other items which can be deducted include tax (UK and foreign) paid on behalf of the policyholder, bonus allocations and the present value of the cost of reversionary bonuses.
3. If at the year end the life company has a surplus (as determined by the actuarial investigation), it may set aside that part of the surplus which can be demonstrated to be needed to meet PRE.

[8.36]
An anomaly still occurs even in taxing an insurance company under the modified rules of Sch D, Case I. It is standard to tax income only when received, and gains and losses on investments when they are realised. However, actuarial liabilities are calculated on accrued but unrealised investment income and unrealised profits. At **[8.35]** point 1 above, the actuarial liability is deducted in full and profits are to be calculated using investment income and gains, whether or not realised or unrealised. It is the deduction of actuarial liabilities that usually results in a lower tax charge under Sch D, Case I than under the I – E method.

[8.37]
Tax is charged at the normal rate of corporation tax, determined in accordance with the amounts of profits of the company.

(ii) I – E method

[8.38]
Tax on life assurance business assessed under the income less expenses method is payable on:

(a) investment income and capital gains attributable to basic life assurance and general annuity business, less management expenses attributable to that business; and
(b) profits made on pensions business, overseas life assurance business and life reinsurance business assessed under Sch D, Case VI.

[8.39]
The calculation of profits for pensions business in **[8.38]**(b) is complex. Income is defined as premiums received plus gains less losses on investments attributable to pensions business. Investment income for pension business is tax exempt and any tax deductions are repaid; but the income is brought into the computation to see if any Sch D, Case VI profits emerge. Pension annuities, bonus allocations and a percentage of general trading expenses are deducted from the profits.

[8.40]
Management expenses in **[8.38]**(a) are subject to various restrictions. They can only be set off against investment income and gains attributable to basic life assurance and general annuity business; any excess in any particular year is carried forward to be set against such profits in future years. Furthermore, management expenses are restricted by reference to a notional Sch D, Case I computation. This means that where a tax charge calculated under the I – E method would be lower than it would have been under the Sch D, Case I method, such expenses are restricted until there is no advantage in applying the I – E method. Expenses restricted in this manner will also be available to set against profits in (a) in future years (FA 1989, s 47).

[8.41]
Chargeable profits computed under the I – E method are potentially taxable at three different rates:

(a) the normal rate of corporation tax in respect of profits attributable to shareholders (this rate is determined in accordance with the amount of profits of the company);
(b) a rate equal to the lower rate of income tax in respect of profits attributable to policyholders' share of basic life assurance and general annuity business; and
(c) a rate equal to the basic rate of income tax in respect of other profits attributable to policyholders (FA 1989, ss 88, 88A, 89).

4. VAT

[8.42]
Carrying on insurance business or reinsurance is exempt for VAT purposes (Value Added Tax Act 1994 (VATA 1994), Sch 9 as amended by FA 1997, s 38). This means that insurance companies do not need to register for VAT and cannot charge VAT to customers for their services, but must pay VAT when purchasing any 'vatable' services or goods. There is, therefore, no set off as in the case of companies registered for VAT, where input and output VAT can be set off and any difference paid to or reclaimed from Customs and Excise.

[8.43]
Two or more companies may be registered for VAT purposes as members of a group where, broadly:

(a) they are resident in the UK; and
(b) they are in control of the other or are under common control (VATA 1994, s 43A).

[8.44]
However, Customs and Excise have wide powers to refuse a group application or to vary or dissolve VAT groups where this is necessary 'for the protection of the revenue' (VATA 1994, ss 43B, 43C). There are two

main effects of group registration (VATA, s 43(1)). First, one company in the group acts as the representative member and assumes all the rights and duties of the group as a whole in relation to VAT. Secondly, transactions within the group are not subject to VAT. Therefore, where an insurance company is part of a group with other companies, it does not charge VAT on any intra-group transactions it makes and it need not pay VAT on supplies or goods received from other group members. Group registration does not, however, affect the VAT rules for supplies made by a group member to a person outside the group or vice versa.

[8.45]
In Chapter 2 it was explained that because of ICA 1982, s 16 many insurance companies inevitably chose to set up subsidiary companies in order to extend their range of activities. The VAT treatment has been aimed at trying to create a parity between companies choosing to structure on a divisional or departmental way and those which prefer a group structure.

5. STAMP DUTY

[8.46]
Stamp duty is payable on the transfer of shares (FA 1999, Sch 15). On demutualisation (post 19 March 1997), relief is given where transfers of all or part of the insurance business carried on by a mutual insurance company (ie one with no share capital) is transferred. There are three conditions:

1. The shares must be offered to at least 90% of the persons who are members of the mutual immediately prior to transfer.
2. All the shares in the acquiring company which will be in issue immediately after the transfer, other than shares subject to public offer, must be offered to persons who are at the time of the offer, members of the mutual or persons entitled to become members or employees, former employees or pensioners of the mutual or a subsidiary company which is wholly owned by the mutual.
3. The transfer must be in terms of ICA 1982, Sch 2C (see Chapter 9) (FA 1997, s 96).

[8.47]
Instruments which are not chargeable to stamp duty still need to be adjudicated and stamped to show they are not chargeable to duty (Stamp Act 1891, s 12).

6. SUMMARY

[8.48]
1. Changes were introduced in 1993 to the way insurance accounts were prepared and the current requirements are set out in CA 1985, Sch 9A. The main changes were:

(i) life companies were previously exempt from stating the accounts were 'true and fair' and this exemption has now been removed;
(ii) deferred acquisition costs were introduced to make the emergence of profits more realistic; and
(iii) insurance companies were given the option to report on a modified statutory solvency basis or an embedded value basis: most life companies use the former and parent companies of life companies use the latter.

2. The format of the life company's annual returns are set out in IC(AS)R 1996, SI 1996/943.
3. Life companies are normally taxed on an I – E basis but still have to produce notional Sch D, Case I calculations in order to determine whether management expenses are to be restricted.
4. Carrying on insurance business is exempt for VAT purposes.
5. Transfers of long-term business are exempt from stamp duty if a number of conditions are satisfied, the main one being that the transfer is in terms of ICA 1982, Sch 2C.

Chapter 9
Corporate changes

I. SALE AND ACQUISITION OF AN INSURANCE COMPANY

A. Introduction

[9.1]
When an insurance company is being purchased or sold, it can be achieved in much the same way as any other company sale or acquisition. There are some additional features which are worth noting.

B. Demutualisation

[9.2]
If the company is a mutual, it can only be sold or acquired if all or a percentage of the policyholders agree: the exact number should appear in the memorandum and articles or other establishment document or, alternatively, passed in a special resolution of the company. The articles should also specify which classes of policyholders are eligible to vote, ie it may be limited to with profit policy holders only. A new company is set up which will purchase the rights of the policyholders to participate in the profit of the mutual for cash or shares in the new company. If the requisite number of policyholders agree, the long-term business of the mutual can be transferred to the new company in terms of ICA 1982, Sch 2C (see **[9.4]–[9.17]** below). The mutual would normally hold a meeting in terms of the relevant establishment document, at which policyholders vote on the purchase of their rights, the transfer of business, any changes to the mutual's establishment documents and any other relevant matters.

C. Change of directors or controllers

[9.3]
If there are any changes to the directors or controllers of a life company then ICA 1982, ss 60–64 apply. There is a duty to notify the Treasury and the information to be supplied is set out in ICR 1994, SI 1994/1516, Sch 6. The Treasury have three months in which to object to any new appointment on the grounds that the fit and proper test has not been met (Chapter 7 below).

2. TRANSFER OF INSURANCE BUSINESS

A. Introduction

[9.4]
Merging the funds of two insurance companies or moving insurance business from a mutual to a proprietory company involves following the procedures set out at ICA 1982, Sch 2C. Provided the transfer is done in terms of ICA, Sch 2C, stamp duty is usually avoidable. The procedure is not mandatory: technically, the transfer could also be effected by assigning all the contracts and transferring all the assets to the purchaser, who would agree to assume the liabilities all with the consent of the policyholders. This latter approach would in the majority of circumstances be more costly and onerous than following the statutory procedure.

[9.5]
The relevant section is ICA 1982, s 49. Basically, the insurance company has to draw up a scheme narrating in detail how the transfer of funds is to take place and comment on the effect of the transfer on all the different classes of policyholders. The appointed actuary then has to produce a report to the Board on the proposed scheme stating that, in his opinion, the scheme should go ahead and that no class of policyholder will suffer any disadvantage as a result of the scheme. An independent actuary has to prepare a similar report. A petition is then made to the High Court of Justice in England or the Court of Session in Scotland or the High Court of Justice in Northern Ireland to sanction the scheme. Various other documents (discussed in more detail below) are prepared to inform policyholders and other relevant parties about the terms of the scheme and advertisements are placed in national newspapers. The court will usually appoint a reporter to examine the documentation and consider whether all the requirements of ICA 1982, Sch 2C have been met and report back to the court. A strict timetable is adhered to. Further, a great deal of planning both before and after the transfer is necessary. The whole process is discussed in more detail below.

B. Procedure

[9.6]
This paragraph and **[9.7]–[9.16]** deal with the procedure relating to transfers within the UK. **[9.17]** deals with the variations on this procedure where there is a European dimension. The court will not sanction the scheme unless the following requirements have been complied with:

1. The petition is accompanied by the independent actuary's report. Normally, the scheme document and the appointed actuary's report will also be lodged with the petition, together with documents evidencing that the requirements at 2 below have been met.
2. A notice is placed in the London, Edinburgh and Belfast Gazettes stating the addresses of the offices where copies of the petition and independent actuary's report are available for inspection. The notice

should also state the period during which the documents can be inspected. The period must be at least 21 days from the date the notice is published.

3. Unless a successful application is made by the petitioner to dispense with this requirement, the court will also direct that the notice at 2 above is also published in two national newspapers in the UK.
4. Unless a successful application is made by the petitioner to dispense with this requirement, a statement setting out the terms of the scheme and a summary of the independent actuary's report, covering, especially, the likely effects of the scheme on the long-term policyholders, is sent to each of the policyholders of the transferring and transferee companies. It is possible to dispense with or reduce this requirement if, for example, only a partial transfer is contemplated.
5. A copy of the petition and independent actuary's report together with a copy of the statement, if any at 4 above is served on the Treasury and a period of not less than 21 days have elapsed since the date of service.
6. Prior to the scheme being sanctioned, the transferring and transferee companies must make available on request by any one, a copy of the petition and independent actuary's report. The companies can charge a fee (prescribed by the court) for this.
7. Those entitled to object or be heard by the court include the Treasury and any person who might be adversely affected by the scheme (ie policyholders and employees of all the companies involved, creditors etc).
8. The court must be satisfied that the transferee company is, or will be immediately after the order sanctioning the scheme, authorised under ICA 1982, s 3 or 4 to carry on the classes of long-term business transferred under the scheme.
9. The Treasury has certified that the transferee company will have the necessary margin of solvency post transfer.

C. Powers of court

[9.7]

In granting an order sanctioning the scheme, the court may in that order or subsequent orders make provision for any of the following:

1. The transfer to the transferee company of the whole or any part of the undertaking and of the properties or liabilities of the transferor company.
2. The allotment or appropriation by the transferee company of any shares, debentures, policies or interests.
3. The continuation of any legal proceedings.
4. The dissolution without winding up of the transferor company.
5. Any incidental measure needed to fully implement the scheme.

[9.8]

In *Re Hill Samuel Life Assurance Ltd; Re Ambassador Life Co Ltd* [1998] 3 All ER 176 it was held on an application under ICA 1982, Sch 2C that in granting the petition the court had to have regard to the following:

1. the fact that the transferor's board had considered the transfer commercially beneficial;
2. whether any policyholders, employees or others might be adversely affected by the decision (although it did not follow that if they were the scheme had to be rejected); and ultimately
3. whether the scheme was fair between the affected persons, which issue required an independent actuary's report; and
4. policies which were not being transferred and to which ICA 1982, Sch 2C, para 5(1)(e) applied (ie 'such incidental, consequential and supplementary matters as are necessary to secure that the scheme shall be fully and effectively carried out').

D. The effect of the order

[9.9]
In relation to the transfer of assets and liabilities, the order effectively vests assets in the transferee company and transfers liabilities. There will usually be a great deal of post-order paperwork to carry out to ensure assets and liabilities are in the name of the transferee company. When assets are being sold or transferred the court order acts as a link in title.

E. Documentation

[9.10]
The following documents need to be prepared.

(i) The scheme

[9.11]
This should include:

1. A definitions section.
2. A brief description of the companies involved; that they are all authorised under ICA 1982 and that they are all bound by the scheme and that they will take all necessary steps to ensure the scheme is implemented.
3. Details of when and how the transfer of assets and liabilities is to be effected; the price; that if there is a delay in effecting the transfer of assets that they will be held by the transferor on trust for the transferee company; that any payments made to the transferor company in respect of the transferred assets after the transfer will be paid to the transferee company; indemnities from the transferee company.
4. A description and undertaking of how the internal funds of the transferee company will be managed post transfer.
5. A description and undertaking of how the value of the any merged funds will be calculated and the principles underlying any adjustment to the values.
6. Mandates for premiums relating to the transferred policies will automatically be deemed to be in favour of the transferee company;

similarly any mandate on the method of payment of annuities or other sums will be binding on the transferee company.

7. The date on which the scheme is to become effective and any conditions precedent, for example, obtaining a waiver from the IR on stamp duty and other taxes on any of the assets transferred.
8. The power to modify the scheme by agreement and with the court's approval.

(ii) The independent actuary's report

[9.12]

It should be kept in mind that the independent actuary's duty is to the court and not to the petitioning company, who would normally appoint him. The independent actuary, in preparing his report should:

(a) Refer to GN 15; and

(b) Have copies of the following documents:

1. The Memorandum and Articles of all the companies involved in the scheme, the Annual Reports and Accounts for the previous year and the annual returns to HMT for the previous year (GN 15, s 3.8.1).
2. Reports by the appointed actuary on the most recent actuarial investigation.
3. Samples of quotations, charges and policy documents and any other reports on policyholders reasonable expectations.
4. Sample Reassurance Agreements, if relevant.
5. With Profit Guide issued to policyholders.
6. The Scheme.
7. Reports on recent investment policy and reports on alternative strategies may be useful.
8. Reports evaluating alternative schemes, if any, and any other documents associated with the transfer.

(c) The report should cover the following:

1. The qualifications of the independent actuary, his remit and the documents he has examined, any interests with any of the parties involved and who is paying his costs.
2. A summary of the history of the companies involved and their financial position (ie classes of business and number of contracts in force, their value).
3. A detailed summary of the scheme and its purpose.
4. The effect of the transfer on all the policyholders (ie those transferring, those remaining with the transferor and those with the transferee). The effects should include:
   - security of their investments;
   - their reasonable expectations including bonus prospects;
   - costs and tax consequences of scheme if they impact on the policyholder funds;
   - the effect on any rights to participate in profits charges and values;

  - whether any compensation payments are equitable; and
  - the ability of the company to continue to meet the PRE for the duration of the contracts; if the company is a mutual, the effect on the members rights regarding any further constitutional changes.

  (See generally GN 15, para 5.)

5. Statement that in his opinion the scheme will not adversely effect the expectations of the policyholders and in particular:

   > '. . . is satisfied that for each of the companies concerned the scheme is equitable to all classes and generations of policyholders; and whether for each relevant company the scheme places obligations on the directors, or provides for future certification by its Appointed Actuary, sufficient . . . for the protection of those expectations.' (GN 15 4.6.)

[9.13]
Before finalising the report, the independent actuary should speak to all the appointed actuaries involved and to the regulator, to see if they have any issues which he or she should be aware of.

(iii) The petition

[9.14]
A barrister (England) or advocate (Scotland) should be instructed to draft the petition to the relevant court (ICA 1982, Sch 2C, Pt 1, para 1(4)).

(iv) The appointed actuary report

[9.15]
This really is a report to the Board on the feasibility, mechanics and benefits of effecting a transfer. The other documents are factually based on this and amendments made by the Board. It is not a legal requirement to include it with the petition, but if the scheme is complex (eg includes fund mergers), it should be included.

(v) Miscellaneous documentation

[9.16]
The following documents will also be required:

1. The report by the court reporter, if one is appointed.
2. An undertaking by the transferee company that any compensation payments or shares in surplus to relevant categories of policyholder in terms of the scheme will be made; and a corresponding letter from the independent actuary confirming that the undertakings provide the necessary protection to policyholders.
3. The letter to policyholders summarising the scheme, the appointed actuary's and independent actuary's reports and a corresponding affidavit from the independent actuary confirming the accuracy of the summary.

4. An affidavit by the appointed actuary, or some officer of the transferring company, confirming that the letter at 3 was sent to the policyholders and the availability of addresses or any other problems associated with this.
5. A certificate from the Treasury pursuant to ICA 1982, Sch 2(c), s 3(1)(b) that the transferee company after the transfer has the necessary solvency margin; list of classes of insurance business for which each company is authorised and that, on the basis of the information before them, they do not wish to be heard in respect of the petition.

F. The European dimension

[9.17]
Where one of the companies is located in the EEA or EFTA, or if all the companies involved are located in the UK but have policies where the 'State of the commitment' is in the EEA or EFTA, a system of certification by HMT and notification to regulatory authorities in other member states apply (ICA 1982, Sch 2C).

3. WINDING UP INSURANCE COMPANIES

[9.18]
This is covered by ICA 1982, ss 53–59. There are essentially only two methods by which an insurance company can be wound up:

1. An insurance company can be wound up on the petition of ten or more policyholders owning policies worth in total £10,000 or more. Leave of the court is needed before presenting the petition and it will only be granted if a prima facie case is made out to the satisfaction of the court and security for costs at a level the court determine reasonable are provided.
2. The Treasury can petition the court for a winding-up order on the following three grounds namely, that the company:
   (a) is unable to pay its debts in terms of the Insolvency Act 1986, ss 123, 222–224;
   (b) has failed to satisfy an obligation under ICA 1982, or previous insurance legislation, or where the company has been authorised in another member state under the legislation giving effect to the insurance directives or other applicable legislation; or
   (c) failed to produce accounting records in terms of CA 1985, ss 221 and 222.

[9.19]
Once the winding-up order has been granted, the liquidator can, unless the court directs otherwise, carry on the long-term business of the company with a view to transferring it to another company as a going concern. Any deficit to policyholders on liquidation would be made good (at least 90%) in terms of the PPA 1975 (see Chapter 7).

[9.20]
There is, at present, a prohibition on the voluntary winding up of insurance companies. The Financial Services and Markets Bill proposes to remove this outright prohibition and allow voluntary winding up subject to the Financial Services Authority granting permission. Any notice of a general meeting of creditors to propose a winding up resolution must be notified to the Financial Services Authority. Failure to notify will constitute a criminal offence. The draft Bill also proposes to allow insurance companies to be subject to administration orders.

4. CROSS-BORDER BUSINESS

A. Formal requirements

[9.21]
UK life companies can do cross-border business in the other 14 member states by setting up a branch (establishment business) or selling directly to customers in the other member states (services business). They can also provide services business to countries in the EFTA (ie the 15 member states and Norway, Iceland and Liechtenstein) and sell back into the UK from branches established in the EEA (ie the 15 member states and Norway, Iceland Liechtenstein and Switzerland). Complimentary provisions exist to cover EC and EFTA life companies doing business in the UK (ICA 1982, s 81A and 81B and Sch 2F and 2G).[1]

1 To some extent the single market depends on all the states having implemented the relevant directives.

[9.22]
The procedure is based on the 'single passport' system, which in effect means that once authorised, a life company has the right to conduct business throughout the EC and EFTA. The formalities of the procedure involve a system of notification to the home and host states' supervisory bodies, together with detailed information, 'the requisite details', on the nature and extent of the proposed cross-border business. The requisite details are more extensive in the case of establishment business than services business. The only grounds on which the host member state can refuse to allow an authorised insurer to conduct business is if the proposed operations somehow conflict with the 'general good'.[1] The UK supervisory authority has a discretion to refuse to allow the insurer to carry on business in another state if it appears to them that the business would fail the sound and prudent management test.

1 Commission Interpretative Communication 'Freedom to Provide Services and the General Good in the Insurance Sector' 97/C 365/04, see Appendix 2.

(i) UK insurers carrying on business in other member states

[9.23]
ICA 1982, Sch 2G, Pt I deals with UK insurers selling in other member states. The notification procedure and timetable is virtually identical for

both establishment and services business: the differences are (a) a shorter time-scale for services business; (b) the ability to combine services business in different states on one notice; (c) no general good requirement or waiting period from host state supervisory body for services business; and (d) less in the way of requisite details for services business. The procedure is as follows:

1. The insurer must be authorised under ICA 1982, s 3 or 4.
2. The insurer gives the Treasury a notice containing UK and EC requisite details (establishment business); requisite details (services business). ICA 1982, Sch 2G, Pt I, paras 4 and 7 respectively.
3. The Treasury within three months (establishment business) or one month (services business) from the date of receipt of the notice, gives the supervisory authority in the state where the branch is to be established, or the states in which services are to be provided, the notice and a certificate stating:
   (a) that the insurer has the minimum margin of solvency calculated in accordance with arts 18, 19 and 20 of the First Long-Term Insurance Directive 79/267/EEC, and
   (b) the classes of insurance business which the insurer is authorised to carry out in the UK.
4. The Treasury must also, within the three or one month period, notify the insurer that the notice and certificate have been given to the supervisory authority in the other state/s or refuse to do this. The only grounds for refusal is if 'having regard to the business to be carried on' through the branch or provided in the member state 'it appears to them that the criteria of sound and prudent management would not or might not continue to be fulfilled in respect of the company'.
5. The supervisory authority of the state of the branch or services, on receipt of the notice and certificate, must inform the Treasury of the conditions which, in the interests of the 'general good', the insurer must comply with or a period of two months have elapsed since the Treasury gave the supervisory authority the notice and certificate (note: this only applies to establishment business).

[9.24]
Once these formalities are completed, the insurer can commence business in the host member state. Any proposed change to the requisite details once the branch has been established or services commenced must be notified to the Treasury in the case of the branch not less than one month before the change (there is no time limit for services business) and in both cases, if the change is outwith the control of the company a notice must be given as soon as possible afterwards. An abridged notification procedure follows.

(ii) UK insurers providing insurance in EFTA states

[9.25]
This is covered at ICA 1982, Sch 2G, paras 9 and 10. Essentially, the company must notify the Treasury of the state in which insurance business is to be

provided and the class of insurance business. The company may also apply to the Treasury for a certificate stating that the company has a minimum solvency margin, the classes of business for which it has authorisation and that it extends to carrying on business outside the UK, and that the Treasury have no objection to the company carrying on insurance business outside the EEA state of establishment. If the Treasury refuse to grant the certificate, they must state their reasons for refusal in writing.

B. Obstacles to completion of single market

(i) Introduction

[9.26]
The EU comprises 15 member states, with additional countries in the EEA and EFTA, each with different cultural heritage, traditions (including traditions relating to the provision of financial services) and language. Moreover, each member state has different legal, political and fiscal systems. The Commission has tried to create a 'level playing field' in life insurance through the three Life Directives, but realised that this in itself was insufficient and so over the past seven years has made numerous attempts, some more successful than others, to decrease differences between member states in a number of areas dealt with below.

(ii) Tax

[9.27]
The fear was that once a single market was established, national governments would compete on the tax front to attract foreign investment using tax incentives and lower tax regimes. It was recognised that although this may not cause vast increases in the revenue of the host country, it might deplete the resources of the other countries.

Company taxation

[9.28]
In 1991, a committee of taxation experts was set up by the Commission under Mr Onno Ruding. Their brief was to:

> '. . . evaluate . . . the importance of taxation for business decisions with respect to the location of investment and the international allocation of profits between enterprises. An assessment of the impact of taxation relative to other factors is necessary to determine whether existing differences in corporation tax and the burden of business taxes among member countries leads to major distortions affecting the functioning of the internal market.'

[9.29]
The Ruding Committee conducted a survey of multinational companies within 17 countries including the then 12 member states. Separate figures

were produced for different sectors. In financial services, 78% of companies claimed that differences in taxation was a major factor in their decision on where to locate. The Committee recommended that minimum harmonisation at Community level in certain key areas would lessen distortions while leaving national governments a real degree of flexibility over direct taxes. Various Directives were introduced to achieve this. Member states are currently discussing tax on savings but have not reached agreement as yet.

Insurance policy taxation

[9.30]

The European Court of Justice decision in *Bachmann v Belgium* C-204/90 [1992] ECR I-249 contradicted to some extent the aims of the Commission. The case dealt with whether or not the tax system in Belgium relating to contributions (premiums) to or proceeds from insurance policies taken out in other member states constituted an obstacle to the freedom of movement of persons under the EC Treaty, arts 39 and 49.[1] The facts were that Mr Bachmann was a German national working in Belgium. He had a German insurance policy and wanted to continue paying premiums to it, but the Belgium tax authorities would not allow tax relief on the contributions because the policy had not been taken out with a Belgium authorised insurer.

1 Formerly the Treaty of Rome, arts 48 and 59.

[9.31]

The court argued that if one member state allowed relief on contributions, then that member state should be entitled to tax the proceeds, even although these were paid in another member state. The principle underlying the court's decision was stated as preserving the integrity of each member states' tax system:

> 'Articles 48 and 59 of the EC Treaty preclude the legislation of a member state from subjecting the deductibility of sickness and invalidity insurance contributions or pensions and life insurance contributions to the condition that the contributions are paid in that state. However, such a condition is permissible if it is necessary in order to ensure the cohesion of the relevant fiscal system.'

So, as the Belgium authorities were unable to tax the proceeds of the policy, they need not give tax relief on the premiums.

[9.32]

In the later case of *Wielockx v Inspecteur der Directe Belastingen* C-80/94 [1995] All ER (EC) 769, the facts were similar to *Bachmann v Belgium* Case C-204/90 [1992] ECR I-249 but the ECJ held that as there was a taxation convention between the two member states involved, there already existed a system of fiscal cohesion and tax relief could not be refused.

[9.33]
As similar tax conventions (based on the OECD model) exist between most member states, any attempt by a member state to discriminate against foreign nationals or institutions can be challenged.

[9.34]
The position was further clarified in the case of *Safir v Skattemyndigheten I Dalarnas Län* Case C-118/96 [1992] ECR I-1897. The facts were that Swedish legislation differentiated between national and foreign insurers by imposing tax of 27% on the yield from capital insurance business of foreign companies and also 15% premium tax on policyholders and requiring policyholder to register with the tax authorities. The tax authorities could exempt or reduce the premium tax, but only if the company provided details of its tax position. The European Court of Justice held that the Swedish national legislation was likely to dissuade other EC companies from selling insurance in Sweden and also dissuade people from taking out policies with companies established elsewhere in the EC and was in breach of the EC Treaty, art 49.[1]

1 The EC Treaty, art 49 provides: '. . . restrictions on freedom to provide services within the Community shall be progressively abolished . . .' (Formerly The Treaty of Rome, art 59).

(iii) Legal systems

[9.35]
Different legal systems also represent a barrier to the single market. There are differences in the law of insurance (eg UK law insists on disclosure by policyholder, whereas in France and Germany this is not a requirement for policy validity); differences in contract and trust law (some states do not have the concept of trust) and in the regulatory environment relating to marketing and selling and investment practices. ICA 1982, s 94A and Sch 3B, Pt II lays down rules for determining the law of the contract. In the case of disputes, jurisdiction would be determined by the Civil Jurisdiction and Judgments Act 1982.

[9.36]
The introduction of the concept of 'general good' has also caused some difficulties and the Commission drafted a communication on 'Freedom to provide services and the general good in insurance' 97/c 365/04, OJEC no C365/7 of 3 December 1997. It lists some national provisions considered to qualify as a 'general good'.

(iv) Other differences

[9.37]
Other obstacles include differences in accounting standards and practices, marketing environments and currency differences. Attempts are being made to address these.

(v) Conclusions

[9.38]
EU enlargement (another ten countries from central and eastern Europe and Cyprus are hoping to join the EC) and the different stages of implementation of much of the legislation adds to the difficulty of cross border trade. This is borne out by recent statistics which show that levels of cross border trade are relatively modest.

5. COMPETITION POLICY

A. Background

(i) EC Treaty, arts 81 and 82[1]

[9.39]
The core of EU competition law is contained in the EC Treaty, arts 81 and 82 together with the Merger Regulations. The EC Treaty, art 81(1) prohibits all agreements between undertakings, decisions by associations of undertakings and concerted practices which have as their object or effect the prevention, restriction or distortion of competition within the EC. The EC Treaty, art 82 prohibits abuse by any undertaking in a dominant position in the market.

1 Formerly the Treaty of Rome, arts 85 and 86.

(ii) The merger regulation

[9.40]
The merger regulation covers mergers and joint ventures where the turnover of all the parties concerned is over 5,000m Ecus and where 250 Ecus are located in the EU.

(iii) Exemptions to the EC Treaty, art 81(1)

[9.41]
Block exemption Regulations exist under the EC Treaty, art 81(3) which exempt categories of agreement from the EC Treaty, art 81(1). The Commission also provides 'negative clearances' or individual exemptions or comfort letters. These, however, do not have the force of law and although they may prevent the Commission taking action, they would not bind the European Court of Justice if the company with the individual exemption were sued by another company for infringement of EU competition law.

[9.42]
In relation to the life assurance industry, there are two relevant regulations:

1. OJ No L173 (30 June 1983) p 1, which exempts certain categories of exclusive distribution agreements.

2. 1534/91 OJ L 143 on the application of the EC Treaty, art 81(1) to information agreements, decisions and concerted practices in the insurance sector.

Both of these regulations are discussed in more detail below.

[9.43]
There are also four relevant notices by the Commission which would informally take other categories of agreement outwith the ambit of the EC Treaty, art 81:

1. Notice on Agreements of Minimal Importance OJ (1986) C231/2 (updated 97/C 372/04).
2. Notice on Co-operation Agreements OJ (1968) C75/3.
3. Notice on Principal and Agent Agreements OJ (1962) 139/2921.
4. Notice on Firms and Sub-contractors OJ (1979) C1/2.

[9.44]
The principle underlying the first two notices is the de minimis doctrine: agreements of minor importance, and co-operation agreements between small and medium sized firms are unlikely to have an appreciable effect on EU trade and so can be excluded from the EC Treaty, art 81(1). In relation to the last two notices, the argument is that these agreements can be viewed as between two members of a single economic unit and really involve an allocation of functions within a single entity rather than restricting trade. It had already been decided in *Béguelin Import Co v GL Import Export SA* 22/71 [1971] ECR 949, ECJ that the EC Treaty, art 81 would not apply between a parent and a subsidiary 'which although having separate legal personality, enjoys no economic independence'. The two notices simply extend this principle to principals and agents and contractors and subcontractors.

B. Vertical and horizontal restraints of the EC Treaty, art 81(1)

[9.45]
It has been argued unsuccessfully that the EC Treaty, art 81(1) only applies to horizontal agreements between two or more undertakings. This argument was rejected in *Etablissements Consten SARL and Grundig-Verkaufs-GmbH v EC Commission* 56,58/64 EC Treaty, art 81(1), where it was held that agreements giving absolute territorial protection to distributors were caught by the EC Treaty, art 81(1). The following lists indicate the types of agreements that will fall foul of the EC Treaty, art 81(1):

Vertical Restraints
Exclusive distribution agreements.
Exclusive purchasing agreements.
Selective distribution agreements.
Franchising agreements.
Agency agreements.

Horizontal restraints
Horizontal price fixing agreements.

Horizontal geographical market division.
Quotas and other restrictions on production.
Collusive tendering.
Agreements on terms and conditions.
Information agreements.
Advertising agreements.
Research and development agreements.
Specialisation agreements.
Restructuring agreements and crisis cartels.
Standardisation agreements.
Restrictive covenants.
Miscellaneous.

[9.46]
The following two sections deal with an agreement from each of the above two categories which are used frequently within the insurance industry, namely exclusive distribution agreements and information agreements.

(i) Exclusive distribution agreements

[9.47]
Unless these are drafted to fall within the Block Exemption Regulation, they will normally be treated as infringing the EC Treaty, art 81(1). The Regulation, however, only exempts agreements relating to goods and not services, but the Commission, in their Notes of Guidance, indicate that the rationale underlying the exemptions could equally apply to agreements relating to the provision of services. The best practice if a company is in doubt about whether a distribution agreement infringes the EC Treaty, art 81(1) is to apply to the Commission for an individual exemption. Standard Life and the Halifax adopted this course in the early 1990s and the Commission (about three years later) produced a decision, basically excluding two clauses from the agreement which related to (a) the prohibition on Standard Life appointing other Building Societies as its appointed representative and (b) the prohibition on commission rebating. The Commission stated they would take a 'favourable view' of the rest of the agreement.

(ii) Information agreements

[9.48]
The exchange of information can be beneficial and to that extent is accepted business practice: where it amounts to businesses acting in concert, it is viewed as having a detrimental effect on competition. The Notice on Co-operation Agreements exempts agreements on exchanges of opinion, joint market research, joint comparative studies, joint preparation of statistics and calculation models. As a result of successful lobbying on the part of the insurance industry, a Block Exemption Regulation allowed insurance companies to co-operate on the following matters:

1. The establishment of common risk premium tariffs based on collectively ascertained statistics or the number of claims.
2. The establishment of common standard policy conditions.
3. The common coverage of certain types of risk.
4. The settlement of claims.
5. The testing and acceptance of security devices (applicable to general insurance business).
6. Registers of and information on aggravated risks, providing that the keeping of these registers and the handling of this information is carried out subject to the proper protection of confidentiality.

C. Conclusion

[9.49]
The insurance industry, therefore, has a certain amount of latitude as far as EU competition law is concerned. The Competition Act 1998 brings the UK domestic law on competition more closely in line with the EU model.

[9.50]
A more exhaustive analysis on competition law can be found in *Butterworths Competition Law Service*.

6. JOINT VENTURES

[9.51]
The regulatory difficulties associated with joint ventures are that the insurance company must not by default or design be seen to be engaged in non-insurance activities (ICA 1982, s 16); nor must the partner in the joint venture be seen as a 'controller' of the insurer unless it does want to take on the responsibilities of a controller. Non-regulatory issues will include access to databases; the ownership of intellectual property; whether the venture breaches the competition rules; protection of reputation.[1]

1 See Prime, Gale and Scanlon *The Law and Practice of Joint Ventures* (2nd edn, 1997).

7. SUMMARY

[9.52]
There are special features when purchasing an insurance company and a procedure for transferring or merging insurance business under ICA 1982. There are also special rules for doing business in the EC, although some of the remaining obstacles to the single market have resulted in low levels of cross border business. Insurance companies benefit form a number of exemptions to the EC Competition regime. Care has to be taken with joint venture agreements.

Chapter 10
Future developments

1. SUPERVISORY AUTHORITIES AND THE FINANCIAL SERVICES AND MARKETS BILL

A. Introduction

[10.1]
It is generally accepted throughout the financial services industry that the plethora of regulatory bodies and rules and variety of complaint mechanisms and compensation schemes resulted in a system which was needlessly complicated; not only for those working in the industry, but also for consumers. Following a number of spectacular failures of the system, notably in the collapse of Barings and the pensions mis-selling scandal, it was accepted that the consumer had not been given the level of protection it had been hoped the system would provide. It was recognised that a fragmentary approach to supervision was not the best method of overseeing a consolidating industry.[1]

> 'A modern financial services industry needs an up to date regulatory system. In today's world regulation is a key source of competitive advantage – or disadvantage. Britain's old system of financial regulation – with 9 different regulators – has not prevented us from developing a highly innovative and successful industry. But is has not always served the consumer well. And it is increasingly inappropriate in a world where technology and competitive pressures are dissolving the boundaries between the old financial services sectors and companies.' ('Financial Services and Markets Bill' Progress Report, HMT, March 1999.)

1 The Maxwell scandal had different causes, mainly the lack of power of the Occupational Pensions Board (the OPB) and the lack of real employee participation at trustee level. These were addressed in PA 1995, following a lengthy report by Professor Goode.

[10.2]
The Financial Services and Markets Bill (FSM Bill) was drafted and passed to relevant bodies for comment in 1998. The Bill is scheduled to come into force around autumn 2000. The purpose of the Bill is to move supervision of different areas of financial services to a new single regulator, the Financial Services Authority, rationalise and consolidate the existing systems of supervision, to strengthen the powers of the Financial Services Authority, increase consumer input to the system and develop new regimes in certain areas. The Bill is enabling legislation and is to be supplemented

by regulations and rules.[1] These are commented on more fully below and are based on a Treasury Progress Report dated March 1999 and Financial Services Authority consultation papers 31 and 41 on the changes to the prudential supervision of insurance companies.

1 The Financial Services Authority has produced numerous consultative documents on proposed rules and guidance.

B. Moving supervision to the Financial Services Authority

[10.3]
The Financial Services Authority, which was established in October 1997, will eventually replace the SIB and all the SROs, and also replace other prudential supervisory authorities like the Building Societies Commission, and Friendly Societies Commission and the professional bodies in so far as they supervise regulated activities. Supervision for the Bank of England was passed to the Financial Services Authority by the Bank of England Act 1998. Supervision for insurance companies was moved from the DTI to the Treasury, but will move to the Financial Services Authority when the FSM Bill becomes law. Supervision over the marketing and selling of mortgages and deposit accounts is to pass to the Financial Services Authority.

C. Consolidating existing systems

[10.4]
Bringing regulatory supervision under one roof provides an opportunity to standardise many of the regulations and rules on an industry wide basis and it allows the legislature an opportunity for stripping away layers of bureaucracy: there are at present several different systems of authorisation, ombudsman schemes and compensation schemes. These are to be reduced to one single authorisation procedure, one ombudsman scheme and one compensation scheme. The compensation scheme will be subdivided for deposits insurance and investment; the sub-scheme for insurance will replicate PPA 1975 (97). The danger is that the hoped for uniformity of approach in supervision may break down: it is thought that by setting out in detail the remit of the Financial Services Authority and making it more accountable to industry and consumers this may be avoided.

(i) Single authorisation

[10.5]
The Financial Services Authority will be responsible for granting authorisation and permission for certain activities. In reaching its decision it will have to have regard to a range of issues outlined at FSM Bill, Sch 6. It is intended that FSM Bill, Sch 6 will be supplemented by detailed Financial Services Authority rules. In addition, the Financial Services Authority will maintain a public register of authorised persons and the activities they are permitted to carry out. The Financial Services Authority will have power to impose time limits on the carrying out of permitted activities and a time limit will be imposed on the Financial Services

Authority in considering applications. It is unlikely that contracts entered into with unauthorised persons will be unenforceable, as the Financial Services Authority will have wide range of powers of restitution and compensation.

(ii) Prudential supervision

[10.6]
A consultation paper (CP 31) was published in November 1999 and follows up a previous paper issued in March 1999 (CP 8). The proposals are designed to meet the EU directives on prudential supervision (ie adequacy of financial resources and risk management systems) and also tie in with the Financial Services Authority's statutory objectives of protecting consumers, maintaining market confidence and preventing financial crime.

[10.7]
The main thrust of the proposals is to move away from sector based prudential supervision to risk-based supervision covering:

- credit risk;
- market risk;
- operational risk; and
- insurance risk.

[10.8]
These will apply across sectors such as banking, investment and insurance. The Financial Services Authority concede that where some sector difference justifies a difference in treatment, this will be taken into account. Some of the reasons given as grounds for a difference in treatment include:

- whether or not firms incur any liabilities to customers;
- where EU legislation or international standards make distinction; and
- the degree of complexity of a firm's business;

[10.9]
Minimum standards will be set for financial resources or capital adequacy but the Financial Services Authority will have power under FSM Bill to vary this. How this power will be exercised is to be set out in the Supervision Manual.

[10.10]
The Financial Services Authority realise that this will involve major system changes for firms and so have proposed an interim period where very little in the existing regimes will change, apart from regimes relating to banks and building societies, and an extended timetable for implementation of their proposed Integrated Prudential Sourcebook.

[10.11]
The prudential rules will also link in to other sections of the Financial Services Authority Handbook of Rules and Guidance, such as Principles

for Business, the Qualifying Conditions for Authorisation and Authorisation Manual, Supervision Manual and Enforcement Manual.

[10.12]
The interim arrangements will take effect on the FSM Bill becoming law in 2000. The main changes will not take effect until March 2002. The later date is to tie up with the timetable being followed by the Basel Committee on Banking Supervision and EU.

[10.13]
The existing regimes will remain much as they are, except for formal changes to make them consistent with the new legislation and changes to the regimes for banks and building societies. Authorised or exempt firms will have to confirm existing permissions to the Financial Services Authority (as notified to them by the Financial Services Authority) and then the Financial Services Authority will tell them which prudential rules they should meet prior to the FSM Bill becoming law. Newly authorised firms will also be told which requirements they need to meet. Section 5 of the consultation paper outlines potential changes on a sector by sector basis.

[10.14]
The 'Insurance draft Interim Prudential Sourcebook' (IDPIS) was published in January 2000. The current Insurance legislation, together with DTI guidance, is to be rationalised and incorporated into appropriate sections of the Financial Services Authority Handbook. The following is a brief summary of CP 41.

(a) There will be no new substantive requirements until at least March 2002. The IDPIS will form part of the Financial Services Authority Handbook and largely restate existing legislative provisions and guidance. The material in the IDPIS will cover:
   - Capital adequacy and other financial requirements
   - The separation of long term assets
   - Prudential systems of control
   - Restrictions on the conduct of non-insurance activity

   Remaining legislative material and guidance will be located at other parts of the Handbook. The high level requirements also replace the criteria of prudent management in the Insurance Companies Act 1982 and Principle 6, namely the duty to 'pay due regard to the interests of customers and treat them fairly' replaces the policyholders' reasonable expectations requirement although there will be separate consultation on this. Also the enforcement methods under the new regime will contain differences and include powers to:
   - Investigate a firm's business or suspected rule breach
   - Vary and cancel a firm's permission
   - Take disciplinary action
   - Apply to courts for injunction

(b) The IPSB will replace the following legislation:
   - Prudential provisions within ICA 1982

- ICR 1994, SI 1994/1516 relating to deposits by overseas insurers, margins of solvency, currency matching and localisation, linked long term policies, valuation of assets, determination of liabilities and statistical information
- IC(AS)R 1996, SI 1996/943 on HMT returns
- Insurance Companies (Reserves) Regulations 1996, SI 1996/943
- Insurance Directorate Prudential Guidance Notes on hybrid capital, systems and controls over investments, the valuation of assets, the use of derivatives, general business claims provisions, linked long term policies and the preparation of the annual regulatory returns
- The Dear Director letter on the use of derivatives-listed products
- Dear Appointed Actuary letters on resilience testing, aids reserving policy and reserving for guaranteed annuity products

The Financial Services Authority will take the opportunity to rationalise existing requirements

(c) Proposed key changes:

- Implementation of the new Insurance Groups Directive
- Enhancing disclosure re with-profits long term insurance business
- Reduction of lodgement period for regulatory returns
- To accommodate legislative transition on frequently granted concessions

The first two changes are to be the subject of separate consultation. The third change was outlined in CP31 and proposes that for financial years ending on or after 31.12.01, four-month period for electronic and 3.5-month period for paper returns; for financial years on or after 31.12.02, 3 months and 2.5 months respectively. In respect of the fourth matter, the Financial Services Authority propose four changes to the operation of s 68 waivers under the ICA 1982 or the Friendly Societies Act 1992, s 103 in order to reduce the need for waivers. The four changes proposed are:

- Specialist reporting forms for specialist marine insurers
- The limitation of admissible assets to fixed percentages of total portfolio of admissible assets rather than of the long term business amounts
- Raising the limits on bank deposits
- Raising the limit for equities used for tracker funds.

(iii) Single ombudsman scheme

[10.15]

The main features are:

(a) There will be no appeal on a point of law, as it is felt this would undermine the idea that the scheme provides a quick, cheap method of redress; the scheme procedure will comply with the European Convention on Human Rights and judicial review will be available to both firm and consumers.

(b) The scheme operator will have the power to make rules on awards of costs based on the discretion of the ombudsman, but it is likely these will relate to the scheme operator's costs and not the costs of the other side.

[10.16]
The thinking on the compulsory and voluntary jurisdictions of the ombudsman needs more clarity, but it looks as though the Financial Services Authority may have a discretion to include activities which are not regulated (eg unsecured lending) and activities by unauthorised persons within the voluntary jurisdiction.

(iv) Single compensation scheme

[10.17]
Different funds will be maintained for meeting claims from different types of business (eg insurance, investment and deposits). The scheme manager will have power to impose levies on authorised persons for the purpose of meeting expenses and payments of compensation. This will be structured so that there is a correlation between types of firm and particular sub-funds. The draft FSM Bill allows the Financial Services Authority to provide detailed rules on the assessment and payment of compensation and the FSM Bill will also cover the interaction of the scheme with insolvency law. For insurance, the sub scheme will be based on PPA 1975.

D. Scope of the Financial Services Authority

[10.18]
Regulated activities will be detailed at FSM Bill, Sch 2. A current list of what is to be included can be found in a draft statutory instrument published as part of the consultation document in February 1999.

[10.19]
The remit of the Financial Services Authority can be broken down into three main areas: its objectives, the principles to be adhered to, and its rule making powers.

(i) Objectives

[10.20]
These are set out at the beginning of the FSM Bill and are: (a) to increase market confidence; (b) to promote public awareness; (c) to protect consumers; and (d) to reduce financial crime.

(ii) Principles

[10.21]
The Financial Services Authority must take into account the following principles when discharging their obligations:

(a) The need to use resources economically and efficiently.
(b) The responsibility of firms' senior management.
(c) The cost of regulation is to be proportionate to the benefits.
(d) Facilitating innovation.
(e) The international dimension to financial services.
(f) Maintaining the UK's competitiveness.
(g) Competition not to be distorted unnecessarily.

[10.22]
An overall balance has to be struck between the firms' responsibility of providing advice and the consumers' responsibility for making decisions.

(iii) Rules

[10.23]
The Financial Services Authority's power to make rules under the FSM Bill is set against a background of greater accountability and consultation. When the Financial Services Authority make new rules or amend existing ones, they have to include an explanatory memorandum setting out the purposes of the rules or amendments and their compatibility with the regulatory objectives and principles. When the final rules are published, the Financial Services Authority must publish a statement of any alterations from the original proposal and a revised cost benefit analysis.

[10.24]
The government ultimately hopes to rationalise the procedural requirements relating to publication, consultation, informing the Treasury and the provision of cost/benefit analysis across a range of Financial Services Authority activities (eg issuing statements of principle; publishing or altering codes for market abuse; making rules; and issuing standing guidance). Some activities, such as deposits and general insurance, may be excluded from the Financial Services Authority's rule making powers.

E. Accountability of the Financial Services Authority

[10.25]
It is now generally held that self-regulation under FSA 1986 is no longer satisfactory and that the government wishes to create a regulatory authority which acts in the broader public interest. With that in mind, a number of far-reaching measures are being proposed to ensure the continuing accountability of the Financial Services Authority, not only to the Treasury and Parliament, but also to regulated firms and consumers.

[10.26]
These measures are as follows:

1. The Financial Services Authority Chairman and Board are to be appointed and removable by the Treasury. The majority of the board

will be non-executive and the board's rule making powers cannot be delegated.

2. The Financial Services Authority, in discharging its obligations, must work within the regulatory objectives and principles.
3. The Financial Services Authority is to prepare an annual report for the Treasury and Parliament and hold an annual public meeting to discuss the report.
4. The Treasury Committee can ask the Financial Services Authority and the Treasury to provide evidence periodically.
5. The finances of the Financial Services Authority are to be kept under review by a committee of non-executive directors of the Financial Services Authority board (a chairman from among them will be appointed by the Treasury), which will also have the power to set remuneration for the Financial Services Authority chairman and executive board members. The committee will be required to report on its functions within the annual Financial Services Authority report.
6. The Treasury will have the power to commission inquiries into regulatory matters of public concern and commission independent reports into the efficiency and economy of the Financial Services Authority operations.
7. The Financial Services Authority is to provide the Treasury with copies of any rules or standing guidance it makes.
8. The Treasury will also have the power to direct the Financial Services Authority to alter its rules, procedures or practices in response to any adverse competition report by the Director General of Fair Trading or to comply with the UK's international obligations.
9. There will be extensive requirements on the Financial Services Authority to consult practitioners and consumers on a range of issues (eg rules including fees, standing guidance, fining policies and complaint handling procedures). There will also be a duty to consult on its arrangements for independent investigations of complaints made against it and the investigator will have the power to publish his findings and any responses to his recommendations made by the Financial Services Authority. In addition, it is likely that the Financial Services Authority will be required to maintain consumer and practitioner panels to oversee the performance of the Financial Services Authority against its statutory objectives.
10. An independent tribunal will be established under the jurisdiction of the Lord Chancellor's Department to deal with hearings on disciplinary decisions, the exercise of powers of intervention and refusal of authorisation. It is intended that this be a court of first instance, whose decisions can be appealed to the Court of Appeal in England, Wales and Northern Ireland and the Court of Session in Scotland. The Lord Chancellor will be consulting on draft rules for the tribunal procedures shortly. This will, it is hoped, result in some consistency of approach in dealing with breaches and imposing fines.

[10.27]

It is thought that the current statutory immunity enjoyed by the Financial Services Authority should remain.

F. Powers of the Financial Services Authority

[10.28]

The current powers of the Financial Services Authority include powers to issue public statements on misconduct, withdrawal of authorisation and the power to impose civil fines, for example, for market abuse. These powers are to be supplemented and procedures improved to answer the perceived lack of fairness and transparency in the existing systems.

(i) Improving disciplinary procedures

[10.29]

The Financial Services Authority published a consultation document in December 1998 entitled 'Financial Services Regulation: Enforcing the New Regime', which included proposed new requirements for the Financial Services Authority to issue warning notices, disclose their reasons for intended disciplinary action and to allow a period for representations before any final decision is made. In addition, the FSM Bill will be amended to include further changes to increase transparency and fairness, such as:

(a) a duty on the Financial Services Authority to establish and publish procedures and to act in accordance with these;
(b) a right to see relevant evidence and a duty on the Financial Services Authority to produce such evidence;
(c) a duty to wait until the enforcement procedure is completed (including any hearing by the tribunal) before publishing any enforcement action; and
(d) to abandon the proposal that the Financial Services Authority can make rules on the admissibility of evidence.

(ii) Further investigative powers

[10.30]

The Treasury propose to revise the FSM Bill by including the following powers:

(a) To require an authorised person to provide documents and information as part of continuous supervisory process.
(b) To require an authorised person to commission a report from an accountant or other professional (see cls 96 and 197 of consultation draft).
(c) To enter premises, whether business or domestic, on the production of a warrant.
(d) To appoint investigators to verify information and compel information from the authorised person and specified connected parties.
(e) To appoint investigators to cover possible contraventions or criminal offences by unauthorised and authorised persons and compel information from these persons and third parties.

[10.31]
Oral evidence from witnesses under these compulsory powers will not generally be admissible in criminal proceedings.

G. Other developments

[10.32]
The draft FSM Bill also covers new regimes for regulation of:

(a) employers and controllers;
(b) financial promotion;
(c) market abuse;
(d) investment exchanges and clearing houses;
(e) Lloyd's;
(f) competition; and
(g) the role of auditors and actuaries (FSM Bill, Pt XVII), which is still under discussion.

[10.33]
In the following areas, the government simply stated their intention in the draft FSM Bill, with more details to follow the consultation process:

(h) the registration of mutuals;
(i) collective investment schemes;
(j) the competent authority for official listing;[1]
(k) insolvency and winding up; and
(l) protection of confidential information.

1 Responsibility for this passed from the London Stock Exchange to the Financial Services Authority on 1 May 2000.

H. Conclusions

[10.34]
The draft FSM Bill, once law, will have a major impact on the operations of all financial services companies, including life companies. There will no doubt be a transitional period as companies move from the old FSA 1986 and ICA 1982 regime into the new FSM regime. The prudential regulations governing insurance companies will remain intact. The key area will be managing the relationship with the new supervisory authority: it would seem likely that, given the increase in powers and transparency of the new regime, this relationship may be more demanding than current supervisory relationships. There is also some concern within the actuarial profession regarding the future role of the appointed actuary: if the responsibilities of this role become too prescriptive, the role may diminish from that of assisting in the running of the life company to that of a technical adviser.

2. PENSIONS REFORM

A. Introduction

[10.35]
The Welfare Reform and Pensions Act 1999 will introduce, amongst other things, stakeholder pensions by April 2001. These are designed to encourage people to save for retirement. A period of one year is being considered before employers, if they have not already established an occupational pension scheme for their employees, have to nominate a stakeholder scheme and allow employees access to it. Life companies will be able to establish these schemes from new or register a suitable existing PP scheme as a stakeholder scheme. The details of these schemes are outlined at Chapter 5. Additional changes to pensions include the effect of insolvency on pension rights and pension sharing on divorce.

3. INDUSTRY PROBLEMS

A. Pensions mis-selling

[10.36]
This arose as a result of advising members or potential members of final salary occupational pension schemes (FS scheme) to move to, or invest in, a personal pension (PP). It is broadly argued that because benefits are guaranteed in the first arrangement (and usually employers contribute to these, although they can also contribute to a PP), whereas benefits under a PP are uncertain, advising someone to move from an FS scheme to a PP, or invest in a PP when they have a right to membership in an FS scheme, is not best advice.

[10.37]
It is possible if the performance of the PP investments is high and annuities are inexpensive when a PP holder retires, that the PP holder can obtain a better pension than someone in an FS scheme, but there is a significant risk that he might obtain less. The other perceived advantage of a PP is its 'portability': it could be maintained through changes in employment, whereas membership of an FS scheme terminates on leaving the employment to which the scheme relates. Lastly, under an FS scheme the benefits must not exceed IR limits (eg the scheme cannot fund pensions in excess of two-thirds final pensionable salary without losing tax advantages), whereas in the PP arrangement there are limits on contribution levels (ie a percentage of salary increasing with age) but none on benefits. So PPs may suit some employees – for example, high earners who are likely to change employment and are willing to accept some risk.

B. Pensions drawdown

[10.38]
This arrangement was really a Revenue concession in order to alleviate the effect of the increased cost of annuities. Prior to allowing drawdown, a

PP holder on retirement (normally aged between 50 and 75) had to purchase an annuity (ie a compulsory purchase annuity: see Chapter 5) and would, therefore, be subject to the annuity rates at that time. Permitting the PP holder to draw down some capital from the pension fund gave the PP holder time to wait for better rates before purchasing an annuity. These arrangements are currently under scrutiny.

C. Endowment mortgages

[10.39]
There is mounting consumer concern over these products as insurers ask policyholders to increase premiums in order to achieve the necessary fund size to repay the outstanding mortgage. The problem really highlights the fact that it is difficult to predict investment returns over a period of, typically, 25 years.

D. Equitable Life and guaranteed annuities

[10.40]
This is discussed at Chapter 5.

4. OTHER DEVELOPMENTS

A. Institutional investors

[10.41]
The Hampel Report recommended, inter alia:

> '. . . that institutional investors have a responsibility to their clients to make considered use of their votes; and . . . institutional investors of all kinds, where practicable, to vote on the shares under their control.'

The report stopped short of making voting by institutional investors compulsory. NAPF then set up an inquiry into the voting execution system and the voting policies of pension funds and institutional investors. The report was published in July 1999 and the key recommendations were:

(a) voting should be considered a fiduciary responsibility;
(b) voting policies should be established;
(c) the UK's voting system should be modernised;
(d) companies should actively encourage voting;
(e) registrars should support electronic voting arrangements;
(f) custodians should co-operate in the voting process; and
(g) voting under stock lending arrangements needs review.

[10.42]
To implement these recommendations requires a system for tracking AGMs and co-ordinating voting policy, which would then be up to the investment managers to carry out.

B. Disability Discrimination Act 1995

[10.43]
The duties of service providers is being phased in three stages:

1. From 2 December 1996, service providers were prohibited from:
   (a) refusing to provide a service which was offered to others;
   (b) offering a lower standard of service; and
   (c) offering the service on less favourable terms.
   (SI 1996/1836 introduced special rules for the provision of insurance, guarantees and deposits.)
2. From 1 October 1999, the following more active duties were placed on service providers under the Disability Discrimination Act 1995 1995, Pt III:
   (a) to make reasonable adjustments to policies, procedures and practices which exclude disabled people or make it unreasonably difficult for disabled people to use the service (Disability Discrimination Act 1995, s 21(1));
   (b) where a physical feature is a barrier to the service, finding a reasonable alternative method of delivering the service (Disability Discrimination Act 1995, s 21(2)(d));
   (c) to provide auxiliary aids and services to enable disabled persons to use the service (eg contracts and key feature documents in Braille, audio cassette, signed and subtitled video and version for people with learning disabilities) (Disability Discrimination Act 1995, s 21(4)).
3. From 2004, where a physical feature is a barrier to the service, the feature must be removed or altered so that it no longer has that effect or provide a reasonable means of avoiding the feature (Disability Discrimination Act 1995, s 21(2)(a),(b),(c)).

[10.44]
There is a Code of Practice published by the DSS which lists the steps insurers should take in order to comply with the Disability Discrimination Act 1995.

C. E-commerce

[10.45]
The E-commerce Bill is to be amended after the recent consultation process resulted in the government abandoning the requirement for key escrow and licences for firms providing encryption services. The Bill is now primarily concerned with the legal status of electronic signatures.[1]

1 (This is not the Electronic Communications Act 2000)

D. EU developments

(i) Introduction

[10.46]
It is the Financial Services Policy Group which is responsible at EU level for advising on the single market in financial services. This group was set

up in 1999, following a Communication entitled 'Financial Services: Building a Framework for Action' dated 28 October 1998. The group is made up of economic and finance ministers and the European Central bank and chaired by the Commissioner for DGXV.

(ii) Proposed European legislation

[10.47]

The following Commission Proposals and improvements to existing legislation affecting insurance are hoped to be taken forward this year on the recommendation of the above group:[1]

1. A directive on the winding up and liquidation of insurance companies. The following outstanding points still have to be resolved:
   (i) How to rank the different categories of creditor: the suggested ranking is staff, tax authorities, social security authorities, guarantee fund beneficiaries, insurance clients and victims with claims ahead of all other creditors.
   (ii) Whether the proposed measures should cover only liquidation and insolvency or also, for example, where authorisation has been withdrawn.
   (iii) Whether to include a requirement to maintain a register of assets.
2. An electronic money directive which covers, inter alia, protection of personal data, electronic signatures, electronic money and distance marketing techniques.
3. A directive on distance selling of financial services, which has met with fierce opposition, mainly because it is thought to run counter to the directive on e-commerce and does not provide a coherent legal framework for distance selling, but also because of the cooling off period, which is divided into a period for reflection and a period of withdrawal from the contract. The insurance industry considers that the withdrawal period makes it impossible to provide immediate cover.
4. Improvements in the solvency requirement for long-term business, indexation of the minimum guarantee fund, and treatment of reassurance which is not as yet regulated by the EU.

1 Further developments which may affect insurers are a directive on the European Company Statute, two directives on UCITS, an amendment to the money laundering directive and improvements to the public offer and listing prospectus directives.

(iii) Financial conglomerates

[10.48]

It is recognised that supervisory authorities may have difficulty overseeing financial conglomerates and, consequently, be unable to adequately assess risks. Further, the impact of any regulatory failure by the larger conglomerates may have serious knock on effects for the rest of the industry. Two proposals exist for the supervision of insurance groups and for financial conglomerates.

5. THE EURO

A. Introduction

[10.49]
The introduction of the euro in 11 member states at the beginning of 1999, and the possibility of the UK joining in the near future, has had, and continues to have, an effect on the financial services industry. It is recognised that wholesale services provided by banks will experience most of the impact sooner than retail financial services like insurance. The following is a brief summary of the background to the euro and the legal framework within which it has been introduced.

B. History

[10.50]
Since early 1990, an action plan was drawn up for the eventual introduction of a single European currency. In 1990, capital restrictions within the EU were abolished and economic convergence on inflation, long-term interest and public finance commenced. By mid-1994, member state budgets were monitored and recommendations made, Central Bank credits were made to public authorities and government bodies and the European Monetary Institute set up what is now the European Bank. The Maastricht Treaty set out convergence criteria and at Madrid in 1995 a timetable was set for the introduction of the euro.

C. Timetable

[10.51]
On 1 January 1999, the European Council allowed 11 member states to join the single currency. The European Central Bank was established, but National Banks are still responsible for local currency. The exchange rates between national currencies and the euro were fixed.

[10.52]
A three-year transition period to 1 January 2002 follows, referred to as the 'no compulsion no prohibition' period because although transactions can be in euro if the parties agree, no one can impose the euro on anyone else unilaterally. The European Central Bank has responsibility for monetary policy and new issues of public debt are in euro.

[10.53]
From 1 January 2002, for a period yet to be determined, euro notes and coins will be introduced and local currencies withdrawn.

D. Stability and growth pact

[10.54]
At Amsterdam in 1998, member states agreed the above pact for keeping the member states which join the single currency on target. Member states

must produce a convergence programme and forecast and the Council can make recommendations to the member state. If the member state does not follow the recommendations, sanctions can be imposed, eg a non-interest bearing deposit of 5% GDP: if the recommendation is repeatedly ignored, the deposit becomes a fine and a new deposit is required. It is not thought that these sanctions will ever be needed in practice.

[10.55]
The relationship between those member states which join the single currency and those who do not is similar to the ERM arrangements.

E. The legal framework

[10.56]
Two regulations were prepared under the Maastricht Treaty. The main legal points are that:

1. contracts referring to national currencies are to be read as referring to euros at the official conversion rate;
2. contracts referring to ECU will be converted one for one into euros;
3. the introduction of the euro will not give either party to a contract the right to terminate it or alter it unilaterally;
4. the provisions in the regulation can be overridden by anything the parties may agree;
5. euro conversion rates will be expressed as one euro per number or part of each national currency unit within EMU, accurate to six figures excluding initial zeros and these rates cannot be rounded or truncated when converting (it is accepted this may cause some difficulty for IT departments); and
6. originally, it was intended that to convert from one national currency to another an intermediate conversion to the euro was necessary (ie 'triangulation'), but this has now been abandoned.

6. SUMMARY

[10.57]
There is much legislative activity, both at UK level and EC level, to present further challenges and opportunities for life companies, in particular:
1. The new supervisory regime with its emphasis on transparency and accountability may increase public confidence in the system.
2. New products, such as stakeholder pension schemes, may widen the market for financial services products.
3. Dealing with the problems of bad advice and possibly badly designed products.
4. Dealing with UK developments in e commerce and the possible introduction of the euro in the UK.

Appendix I

First Council Directive on life assurance business, article I

[11.1]
79/267/EEC
5 MARCH 1979

TITLE I GENERAL PROVISIONS

Article 1

This Directive concerns the taking up and pursuit of the self-employed activity of direct insurance carried on by undertakings which are established in a Member State or wish to become established there in the form of the activities defined below–

1. The following kinds of insurance where they are on a contractual basis–
   (a) life assurance, that is to say, the class of insurance which comprises, in particular, assurance on survival to a stipulated age only, assurance on survival to a stipulated age or on earlier death, life assurance with return of premiums, marriage assurance, birth assurance;
   (b) annuities;
   (c) supplementary insurance carried on by life assurance undertakings, that is to say, in particular, insurance against personal injury including incapacity for employment, insurance against death resulting from an accident and insurance against disability resulting from an accident or sickness, where these various kinds of insurance are underwritten in addition to life assurance;
   (d) the type of insurance existing in Ireland and the United Kingdom known as permanent health insurance not subject to cancellation.

2. The following operations, where they are on a contractual basis, in so far as they are subject to supervision by the administrative authorities responsible for the supervision of private insurance . . . –
   (a) tontines whereby associations of subscribers are set up with a view to jointly capitalising their contributions and subsequently distributing the assets thus accumulated among the survivors or among the beneficiaries of the deceased;
   (b) capital redemption operations based on actuarial calculation whereby, in return for single or periodic payments agreed in advance, commitments of specified duration and amount are undertaken;
   (c) management of group pension funds, ie operations consisting, for the undertaking concerned, in managing the investments, and in particular the assets representing the reserves of bodies that effect payments on death or survival or in the event of discontinuance or curtailment of activity;
   (d) the operations referred to in (c) where they are accompanied by insurance covering either conservation of capital or payment of a minimum interest;

(e) the operations carried out by insurance companies such as those referred to in Chapter 1, Title 4 of Book IV of the French "Code des assurances".

3. Operations relating to the length of human life which are prescribed by or provided for in social insurance legislation, when they are effected or managed at their own risk by assurance undertakings in accordance with the laws of a Member State.

Notes

Para (2): words omitted repealed by Council Directive 92/96/EEC of 10 November 1992, art 2(2).

Appendix 2
Draft commission interpretative note on insurance services

[12.1]
DRAFT COMMISSION INTERPRETATIVE COMMUNICATION

Freedom to provide services and the general good in the insurance sector

(97/C 365/04)

(TEXT WITH EEA RELEVANCE)

The third Council Directives 92/49/EEC and 92/96/EEC[1] completed the establishment of the single market in the insurance sector. They introduced a single system for the authorization and financial supervision of the insurance undertaking by the Member State in which it has its head office (the home Member State). Such authorization issued by the home Member State enables the insurance undertaking to carry on its insurance business anywhere in the European Community, either under the rules on establishment, i.e. by opening agencies or branches in all the Member States, or under the rules on the freedom to provide services. Where it carries on business in another Member State, the insurance undertaking must comply with the conditions in which, for reasons of the general good, such business must be conducted in the host Member State. Under the system set up by the Directives, the financial supervision of the business carried on by the insurance undertaking, including business carried on under the rules on establishment or on the freedom to provide services, is always a matter only that insurance undertaking's home Member State.

In the course of its contacts with numerous economic agents, the Commission has come to realize that the continuing uncertainty surrounding the interpretation of the basic concepts of freedom to provide services and the general good seriously undermines the workings of the machinery set up by the third Directives on the coordination of insurance and is likely to deter certain insurance undertakings from exercising the freedoms created by the Treaty which the third Directives set out to promote and, hence, to restrict the free movement of insurance services in the Union.

This draft communication is the Commissions, contribution to the discussions under way on the problems associated in the insurance industry with the freedom to provides serves (**Part I**) and the general good (**Part II**), in the light in particular of the third Council Directives on insurance (92/49/EEC and 92/96/EEC).

To date, these discussions have been restricted to the Member States, particularly within the framework of the Insurance Committee and the sub-group on the interpretation of insurance directives.

The Commission now takes the view that the broadest possible consultations should be held on its interpretative work and, accordingly, it invites all interested parties to submit their comments on this draft communication within four months of its being published in the *Official Journal of the European Communities*.

Comments should be sent in writing to the following address:

European Commission
Directorate-General XV, Unit C-2
Rue de la Loi/Wetstraat 200
B-1049 Brussels
Fax: (32 2) 295 65 00
Internet address: john.mogg@dg15.cec.be

In the light of the contributions received, the draft will, if necessary, be transformed into a Commission interpretative communication, which will enable economic agents and the Member states to determine the stance that the Commission would be likely to adopt in the event of a particular problem being brought to its attention.

The Commission deems it desirable to draw attention to and to systematize the principles governing the rights of establishment and the freedom to provide services, as elucidated by the Court of Justice, and to consider how they apply to the third Insurance Directives. This interpretation is based on the provisions of the Treaty, the texts of the Community Insurance Directives and on the decisions of the Court of Justice, which has set out a large number of principles essential to the observance of the freedom of establishment and the freedom to provide services.[2]

In publishing this interpretative communication, the Commission is seeking to make transparent and to clarify the common rules which it is its task to see and be observed. It is supplying all those concerned, national administrations, economic agents and consumers, with a reference tool which explains the Commission's opinion with regard to the legal framework in which insurance business may be carried on.

The interpretations and ideas set out in this draft communication, which concern only the specific problems of the insurance sector,[3] do not claim to cover all possible situations, but merely the most frequent or most likely.

They do not necessarily represent the often very divergent views put forward by the Member States and should not, in themselves, impose any new obligation on them.

It goes without saying that the Commission's interpretations do not prejudge the interpretation that the Court, which is responsible in the final instance for interpreting the Treaty and secondary legislation, might place on the matters at issue.

It should be explained straightaway that the interpretations contained in this draft communication do not affect the Commission's subsequent interpretations of the principles of establishment and freedom to provide services with regard to the development of communication technology and its use in the insurance business. Community policy on the information society is designed to promote the expansion of information society services and their movement between the Member States, especially electronic commerce.[4] Clearly, with the development of the information society, use of the opportunities afforded by new technology for the performance of insurance and financial business should become very important and should eventually change the machinery for distributing insurance products in the Community.

The current legal framework for the single market in insurance is based on machinery where consideration has not yet been given to how to use this new technology for carrying out insurance business in the single market.

The initiatives which the Commission has just launched on electronic commerce[5] and the work carried out in the Insurance Committee on the implications of electronic commerce technology for insurance will provide new elements which will have to be taken into account in the interpretation of the insurance Directives. The Commission considers, therefore, that the evolution of this technology could lead it later to alter its interpretation or issue a supplementary interpretation.

PART I

I. DEMARCATION BETWEEN THE RIGHT OF ESTABLISHMENT AND THE FREEDOM TO PROVIDE SERVICES[6]

1. Freedom to provide services

(a) Temporary nature

Article 59 *et seq.* of the Treaty establish the principle of the free movement of services. The principle acquired direct, unconditional effect on the expiry of the transitional period.[7]

It should be noted that, according to the decisions of the Court of Justice, the freedom to provide services may involve the movement of the provider of the service, as envisaged in the third paragraph of Article 60 of the Treaty, or the movement of the recipient of the service within the Member State of the provider; the service may, however, also be carried out without any movement, either of the supplier or of the recipient.[8]

Where a business is carried on under the freedom to provide services with the provider present on the territory of the Member State of provision, the concept of the provision of services is basically distinguished from that of establishment by its temporary character while the right of establishment presupposes a lasting presence in the host country.

The distinction stems from the Treaty itself, where the third paragraph of Article 60 stipulates that a person providing a service may, in order to do so, 'temporarily' pursue his activity in the State where the service is provided.

According to the most recent case-law of the Court of Justice, the temporary nature of the provision of services is to be determined in the light of its duration, regularity, periodicity and continuity.[9]

(b) Prohibition of circumvention

The Court has acknowledged that a Member State is entitled to take steps to prevent a service provider whose activity is entirely or mainly directed towards its territory from exercising the freedom enshrined in Article 59 of the Treaty in order to circumvent the rules of professional conduct which would be applicable to him if he were established in that State[10]. It adds that such a situation may fall within the ambit of the chapter on the right of establishment and not of that on the freedom to provide services.[11]

The criterion of frequency is important in order to determine whether there may be an attempt at 'circumvention' while using the right conferred pursuant to Article 59, but it is not sufficient to define the service provided (an establishment may also operate on an occasional basis).

However, this reasoning is valid only for those forms of provision of services which involve movement by the service provider towards the Member State of provision, as referred to in the third paragraph of Article 60 of the Treaty.

Thus, a situation where an insurance undertaking is constantly being approached within its territory by consumers residing in other Member States could not be regarded as a circumvention. In such a case there would be no intention on the part of the provider of services to carry out such a circumvention.

2. Right of establishment

If an undertaking maintains a permanent presence in the Member State where it carries on its business, it is covered in principle by the provisions of the Treaty on the right of establishment. The Court has held that:

> '... a national of a Member State who pursues a professional activity on a stable and continuous basis in another Member State where he holds himself out from

an established professional base to, amongst others, nationals of that State comes under the chapter relating to the right of establishment and not the chapter relating to services.'[12]

In Commission v. Germany of 4 December 1986[13] the Court held that:

> '. . . an insurance undertaking of another Member State which maintains a permanent presence in the Member State in question comes within the scope of the provisions of the Treaty on the right of establishment, even if that presence does not take the form of a branch or agency, but consists merely of an office managed by the undertaking's own staff or by a person who is independent but authorized to act on a permanent basis for the undertaking, as will be the case with an agency'.

The Court has therefore acknowledged that, in principle, an undertaking which has recourse to an intermediary on the territory of another Member State on a permanent basis to carry on activities in that Member State may lose the benefit of the freedom to provide services and come under the right of establishment. The Court has sought thereby to avoid the freedom to provide services being used abusively in order to circumvent the rules that would apply in the host Member State if the undertaking were established there.[14]

This risk of abuse has nevertheless been eliminated in the insurance sector as a result of the harmonization achieved since the above judgment by the Community Directives concerning the conditions for taking up and carrying on insurance activities. The prudential and supervisory rules for insurance undertakings are equivalent, whichever way insurance activities are carried out: by way of establishment or through the provision of services.

With regard to the insurance sector, the Community Directives, which are based on the Court's judgment in Commission v. Germany, treat in the same way as an agency of branch of an insurance undertaking 'any permanent presence of an undertaking in the territory of a Member State, even if that presence does not take the form of a branch or agency, but consists merely of an office managed by the undertaking's own staff or by a person who is independent but has permanent authority to act for the undertaking as an agency would.[15]

Nevertheless, in view of the most recent decisions of the Court of Justice[16] the Commission considers that the Member State of the provision of services may not rely on that judgment in order to assimilate any permanent presence of the provider of services on its territory to an establishment and subject it in any event to the rules relating to the right of establishment.

The Court of Justice recently acknowledged that the temporary character of the freedom to provide services does not mean that the provider may not equip himself with some form of infrastructure (chambers, office, etc.) in the host Member State in so far as it is necessary for the purposes of performing the services in question without coming under the right of establishment.[17] The Court took the view that in such cases the temporary character of the services provided should be determined by reference to their duration, frequency, periodicity and continuity.[18]

3. Grey area

It is not always easy to draw the line between the two concepts of provision of services and establishment. Some situations are difficult to classify, in particular where the insurer, in order to carry on its insurance business, uses a permanent infrastructure in the Member State of provision. This arises in particular in the following cases:

(a) recourse to independent intermediaries;
(b) permanent presence of the undertaking's own staff.

On the strength of the Court's case-law, the Commission departments propose the following interpretations:

(a) Recourse to independent intermediaries[19]

The problem is to define the arrangements applicable to an independent intermediary established in Member State A to whom insurance undertakings established in Member State B may have recourse in order to do business in Member State A, the conditions under which that independent intermediary may be regarded as himself exercising a permanent activity in that Member State and hence be assimilated to an establishment of the insurance undertaking in the host Member State, instead of as an insurance activity carried on under the rules on the freedom to provide services, and the resulting legal implications.

In De Bloos case of 6 October 1976[20] the Court held that:

> 'One of the essential characteristics of the concepts of branch or agency is the fact of being subject to the direction and control of the parent body'.

In even more precise terms, in Somafer case of 22 November 1978[21] the Court held that:

> 'The concept of branch, agency or other establishment implies a place of business which has the appearance of permanency, such as the extension of a parent body, has a management and is materially equipped to negotiate business with third parties, so that the latter, although knowing that there will if necessary be a legal link with the parent body, the head office of which is abroad, do not have to deal directly with such a parent body but may transact business at the place of business constituting the extension'.

It concluded that a sole concessionaire not subject to the control and direction of a company could not be regarded as a branch, agency or establishment.

In Blanckaert and Willems case of 18 March 1981[22] the Court held that:

> 'An independent commercial agent who merely negotiates business, inasmuch as his legal statutes leaves him basically free to arrange his own work and decide what proportion of his time to devote to the interests of the undertaking which he agrees to represent and whom that undertaking may not prevent from representing at the same time several firms competing in the same manufacturing or marketing sector, and who, moreover, merely transmits orders to the parent undertaking without being involved in either their terms or their execution, does not have the character of a branch, agency or other establishment . . .'.

Moreover, in his opinion in Shearson Lehman Hutton of 27 October 1992[23] Mr Advocate-General Darmon stated that:

> 'The link of dependence *vis-à-vis* the company established in another signatory State[24] is not the determining criterion here. In our opinion, that criterion resides in the fact that the secondary establishment has the power to enter into contracts with third parties'. Lastly, in his report on the Brussels Convention, Mr Jenard notes that there is an agency or branch only 'where the foreign company is represented by a person capable of acting in a manner that is binding on it *vis-à-vis* third parties'.[25]

On the basis of these precedents, the Commission considers that, for the links between an independent intermediary and an insurance undertaking to be regarded as meaning that the insurance undertaking falls within the scope of the arrangements governing an establishment, the intermediary must meet the following three cumulative conditions:

(i) the intermediary must be subject to the management and the supervision of the insurance undertaking it represents,
(ii) it must be able to commit the insurance undertaking, and
(iii) it must have received a permanent brief.

It is, therefore, only where the intermediary acts as a genuine extension of the insurance undertaking that the insurance undertaking falls within the scope of the arrangements applicable to the establishment of a branch.

(I) THE INTERMEDIARY MUST BE SUBJECT TO THE MANAGEMENT AND THE SUPERVISION OF THE INSURANCE UNDERTAKING HE REPRESENTS

To verify if this criterion is met, a check should be made in particular to see whether, in the light of the links established between the insurance undertaking and the independent intermediary, the latter has sufficient freedom to organize his activities, to decide how much time he will devote to the insurance undertaking and, in particular, to represent competitors at the same time.

An exclusive brief received by an intermediary from a single insurer is an essential indication that the independent intermediary is subject to the direction and control of that insurer. It is nevertheless not uncommon in the insurance sector for intermediaries to represent several competing insurers at the same time. In most cases, such representation concerns different classes of insurance for different insurers.

Thus, in such cases, an intermediary who works for several insurers, only one of which has given him an exclusive brief, would be assimilated to a branch of that insurance undertaking to the extent that the brief subjects the intermediary to the direction and control of that insurer.

In any event, the remaining two conditions mentioned should also be satisfied in order for the intermediary to be assimilated to a branch of an insurance undertaking in the host Member State and for the activities of that insurer to be covered by the rules on establishment.

The above considerations apply irrespective of whether the intermediary is a natural person or a legal person.

(II) THE INTERMEDIARY MUST COMMIT THE INSURANCE UNDERTAKING

To determine whether this condition requiring a commitment has been satisfied, it has to be examined, in accordance with the Court's case-law, whether, in their contacts with an intermediary, third parties do not need to deal with the insurance undertaking itself and may conclude business with the intermediary.

The commitment of the insurance undertaking *vis-à-vis* the insured results primarily from the brief given to the intermediary to conclude insurance policies with those seeking insurance on behalf, and for the account, of the insurance undertaking not established in the host Member State. The specific purpose of an agency or a branch is to conclude policies with third parties on behalf, and for the account, of the head office, which is thus directly committed, since the agency is an extension of the head office.

In some cases, however, other elements of the brief given by the insurance undertaking to the intermediary may show the intention of the insurance undertaking to be directly committed to the policy holder. An insurance undertaking can thus be bound by the act of an intermediary even if the latter cannot sign policies. If, for instance, an intermediary can make a complete offer on behalf of the insurance undertaking, but it is the latter which retains the power to sign the policy, the commitment criterion may still be satisfied. If the insurance undertaking can refuse the proposal submitted by the intermediary and signed by the client, the criterion of the ability to commit will not be met.

Another case which could prove the intention of the insurance undertaking to be directly bound by the activity of its intermediary would be the power granted to the latter to decide to accept and settle a claim submitted to it, since decisions taken by the intermediary bind the insurer. This function must, however, be distinguished from the brief given to the intermediary simply to manage files relating to claims; this may include, where appropriate, the payment of indemnities pursuant to the instructions given by the insurer himself.

It is thus the margin of manoeuvre which the insurer has kept for itself with regard to the activities carried on by the intermediary on behalf of that insurer that makes it possible to know if a decision taken by the intermediary formally commits it or not.

The Commission considers that an insurance undertaking that decides to transport insurance business under the freedom to provide services must be able to use certain services either upstream or downstream of the transaction in the Member State of provision. For example, an insurance undertaking should be able to use for its business under the freedom to provide services:

- a local expert to assess the risks to be covered under the freedom to provide services,
- a local expert to assess damage caused under risks covered by insurance policies negotiated under the freedom to provide services,
- canvassers who do not conclude insurance policies and whose activity is limited to sending insurance proposals received from potential policy holders to the insurance undertaking for acceptance,
- local legal services, or medical services established in the Member State of provision,
- a permanent structure for collecting the premiums for insurance policies entered into under the freedom to provide services (e.g. a credit institution or a factoring company),
- a permanent structure for receiving notices of claims relating to policies concluded under the freedom to provide services for transmission to the insurance undertaking for a decision to accept or refuse a claim.

It should be made clear that the only brief which results in treating a permanent presence in the same way as a branch of the insurance undertaking in the Member State of provision is one which concerns the activities that are part of the undertaking's objects, i.e. the business of insurance. A brief given to persons established in another Member State to carry out activities other than insurance cannot be taken into account when assessing the arrangements for carrying on the insurance activity in the host Member State. This could be the case with a brief given to an investment company to manage the insurance undertaking's securities portfolio, or with a company instructed to manage real estate which the undertaking owns in a Member State and which it uses as cover for technical provisions.

(III) THE INTERMEDIARY MUST HAVE RECEIVED A PERMANENT BRIEF

The capacity of an intermediary established in the host Member State to commit an insurance undertaking must be based on a long-term, continuous brief and not just a one-off instruction. This stable and continuous quality shows that the insurance undertaking intends to integrate into the economy of the host Member State the insurance activities which it carries on there.

Conclusion

The Commission takes the view that it is only where the above three conditions are met that the insurance undertaking, using the intermediaries permanently established in the host Member State, must be treated as if it had a branch in the host Member State, with all that this implies from the legal point of view. Accordingly, the insurance undertaking will have to follow the procedure for opening a branch laid down by Article 10 of the first Insurance Directives 73/329/EEC and 79/267/EEC, as amended by Article 32 of the third Insurance Directives 92/49/EEC and 92/96/EEC (specifying that the activities envisaged will be carried on through an independent intermediary). The intermediary's activities must be carried on with due regard for the rules on branches adopted in the interest of the general good by the host State.

The fact that these conditions may involve the subjection of the insurance undertaking to the right of establishment does not mean that the intermediary itself constitutes a branch of the said insurer. A branch is 'a place of business which forms a legally dependent part of an insurance undertaking'.[26] Since an intermediary is assumed to be independent, he cannot be a 'part' of an insurance undertaking.

(b) Permanent presence of the insurance undertaking's staff

A distinction should be drawn here between two possible scenarios:

(b.1) The insurance undertaking's staff established on a permanent basis in another Member State do not engage in any insurance activity

Such an arrangement is commonly referred to as a 'representative office', a flexible structure traditionally regarded simply as a means of reconnoitring the market, establishing contacts and examining to what extent establishment in the country concerned might prove viable.

Such offices are to be regarded as *sui generis* cases.

The Commission takes the view that such offices cannot, of course, be regarded as branches, the establishment of which would, on the basis of Article 10 of the first Insurance Directives as amended by the third Insurance Directives, be subject to the prior notification requirement.

(b.2) The permanent staff engage in insurance activities

The situation here is quite clear. The insurance undertaking is regarded as having a branch which, after 1 July 1994, should have been notified in advance under the first Directives, as amended by the third Directives. If the branch was operational before 1 July 1994 in accordance with the provisions in force in the Member State of establishment, it is deemed to have complied with the prior notification procedure laid down by Article 10 of the first Directives, and may avail itself of the acquired rights granted by Article 52(1) of the third Directive 92/49/EEC and Article 48(1) of the third Directive 92/96/EEC.

II. NATURE OF THE PROCEDURE FOR NOTIFYING THE OPENING OF A BRANCH OR THE INTENTION TO CARRY ON A BUSINESS UNDER THE FREEDOM TO PROVIDE SERVICES

The Commission considers that the notification procedure laid down in the third Insurance Directives (both for branches and for provision of services)[27] pursues a simple objective of exchange of information between supervisory authorities and is not a consumer protection measure. It should not, in the Commission's view, be considered a procedural condition affecting the validity of an insurance policy.

III. ADVERTISING INSURANCE SERVICES

The third Insurance Directives lay down that insurance undertakings with head offices in Member States may advertise their services, through all available means of communication, in the Member State of the branch or the Member State of the provision of services, subject to any rules governing the form and content of such advertising adopted in the interest of the general good.[28]

The Commission believes it is out of the question to make the right to advertise[29] conditional on the need to comply with the notification procedure laid down in Article 34 *et seq.* of the third Directives in order to carry on insurance business under the freedom to provide services.

Such a link would be artificial, since it is not explicitly provided for by the third Directives. Article 34 *et seq.* of the third Insurance Directives subject to the notification procedure not advertising activities in the host Member State, but the intention to pursue an insurance activity on the territory of another Member State under the freedom to provide services.

Similarly, to link advertising and the notification procedure provided for the pursuit of activities under the freedom to provide services could lead to absurd situations where an insurance undertaking finds itself invited to notify the authorities of all the Member States in which its advertising may in theory be received, when it may be that the undertaking does not plan to pursue its activities in all Member States where such advertising is received.

The Commission believes, therefore, that, in accordance with the third Directives, all forms of advertising by whatever means (mail, fax, electronic mail, etc.) should not be subject to the notification procedure referred to in Article 34 *et seq.* of the third Directives. Only if the insurance undertaking plans to pursue its activities on the client's territory under the freedom to provide services, must it comply with the notification procedure.

The above considerations concern only the problem of advertising seen from the formal angle and do not affect the right of Member States to enforce, on their territory and subject to current Community law, their general-good rules on the content of advertising, pursuant to Article 41 of the third Directives.

PART II

IV. THE GENERAL GOOD IN THE THIRD INSURANCE DIRECTIVES APPLICABILITY OF RULES PROMOTING THE GENERAL GOOD

The third Insurance Directives reflect the case-law of the Court of Justice and contain many references to the concept of the general good, providing in particular that an insurance undertaking operating under a single licence must comply with host-country rules adopted in the interest of the general good.

Such compliance is required either in the specific context of freedom of establishment (Article 32(4) of Directives 92/49/EEC and 92/96/EEC) or indiscriminately in connection with the freedom of establishment and the freedom to provide services (Articles 28 and 41 of Directives 92/49/EEC and 92/96/EEC).

Since the entry into force of the third Directives (1 July 1994), the host Member State may require an insurance undertaking operating under a single licence to comply with the same general-good provisions whether the undertaking carries on its activity under establishment (through a branch) or under the freedom to provide services.

It should be noted that, in mentioning the concept of the general good for activities carried on under the rules on establishment (branch), the third Directives anticipated the trend of decisions handed down at that time by the Court of Justice.

After the third Insurance Directives had been adopted, the Court applied its case-law on the general good both to the freedom of establishment and to the freedom to provide services.

1. The concept of the general good

(a) Case-law principles[30]

The concept of the general good is based in the Court's case-law. It was developed first in the context of the free movement of services and goods.

In the abovementioned Säger case[31] the Court held that.

> '. . . as a fundamental principle of the Treaty, the freedom to provide services may be limited only by provisions which are justified by imperative reasons

relating to the general good and which apply to all persons or undertakings pursuing an activity in the State of destination, in so far as that interest is not protected by the rules to which the person providing the services is subject in the Member State in which he is established, In particular, those requirements must be objectively necessary in order to ensure compliance with professional rules and to guarantee the protection of the recipient of services and they must not exceed what is necessary to attain those objectives'.

The Court therefore established, initially in the field of provision of services, a number of criteria which the host Member State must meet before requiring the provider of services to comply with a national measure restricting the pursuit of an activity under the freedom to provide services.

Such a restrictive measure must:

- come within a field which has not been harmonized. Measures relating, for example, to the calculation of technical provisions and the solvency margin, the conditions for taking up insurance business, and financial and prudential supervision may no longer be covered by the general good of a Member State. The level of harmonization achieved by the Directives could be considered as the 'Community general good',
- pursue an objective of the general good,
- be non-discriminatory,
- be objectively necessary,
- be proportionate to the objective pursued,
- it is also necessary for the general-good objective not to be safeguarded by rules to which the provider of services is already subject in the Member State where he is established.

These conditions are cumulative. A national measure which is claimed to be compatible with the principle of the freedom of movement must accordingly satisfy all the conditions. If a national measure does not meet one or other condition, it is not compatible with Community law.

Court decisions have progressively extended the concept of the general good to the right of establishment.[32] Initially, the court used the concept in cases relating to the professional qualifications needed in order to take up an activity. In this context, the Court applied two elements of flexibility to the principle of non-discrimination:

- firstly, it held that the rules on the equality of treatment also prohibit all hidden forms of discrimination which, by applying other distinguishing criteria, actually lead to the same result.[33]
- secondly, it has gradually moved away from its traditional approach, which was limited to strict equality of treatment, at first with regard to the professional qualifications needed in order to take up an activity[34] and subsequently with regard also to the conditions for carrying on an activity by way of establishment.[35] In this respect, the Court proceeded from the premise that any restriction is in principle contrary to Article 52 unless it is in the general good and is necessary and proportionate.

In two subsequent judgments, which followed adoption of the third Insurance Directives, the Court definitively established the principle whereby freedom of establishment is not confined to compliance with the principle of non-discrimination but also prohibits any restrictions which apply indiscriminately to its exercise beyond the area of the recognition of professional qualifications.[36]

Thus, in Gebhard of 30.11.1995[37] the Court extended to the freedom of establishment the reasoning it had already applied in the field of the free movement of goods and the freedom to provide services as regards recourse by the host Member State to rules protecting the general good. The Court ruled:

'. . . national measures liable to hinder or make less attractive the exercise of fundamental freedoms guaranteed by the Treaty must fulfil four conditions: they must be applied in a non-discriminatory manner; they must be justified by imperative requirements in the general interest; they must be suitable for securing the attainment of the objective which they pursue, and they must not go beyond what is necessary in order to attain it.[38]

This case-law was subsequently confirmed by the Court in Bosman[39] and Futura.[40]

(b) The concept of the general good in the third Insurance Directives

The third Insurance Directives refer to the general good in several places.

(b.1) Setting up a branch establishment

The host Member State has two months from the receipt of the file sent by the home Member State, to indicate to the insurance undertaking the conditions in which, for reasons of the general good, such activities must be carried on in the Member State of the branch.

(b.2) Marketing insurance policies

The Member State of the commitment or that in which the risk is situated must allow insurance policies (non-life or life) to be concluded with insurance undertakings authorized in other Member States, whether under the rules on branches or under the freedom to provide services, provided that such insurance polices do not conflict with the statutory provisions protecting the general good in force (in the Member State of the commitment or that in which the risk is situated) (Article 28 of Directive 92/49/EEC and Article 28 of Directive 92/96/EEC).

The above provisions apply to activities carried on under the rules on branches and to those carried on under the freedom to provide services. In other words, they apply to every insurer which, using its single licence issued by its home Member State, carries on insurance business in Member States other than its home State.

(b.3) Health insurance taken out as an alternative to the cover provided by a statutory system of social security

Article 54 of the third Non-life Directive (92/49/EEC) states that each Member State in which health insurance policies can be substituted either wholly or in part for the sickness cover provided by a statutory system of social security may require such policies to comply with the statutory provisions protecting the general good in that Member State for that class of insurance. The Member State may also require prior notification of policy conditions before such policies are marketed.[41]

(b.4) An insurance undertaking authorized in its home Member State may advertise its services

An insurance undertaking authorized in its home Member State may advertise its services by any means of communication available in the Member State of branch or the provision of services, provided it complies with any general-good rules on the form and content of the advertisement (Article 41 of Directive 42/49/EEC and Article 41 of Directive 92/96/EEC).

While they make clear that the provision of services may be restricted only by rules protecting the general good of the host Member State in areas which have not been harmonized at Community level, the third Directives do not innovate in relation to the established case-law of the Court of Justice. The Court has held, as has been pointed out above, that even a non-discriminatory rule in the host country may be discounted to the advantage of a provider of services, if that provision is not in the interest of the general good or, if it is not necessary or proportional to the objective pursued.

The third Insurance Directives do not distinguish, with regard to the conditions for carrying on such an activity, between setting-up a branch and the provision of services.[42] The differences which they introduce concern only the notification procedure, which is more detailed for the establishment of a branch (Article 32 of Directives 92/49/EEC and 92/96/EEC) than for the conduct of insurance business under the freedom to provide services (Article 34 *et seq.* of Directives 92/49/EEC and 92/96/EEC).

The Commission considers that, since the entry into force of the third Insurance Directives, the assessment of conformity with Community law of a national measure restricting one of the activities referred to in the Annex to the first Directives must be made in the light of the requirements of the concept of the general good, both for activities carried on through a branch and for those carried on under the freedom to provide services.

The fact that the Community legislator did not intend to differentiate in this respect between the arrangements applicable to branches and those applicable to the provision of services[43] is clear from the 19th recital of Directive 92/49/EEC and from the twentieth recital of Directive 92/96/EEC, which state that:

> '. . . it is for the Member State of the commitment (or in which the risk is situated) to ensure that there is nothing to prevent the marketing within its territory of all the insurance products offered for sale in the Community as long as they do not conflict with the legal provisions protecting the general good in force in the Member State of the commitment (or in which the risk is situated)'.

Since the recitals to a directive have legal force as an aid to interpretation, they shed light for the reader on the intentions of the Community legislator.[44]

2. Conditions under which the host country rules promoting the general good may be enforced

Discriminatory restrictions

As a general rule, if the restriction in question is discriminatory, it can be justified only on the grounds set out in Article 56 of the Treaty (public policy, public security and public health;[45] economic grounds are not included.[46] It follows that there is no need to rely on rules promoting the general good in such cases.

Non-discriminatory restrictions

The situation is different, however, in the case of non-discriminatory restrictions. It can be deduced from the principles laid down in the third Directives and confirmed by the Court's general-good case-law that any non-discriminatory national measure which restricts an insurance activity benefiting from mutual recognition and carried on either through a branch or under freedom to provide services must, if it is to be capable of being lawfully enforced against a Community insurance undertaking, be in the interest of the general good, be necessary and proportionate and must not duplicate the rules of the home country.

In any event, in the event of a dispute, it is for the Member State imposing the restriction to prove that the measure in question meets these conditions.

The Court has provided a number of pointers as to the areas covered by the concept of the general good and the principles to be applied.

(a) Areas covered by the general good

The Court has so far recognized the following areas as possibly being covered by the general good, in the absence of harmonization:[47]

— professional rules intended to protect the recipient of services,[48]

— the protection of workers[49] including social protection,[50]
— the protection of consumers,[51]
— preservation of the good reputation of the national financial sector,[52]
— the prevention of fraud,[53]
— social order,[54]
— the protection of intellectual property,[55]
— the preservation of the national historical and artistic heritage,[56]
— cultural policy and safeguarding cultural diversity in the audiovisual sector,[57]
— the cohesion of the tax system,[58]
— road safety,[59]
— the protection of creditors,[60] and
— the protection of the proper administration of justice.[61]

The list is not exhaustive, and the Court reserves the right to add to it at any time.

(b) Principles applicable

For it to be compatible with Community law, it is not sufficient that the national measure invoked be recognized as being in the interest of the general good. The host Member State must also respect certain principles.

These principles are those established by the Court in its case-law on the general good (non-discrimination, non-duplication, necessity, proportionality, etc.) and already outlined in this communication. In accordance with that case-law, however, the concept of the general good is an exception to the fundamental principles of the Treaty in the area of freedom of movement and should therefore be interpreted strictly so that it is not relied on excessively or misused.

A host Member State should therefore satisfy itself that a national measure which it plans to introduce is in the interest of the general good and is necessary and proportionate.[62]

In this context, it follows that the inclusion by some Member States of whole areas of their national law in the list of provisions adopted in the interest of the general good could prove to constitute a misuse of the concept; several Member States are tending to treat as rules adopted in the interest of the general good all their legislation on consumer protection, their tax or commercial law or their competition law. The Commission takes the view that the principles of necessity, non-duplication and proportionality mean that Member States should indicate, when a Bill is adopted in the case of new legislation or, where appropriate, when the conditions referred to in Article 32(4) of Directives 92/49/EEC and 92/96/EEC are notified, the specific provisions in each national legislative instrument which could be in the interest of the general good.

However, although the reasoning is identical and the questions are the same whether the insurance undertaking operates through a branch or under the freedom to provide services, the answers may vary depending on the mode of operation.

The assessment of the proportionality of a restriction may differ depending on the mode of operation.

There are undoubtedly differences of kind between the provision of services and establishment; consequently, a restriction could be more easily regarded as proportionate where an operator carries on his activities permanently within a territory than where he does so only temporarily.

The Court recognized this difference by imposing a less restrictive and more 'lightweight' legal framework for provision of services than for establishment.

It has consistently held that a Member State:

'may not make the provision of services in its territory subject to compliance with all the conditions required for establishment and thereby deprive of all practical effectiveness the provisions of the Treaty whose object is, precisely, to guarantee the freedom to provide services.'[63]

The Court has likewise consistently held that it does not follow from Article 60(3) of the Treaty that

> 'all national legislation applicable to nationals of that State and usually applied to the permanent activities of undertakings established therein may be similarly applied in its entirety to the temporary activities of undertakings which are established in other Member States.'[64]

Thus, depending on the circumstances, the same restriction applied in the interest of the general good could be adjudged proportionate in respect of a branch but disproportionate in respect of a service provider.

(c) Examples in the insurance sector

Having identified the main characteristics of the general good, the Commission regards it as appropriate to state its interpretation of the concept as it applies to insurance, giving a few examples of national rules where compliance could be required by the authorities of the host Member State on the grounds of their supposed compatibility with the general good. Once again it should be explained that this interpretation does not prejudge that which the Court, competent in the last analysis for the interpretation of the Treaty and secondary legislation, could be asked to give of the questions raised. Such rules may concern, for instance:
(i) prior notification of policy conditions;
(ii) capital redemption operations of insurance undertakings;
(iii) uniform no-claims bonus systems;
(iv) the language of the insurance policy;
(v) professional codes of conduct;
(vi) maximum technical interest rates for life assurance;
(vii) the imposition of standard clauses or minimum insurance conditions;
(viii) clauses imposing mandatory levels of excess in insurance policies;
(ix) compulsory stipulation of a surrender value in insurance policies;
(x) the prohibition of cold-calling.

(I) Prior notification of policy conditions

The third Directives expressly forbid any prior or systematic substantive control of insurance policies and policy documents,[65] irrespective of the name given by the national authorities to the system used, whether it involves the prior approval of policies and scales of premiums or their simple, systematic notification with tacit approval or with the simple deposit of documents before they can be used. Prior, systematic approval is henceforward authorized only in those cases explicitly provided for in the Community Directives. Such is the case, for instance, with compulsory insurance (e.g. compulsory third-party motor insurance[66] or health insurance which is a substitute for a statutory system of social security.[67]

The Member States may only use systems of *ex post*, non-systematic control of insurance conditions, without in any event, such a requirement constituting a condition which an insurance undertaking must satisfy before carrying on its business, in order to ensure that their general-good provisions concerning insurance conditions are complied with by the policies marketed on their territory. Since the Community legislator has already determined the systems of substantive control that may be applied by the Member States and their conditions of application, this is an area which is already the subject of harmonization at Community level.

Nevertheless, certain Member States with a tradition of prior approval of policy conditions continue to require prior notification of these particulars. They argue that this is necessary to protect their consumers and to guarantee transparency of the products available on their national markets. In most cases, a sheet describing the insurance policy conditions has to be submitted.

The Commission takes the view that maintaining such systems of prior or systematic control of insurance policies is not consistent with the third Insurance Directives. It also considers that Member States may not justify such requirements on grounds of the general good, since the conditions set by the Court of Justice have not been met, inasmuch as this is an area which is already the subject of harmonization at Community level.

(II) Capital redemption operations of insurance undertakings

The system of a single administrative licence for an insurance undertaking in respect of those activities which fall within the scope of the Insurance Directives has meant that a life assurance undertaking may carry on anywhere in the Community those activities for which it was authorized in its home Member State. Such activities may be carried on in any Member State either under the rules on establishment or under the freedom to provide services.

'Capital redemption operations based on actuarial calculations, whereby, in return for single or periodic payments agreed in advance, commitments of specified duration and amount are undertaken' figure among the activities covered by the single licence, where such operations are the result of a contract and are subject to supervision by the insurance monitoring authority in the home Member State. Such activities, like any other activity falling within the scope of the Life Directives, may be carried on anywhere in the Community, including in a Member State in which they are not authorized for local life assurance undertakings on the grounds, for instance, that in the host Member State, such operations are regarded as banking operations and are therefore reserved for credit institutions.

The Commission considers, therefore, that there is no reason to prohibit the marketing of capital redemption products which fulfil the conditions of the first Life Directive 79/267/EEC, as amended by Directive 92/96/EEC, and which are marketed in a Member State by an insurer authorized in its home Member State to pursue such activities. The fact that, in the host Member State, such activities are not regarded as insurance activities and are not therefore permitted for insurers which have their head office there does not prevent insurers from other Member States from pursuing those activities which, having been the subject of mutual recognition between the Member States, benefit from the single licence system introduced by the third Life Directive 92/96/EEC.[68]

In the exercise of these activities, capital redemption products that are made available in the host Member State by a life insurance undertaking should respect, as in any other life insurance activity, the regulations in force in the host Member State that are justified on general grounds, notably as regards the taxation of these products or rules on advertising.

(III) Mandatory systems for reducing/increasing premium coefficients in compulsory third-party motor insurance (no-claims bonus)

In some Member States, detailed national legislative instruments establish the criteria to be taken into account when calculating the premiums for third-party motor insurance. The instruments prescribe, *inter alia*, coefficients for the reduction/increase of premiums (no-claims bonus schemes). The method laid down consists in determining a compulsory scale for calculating the annual premium. The scale applies both at the time the third-party motor insurance policy is concluded and when subsequent movements up or down the scale occur, depending on the frequency with which the insured submits a claim. The increase or reduction of the premium is not liberalized; on the contrary, it must comply with specific criteria laid down in the Member State's legislation. From the technical insurance perspective, such schemes are tariff measures and are therefore contrary to both the letter and the spirit of the third Directives.

The main argument advanced by Member States that have such a mandatory no-claims bonus system is that of prevention. According to these States, drivers who face an increased premium in the event of an accident will drive more carefully.

The third Non-life Directive 92/49/EEC introduced not only freedom as regards scales of premiums and the abolition of prior or systematic approval of scales and policies; it also introduced the concept of home country control in the field of financial supervision.[69]

To the extent that such mandatory no-claims bonus systems are tariff provisions, they are contrary to the third Non-life Directive. In the circumstances, the Commission takes the view that the Member States cannot therefore invoke the general good in order to preserve the mandatory character of these systems, since they concern rules which have already been coordinated at Community level.

(IV) The language of the insurance policy

Some Member States require insurance policies taken out or performed on their territory to be drafted exclusively in their official language(s). Other languages, Community or otherwise, may be used only for simple translations, even if the Contracting Parties would have liked to use such languages for the original policy.

This absolute and unconditional requirement is justified by the linguistic sovereignty of the Member States and a desire to protect consumers and by the need for any proceedings brought before local courts to be properly conducted.

The Commission is not calling into question the linguistic sovereignty of the Member States.[70]

The Commission considers in this respect that a distinction should be drawn between large industrial and commercial risks and mass risks. In the former case, consumer protection is not a valid concern. As regards mass risks and individual life assurance, provisions on the language of an insurance policy should also take account of certain circumstances. Thus, the first thing to take into consideration are policies with an international dimension, i.e. those where the law applicable to the insurance policy is not the law of the Member State where the risk/commitment is situated. For instance, exemptions from the principle that a policy must be drawn up in the official language(s) of the Member State where the risk/commitment is situated should be provided for in those cases where the insured person is of foreign origin. In all, 5 million citizens of the European Union live in a Member State which is not their own. Such persons would probably be better protected if they could take out policies in their own language instead of that of the Member State of residence or location of the risk they seek to cover. Secondly, exemptions should also be available for those cases where, pursuant to Articles 8 to 10 of the Brussels Convention of 27 September 1968 on Jurisdiction and the Enforcement of Judgments in Civil and Commercial Matters, a dispute may be heard by a court other than in the country of the commitment.

(V) Professional codes of conduct

Professional codes of conduct, which are valid on the territory of a Member State of the European Union, are in principle also valid with regard to foreign insurers; failure to observe them often incurs a penalty, especially of a commercial nature. Compliance with codes of conduct is justified by the signatory parties on grounds of consumer protection or contribution to market discipline.

It should be pointed out that the restrictions of private origin covered by Articles 48, 52 and 59 of the Treaty are different from those covered by the Treaty's competition rules (Article 85 *et seq.*). In the former case, it is a question of a vertical relation between the private body from which the restrictive measure emanate and the Member State: the public authority cedes part of its prerogatives to a private body with a well-defined task and the authority to adopt measures which bind individuals. By contrast, in the latter case it is a question of a horizontal relation between economic agents: the origin of the restriction lies entirely in the agreement concluded, *de jure* or *de facto*, between private undertakings. The only role which the State may play in this case is to tolerate or encourage such a restriction.[71]

The Commission takes the view that a distinction should be made between codes promulgated by national authorities and those drawn up by professional associations. The former should be examined on a case-by-case basis to ensure their compatibility with Articles 52 and 59 of the EC Treaty and in particular to see if the general-good conditions are met.

The latter type of code should normally be examined in the light of the Treaty's competition rules (Articles 85 and 86). In such cases and without prejudice to an examination of the requirements for the application of Article 85(3), it should not always be possible to impose the codes on foreign operators, who, since they would not be Members of the professional association which drew them up, will not have discussed their substance and means of application. It is possible, however, that the substance of such codes of conduct should also be examined in the light of Articles 52 and 59 of the Treaty.

(VI) Maximum technical interest rates for life assurance

The third Life Directive 92/96/EEC coordinated the actuarial principles governing the calculation of mathematical provisions.

Concerning the definition of technical interest rates, the third Life Directive provides[72] firstly, that the home Member State may set a maximum technical interest rate which the insurance undertakings it supervises must apply in order to calculate the bases for their technical provisions. It provides secondly that the home Member State may require insurance undertakings with their head office on its territory to notify systematically the technical bases used to calculate tariffs and technical provisions.

The Commission would point out that, in view of the provisions of the third Directive and the rules on supervision, which give exclusive competence for financial supervision to the insurance undertaking's home Member State, the branches of insurance undertakings and the insurers operating under the freedom to provide services are not bound by the provisions of the host Member State on maximum technical interest rates. Since the host Member State has no competence as regards financial supervision, it cannot impose compliance with its own prudential principles or check such compliance through substantive control of premium scales.

(VII) Imposition of standard clauses or minimum insurance conditions

Member States which have rules laying down compulsory clauses for insurance policies justify them by a concern to protect the weaker party in the contractual relationship and to preserve the balance in the latter by imposing a given content for the rights and obligations of the parties, and by a desire to protect third-party victims in the event of an accident.

The Commission believes that, in any event, protection of the weaker party should be imposed only in those cases where it is objectively necessary, for in insurance policies where the policy holder, by virtue of his nature or size, has a particular need or protection in order to preserve the contractual balance. It will also be necessary to consider the proportionality of such measures and analyse whether the inclusion in insurance policies of standard clauses laid down by the rules of a host Member State is a more difficult condition in practice for insurance undertakings from other Member States to fulfil than for insurance undertakings from the host Member State. This would be the case in particular if those insurance undertakings were deterred from prospecting anew market because they would be forced to create an entirely new insurance product in order to sell it on the market concerned instead of using an insurance product which is already used in their home Member State.

Similarly, the obligation to comply with standard clauses or minimum insurance conditions should not mean, either, that insurance policies cannot be worded differently.

(VIII) NATIONAL RULES IMPOSING A COMPULSORY EXCESS IN INSURANCE POLICIES

Member States with rules of this kind believe the compulsory excesses were introduced in the interest of the consumer, enabling him to take out insurance at a reasonable price, since, without this mechanism, which obliges the insured to bear part of the costs of the claim, premiums would increase in a completely unreasonable manner, because the insurer would have to act in the case of claims with a low economic cost. A second argument put forward by Member States which have adopted such rules is that the compulsory excess makes it possible to combat insurance fraud, which would otherwise be very frequent in the case of small claims. In such cases, the mandatory rule is designed to safeguard the profits of the insurer faced with a multitude of small claims.

The two arguments clearly establish that the introduction of a compulsory excess meets a need to discipline the market so as to avoid undue competition over premiums charged by insurance undertakings. It may also be asked whether the aim of a compulsory excess is not to preserve the profits of the insurer faced with a multitude of small claims rather than safeguard the interests of the policy holder or uphold public morality. It should be pointed out, however, that Community law excludes from reasons of the general good any consideration based on strictly economic grounds.[73]

In addition, as with the imposition of standard clauses or minimum conditions in insurance policies, the rigid application of such rules by the host Member State may have a restrictive effect on insurance undertakings operating under the rules on establishment or under the freedom to provide services, since they would be prevented from marketing insurance policies already correctly used in their home Member State without such excesses.

Lastly, while it could be admitted that the introduction of excesses reflects the choice of management method by the insurance undertaking, it still has to be examined whether the imposition of compulsory excesses through binding rules is consistent with the objectives of the third Insurance Directives as regards policies and scales of premiums.

Insurance undertakings should therefore be free to assess the advisability of including an excess in the policies which they market. Where an insurance undertaking satisfies the solvency requirements laid down by its home Member State, which has given it its approval and is responsible for its financial supervision, it should be free to decide to market insurance policies, with or without excesses, in the host Member State, clearly indicating to customers that it is doing so, without being forced into this by binding national rules.

(IX) NATIONAL RULES IMPOSING THE OBLIGATION TO PROVIDE IN ALL LIFE ASSURANCE POLICIES FOR A SURRENDER RIGHT AND/OR A BONUS

The Member States advance very different reasons why such rules are compatible with the concept of the general good. Some consider that the obligation to fix a surrender value in a life assurance policy meets the interests of consumers, who thus have the flexibility and liberty necessary in such policies, most often long-term, and are able to mobilize their savings. On the other hand, in other Member States, which wish to guarantee the stability of the insurer's portfolio and promote long-term saving, the early cancellation of a life insurance policy by the policy holder adversely affects the interests of the insured person. As for the rules making it compulsory to provide in life assurance policies for the insured to receive a bonus, these are also justified, depending on the Member State, by a desire to protect the economic interests of the insured.

Although the situation in each Member State must be assessed separately, it should be pointed out that the third Life Directive 92/96/EEC lays down, as part of the actuarial principles which the home Member State imposes on insurance undertakings for the establishment of their mathematical reserves, specific provisions for policies with a guaranteed surrender value and provisions for policies with bonuses. Furthermore, among the information to be given to policy holders before the policy is concluded and during the term of the policy, Annex II to the third Directive specifies 'the indication of surrender and paid-up values and the extent to which they are guaranteed, and the means of calculation and distribution of bonuses'.

It may be wondered, therefore, whether a national rule of the host Member State which imposes in a general and absolute manner the obligation to provide for a surrender value or a bonus in life assurance policies marketed on its territory is objectively necessary and proportionate to the objective of protecting the economic interests of policy holders, or on the contrary whether this objective cannot be achieved by other less restrictive means, for example the obligation to give detailed information to the policy holder prior to the conclusion of the policy.

(x) Prohibition of cold-calling

As regards this last example, the Court has already recognized the right to prohibit this marketing practice in the case of other financial products after examining a provision of Dutch law which was designed to protect the good reputation and reliability of the financial market in the Netherlands.[74] Consumer protection is also an argument that is often put forward in support of banning this marketing method. The reasoning followed by the Court in the Dutch case can also be applied to insurance products. Nevertheless, one should avoid trying to establish a general rule for the compatibility of this marketing method as far as insurance products are concerned, and each case should be assessed individually.

(xi) General

It is the Commission's duty to point out that national rules designed to protect the consumer (even if in principle invoked as promoting the general good, which is most often the case), or other considerations promoting the general good, must always satisfy the criteria laid down by the Court of Justice. Since the mandatory application of such rules in the host Member State may make it more difficult for risks located in that country to be covered by foreign insurers who carry on their business there under the rules on branches or under the freedom to provide services, their legitimacy must be examined in the light of the general-good test. In each case, the objectives pursued by the national rule invoked (consumer protection, protection of third-party victims, desire to make it possible for a risk to be insured by making its cover collective) must be examined, and a check should be made to see whether the conditions justifying recourse to the concept of the general good, set out in this document, have been met.

3. Rules relating to the law applicable to insurance contracts and the concept of the general good

The Insurance Directives[75] lay down specific rules for determining the substantive law applicable to insurance policies covering risks situated within the European Economic Area.[76] They make it possible to define what substantive law will govern the insurance policy. The rules apply both to insurance activities carried on under the rules on establishment and to those carried on under the freedom to provide services.

As a general rule and in a concise manner, in respect of non-life insurance policies relating to 'major risks' within the meaning of Article 5(d) of the first Non-life Directive 73/239/EEC[77] the parties have a free choice as to the law applicable to the insurance policy. As regards mass risks and policies which fall within the scope of the Life Directives, the established rules authorize the Member State where the risk/commitment which is the subject of the insurance policy is situated to submit the said policy to its own legislation. As regards compulsory non-life insurance, the Member State imposing the obligation to take out insurance may lay down that its legislation will apply to the said insurance policy.[78]

The second Insurance Directives also provided specific rules for determining the law applicable, where the Contracting Parties have a choice and the latter is not expressly established or demonstrated with reasonable certainly by the terms of the insurance policy. They also lay down rules relating to the application of the 'policing laws' of the forum and the Member State of the risk/commitment and to the 'public policy' provisions.[79]

The application, under the rules on the conflict of laws laid down by the Insurance Directives, by a Member State of its own 'mandatory' substantive provisions, its 'policing laws' and its 'public policy provisions' to insurance policies is likely, if it results in a restriction, to be examined from the viewpoint of the general good. The concept of the general good acts as a filter of national legislation. It obliges the authorities of the Member States to analyse their national legislation for compliance with the Treaty's principles of free movement.

It is essential that any rules of national law, whatever the field it relates to, should be compatible with Community law. Thus, in SAIL, the Court held that:

> 'The effectiveness of Community law cannot vary according to the various spheres of national law with it may affect.'[80]

Community law takes precedence therefore, if necessary, over national rules in the sphere of private law.

In particular, it has fallen to the Court to verify compatibility with Community law of national rules of civil law[81] and civil procedure.[82]

Consequently, and as has already been stated above, it is not sufficient that the host Member State's entire legislation on insurance policies be immediately declared mandatory for the authorities to think that it must be observed in full.[83] Such provisions must also satisfy the requirements of the general good if the host Member State is to be able to require compliance with them by insurers operating through a branch or under the freedom to provide services.

Since these are rules which were adopted in order to protect the consumer, there is a strong possibility that such rules of substantive law will pass the general-good test. The Court has recognized that consumer protection is an objective of the general good which justifies restrictions of fundamental freedoms. It cannot be presumed, however, that the test will be passed. It was seen above that national laws adopted with the declared aim of protecting the consumer can be subjected to the control of the Court and, where appropriate, 'disqualified', for example if they are not necessary or are disproportionate.

This additional level of reasoning is therefore essential, in the context of a single market, in order to verify if, in the absence of harmonization, national measures are not, under the pretext of consumer protection, being maintained simply to restrict or prevent the entry of insurance services which are different or unknown on the national territory.

If a Member State could invoke non-conformity with its own legislation in the case of an insurance product marketed in another Member State in order to restrict the marketing thereof on its territory, it would be hindering competition between insurance undertakings.

4. Action to be taken when faced with national rules regarded as being in the general good by the host Member State

To apply the principle just mentioned to a national rule which in his view is an unjustified restriction, the economic agent (insurance undertaking, intermediary or policy holder) must normally resort to the courts or inform the Commission, for example by lodging a complaint.

In practice, if for instance an insurance undertaking believes that the rules of a Member State where it proposes to carry on business contain restrictions that cannot satisfy the tests of the general good (e.g. binding provisions which are to be included in any policy and which are unknown, or different to those, in its home State), various possibilities are open to it:

- to avoid any potential conflict, it may of course adapt its services in all respects to the rules of the host country,
- if, all the same, it offers insurance products that do not comply exactly with the binding provisions of the host country, it may well be prosecuted by the national authorities or by one of its clients. The insurance undertaking will have to assert its Community-law arguments before a national court or authority in order to establish that the rule which the Member State intends to invoke against it does not satisfy the conditions identified by the Court. It is the national court which will assess the validity of the parties' arguments, having possibly referred the matter to the Court of Justice for a preliminary ruling pursuant to Article 177 of the Treaty,
- it may, at any moment, inform the Commission, which, if it thinks the restrictions are unjustified and hence contrary to Community law, could institute proceedings pursuant to Article 169 against the Member State concerned for failure to fulfil its obligations. In this context, it will be for the Commission to provide evidence of the alleged failure to fulfil obligations.[84] Where appropriate, it is the Court of Justice which will decide in the last instance whether the disputed national measure satisfies the tests of the general good or not.

1 Directive 92/49/EEC (OJ L 228, 11.8.1992, p. 1) and Directive 92/96/EEC (OJ L 360 L 9.12.1992, p. 1) as last amended by Parliament and Council Directive 95/26/EEC (OJ L 168, 18.7.1995, p. 7).

2 Where different interpretations of the Insurance Directives are possible, this document follows the interpretation which in the opinion of the Commission is closest to the EC Treaty. It should be noted in this respect that, in accordance with the Court's case-law, where a text of secondary legislation can be interpreted differently, preference should be given to the interpretation which would align it with the Treaty, rather than one which would render it incompatible (see Case 205/84 Commission v. Germany [1986] ECR 3755).

3 As regards the banking sector, the Commission has published an interpretative communication on the freedom to provide services and the general good in the second Banking Directive (SEC(97) 1193 final, 20.6.1997).

4 Council resolution on the new priorities concerning the information society, adopted on 8 October 1996; Commission communication to the European Council entitled 'Putting services to work' (CSE(96) 6 final, 27.11.1996); communication from the Commission to the European Parliament, the Council and the Economic and Social Committee concerning regulatory transparency in the internal market for information society services and proposal for a European parliament and Council Directive amending for the third time Directive 83/189/EEC laying down a procedure for the provision of information in the field of technical standards and regulations (COM(96) 392 final, 30.8.1996).

5 Communication from the Commission on a European initiative in electronic commerce (COM(97) 157, 15.4.1997). In this context, it should also be pointed out that the Commission plans to present in the very near future a proposal for a Council and Parliament Directive on contracts negotiated at a distance in the field of financial services.

6 For the purpose of this communication, the terms 'Member State of the provision of services', 'Member State where the risk is situated', 'home Member State', 'Member State of the branch', etc. are used in accordance with the definitions given in Directives 88/357/EEC, 90/619/EEC, 92/49/EEC and 92/96/EEC.

Member State of the provision of services: the Member State where the risk is situated pursuant to Article 2 (d) of Directive 88/357/EEC, where it is covered by an insurance undertaking or branch situated in another Member State, or the Member State of the commitment pursuant to Article 2 (e) of Directive 90/619/EEC, where the commitment is covered by an insurance undertaking or branch situated in another Member State (Article 1 (e) of Directive 92/49/EEC and Article 1 (f) of Directive 92/96/EEC).

Home Member State: the Member State in which the head office of the insurance undertaking covering the risk or the commitment is situated (Article 1 (c) of Directive 92/49/EEC and Article 1 (d) of Directive 92/96/EEC).

Member State of the branch: the Member State in which the branch covering the risk or commitment is situated (Article 1 (d) of Directive 92/49/EEC and Article 1 (e) of

Directive 92/96/EEC). *Branch:* any agency or branch of an insurance undertaking. Any permanent presence of an undertaking in the territory of a Member State is treated in the same way as an agency or branch, even if that presence does not take the form of a branch or agency, but consists merely of an office managed by the undertaking's own staff or by a person who is independent but has permanent authority to act for the undertaking as an agency would (Article 1 (b) of Directive 92/49/EEC and Article 1 (b) of Directive 92/96/EEC, and Articles 3 of Directives 88/357/EEC and 90/619/EEC).

7 Case 205/84 Commission v. Germany [1986] ECR 3755.

8 Joined Cases 262/82 and 26/83 Luisi and Carbone [1984] ECR 377. Case C-76/90 Säger [1991] ECR I-195.

9 Case 55/94 Gebhard [1995] ECR I-4195.

10 Case 205/84 Commission v. Germany [1986] ECR 3755, *supra*; Case 33/74 Van Binsbergen [1974] ECR 1299; Case C-148/91 Veronica [1993] ECR I-487; Case C-23/93 TV 10 [1994] ECR I-4795.

11 Case 205/84, paragraph 22, *supra*; Case 33/74 Van Binsbergen [1974] ECR 1299, paragraph 13.

12 See Gebhard, *supra*.

13 Case 205/84 [1986] 3755.

14 Case 205/84 [1986] ECR 3755, paragraphs 21 and 22; Case C-148/91 Veronica [1993] ECR I-487.

15 Article 1 (b) of Directives 92/49 EEC and 92/96/EEC and Article 3 of Directives 88/357/EEC and 90/619/EEC.

16 See, in particular, Gebhard of 30.11.1995, *supra*.

17 Case C-55/94 Gebhard, of 30.11.1995 *supra*. It should be pointed out that, in his opinion on Case 205/84 Commission v. Germany, *supra*, the Advocate-General stated that the appointment of an agent or representative (in the host Member State) did not in itself necessarily constitute establishment.

18 Case C-55/94 Gebhard of 30.11.1995, *supra*.

19 It should be pointed out straight away that the notion of 'independent intermediary' refers to structures (natural or legal persons) that are legally separate from the insurance undertaking they call on, irrespective of their form or designation. It is not used therefore in the more restrictive sense of Council Directive 77/92/EEC (OJ L 26, 31.1.1977) to distinguish between insurance agents (who act on behalf, and for the account, of, or solely on behalf of, one or more insurance undertakings) and insurance brokers (whose professional activity consists in particular in bringing together persons seeking insurance and insurance undertakings without being bound in the choice of the latter, with a view to covering risks to be insured, and who carry out work preparatory to the conclusion of policies of insurance and assist in the administration and performance of such policies, in particular in the event of a claim).

20 Case 14/76 [1976] ECR 1497. It should be noted that this judgment, together with those cited in footnotes 21, 22 and 23, were delivered in cases concerning the interpretation of the concept of a branch in accordance with the Brussels Convention on Jurisdiction and the Enforcement of Civil and Commercial Judgments.

21 Case 33/78 [1978] ECR 2183. See also Case C-439/93 Lloyd's Register of Shipping v. Société Campenon Bernard [1995] ECR I-961.

22 Case 139/80 [1981] ECR 819.

23 Case C-89/91 [1993] ECR I-165.

24 The term 'signatory State' is used here because the case concerned the Brussels Convention on Jurisdiction and the Enforcement of Judgments in Civil and Commercial Matters.

25 OJ C 59, 5.3.1979, p. 1.

26 See in this respect the concept of a branch given in Article 1(3) of the second Banking Directive 89/646/EEC (OJ L 386, 30.12.1989) and Article 1(8) of the Directive on investment services in the securities field (OJ L 141, 11.6.1993).

27 See Article 10 of first Directive 73/239/EEC, as amended by Article 32 of Directive 92/49/EEC, as regards non-life insurance and Article 10 of the first Directive 79/267/EEC, as amended by Article 32 of Directive 92/96/EEC, as regards life assurance for the procedure to be followed for opening a branch.

See Articles 14, 16 and 17 of Directive 88/357/EEC, as amended by Articles 34, 35 and 36 of Directive 92/49/EEC, as regards non-life insurance, and Articles 11, 14, and 17 of Directive 88/357/EEC, as amended by Articles 34, 35 and 36 of Directive 92/96/EEC, as regards life assurance, for the procedure relating to activities under the freedom to provide services falling within the scope of these Directives.

28 Article 41 of the third Non-life Directive (92/49/EEC) and Article 41 of the third Life Directive (92/96/EEC).

29 By advertising is meant 'the making of a representation in any form in connection with a trade, business, craft or profession in order to promote the supply of goods or services, including immovable property, rights and obligations' (Directive 84/450/EEC of 10 September 1984 on misleading advertising (OJ L 250, 19.9.1984, p. 17).

30 The Commission's analysis may of course be modified to reflect changes in the Court's case-law.

31 Case C-76/90 [1991] ECR I-4221.

32 See Case C-55/94 Gebhard, *supra.*

33 See, for example, Case C-1/93 Halliburton [1994] ECR I-1137, or Case C-330/91 Commerzbank [1993] ECR I-4017.

34 Case C-340/89 Vlassopoulou [1991] ECR I-2357. See also Case C-104/91 Colegio Oficial [1992] ECR I-3003.

35 Case C-19/92 Kraus [1993] ECR I-1663, paragraph 2.

36 Case C-55/94 Gebhard, *supra*; Case C-415/93 Bosman [1995] ECR I-4921.

37 Case C-55/94, *supra.*

38 It is interesting to note that the Court's judgment in Gebhard relates to an area (access to the profession of lawyer) in which harmonization of the conditions for taking up and carrying on the activity is very limited in comparison with insurance. In the insurance sector, these conditions have been very extensively harmonized and the possibilities for relying on general-good rules are, hence, much more limited.

On the other hand, with regard to the law of insurance policies, which is a field that has not been harmonized by secondary Community legislation, the discretion of the Member States is much wider. It is above all in this field that the test of the general good is likely to be applied.

39 Case C-415/93 [1995] ECR I-4921.

40 Case C-250/95 Futura, not yet reported.

41 It should be noted here that where the technique of health insurance is similar to that in the field of life assurance, Article 54(2) of the third Directive 92/49/EEC has already established the conditions that can be applied to insurers exercising such activities. As regards compulsory insurance for accidents at work, the Member States concerned may require every insurance undertaking to respect the specific provisions in their national law for such instance, with the exception of provisions concerning prudential supervision, which belong to the competence of the home Member State (Article 55 of Directive 92/49/EEC).

42 It should be pointed out that the principle of single authorization and supervision by the home Member State does not obstruct the application of other areas of the national law of the host Member State, e.g. tax law, social security law or labour law, which may accord differentiated treatment to Community firms depending on the way in which they choose to conduct their business, i.e. under the freedom to provide services or as a branch. In any event, the compatibility of such provisions with Community law will always be assessed on the basis of established case-law criteria especially where the general good is concerned, i.e. non-discrimination, non-duplication, necessity, proportionality, etc.

43 It should be pointed out that the uniform application of the mutual recognition principle to both branches and service providers was not introduced for the first time by the third Insurance Directives but appears also in the other Directives relating to financial services: the second Banking Directive 89/646/EEC (OJ L 386, 30.12.1989), as last amended by Directive 92/30/EEC (OJ L 110, 28.4.1992, p. 52) and Directive 93/22/EEC on investment services in the securities field (OJ L 141, 11.6.1993, p. 27).

44 See in particular Case 76/72 Michel [1973] ECR 457 and Case C-238/94 Garcia [1996] ECR I-1673.

45 See most recently Case C-17/92 Federación de Distribuidores Cinematográficos [1993] ECR I-2239.

46 Case 352/85 [1988] ECR 2085; Case C-17/92 [1993] ECR I-2239; Case C-483/93 Svenssonn [1995] ECR I-3955.

47 To this list must be added *a fortiori* the provisions of Article 56, i.e. public policy, public security and public health.

48 Joined Cases 110/78 and 111/78 Van Waesmael [1979] ECR 35.

49 Case 279/80 Webb, *supra.*

50 Case C-272/94 Guiot [1996] ECR I-1905.

51 Case 205/84 Commission v. Germany, *supra.*

52 Case C-384/93 Alpine Investments BV [1995] ECR I-1141.

53 Case C-275/92 Schindler [1994] ECR I-1039.

54 Ibid.

55 Case 62/79 Coditel [1980] ECR 881.

56 Case C-180/89 Commission v. Italy [1991] ECR 709.
57 Case C-288/89 Collectieve Antennevoorziening Gouda [1991] ECR I-4007; Case C-353/89 Commission v. Netherlands [1991] ECR I-4069; Case C-148/91 Veronica Omroep Organisatie [1993] ECR I-487.
58 Case C-204/90 Bachmann [1992] ECR 249.
59 Case C-55/93 Johannis Gerrit [1994] ECR 4837.
60 Case C-3/95 Reisebüro Broede, not yet reported.
61 Ibid.
62 See, in the context of the free movement of goods, Case 304/84 Muller [1986] ECR 1511, paragraph 25 and Case C-17/93 Van der Veldt [1994] ECR I-3537.
63 Case C-76/90 Säger, *supra*. See also Case C-198/89 Commission v. Greece [1991] ECR I-735.
64 Case 205/84 Commission v. Germany, *supra*. See also Case 279/80 Webb, *supra*.
65 Articles 6(3), 29 and 39 of Directive 92/49/EEC and Articles 5(3), 29 and 39 of Directive 92/96/EEC.
66 Article 30(2) of Directive 92/49/EEC.
67 Article 54(1) of Directive 92/49/EEC.
68 The same condition applies *mutates mutandis* to the other operations referred to in Article 1(2) of the first Life Assurance Directive 79/267/EEC and contained in points V (Tontines) and VII (Management of group pension funds) of the Annex to the first Directive.
69 Articles 6(3), 29 and 39 of Directive 92/49/EEC and Articles 5(3), 29 and 39 of Directive 92/96/EEC.
70 See point 2 of the communication from the Commission to the Council and the European Parliament concerning language use in the information of consumers in the Community (COM(93) 456 final, 10.11.1993).
71 See Case 229/83 Centres distributeurs E. Leclerc [1985] ECR 1; Case 83/231 H. Cullet [1985] ECR 305; Joined Cases 209 to 213/84 Asjes [1986] 1425; Case C-70/95 Sodemare, not yet reported.
72 See Article 17(1)(B) of the first Directive 79/267/EEC, as amended by Article 18 of the third Directive 92/96/EEC.
73 See footnote 46.
74 Case C-384/93 Alpine Investments v. Minister van Financiën [1995] ECR I-1141.
75 Non-life insurance: see Articles 7 and 8 of the second Directive 88/357/EEC, as amended by the third Directive 92/49/EEC. Life assurance: Article 4 of the second Directive 90/619/EEC.
76 It should be pointed out that the Rome Convention on the Law Applicable to Contractual Obligations (OJ L 226, 9.10.1980, p. 1) excludes from its scope insurance policies covering risks situated in the territories of the Member States (Article 1(3)).
77 Article 5(d) of Directive 73/239/EEC, introduced by Directive 88/357/EEC and amended in this respect by Directive 90/618/EEC (OJ L 330, 29.11.1990, p. 44).
78 Article 8(4) of the second Directive 88/357/EEC.
79 Non-life insurance: Article 7(1) of the second Directive 88/357/EEC.
80 Case 82/71 [1972] ECR 119. See also Case 20/92 Hubbard [1993] ECR I-3777.
81 Case C-168/91 Konstantinidis [1993] ECR I-1191; Case C-339/89 Alsthom Atlantique [1991] I-107; Case C-93/92 Motorradcenter [1993] ECR I-5009.
82 See in this respect Case C-398/92 Case C-398/92 Mund and Fester [1994] ECR I-467; Case C-43/95 Data Delecta [1996] ECR I-4661; Case C-177/94 Perfili [1996] ECR I-161. See also Hubbard (footnote 65).
83 *Supra*, point 2(b).
84 Case C-157/91 Commission v. Netherlands [1992] ECR I-5899.

Appendix 3 Insurance Companies Act 1982, Schedule 1

[13.1]
1982 CHAPTER 50

SCHEDULE 1
CLASSES OF LONG TERM BUSINESS

SECTION 1

Number	Description	Nature of business
I	Life and annuity.	Effecting and carrying out contracts of insurance on human life or contracts to pay annuities on human life, but excluding (in each case) contracts within Class III below.
II	Marriage and birth.	Effecting and carrying out contracts of insurance to provide a sum on marriage or on the birth of a child, being contracts expressed to be in effect for a period of more than one year.
III	Linked long term.	Effecting and carrying out contracts of insurance on human life or contracts to pay annuities on human life where the benefits are wholly or partly to be determined by reference to the value of, or the income from, property of any description (whether or not specified in the contracts) or by reference to fluctuations in, or in an index of, the value of property of any description (whether or not so specified).
IV	Permanent health.	Effecting and carrying out contracts of insurance providing specified benefits against risks of persons becoming incapacitated in consequence of sustaining injury as a result of an accident or of an accident of a specified class or of sickness or infirmity, being contracts that– (a) are expressed to be in effect for a period of not less than five years, or until the

		normal retirement age for the persons concerned, or without limit of time, and
		(b) either are not expressed to be terminable by the insurer, or are expressed to be so terminable only in special circumstances mentioned in the contract.
V	Tontines.	Effecting and carrying out tontines.
VI	Capital redemption.	Effecting and carrying out capital redemption contracts.
VII	Pension fund management.	Effecting and carrying out–
		(a) contracts to manage the investments of pension funds, or
		(b) contracts of the kind mentioned in paragraph (a) above that are combined with contracts of insurance covering either conservation of capital or payment of a minimum interest.
[VIII	Collective insurance etc.	Effecting and carrying out contracts of a kind referred to in Article 1(2)(e) of the first long term insurance Directive.
IX	Social insurance.	Effecting and carrying out contracts of a kind referred to in Article 1(3) of the first long term insurance Directive.]

NOTES

Derivation

This Schedule derived from the Insurance Companies Act 1981, Sch 1.

Amendment

Entries VIII, IX: inserted by SI 1994/1696, reg 3.

Appendix 4
Income and Corporation Taxes Act 1988, sections 590-612 and Schedule 15

[14.1]
PART XIV

PENSION SCHEMES, SOCIAL SECURITY BENEFITS, LIFE ANNUITIES ETC

CHAPTER I

RETIREMENT BENEFIT SCHEMES

Approval of schemes

590 Conditions for approval of retirement benefit schemes

(1) Subject to section 591, the Board shall not approve any retirement benefits schemes for the purposes of this Chapter unless the scheme satisfies all of the conditions set out in subsection (2) below.

(2) The conditions are—
- (a) *that the scheme is bona fide established for the sole purpose of providing relevant benefits in respect of service as an employee, being benefits payable to, or to the widow, [widower,] children or dependants or personal representatives of, the employee;*
- [(a) that the scheme is bona fide established for the sole purpose (subject to any enactment or Northern Ireland legislation requiring or allowing provision for the value of any rights to be transferred between schemes or between members of the same scheme) of providing relevant benefits in respect of service as an employee;]
- [(aa) that those benefits do not include any benefits payable to a person other than—
  - (i) the employee or a scheme member's ex-spouse,
  - (ii) a widow, widower, child, or dependant of the employee or of a scheme member's ex-spouse, or
  - (iii) the personal representatives of the employee or of a scheme member's ex-spouse;]
- (b) that the scheme is recognised by the employer and employees to whom it relates, and that every employee who is, or has a right to be, a member of the scheme has been given written particulars of all essential features of the scheme which concern him;
- (c) that there is a person resident in the United Kingdom who will be responsible for the discharge of all duties imposed on the administrator of the scheme under this Chapter;
- (d) that the employer is a contributor to the scheme;
- (e) that the scheme is established in connection with some trade or undertaking carried on in the United Kingdom by a person resident in the United Kingdom;

(f) that in no circumstances, whether during the subsistence of the scheme or later, can any amount be paid by way of repayment of an employee's contributions under the scheme.

(3) Subject to subsection (1) above, the Board shall approve a retirement benefits scheme for the purposes of this Chapter if the scheme satisfies all the conditions of this subsection, that is to say—

(a) that any benefit for an employee is a pension on retirement at a specified age not earlier than 60 [and not later than 75], which does not exceed one-sixtieth of the employee's final remuneration for each year of service up to a maximum of 40;

(b) that any benefit for any widow [or widower] of an employee is a pension payable on his death after retirement such that the amount payable to the widow [or widower] by way of pension does not exceed two-thirds of any pension of pensions payable to the employee;

(c) that no other benefits are payable under the scheme;

[(ba) that any benefit for an ex-spouse, or for the widow or widower of an ex-spouse, is a benefit in relation to which the scheme satisfies the conditions set out in subsection (3A) below;

(bb) that the scheme does not allow any rights debited to a scheme member as a consequence of a pension sharing order or provision to be replaced with any rights which that scheme member would not have able to acquire (in addition to the debited rights) had the order or provision not been made;

(c) that no benefits are payable under the scheme other than those mentioned in paragraphs (a), (b) and (ba) above;]

(d) that no pension is capable in whole or in part of surrender, commutation or assignment, *except* [except—

(i) for the purpose of giving effect to a pension sharing order or provision, or

(ii) in so far as the commutation of a benefit for an ex-spouse is allowed by virtue of subsection (3A) below, or

(iii)] in so far as the scheme allows an employee on retirement to obtain, by commutation of *his pension* [*a pension provided for him*],

a lump sum or sums not exceeding in all three-eightieths of his final remuneration . . . for each year of service up to a maximum of 40;

[(da) that, in a case in which—

(i) a lump sum may be obtained by the commutation of a part of a pension provided for an employee, and

(ii) the amount of that pension is affected by the making of a pension sharing order or provision,

the lump sum does not exceed the sum produced by multiplying by 2.25 the amount which (after effect has been given to the pension sharing order or provision) is the amount of that pension for the first year in which it is payable;]

[(e) that, in the case of any employee who is a member of the scheme by virtue of two or more relevant associated employments, the amount payable by way of pension in respect of service in any one of them may not, when aggregated with any amount payable by way of pension in respect of service in the other or others, exceed the relevant amount;

(f) that, in the case of any employee who is a member of the scheme by virtue of two or more relevant associated employments, the amount payable by way of commuted pension in respect of service in any one of them may not, when aggregated with any amount payable by way of commuted pension in respect of service in the other or others, exceed the relevant amount;

(g) that, in the case of any employee in relation to whom the scheme is connected with another scheme which is (or other schemes each of which is) an approved scheme, the amount payable by way of pension under the scheme may not, when aggregated with any amount payable by way of pension under the other scheme or schemes, exceed the relevant amount;

(h) that, in the case of any employee in relation to whom the scheme is connected with another scheme which is (or other schemes each of which is) an approved scheme, the amount payable by way of commuted pension may not, when aggregated with any amount payable by way of commuted pension under the other scheme or schemes, exceed the relevant amount.]

[(3A) The conditions mentioned in subsection (3)(ba) above are—

(a) that any benefit for an ex-spouse takes the form of a pension (with or without an entitlement to commute a part of that pension);

(b) that any benefit for an ex-spouse is a pension payable only on the attainment by the ex-spouse of a specified age of not less than 60 and not more than 75;

(c) that any entitlement to commute a part of the pension is exercisable only on its becoming payable;

(d) that any benefit for the widow or widower of an ex-spouse is confined to a non-commutable pension payable on the death of the ex-spouse at a time when the ex-spouse is already entitled to receive a pension under the scheme;

(e) that any pension provided for the widow or widower of an ex-spouse is of an amount not exceeding two-thirds of the pension payable to the ex-spouse;

(f) that, in a case in which a lump sum may be obtained by the commutation of a part of a pension provided for an ex-spouse, the lump sum does not exceed the sum procured by multiplying the sum of the pension for the first year in which it is payable by 2.25.]

(4) The conditions set out in *subsections (2) and (3)* [subsections (2) to (3A)] above are in this Chapter referred to as “the prescribed conditions”.

[(4A) In subsection (3)(c) above “benefits” does not include any benefits for whose payment the scheme makes provision in pursuance of any obligation imposed by legislation relating to social security.]

[(4B) For the purposes of this section a benefit provided under any scheme is provided for an ex-spouse or the widow or widower of an ex-spouse, and shall be treated as not provided for an employee or the widow or widower of an employee, to the extent (and to the extent only) that—

(a) it is provided for a person who is, or is the widow or widower of, either—

(i) an employee who is an ex-spouse; or

(ii) a scheme member’s ex-spouse; and

(b) it is as an ex-spouse, or as the widow or widower of an ex-spouse, that that person is the person for whom the benefit is provided.

(4C) For the purposes of this section a benefit provided for any person under any scheme is provided for that person as an ex-spouse, or as the widow or widower of an ex-spouse, to the extent (and to the extent only) that—

(a) the benefit is provided in respect of rights of an ex-spouse that are or represent rights conferred on the ex-spouse as a consequence of a pension sharing order or provision; and

(b) the scheme makes provision for the benefit to be treated as provided separately from any benefits which are provided under the scheme for the same person as an employee or as the widow or widower of an employee.

(4D) In this section “scheme member”, in relation to a scheme, means—

(a) an employee; or

(b) a person entitled to any relevant benefits under the scheme as a consequence of a pension sharing order or provision.

(4E) The following rules shall apply in calculating for the purposes of subsection (3)(da) or (3A)(f) above the amount of a person’s pension for the first year in which

it is payable—
- (a) if the pension payable for the year changes, the initial pension payable shall be taken;
- (b) it shall be assumed that that person will survive for the year; and
- (c) the effect of commutation shall be ignored.

(4F) A pension provided for an ex-spouse who is an employee, or for the widow or widower of such an ex-spouse, shall be disregarded in any determination of whether the conditions set out in subsection (3)(e) to (h) above are satisfied or continue to be satisfied in the case of that employee.]

(5), (6) . . .

[(7) Subsections (8) to (10) below apply where the Board are considering whether a retirement benefits scheme satisfies or continues to satisfy the prescribed conditions.

(8) For the purpose of determining whether the scheme, so far as it relates to a particular class or description of employees, satisfies or continues to satisfy the prescribed conditions, that scheme shall be considered in conjunction with—
- (a) any other retirement benefits scheme (or schemes) which relates (or relate) to employees of that class or that class or description and which is (or are) approved for the purposes of this Chapter,
- (b) any other retirement benefits scheme (or schemes) which relates (or relate) to employees of that class or description and which is (or are) at the same time before the Board in order for them to decide whether to give approval for the purposes of this Chapter.
- (c) any section 608 scheme or schemes relating to employees of that class or description, and
- (d) any relevant statutory scheme or schemes relating to employees of that class or description.

(9) If those conditions are satisfied in the case of both or all of those schemes taken together, they shall be taken to be satisfied in the case of the scheme mentioned in subsection (7) above (as well as the other or others).

(10) If those conditions are not satisfied in the case of both or all of those schemes taken together, they shall not be taken to be satisfied in the case of the scheme mentioned in subsection (7) above.

(11) The reference in subsection (8)(c) above to a section 608 scheme is a reference to a fund to which section 608 applies.]

NOTES

Derivation

This section, as originally enacted, derived as follows: subs-ss (1), (6) derived from the Finance Act 1970, s 19(1), (4), and the Finance Act 1971, s 21(2), Sch 3, para 12(1); sub-ss (2), (7) derived from the Finance Act 1970, s 19(2), (5); sub-ss (3), (4) derived from the Finance Act 1970, s 19(2A), (2B), the Finance Act 1971, s 21(3), and the Finance (No 2) Act 1987, Sch 3, para 1; sub-s (5) derived from the Finance Act 1970, s 19(3), and the Finance (No 2) Act 1987, Sch 3, para 2.

Amendment

Sub-s (2): para (a) substituted by the Finance Act 1999, s 79, Sch 10, para 2(1).

Date in force: this amendment applies for the purposes of the grant or withdrawal of any approval of a retirement benefits scheme (whenever made or approved) at any time on or after a day to be appointed: see the Finance Act 1999, s 79, Sch 10, para 18(1), (3) (for further provision see sub-para (4) thereto).

Sub-s (2): in para (a) word "widower," in square brackets inserted by the Finance Act 1988, s 35, Sch 3, Part I, para 18, with effect on and after 6 April 1990.

Sub-s (2): para (aa) inserted by the Finance Act 1999, s 79, Sch 10, para 2(2).

Date in force: this amendment applies for the purposes of the grant or withdrawal of any approval of a retirement benefits scheme (whenever made or approved) at any time on or after a day to be appointed: see the Finance Act 1999, s 79, Sch 10, para 18(1), (3) (for further provision see sub-para (4) thereto).

Sub-s (3): in para (a) words "and not later than 75" in square brackets substituted, in relation to a scheme not approved by the Board before 25 July 1991, by the Finance Act 1991, s 34(2), (4).

Sub-s (3): in para (b) words "or widower" in square brackets in both places they occur inserted by the Finance Act 1988, s 35, Sch 3, Part I, para 18, with effect on and after 6 April 1990.

Sub-s (3): para (c) substituted, by subsequent paras (ba)–(c) in square brackets, by the Finance Act 1999, s 79, Sch 10, para 2(3).

Date in force: this amendment applies for the purposes of the grant or withdrawal of any approval of a retirement benefits scheme (whenever made or approved) at any time on or after a day to be appointed: see the Finance Act 1999, s 79, Sch 10, para 18(1), (3) (for further provision see sub-para (4) thereto).

Sub-s (3): in para (d) words "except" and "his pension" in italics repealed and subsequent words in square brackets substituted by the Finance Act 1999, Sch 10, para 2(4).

Date in force: these amendments apply for the purposes of the grant or withdrawal of any approval of a retirement benefits scheme (whenever made or approved) at any time on or after a day to be appointed: see the Finance Act 1999, s 79, Sch 10, para 18(1), (3) (for further provision see sub-para (4) thereto).

Sub-s (3): in para (d) words omitted repealed, in relation to a scheme not approved by the Board before 27 July 1989, by the Finance Act 1989, s 187, Sch 17, Pt IV.

Sub-s (3): para (da) inserted by the Finance Act 1999, s 79, Sch 10, para 2(5).

Date in force: this amendment applies for the purposes of the grant or withdrawal of any approval of a retirement benefits scheme (whenever made or approved) at any time on or after a day to be appointed: see the Finance Act 1999, s 79, Sch 10, para 18(1), (3) (for further provision see sub-para (4) thereto).

Sub-s (3): paras (e)–(h) substituted (for the original sentence following para (d)), in relation to a scheme not approved by the Board before 27 July 1989, by the Finance Act 1989, s 75, Sch 6, paras 3, 18(2).

Sub-s (3A): inserted by the Finance Act 1999, s 79, Sch 10, para 2(6).

Date in force: this amendment applies for the purposes of the grant or withdrawal of any approval of a retirement benefits scheme (whenever made or approved) at any time on or after a day to be appointed: see the Finance Act 1999, s 79, Sch 10, para 18(1), (3) (for further provision see sub-para (4) thereto).

Sub-s (4): words "subsections (2) and (3)" in italics repealed and subsequent words in square brackets substituted by the Finance Act 1999, s 79, Sch 10, para 2(7).

Date in force: this amendment applies for the purposes of the grant or withdrawal of any approval of a retirement benefits scheme (whenever made or approved) at any time on or after a day to be appointed: see the Finance Act 1999, s 79, Sch 10, para 18(1), (3) (for further provision see sub-para (4) thereto).

Sub-s (4A): inserted, in relation to a scheme not approved by the Board before 25 July 1991, by the Finance Act 1991, s 34(3), (4).

Sub-ss (4B)–(4F): inserted by the Finance Act 1999, s 79, Sch 10, para 2(8).

Date in force: this amendment applies for the purposes of the grant or withdrawal of any approval of a retirement benefits scheme (whenever made or approved) at any time on or after a day to be appointed: see the Finance Act 1999, s 79, Sch 10, para 18(1), (3) (for further provision see sub-para (4) thereto).

Sub-ss (5), (6): repealed with retrospective effect by the Finance Act 1991, ss 36(2), (3), 123, Sch 19, Part V.

Sub-ss (7)–(11): substituted, for sub-s (7) as originally enacted, in relation to determinations made on or after 27 July 1989, by the Finance Act 1989, s 75, Sch 6, paras 3(4), 18(3).

See Further

See further, in relation to judicial pensions: the Judicial Pensions and Retirement Act 1993, s 18.

[590A Section 590: supplementary provisions]

[(1) For the purposes of section 590(3)(e) and (f) two or more employments are relevant associated employments if they are employments in the case of which—

- (a) there is a period during which the employee has held both or all of them,
- (b) the period counts under the scheme in the case of both or all of them as a period in respect of which benefits are payable, and
- (c) the period is one during which both or all of the employers in question are associated.

(2) For the purposes of section 590(3)(g) and (h) the scheme is connected with another scheme in relation to an employee if—

- (a) there is a period during which he has been the employee of two persons who are associated employers,
- (b) the period counts under both schemes as a period in respect of which benefits are payable, and
- (c) the period counts under one scheme by virtue of service with one employer and under the other scheme by virtue of service with the other employer.

(3) For the purposes of subsections (1) and (2) above, employers are associated if (directly or indirectly) one is controlled by the other or if both are controlled by a third person.

(4) In subsection (3) above the reference to control, in relation to a body corporate, shall be construed—

- (a) where the body corporate is a close company, in accordance with section 416, and
- (b) where it is not, in accordance with section 840.]

NOTES

Amendment

Inserted, in relation to a scheme not approved by the Board before 27 July 1989, by the Finance Act 1989, s 75, Sch 6, paras 4, 18(2).

See Further

See further, in relation to judicial pensions: the Judicial Pensions and Retirement Act 1993, s 18.

[590B Section 590: further supplementary provisions]

[(1) For the purposes of section 590(3)(e) the relevant amount, in relation to an employee, shall be found by applying the following formula—

$$\frac{(A \times C)}{60}$$

(2) For the purposes of section 590(3)(f) the relevant amount, in relation to an employee, shall be found by applying the following formula—

$$\frac{(3 \times A \times C)}{80}$$

(3) For the purposes of section 590(3)(g) the relevant amount, in relation to an employee, shall be found by applying the following formula—

$$\frac{(B \times C)}{60}$$

(4) For the purposes of section 590(3)(h) the relevant amount, in relation to an employee, shall be found by applying the following formula—

$$\frac{(3 \times B \times C)}{80}$$

(5) For the purposes of this section A is the aggregate number of years service (expressing parts of a year as a fraction), subject to a maximum of 40, which, in the case of the employee, count for the purposes of the scheme at the time the benefits in respect of service in the employment become payable.

(6) But where the same year (or part of a year) counts for the purposes of the scheme by virtue of more than one of the relevant associated employments it shall be counted only once in calculating the aggregate number of years service for the purposes of subsection (5) above.

(7) For the purposes of this section B is the aggregate number of years service (expressing parts of a year as a fraction), subject to a maximum of 40, which, in the case of the employee, count for the purposes of any of the following—
- (a) the scheme, and
- (b) the other scheme or schemes with which the scheme is connected in relation to him, at the time the benefits become payable.

(8) But where the same year (or part of a year) counts for the purposes of more than one scheme it shall be counted only once in calculating the aggregate number of years service for the purpose of subsection (7) above.

(9) For the purposes of this section C is the permitted maximum in relation to the year of assessment in which the benefits in question become payable, that is, the figure found for that year by virtue of subsections (10) and (11) below.

(10) For the years 1988–89 and 1989–90 the figure is £60,000.

(11) For any subsequent year of assessment the figure is the figure found for that year, for the purposes of section 590C, by virtue of section 590C(4) [to (5A)].]

NOTES

Amendment

Inserted, in relation to a scheme not approved by the Board before 27 July 1989, by the Finance Act 1989, s 75, Sch 6, paras 4, 18(2).

Sub-s (11): words "to (5A)" in square brackets substituted, in relation to the year 1994–95 and subsequent years of assessment, by the Finance Act 1993, s 107(6), (8).

See Further

See further, in relation to judicial pensions: the Judicial Pensions and Retirement Act 1993, s 18.

[590C Earnings cap]

[(1) In arriving at an employee's final remuneration for the purposes of section 590(3)(a) or (d), any excess of what would be his final remuneration (apart from this section) over the permitted maximum for the year of assessment in which his participation in the scheme ceases shall be disregarded.

(2) In subsection (1) above "the permitted maximum", in relation to a year of assessment, means the figure found for that year by virtue of subsections (3) and (4) below.

(3) For the years 1988–89 and 1989–90 the figure is £60,000.

(4) For any subsequent year of assessment the figure is also £60,000, subject to [subsections (5) and (5A)] below.

(5) If the retail prices index for the month of [September] preceding a year of assessment falling within subsection (4) above is higher than it was for the previous [September], the figure for that year shall be an amount arrived at by—
- (a) increasing the figure for the previous year of assessment by the same percentage as the percentage increase in the retail prices index, and
- (b) if the result is not a multiple of £600, rounding it up to the nearest amount which is such a multiple.

[(5A) If the retail prices index for the month of September preceding a year of assessment falling within subsection (4) above is not higher than it was for the previous September, the figure for that year shall be the same as the figure for the previous year of assessment.]

(6) The Treasury shall in the year of assessment 1989–90, and in each subsequent year of assessment, make an order specifying the figure which is by virtue of this section the figure for the following year of assessment.]

NOTES

Amendment

Inserted, in relation to a scheme not approved by the Board before 27 July 1989, by the Finance Act 1989, s 75, Sch 6, paras 4, 18(2).

Sub-s (4): words "subsections (5) and (5A)" in square brackets substituted, in relation to the year 1994–95 and subsequent years of assessment, by the Finance Act 1993, s 107(5), (8).

Sub-s (5): word "September" in square brackets in both places it occurs substituted, in relation to the year 1994–95 and subsequent years of assessment, by the Finance Act 1993, s 107(4), (8).

Sub-s (5A): inserted, in relation to the year 1994–95 and subsequent years of assessment, by the Finance Act 1993, s 107(5), (8).

See Further

See further, in relation to judicial pensions: the Judicial Pensions and Retirement Act 1993, s 18.

Subordinate Legislation

Retirement Benefits Schemes (Indexation of Earnings Cap) Order 2000, SI 2000/807 (made under sub-s (6)).

Retirement Benefits Schemes (Indexation of Earnings Cap) Order 1999, SI 1999/592 (made under sub-s (6)).

591 Discretionary approval

(1) The Board may, if they think fit having regard to the facts of a particular case, and subject to such conditions, if any, as they think proper to attach to the approval, approve a retirement benefits scheme for the purposes of this Chapter notwithstanding that it does not satisfy one or more of the prescribed conditions; but this subsection has effect subject to subsection (5) below.

(2) The Board may in particular approve by virtue of this section a scheme—
- (a) which exceeds the limits imposed by the prescribed conditions as respects benefits for less than 40 years; or
- (b) which provides pensions for the widows [and widowers] of employees on death in service, of for the children or dependants of employees; or
- [(ba) which provides pensions for the widows and widowers of ex-spouses dying before the age at which their pensions become payable and for the children or dependants of ex-spouses; or]
- (c) which provides on death in service a lump sum of up to four times the employee's final remuneration (exclusive of any refunds of contributions); or
- (d) which allows benefits to be payable on retirement within ten years of the specified age, or on earlier incapacity; or
- (e) which provides for the return in certain contingencies of employees' contributions; or
- (f) which relates to a trade or undertaking carried on only partly in the United Kingdom and by a person not resident in the United Kingdom; or
- (g) which provides in certain contingencies for securing relevant benefits [falling within subsection (2A) below] (but no other benefits) by means of an annuity contract . . . made with an insurance company of the employee's choice; or
- (h) to which the employer is not a contributor and which provides benefits additional to those provided by a scheme to which he is a contributor.

[(2A) Relevant benefits fall within this subsection if they correspond with benefits that could be provided by an approved scheme, and for this purpose—
- (a) a hypothetical scheme (rather than any particular scheme) is to be taken, and
- (b) benefits provided by a scheme directly (rather than by means of an annuity contract) are to be taken.]

[(3) In subsection (2)(g) above "insurance company" has the meaning given by section 659B.]

(4) In applying this section to a scheme which was in existence on 6th April 1980, the Board shall exercise their discretion, in such cases as appear to them to be

appropriate, so as to preserve—

(a) benefits earned or rights arising out of service before 6th April 1980; and

(b) any rights to death-in-service benefits conferred by rules of the scheme in force on 26th February 1970.

(5) The Board shall not approve a scheme by virtue of this section if to do so would be inconsistent with regulations made [by the Board] for the purposes of this section.

(6) Regulations made [by the Board] for the purposes of this section may restrict the Board's discretion to approve a scheme by reference to the benefits provided by the scheme, the investments held for the purposes of the scheme, the manner in which the scheme is administered or any other circumstances whatever.

NOTES

Derivation

Sub-ss (1), (5), (6) derived from the Finance Act 1970, s 20(1), (4), (5), and the Finance (No 2) Act 1987, Sch 3, para 3(2), (5); sub-s (2) derived from the Finance Act 1970, s 20(2), the Finance Act 1971, s 21(4), the Finance Act 1981, s 32, and the Finance (No 2) Act 1987, Sch 3, para 3(3), (4); sub-s (3) derived from the Finance Act 1970, s 20(2A), the Finance Act 1981, s 32, and the Insurance Companies Act 1982; sub-s (4) derived from the Finance Act 1970, s 20(3), and the Finance Act 1987, Sch 15, para 3.

Amendment

Sub-s (2): in para (b) words "and widowers" in square brackets inserted by the Finance Act 1999, s 79, Sch 10, para 3(a).

Date in force: this amendment came into force on 27 July 1999 in the absence of any specific commencement provision.

Sub-s (2): para (ba) inserted by the Finance Act 1999, s 79, Sch 10, para 3(b).

Date in force: this amendment applies for the purposes of the grant or withdrawal of any approval of a retirement benefits scheme (whenever made or approved) at any time on or after a day to be appointed: see the Finance Act 1999, s 79, Sch 10, para 18(1), (3) (for further provision see sub-para (4) thereto).

Sub-s (2): in para (g) words "falling within subsection (2A) below" in square brackets inserted, in relation to a scheme not approved before 1 July 1994, by the Finance Act 1994, s 107(2).

Sub-s (2): in para (g) words omitted repealed, in relation to a scheme not approved before 1 July 1994, by the Finance Act 1994, ss 107(4), 258, Sch 26, Pt V.

Sub-s (2A): inserted, in relation to a scheme not approved before 1 July 1994, by the Finance Act 1994, s 107(3), (4).

Sub-s (3): substituted, in relation to a scheme not approved by virtue of this section before 1 May 1995, by the Finance Act 1995, ss 59(2), 60(1).

Sub-s (5): words "by the Board" in square brackets inserted with retrospective effect by the Finance Act 1988, s 146, Sch 13, Pt I, para 6.

Sub-s (6): words "by the Board" in square brackets inserted with retrospective effect by the Finance Act 1988, s 146, Sch 13, Pt I, para 6.

See Further

See further, in relation to judicial pensions: the Judicial Pensions and Retirement Act 1993, s 18.

Subordinate Legislation

Retirement Benefits Schemes (Restriction on Discretion to Approve) (Additional Voluntary Contributions) (Amendment) Regulations 1999, SI 1999/1964 (made under sub-s (6)).

[591A Effect on approved schemes of regulations under section 591]

[(1) Subsection (2) below applies where on or after 17th April 1991 regulations are made for the purposes of section 591 ("section 591 regulations") which contain provisions restricting the Board's discretion to approve a retirement benefits scheme by reference to any circumstances other than the benefits provided by the scheme ("relevant provisions").

(2) Any retirement benefits scheme approved by the Board by virtue of section 591 before the day on which the section 591 regulations come into force shall cease to be approved by virtue of that section at the end of the period of 36 months beginning with that day if at the end of that period the scheme—
- (a) contains a provision of a prohibited description, or
- (b) does not contain a provision of a required description,

unless the description of provision is specified in regulations made by the Board for the purposes of this subsection.

(3) For the purposes of this section, a provision contained in a scheme shall not be treated as being of a prohibited description by reason only of the fact that it authorises the retention of an investment held immediately before the day on which the section 591 regulations are made.

(4) In determining for the purposes of this section whether any provision contained in a scheme is of a required description, the fact that it is framed so as not to require the disposal of an investment held immediately before the day on which the section 591 regulations are made shall be disregarded.

(5) In this section—
- (a) references to a provision of a prohibited description are to a provision of a description specified in the relevant provisions of the section 591 regulations as a description of provision which, if contained in a retirement benefits scheme, would prevent the Board from approving the scheme by virtue of section 591;
- (b) references to a provision of a required description are to a provision of a description specified in the relevant provisions of the section 591 regulations as a description of provision which must be contained in a retirement benefits scheme before the Board may approve the scheme by virtue of section 591.]

NOTES

Amendment
Inserted by the Finance Act 1991, s 35.

See Further
See further, in relation to judicial pensions: the Judicial Pensions and Retirement Act 1993, s 18.

Subordinate Legislation
Retirement Benefits Schemes (Restriction on Discretion to Approve) (Additional Voluntary Contributions) (Amendment) Regulations 1999, SI 1999/1964 (made under sub-s (2)).

[591B Cessation of approval: general provisions]

[(1) If in the opinion of the Board the facts concerning any approved scheme or its administration cease to warrant the continuance of their approval of the scheme, they may at any time by notice to the administrator, withdraw their approval on such grounds, and from such date (which shall not be earlier than the date when those facts first ceased to warrant the continuance of their approval or 17th March 1987, whichever is the later), as may be specified in the notice.

(2) Where an alteration has been made in a retirement benefits scheme, no approval given by the Board as regards the scheme before the alteration shall apply after the date of the alteration unless—

- (a) the alteration has been approved by the Board, or
- (b) the scheme is of a class specified in regulations made by the Board for the purposes of this paragraph and the alteration is of a description so specified in relation to schemes of that class.]

NOTES

Amendment

Inserted by the Finance Act 1991, s 36, with retrospective effect.

See Further

See further, in relation to judicial pensions: the Judicial Pensions and Retirement Act 1993, s 18.

[591C Cessation of approval: tax on certain schemes]

[(1) Where an approval of a scheme to which this section applies ceases to have effect, tax shall be charged in accordance with this section.

(2) The tax shall be charged under Case VI of Schedule D at the rate of 40 per cent on an amount equal to the value of the assets which immediately before the date of the cessation of the approval of the scheme are held for the purposes of the scheme (taking that value as it stands immediately before that date).

(3) Subject to section 591D(4), the person liable for the tax shall be the administrator of the scheme . . .

(4) This section applies to a retirement benefits scheme in respect of which [one or more] of the conditions set out below is satisfied.

(5) The first condition is satisfied in respect of a scheme if, immediately before the date of the cessation of the approval of the scheme, the number of individuals who are members of the scheme is less than twelve.

(6) The second condition is satisfied in respect of a scheme if at any time within the period of one year ending with the date of the cessation of the approval of the scheme, a person who is or has been a controlling director of a company which has contributed to the scheme is a member of the scheme.

[(6A) The third condition is satisfied in respect of a scheme if—

- (a) at any time within the period of three years ending with the date of the cessation of the approval of the scheme, the scheme has received a transfer value in respect of any person;
- (b) contributions made by or in respect of that person to any approved pension arrangements (whether or not those from which the transfer value was received) were represented in the transfer value; and
- (c) the contributions so represented were made by or in respect of that person by reference to—

(i) any service by him with a company of which he is or has at any time been a controlling director;
(ii) any remuneration in respect of any such service; or
(iii) any income chargeable to tax under Schedule D and immediately derived by him from the carrying on or exercise by him (whether as an individual or in partnership with others) of a trade, profession or vocation.]

(7) For the purposes of [this section] a person is a controlling director of a company if he is a director of it and within section 417(5)(b) in relation to it.]

[(8) In subsection (6A) above—
(a) the references to the receipt of a transfer value by a scheme are references to the transfer, so as to become held for the purposes of the scheme, of any sum or asset held for the purposes of any other approved pension arrangements; and
(b) the references to contributions to approval pension arrangements include references to—
(i) any contributions made in accordance with, or for the purposes of, the arrangements; and
(ii) anything paid by way of premium or other consideration under an annuity contract for which the arrangements provide.

(9) In this section "approved pension arrangements" means—
(a) any scheme or arrangements approved for the purposes of this Chapter or Chapter IV of this Part or, in relation to a time before 6th April 1988, the corresponding provisions then in force;
(b) any scheme being considered for approval under this Chapter;
(c) any annuity contract entered into for the purposes of any scheme or arrangements falling with in paragraph (a) or (b) above; or
(d) any contract or scheme approved for the purposes of Chapter III of this Part or, in relation to a time before 6th April 1988, the corresponding provisions then in force.]

NOTES

Amendment

Inserted, in relation to any approval of a retirement benefits scheme which ceases to have effect on or after 2 November 1994 other than an approval ceasing to have effect by virtue of a notice given before that day under s 591B(1) hereof, by the Finance Act 1995, s 61(1), (3).

Sub-s (3): words omitted repealed by the Finance Act 1998, s 165, Sch 27, Pt III(20).

Date in force: 31 July 1998: (no specific commencement provision).

Sub-s (4): words "one or more" in square brackets substituted by the Finance Act 1998, s 92, Sch 15, para 1(2).

Date in force: this amendment has effect in relation to any case in which the date of the cessation of the approval is on or after 17 March 1998: see the Finance Act 1998, Sch 15, para 1(6).

Sub-s (6A): inserted by the Finance Act 1998, s 92, Sch 15, para 1(3).

Date in force: this amendment has effect in relation to any case in which the date of the cessation of the approval is on or after 17 March 1998: see the Finance Act 1998, Sch 15, para 1(6).

Sub-s (7): words "this section" in square brackets substituted by the Finance Act 1998, s 92, Sch 15, para 1(4).

Date in force: this amendment has effect in relation to any case in which the date of the cessation of the approval is on or after 17 March 1998: see the Finance Act 1998, Sch 15, para 1(6).

Sub-ss (8), (9): inserted by the Finance Act 1998, s 92, Sch 15, para 1(5).

Date in force: this amendment has effect in relation to any case in which the date of the cessation of the approval is on or after 17 March 1998: see the Finance Act 1998, Sch 15, para 1(6).

[591D Section 591C: supplementary]

[(1) For the purposes of section 591C(2) the value of an asset is, subject to subsection (2) below, its market value, construing "market value" in accordance with section 272 of the 1992 Act.

(2) Where an asset held for the purposes of a scheme a right or interest in respect of any money lent (directly or indirectly) to any person mentioned in subsection (3) below, the value of the asset shall be treated as being the amount owing (including any unpaid interest) on the money lent.

(3) The persons are—

(a) any employer who has at any time contributed to the scheme;

(b) any company connected with such an employer;

[(c) any person who has at any time (whether or not before the making of the loan) been a member of the scheme;

(d) any person connected, at the time of the making of the loan or subsequently, with a person falling within paragraph (c) above.]

(4) Where the administrator of the scheme constituted by persons who include a person who is an approved independent trustee in relation to a scheme, that person shall not be liable for tax chargeable by virtue of section 591C.

(5) A person is an approved independent trustee in relation to a scheme only if he is—

(a) approved by the Board to act as a trustee of the scheme; and

(b) not connected with—

(i) a member of the scheme;

(ii) any other trustee of the scheme; or

(iii) an employer who has contributed to the scheme.

(6) For the purposes of section 596A(9) income and gains accruing to a scheme shall not be regarded as brought into charge to tax merely because tax is charged in relation to the scheme in accordance with section 591C.

(7) The reference in section 591C(1) to an approval of a scheme ceasing to have effect is a reference to—

(a) the scheme ceasing to be an approved scheme by virtue of section 591A(2);

(b) the approval of the scheme being withdrawn under section 591B(1); or

(c) the approval of the scheme no longer applying by virtue of section 591B(2);

and any reference in section 591C to the date of the cessation of the approval of the scheme shall be construed accordingly.

(8) For the purposes of section 591C and this section a person is a member of a scheme at a particular time if at that time a benefit—

(a) is being provided under the scheme, or
(b) may be so provided,

in respect of any past or present employment of his.

(9) Section 839 shall apply for the purposes of this section.]

NOTES

Amendment

Inserted, in relation to any approval of a retirement benefits scheme which ceases to have effect on or after 2 November 1994 other than an approval ceasing to have effect by virtue of a notice given before that day under s 591B(1) hereof, by the Finance Act 1995, s 61(1), (3).

Sub-s (3): paras (c), (d) submitted by the Finance Act 1998, s 92, Sch 15, para 2(1).

Date in force: this amendment has effect in relation to any case in which the date of the cessation of the approval of the scheme is on or after 17 March 1998: see the Finance Act 1998, Sch 15, para 2(2).

Tax reliefs

592 Exempt approved schemes

(1) This section has effect as respects—
(a) any approved scheme which is shown to the satisfaction of the Board to be established under irrevocable trusts; or
(b) any other approved scheme as respects which the Board, having regard to any special circumstances, direct that this section shall apply;

and any scheme which is for the time being within paragraph (a) or (b) above is in this Chapter referred to as an "exempt approved scheme".

(2) Exemption from income tax shall, on a claim being made in that behalf, be allowed in respect of income derived from investments or deposits if, or to such extent as the Board are satisfied that, it is income from investments or deposits held for the purposes of the scheme.

(3) Exemption from income tax shall, on a claim being made in that behalf, be allowed in respect of underwriting commissions if, or to such extent as the Board are satisfied that, the underwriting commissions are applied for the purposes of the schemes and would, but for this subsection, be chargeable to tax under Case VI of Schedule D.

(4) Any sum paid by an employer by way of contribution under the scheme shall, for the purposes of Case I or II of Schedule D and of sections 75 and 76, be allowed to be deducted as an expense, or expense of management, incurred in the chargeable period in which the sum is paid [but no other sum shall for those purposes be allowed to be deducted as an expense, or expense of management, in respect of the making, or any provisions for the making, of any contributions under the scheme].

(5) The amount of an employer's contributions which may be deducted under subsection (4) above shall not exceed the amount contributed by him under the scheme in respect of employees in a trade or undertaking in respect of the profits of which the employer is assessable to tax (that is to say, to United Kingdom income tax or corporation tax).

(6) A sum not paid by way of ordinary annual contribution shall for the purposes of subsection (4) above be treated, as the Board may direct, either as an expense incurred in the chargeable period in which the sum is paid, or as an expense to be spread over such period of years as the Board think proper.

[(6A) Where any sum is paid to the trustees of the scheme in or towards the discharge of any liability of an employer under section 58B of the Social Security Pensions Act 1975 or section 144 of the Pension Schemes Act 1993 (deficiencies in the assets of a scheme) or under Article 68B of the Social Security Pensions (Northern Ireland) Order 1975 or section 140 of the Pension Schemes (Northern Ireland) Act 1993 (which contain corresponding provision for Northern Ireland), the payment of that sum—

(a) shall be treated for the purposes of this section as an employer's contribution under the scheme; and

(b) notwithstanding (where it is the case) that the employer's trade, profession, vocation or business is permanently discontinued before the making of the payment, shall be allowed, in accordance with subsection (4) above, to be deducted as such a contribution to the same extent as it would have been allowed but for the discontinuance and as if it had been made on the last day on which the trade, profession, vocation or business was carried on.]

(7) Any contribution paid under the scheme by an employee shall, in assessing tax under Schedule E, be allowed to be deducted as an expense incurred in the year of assessment in which the contribution is paid.

(8) [Subject to subsection (8A) below,] the amount allowed to be deducted by virtue of subsection (7) above in respect of contributions paid by an employee in a year of assessment (whether under a single scheme or under two or more schemes) shall not exceed 15 per cent, or such higher percentage as the Board may in a particular case prescribe, of his remuneration for that year.

[(8A) Where an employee's remuneration for a year of assessment includes remuneration in respect of more than one employment, the amount allowed to be deducted by virtue of subsection (7) above in respect of contributions paid by the employee in that year by virtue of any employment (whether under a single scheme or under two or more schemes) shall not exceed 15 per cent, or such higher percentage as the Board may in a particular case prescribe, of his remuneration for the year in respect of that employment.]

[(8B) In arriving at an employee's remuneration for a year of assessment for the purposes of subsection (8) or (8A) above, any excess of what would be his remuneration (apart from this subsection) over the permitted maximum for that year shall be disregarded.

(8C) In subsection (8B) above "permitted maximum", in relation to a year of assessment, means the figure found for that year by virtue of subsections (8D) and (8E) below.

(8D) For the year 1989–90 the figure is £60,000.

(8E) For any subsequent year of assessment the figure is the figure found for that year, for the purposes of section 590C, by virtue of section 590C(4) [to (5A)].]

(9) Relief shall not be given under section 266 or 273 in respect of any payment in respect of which an allowance can be made under subsection (7) above.

(10) Subsection (2) of section 468 and subsection (3) of section 469 shall not apply to any authorised unit trust which is also an exempt approved scheme if the employer

is not a contributor to the exempt approved scheme and that the scheme provides benefits additional to those provided by another exempt approved scheme to which he is a contributor.

(11) Nothing in this section shall be construed as affording relief in respect of any sums to be brought into account under section 438.

(12) This section has effect only as respects income arising or contributions paid at a time when the scheme is an exempt approved scheme.

NOTES

Derivation

This section, as originally enacted, derived from the Finance Act 1970, s 21(1)–(9), the Finance Act 1971, s 21(5), and the Finance (No 2) Act 1987, Sch 3, para 4, 5.

Amendment

Sub-s (4): words from "but no other sum" to "contributions under the scheme" in square brackets inserted, in relation to any accounting period or year of assessment ending with a day after 5 April 1993, by the Finance Act 1993, s 112(1), (2).

Sub-s (6A): inserted, in relation to any payment made on or after 27 July 1993, by the Finance Act 1993, 112(6).

Sub-s (8): words "Subject to subsection (8A) below" in square brackets inserted, in relation to the year 1989–90 and subsequent years of assessment, by the Finance Act 1989, s 75, Sch 6, paras 5(2), 18(4).

Sub-s (8A): inserted, in relation to the year 1989–90 and subsequent years of assessment by the Finance Act 1989, s 75, Sch 6, para 5(3), 18(4).

Sub-ss (8B)–(8E): inserted, in relation to the year 1989–90 and subsequent years of assessment, by the Finance Act 1989, s 75, Sch 6, paras 5(4), 18(4), except as regards a person's remuneration in respect of an office or employment in such circumstances as the Board may by regulations provide.

Sub-s (8E): words "to (5A)" in square brackets substituted, in relation to the year 1994–95 and subsequent years of assessment, by the Finance Act 1993, s 107(6), (8).

See Further

See further, in relation to judicial pensions: the Judicial Pensions and Retirement Act 1993, s 18.

593 Relief by way of deductions from contributions

(1) Relief under section 592(7) shall be given in accordance with subsections (2) and (3) below in such cases and subject to such conditions as the Board may prescribe by regulations under section 612(3) in respect of schemes—

(a) to which employees, but not their employers, are contributors; and

(b) which provide benefits additional to benefits provided by schemes to which their employers are contributors.

(2) An employee who is entitled to relief under section 592(7) in respect of a contribution may deduct from the contribution when he pays it, and may retain, an amount equal to income tax at the basic rate on the contribution.

(3) The administrator of the scheme—

(a) shall accept the amount paid after the deduction in discharge of the employee's liability to the same extent as if the deduction had not been made; and

(b) may recover an amount equal to the deduction from the Board.

(4) Regulations under subsection (3) of section 612 may, without prejudice to the generality of that subsection—

(a) provide for the manner in which claims for the recovery of a sum under subsection (3)(b) above may be made;

(b) provide for the giving of such information, in such form, as may be prescribed by or under the regulations;

(c) provide for the inspection by persons authorised by the Board of books, documents and other records.

NOTES

Derivation

This section derived from the Finance Act 1970, Sch 5, Part II, para 6A, and the Finance (No 2) Act 1987, Sch 3, para 12.

See Further

See further, in relation to judicial pensions: the Judicial Pensions and Retirement Act 1993, s 18.

594 Exempt statutory schemes

(1) Any contribution paid by the officer or employee under a [relevant] statutory scheme established under a public general Act shall, in assessing tax under Schedule E, be allowed, to be deducted as an expense incurred in the year of assessment in which the contribution is paid; and relief shall not be given under section 266 or 273 in respect of any contribution allowable as a deduction under this section.

(2) [Subject to subsection (3) below,] the amount allowed to be deducted by virtue of subsection (1) above in respect of contributions paid by a person in a year of assessment (whether under a single scheme or under two or more schemes) shall not exceed 15 per cent, or such higher percentage as the Board may in a particular case prescribe, of his remuneration for that year.

[(3) Where a person's remuneration for a year of assessment includes remuneration in respect of more than one office or employment, the amount allowed to be deducted by virtue of subsection (1) above in respect of contributions paid by the person in that year by virtue of any office or employment (whether under a single scheme or under two or more schemes) shall not exceed 15 per cent, or such higher percentage as the Board may in a particular case prescribe, of his remuneration for the year in respect of that office or employment.]

[(4) In arriving at a person's remuneration for a year of assessment for the purposes of subsection (2) or (3) above, any excess of what would be his remuneration (apart from this subsection) over the permitted maximum for that year shall be disregarded.

(5) In subsection (4) above "permitted maximum", in relation to a year of assessment, means the figure found for that year by virtue of subsections (6) and (7) below.

(6) For the year 1989–90 the figure is £60,000.

(7) For any subsequent year of assessment the figure is the figure found for that year, for the purposes of section 590C, by virtue of section 590C(4) [to (5A)].]

NOTES

Derivation

This section, as originally enacted, derived from the Finance Act 1970, s 22, the Finance Act 1972, s 74(3), and the Finance (No 2) Act 1987, Sch 3, para 6.

Amendment

Sub-s (1): word "relevant" in square brackets inserted, with effect from 14 March 1989, by the Finance Act 1989, s 75, Sch 6, paras 6(2), 18(1).

Sub-s (2): words "Subject to subsection (3) below," in square brackets inserted, in relation to the year 1989–90 and subsequent years of assessment, by the Finance Act 1989, s 75, Sch 6, paras 6(3), 18(4).

Sub-s (3): inserted, in relation to the year 1989–90 and subsequent years of assessment, by the Finance Act 1989, s 75, Sch 6, paras 6(4), 18(4).

Sub-ss (4)–(7): inserted, in relation to the year 1989–90 and subsequent years of assessment, by the Finance Act 1989, s 75, Sch 6, paras 6(5), 18(4), except as regards a person's remuneration in respect of an office or employment in such circumstances as the Board may by regulations provide.

Sub-s (7): words "to (5A)" in square brackets substituted, in relation to the year 1994–95 and subsequent years of assessment, by the Finance Act 1993, s 107(6), (8).

See Further

See further, in relation to judicial pensions: the Judicial Pensions and Retirement Act 1993, s 18.

Charge to tax in certain cases

595 Charge to tax in respect of certain sums paid by employer etc

(1) Subject to the provisions of this Chapter, where, pursuant to a retirement benefits scheme, the employer in any year of assessment pays a sum with a view to the provision of any relevant benefits for any employee of that employer, then (whether or not the accrual of the benefits is dependent on any contingency)—

(a) the sum paid, if not otherwise chargeable to income tax as income of the employee, shall be deemed for all purposes of the Income Tax Acts to be income of that employee for that year of assessment and assessable to tax under Schedule E; and

(b) where the payment is made under such an insurance or contract as is mentioned in section 266, relief, if not otherwise allowable, shall be given to that employee under that section in respect of the payment to the extent, if any, to which such relief would have been allowable to him if the payment had been made by him and the insurance or contract under which the payment is made had been made with him.

(2), (3) . . .

(4) Where the employer pays any sum as mentioned in subsection (1) above in relation to more than one employee, the sum so paid shall, for the purpose of that subsection, be apportioned among those employees by reference to the separate sums which would have had to be paid to secure the separate benefits to be provided for them respectively, and the part of the sum apportioned to each of them shall be deemed for that purpose to have been paid separately in relation to that one of them.

(5) Any reference in this section to the provisions for an employee of relevant benefits includes a reference to the provision of benefits payable to that employee's

wife [or husband] or widow [or widower or], children, dependants or personal representatives.

NOTES

Derivation

This section derived from the Finance Act 1970, s 23(1)–(5).

Amendment

Sub-ss (2), (3): repealed, in relation to the year 1988–89 and subsequent years of assessment, by the Finance Act 1989, ss 75, 187, Sch 6, paras 7, 18(5), Sch 17, Part IV.

Sub-s (5): words "or husband" and "or widower or" in square brackets inserted by the Finance Act 1999, s 79, Sch 10, para 4.

Date in force: these amendments came into force on 27 July 1999 in the absence of any specific commencement provision.

See Further

See further, in relation to judicial pensions: the Judicial Pensions and Retirement Act 1993, s 18.

596 Exceptions from section 595

(1) [Section 595(1) shall not] apply where the retirement benefits scheme in question is—

- (a) an approved scheme, or
- (b) a [relevant] statutory scheme, or
- (c) a scheme set up by a government outside the United Kingdom for the benefit, or primarily for the benefit of, its employees.

(2) [Section 595(1) shall not] apply for any year of assessment—

- (a) where the employee performs the duties of his employment in such circumstances that no tax is chargeable under Case I or II of Schedule E in respect of the emoluments of his employment (or would be so chargeable were there such emoluments), or
- (b) where the emoluments from the employment are foreign emoluments within the meaning of section 192 and the Board are satisfied, on a claim made by the employee, that the retirement benefits scheme in question corresponds to such a scheme as is mentioned in paragraph (a), (b) or (c) of subsection (1) above.

(3) Where, in respect of the provision for an employee of any relevant benefits—

- (a) a sum has been deemed to be income of his by virtue . . . of subsection (1) . . . of section 595, and
- (b) subsequently, the employee proves to the satisfaction of the Board that—
  - (i) no payment in respect of, or in substitution for, the benefits has been made, and
  - (ii) some event has occurred by reason of which no such payment will be made,

  and makes application for relief under this subsection within six years from the time when that event occurred,

the Board shall give relief in respect of tax on that sum by repayment or otherwise as may be appropriate; and if the employee satisfies the Board as mentioned above in relation to some particular part, but not the whole, of the benefits, the Board may give such relief as may seem to them just and reasonable.

[(4) Relief shall not be given under subsection (3) above in respect of tax on any sum if—

(a) the reason for there having been no payment in respect of, or in substitution for, the benefits, or part of the benefits, in question, or

(b) the event by reason of which there will be no such payment,

is a reduction or cancellation, as a consequence of any pension sharing order or provision, of the employee's rights in respect of the benefits.]

NOTES

Derivation

This section derived from the Finance Act 1970, s 24, and the Finance Act 1974, s 21(7).

Amendment

Sub-s (1): words "Section 595(1) shall not" in square brackets substituted, with effect for the year 1988–89 and subsequent years of assessment, by the Finance Act 1989, s 75, Sch 6, paras 8(2), 18(5).

Sub-s (1): in para (b) word "relevant" in square brackets inserted, with effect from 14 March 1989, by the Finance Act 1989, s 75, Sch 6, paras 8(2), 18(1).

Sub-s (2): words "Section 595(1) shall not" in square brackets substituted, with effect for the year 1988–89 and subsequent years of assessment, by the Finance Act 1989, s 75, Sch 6, paras 8(2), 18(5).

Sub-s (3): in para (a) words omitted repealed, except in a case where a sum has been deemed to be income of a person by virtue of s 595(2) of this Act before 6 April 1988, by the Finance Act 1989, ss 75, 187, Sch 6, paras 8(4), 18(6), Sch 17, Part IV.

Sub-s (4): inserted by the Finance Act 1999, s 79, Sch 10, para 5.

Date in force: this amendment came into force on 27 July 1999 in the absence of any specific commencement provision.

See Further

See further, in relation to judicial pensions: the Judicial Pensions and Retirement Act 1993, s 18.

[596A Charge to tax: benefits under non-approved schemes]

[(1) Where in any year of assessment a person receives a benefit provided under a retirement benefits scheme which is not of a description mentioned in section 596(1)(a), (b) or (c), tax shall be charged in accordance with the provisions of this section.

(2) Where the benefit is received by an individual, he shall be charged to tax under Schedule E for that year.

(3) Where the benefit is received by a person other than an individual, the administrator of the scheme shall be charged to tax under Case VI of Schedule D for that year.

(4) [Subject to subsection (9) below] the amount to be charged to tax is—

(a) in the case of a cash benefit, the amount received, and

[(b) in the case of a non-cash benefit, whichever is the greater of—

(i) the amount which would be chargeable to tax under section 19(1) if the benefit were taxable as an emolument of the employment under Case I of Schedule E, or

(ii) the cash equivalent of the benefit determined in accordance with section 596B.]

(5) In the case of the charge under Case VI of Schedule D, the rate of tax is 40 per cent or such other rate (whether higher or lower) as may for the time being be specified by the Treasury by order.

[(6) Tax shall not be charged under this section in the case of—

(a) any pension or annuity which is chargeable to tax under Schedule E by virtue of section 19(1); or

(b) any pension or other benefit chargeable to tax under section 58.]

(7) But where the amount chargeable to tax [as mentioned in subsection (6)(a) above] is less than the amount which would be chargeable to tax under this section—

(a) [subsection (6)(a) above] shall not apply, and

(b) the amount chargeable to tax under this section shall be reduced by the amount chargeable to tax by virtue of [section 19(1)].

[(8) Subject to subsection (9) below, tax shall not be charged under this section (or section 19(1) or 14(8) in the case of a lump sum where—

(a) the employer has paid any sum or sums with a view to the provision of any relevant benefits under a retirement benefits scheme;

(b) an employee has been assessed to tax in respect of the sum or sums by virtue of section 595(1); and

(c) the lump sum is provided under the scheme to the employee, [an ex-spouse of the employee,] any person falling within section 595(5) in relation to the employee or any other individual designated by the employee.

(9) Where any of the income or gains accruing to the scheme under which the lump sum is provided is not brought into charge to tax, tax shall be charged under this section on the amount of the lump sum received less any deduction applicable under subsection (10) or (11) below.

(10) Subject to subsection (11) below, the deduction applicable is the aggregate of—

(a) any sum or sums in respect of which the employee has been assessed as mentioned in subsection (8)(b) above, and

(b) any sum or sums paid by the employee,

which in either case were paid by way of contribution to the provision of the lump sum.

(11) Where—

(a) the lump sum is provided under the scheme on the disposal of a part of any asset or the surrender of any part of or share in any rights in any asset, and

(b) the employee, any person falling within section 595(5) in relation to the employee or any person connected with the employee has any right to receive or any expectation of receiving a further lump sum (or further lump sums) under the scheme on a further disposal of any part of the asset or a further surrender of any part of or share in any rights in the asset,

the deduction applicable shall be determined in accordance with the formula in subsection (12) below.

(12) The formula is—

$$D = S \times (A/B)$$

(13) For the purposes of the formula in subsection (12) above—

D is the deduction applicable;

S is the aggregate amount of any or sums of a description mentioned in paragraphs (a) and (b) of subsection (10) above;

A is the amount of the lump sum received in relation to which the deduction applicable falls to be determined;

B is the market value of the asset in relation to which the disposal or surrender occurred, on the assumption that the valuation is made immediately before the disposal or surrender.

(14) An individual may not claim that a deduction is applicable in relation to a lump sum more than once.

(15) For the purposes of subsections (8) and (9) above, it shall be assumed unless the contrary it shown—

(a) that no sums have been paid, and the employee has not been assessed in respect of any sums paid, with a view to the provision of relevant benefits;
(b) that the income or gains accruing to a scheme under which the benefit is provided are not brought into charge to tax; and
(c) that no deduction is applicable under subsection (10) or (11) above.

(16) Section 839 shall apply for the purposes of subsection (11) above.

(17) In subsection (13) above "market value" shall be construed in accordance with section 272 of the 1992 Act.]]

NOTES

Amendment

Inserted, in relation to payments made and benefits provided on or after 27 July 1989, by the Finance Act 1989, s 75, Sch 6, paras 9, 18(7).

Sub-s (4): words "Subject to subsection (9) below" in square brackets inserted, in relation to retirement benefit schemes entered into on or after 1 December 1993 or before that day if the scheme is varied on or after that day with a view to the provision of the benefit, by the Finance Act 1994, s 108(2), (6).

Sub-s (4): para (b) substituted by the Finance Act 1998, s 93(1).

Date in force: this amendment applies to benefits received in the year 1998–99 and subsequent years of assessment: see the Finance Act 1998, s 93(4).

Sub-s (6): substituted, in relation to retirement benefit schemes entered into on or after 1 December 1993 or before that day if the scheme is varied on or after that day with a view to the provision of the benefit, by the Finance Act 1994, s 108(3), (6).

Sub-s (7): words "as mentioned ins subsection (6)(a) above" in square brackets substituted, in relation to retirement benefit schemes entered into on or after 1 December 1993 or before that day if the scheme is varied on or after that day with a view to the provision of the benefit, by the Finance Act 1994, s 108(4)(a), (6).

Sub-s (7): in para (a) words "subsection (6)(a) above" in square brackets substituted, in relation to retirement benefit schemes entered into on or after 1 December 1993 or before that day if the scheme is varied on or after that day with a view to the provision of the benefit, by the Finance Act 1994, s 108(4)(b), (6).

Sub-s (7): in para (b) words "section 19(1)" in square brackets substituted, in relation to retirement benefit schemes entered into on or after 1 December 1993 or before that day if the scheme is varied on or after that day with a view to the provision of the benefit, by the Finance Act 1994, s 108(4)(c), (6).

Sub-ss (8)–(17): substituted, for sub-ss (8), (9) as originally enacted, in relation to retirement benefit schemes entered into on or after 1 December 1993 or before that day if the scheme is varied on or after that day with a view to the provision of the benefit, by the Finance Act 1994, s 108(5), (6).

Sub-s (8): in para (c) words "an ex-spouse of the employee," in square brackets inserted by the Finance Act 1999, s 79, Sch 10, para 6.

Date in force: this amendment applies to any lump sum provided on or after a day to be appointed by the Treasury: see the Finance Act 1999, s 79, Sch 10, para 18(1), (2), (6).

See Further

See further, in relation to judicial pensions: the Judicial Pensions and Retirement Act 1993, s 18.

[596B Section 596A: supplementary provisions]

[(1) For the purposes of section 596A the cash equivalent of a benefit in kind is—

(a) in the case of a benefit other than living accommodation, the amount which would be the cash equivalent of the benefit under Chapter II or Part V if it were chargeable under the appropriate provision of that Chapter (treating any sum made good by the recipient as made good by the employee), and

(b) in the case of living accommodation, an amount equal to the value of the accommodation to the recipient determined in accordance with the following provisions of this section less so much of any sum made good by him to those at whose cost the accommodation is provided as is properly attributable to the provision of the accommodation.

(2) Where the cost of providing the accommodation does not exceed £75,000, the value of the accommodation to the recipient in any period is the rent which would have been payable for the period if the premises had been let to him at an annual rent equal to their annual value as ascertained under section 837.

(3) But for a period in which those at whose cost the accommodation is provided pay rent at an annual rate greater than the annual value as so ascertained, the value of the accommodation to the recipient is an amount equal to the rent payable by them for the period.

(4) Where the cost of providing the accommodation does exceed £75,000, the value of the accommodation to the recipient shall be taken to be the aggregate of the value of the accommodation to him determined in accordance with subsections (2) and (3) above and the additional value of the accommodation to him determined in accordance with subsections (5) and (6) below.

(5) The additional value of the accommodation to the recipient in any period is the rent which would have been payable for that period if the premises had been let to him at an annual rent equal to the appropriate percentage of the amount by which the costs of providing the accommodation exceeds £75,000.

(6) Where throughout the period of six years ending with the date when the recipient first occupied the property any estate or interest in the property was held by a relevant person (whether or not it was the same estate, interest or person throughout), the additional value shall be calculated as if in subsection (7) below—

(a) the amount referred to in paragraph (a) were the market value of that property as at that date, and

(b) the amount referred to in paragraph (b) did not include expenditure on improvements made before that date.

(7) For the purposes of this section, the cost of providing any living accommodation shall be taken to be the aggregate of—

(a) the amount of any expenditure incurred in acquiring the estate or interest in the property held by a relevant person, and

(b) the amount of any expenditure incurred by a relevant person before the year of assessment in question on improvements to the property.

(8) The aggregate amount mentioned in subsection (7) above shall be reduced by the amount of any payment made by the recipient to a relevant person, so far as that amount represents a reimbursement of any such expenditure as is mentioned in paragraph (a) or (b) of that subsection or represents consideration for the grant to the recipient of a tenancy of the property.

(9) For the purposes of this section, any of the following persons is a relevant person—

(a) the person providing the accommodation;

[(b) the employer or former employer; or

(c) any person, other than the recipient, who is connected with a person falling within paragraph (a) or (b) above.]

(10) In this section—

"the appropriate percentage" means the rate applicable for the purposes of section 160 as at the beginning of the year of assessment in question;

"market value", in relation to any property, means the price which that property might reasonably be expected to fetch on a sale in the open market with vacant possession, no reduction being made, in estimating the market value, on account of any option in respect of the property held by the recipient, or a person connected with him, or by any of the persons mentioned in subsection (9) above;

"property", in relation to any living accommodation, means the property consisting of that living accommodation;

"tenancy" includes a sub-tenancy;

and section 839 shall apply for the purposes of this section.]

NOTES

Amendment

Inserted, in relation to payments made and benefits provided on or after 27 July 1989, by the Finance Act 1989, s 75, Sch 6, paras 9, 18(7).

Sub-s (9): paras (b), (c) substituted, for para (b) as originally enacted, by the Finance Act 1998, s 93(2).

Date in force: this amendment applies to benefits received in the year 1998–99 and subsequent years of assessment: see the Finance Act 1998, s 93(4).

See Further

See further, in relation to judicial pensions: the Judicial Pensions and Retirement Act 1993, s 18.

[596C Notional interest treated as paid if amount charged in respect of beneficial loan]

[(1) This section applies where a person is chargeable to tax under section 596A in any year of assessment on an amount which consists of or includes an amount representing the cash equivalent of the benefit of a loan determined (by virtue of section 596B(1)(a)) in accordance with Part II of Schedule 7.

(2) Where this section applies, the person chargeable is treated as having paid interest on the loan of the same amount as the cash equivalent so determined.

(3) The interest is treated as paid for all the purposes of the Tax Acts (other than those relating to the charge under section 596A) but not so as to make it—
 (a) income of the person making the loan, or
 (b) relevant loan interest to which section 369 applies (mortgage interest payable under deduction of tax).

(4) The interest is treated as accruing during and paid at the end of the year of assessment or, if different, the period in that year during which the loan is outstanding.]

NOTES

Amendment
Inserted by the Finance Act 1998, s 93(3).

Date in force: this amendment applies to benefits received in the year 1998–99 and subsequent years of assessment: see the Finance Act 1998, s 93(4).

597 Charge to tax: pensions

(1) Subject to subsection (2) below, all pensions paid under any scheme which is approved or is being considered for approval under this Chapter shall be charged to tax under Schedule E, and section 203 shall apply accordingly.

(2) As respects any scheme which is approved or is being considered for approval under this Chapter, the Board may direct that, until such date as the Board may specify, pensions under the scheme shall be charged to tax as annual payments under Case III of Schedule D, and tax shall be deductible under sections 348 and 349 accordingly.

[(3) Without prejudice to subsection (1) above, where funds held for the purposes of any scheme which is approved or is being considered for approval under this Chapter are used to acquire an annuity—
 (a) the annuity shall be charged to tax under Schedule E and section 203 shall apply accordingly;
 (b) the annuity shall not be charged to tax under Case III of Schedule D.]

NOTES

Derivation
This section derived from the Finance Act 1970, Sch 5, Part II, para 1.

Amendment
Sub-s (3): inserted, in relation to payments made under annuities on or after 3 May 1994, by the Finance Act 1994, s 110.

See Further

See further, in relation to judicial pensions: the Judicial Pensions and Retirement Act 1993, s 18.

598 Charge to tax: repayment of employee's contributions

(1) Subject to the provisions of this section, tax shall be charged under this section on any repayment to an employee during this lifetime of any contributions (including interest on contributions, if any) if the payment is made under—

(a) a scheme which is or has at any time been an exempt approved scheme, or

(b) a [relevant] statutory scheme established under a public general Act.

(2) Where any payment is chargeable to tax under this section, the administrator of the scheme shall be charged to income tax under Case VI of Schedule D and, subject to subsection (3) below, the rate of tax shall be 10 per cent.

(3) The Treasury may by order from time to time increase or decrease the rate of tax under subsection (2) above.

(4) The tax shall be charged on the amount paid or, if the rules permit the administrator to deduct the tax before payment, on the amount before deduction of tax, and the amount so charged to tax shall not be treated as income for any other purpose of the Tax Acts.

(5) Subsection (1)(a) above shall not apply in relation to a contribution made after the scheme ceases to be an exempt approved scheme (unless it again becomes an exempt approved scheme).

(6) This section shall not apply where the employee's employment was carried on outside the United Kingdom.

(7) In relation to a statutory scheme, "employee" in this section includes any officer.

NOTES

Derivation

This section derived from the Finance Act 1970, Sch 5, Part II, paras 2, 3, the Finance Act 1971, Sch 3, para 7, and the Finance (No 2) Act 1987, Sch 3 para 9.

Amendment

Sub-s (1): in para (b) word "relevant" in square brackets inserted, with effect from 14 March 1989, by the Finance Act 1989, s 75, Sch 6, paras 10, 18(1).

See Further

See further, in relation to judicial pensions: the Judicial Pensions and Retirement Act 1993, s 18.

599 Charge to tax: commutation of entire pension in special circumstances

(1) [Subject to subsection (1A) below,] where a scheme to which this section applies contains a rule allowing, in special circumstances, a payment in commutation of an employee's entire pension, and any pension is commuted, whether wholly or not, under the rule, tax shall be charged on the amount by which the sum receivable exceeds—

(a) the largest sum which would have been receivable in commutation of any part of the pension if the scheme had secured that the aggregate value of the relevant benefits payable to an employee on or after retirement, excluding any pension which was not commutable, could not exceed three-eightieths of his final remuneration (disregarding any excess of that remuneration over the permitted maximum) for each year of service up to a maximum of 40; or

(b) the largest sum which would have been receivable in commutation of any part of the pension under any rule of the scheme authorising the commutation of part (but not the whole) of the pension, or which would have so receivable but for those special circumstances;

whichever gives the lesser amount chargeable to tax.

[(1A) Subsection (1) above shall have effect in relation to the commutation of the whole or any part of a pension the amount of which has been affected by the making of any pension sharing order or provision as if paragraph (a) and the words after paragraph (b) were omitted.

(1B) Where—

(a) a scheme to which this section applies contains a rule allowing, in special circumstances, a payment in commutation of the entire pension provided under the scheme for an ex-spouse, and

(b) any pension is commuted, whether wholly or not, under the rule,

tax shall be charged on the amount by which the sum receivable exceeds the largest sum which would have been receivable in commutation of any part of the pension under any rule of the scheme authorising the commutation of a part (but not the whole) of the pension.

(1C) A pension provided for an ex-spouse shall be disregarded when applying subsection (1) above in relation to the commutation of any pension provided for an employee.

(1D) A pension provided for an employee shall be disregarded when applying subsection (1B) above in relation to the commutation of any pension provided for an ex-spouse.

(1E) Subsections (4B) and (4C) of section 590 apply for the purposes of subsections (1C) and (1D) above as they apply for the purposes of that section.]

(2) This section applies to—

(a) a scheme which is or has at any time been an approved scheme, or

(b) a [relevant] statutory scheme established under a public general Act.

(3) Where any amount is chargeable to tax under this section the administrator of the scheme shall be charged to income tax under Case VI of Schedule D on that amount, and section 598(2), (3) and (4) shall apply as they apply to tax chargeable under that section.

(4) This section shall not apply where the employee's employment was carried on outside the United Kingdom.

(5) In relation to a statutory scheme, "employee" in this section includes any officer.

(6) In applying paragraph (a) or (b) of subsection (1) above [, or in applying subsection (1B) above]—

(a) the same considerations shall be taken into account, including the provisions of any other relevant scheme, as would have been taken into account by the Board in applying section 590; and
(b) where the scheme has ceased to be an approved scheme, account shall only be taken of the rules in force when the scheme was last an approved scheme.

(7) Where the pension has been secured by means of an annuity contract with an insurance company and the sum receivable is payable under that contract by the insurance company, the references to the administrator of the scheme in subsection (3) above and in section 598(2) and (4) as applied by that subsection are to be read as references to the insurance company.

[(8) In subsection (7) above "insurance company" has the meaning given by section 659B.]

(9) In relation to payments made under schemes approved or established before 17th March 1987 to employees who became members before that date, subsection (1)(a) above shall have effect with the omission of the words "(disregarding any excess of that remuneration over the permitted maximum)".

[(10) In subsection (1)(a) above "the permitted maximum" means, as regards a charge to tax arising under this section in a particular year of assessment, the figure found for that year by virtue of subsections (11) and (12) below.

(11) For the years 1988–89 and 1989–90 the figure is £60,000.

(12) For any subsequent year of assessment the figure is the figure found for that year, for the purposes of section 590C, by virtue of section 590C(4) [to (5A)].]

NOTES

Derivation

This section, as originally enacted, derived from the Finance Act 1970, Sch 5, Part II, paras 2, 3, the Finance act 1971, Sch 3, para 7, and the Finance (No 2) Act 1987, Sch 3, para 9.

Amendment

Sub-s (1): words "Subject to subsection (1A) below", in square brackets inserted by the Finance Act 1999, s 79, Sch 10, para 7(1).

Date in force: this amendment came into force on 27 July 1999 in the absence of any specific commencement provision.

Sub-ss (1A)–(1E): inserted by the Finance Act 1999, s 79, Sch 10, para 7(1).

Date in force: this amendment came into force on 27 July 1999 in the absence of any specific commencement provision.

Sub-s (2): in para (b) word "relevant" in square brackets inserted, with effect from 14 March 1989, by the Finance Act 1989, s 75, Sch 6, para 11(2), 18(1).

Sub-s (6): words ", or in applying subsection (1B) above" in square brackets inserted by the Finance Act 1999, s 79, Sch 10, para 7(2).

Date in force: this amendment came into force on 27 July 1999 in the absence of any specific commencement provision.

Sub-s (8): substituted, in relation to tax charged under this section on or after 1 May 1995, by the Finance Act 1995, ss 59(3), 60(2).

Sub-ss (10)–(12): inserted, in cases where the charge to tax under this section arises on or after 14 March 1989, by the Finance Act 1989, s 75, Sch 6, paras 11(3), 18(8).

Sub-s (12): words "to (5A)" in square brackets substituted, in relation to the year 1994–95 and subsequent years of assessment, by the Finance Act 1993, s 107(6), (8).

See Further

See further, in relation to judicial pensions: the Judicial Pensions and Retirement Act 1993, s 18.

[599A Charge to tax: payments out of surplus funds]

[(1) This subsection applies to any payment which is made to or for the benefit of an employee or to his personal representatives out of funds which are or have been held for the purposes of—

(a) a scheme which is or has at any time been an exempt approved scheme, or
(b) a relevant statutory scheme established under a public general Act,

and which is made in pursuance of duty to return surplus funds.

(2) On the making of a payment to which subsection (1) above applies, the administrator of the scheme shall be charged to income tax under Case VI of Schedule D at the relevant rate on such amount as, after deduction of tax at that rate, would equal the amount of the payment.

(3) Subject to subsection (4) below, the relevant rate shall be 35 per cent.

(4) The Treasury may by order from time to time increase or decrease the relevant rate.

(5) Where a payment made to or for the benefit of an employee is one to which subsection (1) applies, it shall be treated in computing the total income of the employee for the year in which it is made as income for that year which is—

(a) received by him after deduction of income tax at the basic rate from a corresponding gross amount, and
(b) chargeable to income tax under Case VI of Schedule D.

(6) But, . . . no repayment of income tax shall be made to, the employee.

(7) . . .

(8) Subsection (5) above applies whether or not the employee is the recipient of the payment.

(9) Any payment chargeable to tax under this section shall not be chargeable to tax under section 598, 599 or 600 or under the Regulations mentioned in paragraph 8 of schedule 3 to the Finance Act 1971.

(10) In this section—

"employee", in relation to a relevant statutory scheme, includes any officer;

references to any payment include references to any transfer of assets or other transfer of money's worth.]

NOTES

Amendment

Inserted, in relation to payments made on or after 27 July 1989, by the Finance Act 1989, s 75, Sch 6, paras 12, 18(9).

Sub-s (6): words omitted repealed, in relation to the year 1996–97 and subsequent years of assessment, by the Finance Act 1996, ss 121(8), 122(7)(b), 205, Sch 41, Part V(6).

Sub-s (7): repealed, in relation to the year 1996–97 and subsequent years of assessment, by the Finance Act 1996, ss 121(8), 122(7)(c), 205, Sch 41, Part V(6).

See Further

See further, in relation to judicial pensions: the Judicial Pensions and Retirement Act 1993, s 18.

Subordinate Legislation

Income Tax (Charge to Tax) (Payments out of Surplus Funds) (Relevant Rate) Order 2000, SI 2000/600 (made under sub-s (4)).

600 Charge to tax: unauthorised payments to or for employees

(1) This section applies to any payment to or for the benefit of an employee [or an ex-spouse], otherwise than in course of payment of a pension, being a payment made out of funds which are . . . held for the purposes of a scheme which is . . . approved for the purposes of—

- (a) this Chapter;
- (b) Chapter II of Part II of the Finance Act 1970; or
- (c) section 208 or Chapter II of Part IX of the 1970 Act.

(2) If the payment [is not expressly authorised by the rules of the scheme or by virtue of paragraph 33 of Schedule 6 to the Finance Act 1989] *the employee (whether or not he is the recipient of the payment) shall* [the employee or, as the case may be, the ex-spouse shall (whether or not he is the recipient of the payment)] be chargeable to tax on the amount of the payment under Schedule E for the year of assessment in which the payment is made.

(3) Any payment chargeable to tax under this section shall not be chargeable to tax under section 598 or 599 or under the Regulations mentioned in paragraph 8 of Schedule 3 to the Finance Act 1971.

(4) References in this section to any payment include references to any transfer of assets or other transfer of money's worth.

NOTES

Derivation

This section derived from the Finance Act 1971, Sch 3, para 9.

Amendment

Sub-s (1): words "or an ex-spouse" in square brackets inserted by the Finance Act 1999, s 79, Sch 10, para 8(1).

Date in force: this amendment applies to any payment made on or after a day to be appointed by the Treasury: see the Finance Act 1999, s 79, Sch 10, para 18(1), (2), (7).

Sub-s (1): first words omitted repealed, in relation to payments made on or after 27 July 1989, by the Finance Act 1989, ss 75, 187 Sch 6, paras 13(2), 18(9), Sch 17, Pt IV.

Sub-s (1): second words omitted repealed, in relation to payments made on or after 27 July 1989, by the Finance Act 1989, ss 75, 187, Sch 6, paras 13(2), 18(9), Sch 17, Pt IV.

Sub-s (2): words from "is not expressly" to "Finance Act 1989" in square brackets substituted, in relation to payments made on or after 27 July 1989, by the Finance Act 1989, s 75, Sch 6, paras 13, 18(9).

Sub-s (2): words from "the employee" to "shall" in italics repealed and subsequent words in square brackets substituted by the Finance Act 1999, s 79, Sch 10, para 8(2).

Date in force: this amendment applies to any payment made on or after a day to be appointed by the Treasury: see the Finance Act 1999, s 79, Sch 10, para 18(1), (2), (7).

See Further

See further, in relation to judicial pensions: the Judicial Pensions and Retirement Act 1993, s 18.

601 Charge to tax: payments to employers

(1) Subsection (2) belo w applies where a payment is made to an employer out of funds which are or have been held for the purposes of a scheme which is or has at any time been an exempt approved scheme and whether or not the payment is made in pursuance of Schedule 22.

(2) An amount equal to 40 per cent of the payment shall be recoverable by the Board from the employer.

(3) Subsection (2) above does not apply to any payment—
- (a) to the extent that, if this section had not been enacted, the employer would have been exempt, or entitled to claim exemption, from income tax or corporation tax in respect of the payment, or
- (b) made before the scheme became an exempt approved scheme; or
- (c) of any prescribed description; or
- (d) made in pursuance of the winding-up of the scheme where the winding-up commenced on or before 18th March 1986; or
- (e) made in pursuance of an application which—
  - (i) was made to the Board on or before that date and was not withdrawn before the making of the payment, and
  - (ii) sought the Board's assurance that the payment would not lead to a withdrawal of approval under section 19(3) of the Finance Act 1970;

(4) Subsection (2) above does not apply where the employer is a charity (within the meaning of section 506).

(5) Where any payment is made or becomes due to an employer out of funds which are or have been held for the purposes of a scheme which is or has at any time been an exempt approved scheme then—
- (a) if the scheme relates to a trade, profession or vocation carried on by the employer, the payment shall be treated for the purposes of the Tax Acts as a receipt of that trade, profession or vocation receivable when the payment falls due or on the last day on which the trade, profession or vocation is carried on by the employer, whichever is the earlier;
- (b) if the scheme does not relate to such a trade, profession or vocation, the employer shall be charged to tax on the amount of the payment under Case VI of Schedule D.

This subsection shall not apply to a payment which fell due before the scheme became an exempt approved scheme or to a payment to which subsection (2) above applies or would apply but for subsection (3)(a) or (4) above.

(6) In this section—
- (a) references to any payment include references to any transfer of assets or other transfer of money's worth; and
- (b) "prescribed" means prescribed by regulations made by the Treasury.

NOTES

Derivation

This section derived from the Finance Act 1970, Sch 5, Part II, para 4, the Finance Act 1971, Sch 3, para 12(5), and the Finance Act 1986, Sch 12, para 1.

See Further

See further, in relation to judicial pensions: the Judicial Pensions and Retirement Act 1993, s 18.

602 Regulations relating to pension fund surpluses

(1) In relation to an amount recoverable as mentioned in section 601(2), the Treasury may by regulations make any of the provisions mentioned in subsection (2) below; and for this purpose the amount shall be treated as if it were—

- (a) an amount of income tax chargeable on the employer under Case VI of Schedule D for the year of assessment in which the payment is made; or
- (b) where the employer is a company, an amount of corporation tax chargeable on the company for the accounting period in which the payment is made.

(2) The provisions are—

- (a) provision requiring the administrator of the scheme or the employer (or both) to furnish to the Board, in respect of the amount recoverable and of the payment concerned, information of a prescribed kind;
- (b) provision enabling the Board to serve a notice or notices requiring the administrator or employer (or both) to furnish to the Board, in respect of the amount and payment, particulars of a prescribed kind;
- (c) provision requiring the administrator to deduct out of the payment the amount recoverable and to account to the Board for it;
- (d) provision as to circumstances in which the employer may be assessed in respect of the amount recoverable;
- (e) provision that, in a case where the employer has been assessed in respect of an amount recoverable but has not paid it (or part of it) within a prescribed period, the administrator may be assessed and charged (in the employer's name) in respect of the amount (or part unpaid);
- (f) provisions that, in a case where the amount recoverable (or part of it) has been recovered from the administrator by virtue of an assessment in the employer's name, the administrator is entitled to recover from the employer a sum equal to the amount (or part);
- (g) provision enabling the employer or administrator (as the case may be) to appeal against an assessment made on him in respect of the amount recoverable;
- (h) provision as to when any sum in respect of the amount recoverable is payable to the Board by the administrator or employer and provision requiring interest to be paid on any sum so payable;
- (j) provision that an amount paid to the Board by the administrator shall be treated as paid on account of the employer's liability under section 601(2).

(3) For the purpose of giving effect to any provision mentioned in subsection (2)(c) to (j) above, regulations under this section may include provision applying (with or without modifications) provisions of the enactments relating to income tax and corporation tax.

(4) Subject to any provision of regulations under this section—

- (a) a payment to which section 601(2) applies shall not be treated as a profit or gain brought into charge to income tax or corporation tax and shall not be treated as part of the employer's income for any purpose of this Act; and

(b) the amount recoverable shall not be subject to any exemption or reduction (by way of relief, set-off or otherwise) or be available for set-off against other tax.

(5) If the employer is a company and a payment to which section 601(1) and (2) applies is made at a time not otherwise within an accounting period of the company, an accounting period of the company shall for the purpose of subsection (1)(b) above be treated as beginning immediately before the payment is made.

NOTES

Derivation

This section derived from the Finance Act 1986, Sch 12, para 2(1)(i), (2), (4)–(6).

See Further

See further, in relation to judicial pensions: the Judicial Pensions and Retirement Act 1993, s 18.

603 Reduction of surpluses

Schedule 22 (which provides for the reduction of certain pension fund surpluses) shall have effect.

NOTES

See Further

See further, in relation to judicial pensions: the Judicial Pensions and Retirement Act 1993, s 18.

Supplementary provisions

604 Application for approval of a scheme

(1) An application for the approval for the purposes of this Chapter of any retirement benefits scheme shall be made in writing by [the appropriate applicant] to the Board before the end of the first year of assessment for which approval is required, and shall be accompanied by—

(a) two copies of the instrument or other document constituting the scheme; and

(b) two copies of the rules of the scheme and, except where the application is being sought on the setting up of the scheme, two copies of the accounts of the scheme for the last year for which such accounts have been made up; and

(c) such other information and particulars (including copies of any actuarial report or advice given to the [appropriate applicant,] administrator or employer in connection with the setting up of the scheme) as the Board may consider relevant.

[(1A) In subsection (1) above "the appropriate applicant" means—

(a) in the case of a trust scheme, the trustee or trustees of the scheme; and

(b) the case of a non-trust scheme, the scheme sponsor or scheme sponsors;

and subsection (9) of section 611AA applies for the purposes of this subsection as it applies for the purposes of that section.]

(2) The form in which an application for approval is to be made, or in which any information is to be given, in pursuance of this section may be prescribed by the Board.

NOTES

Derivation

This section derived from the Finance Act 1970, Sch 5, Part II, paras 6–9, and the Finance (No 2) Act 1987, Sch 3, paras 11, 13–15.

Amendment

Sub-s (1): words "the appropriate applicant" in square brackets substituted by the Finance Act 1998, s 92, Sch 15, para 3(1)(a).

Date in force: this amendment has effect in relation to any application made on or after 31 July 1998: see the Finance Act 1998, Sch 15, para 3(3).

Sub-s (1): in para (c) words "appropriate applicant," in square brackets inserted by the Finance Act 1998, s 92, Sch 15, para 3(1)(b).

Date in force: this amendment has effect in relation to any application made on or after 31 July 1998: see the Finance Act 1998, Sch 15, para 3(3).

Sub-s (1A): inserted by the Finance Act 1998, s 92, Sch 15, para 3(2).

Date in force: this amendment has effect in relation to any application made on or after 31 July 1998: see the Finance Act 1998, Sch 15, para 3(3).

See Further

See further, in relation to judicial pensions: the Judicial Pensions and Retirement Act 1993, s 18.

605 Information

[(1A) The Board may by regulations make any of the following provisions—

- (a) provision requiring prescribed persons to furnish to the Board at prescribed times information relating to any of the matters mentioned in subsection (1B) below;
- (b) provision enabling the Board to serve a notice requiring prescribed persons to furnish to the Board, within a prescribed time, particulars relating to any of those matters;
- (c) provision enabling the Board to serve a notice requiring prescribed persons to produce to the Board, within a prescribed time, documents relating to any of those matters;
- (d) provision enabling the Board to serve a notice requiring prescribed persons to make available for inspection on behalf of the Board books, documents and other records, being books, documents and records which relate to any of those matters;
- (e) provision requiring prescribed persons to preserve for a prescribed time books, documents and other records, being books, documents and records which relate to any of those matters.

(1B) The matters referred to in subsection (1A) above are—

- [(a) a scheme which is or has been an approved scheme;]
- (b) a relevant statutory scheme;
- (c) an annuity contract by means of which benefits provided under an approved scheme or a relevant statutory scheme have been secured;
- (d) a retirement benefits scheme which is not an approved scheme but in relation to which an application for approval for the purposes of this Chapter has been made.

(1C) A person who fails to comply with regulations made under subsection (1A)(e) above shall be liable to a penalty not exceeding £3,000.

(1D) Regulations under subsection (1A) above may make different provision for different descriptions of case.

(1E) In subsection (1A) above "prescribed" means prescribed by regulations made under that subsection.]

(1), (2) . . .

(3) It shall be the duty of every employer—
- (a) if there subsists in relation to any of his employees a retirement benefits scheme to which he contributes and which is neither an approved scheme nor a [relevant] statutory scheme, to deliver particulars of that scheme to the Board within three months beginning with the date on which the scheme first comes into operation in relation to any of his employees, and
- (b) when required to do so by notice given by the Board, to furnish within the time limited by the notice such particulars as the Board may require with regard to—
  - (i) any retirement benefits scheme relating to the employer which is neither an approved scheme nor a [relevant] statutory scheme; and
  - (ii) the employees of his to whom any such scheme relates.

(4) It shall be the duty of the administrator of a retirement benefits scheme which is neither an approved scheme nor a [relevant] statutory scheme, when required to do so by notice given by the Board, to furnish within the time limited by the notice such particulars as the Board may require with regard to the scheme.

NOTES

Derivation

This section derived from the Finance Act 1970, Sch 5, Part II, paras 6–9, and the Finance (No 2) Act 1987, Sch 3, paras 11, 13–15.

Amendment

Sub-ss (1A)–(1E): inserted by the Finance Act 1994, s 105(2).

Sub-s (1B): para (a) substituted by the Finance Act 1998, s 92, Sch 15, para 4.

Date in force: 31 July 1998: (no specific commencement provision).

Sub-ss (1), (2): repealed by the Finance Act 1994, ss 105(3), (5), 258, Sch 26, Part V.

Sub-s (3): word "relevant" in square brackets, in both places it occurs inserted, with effect from 14 March 1989, by the Finance Act 1989, s 75, Sch 6, paras 14, 18(1).

Sub-s (4): word "relevant" in square brackets inserted, with effect from 14 March 1989, by the Finance Act 1989, s 75, Sch 6, paras 14, 18(1).

See Further

See further, in relation to judicial pensions: the Judicial Pensions and Retirement Act 1993, s 18.

[605A False statements, etc]

[(1) A person who fraudulently or negligently makes a false statement or false representation on making an application for the approval for the purposes of this Chapter of—

(a) a retirement benefits scheme, or
(b) an alteration in such a scheme,

shall be liable to a penalty not exceeding £3,000.

(2) In a case where—
(a) a person fraudulently or negligently makes a false statement or false representation, and
(b) in consequence that person, or any other person, obtains relief from or repayment of tax under this Chapter,

the person mentioned in paragraph (a) above shall be liable to a penalty not exceeding £3,000.]

NOTES

Amendment
Inserted, in relation to things done or omitted after 3 May 1994, by the Finance Act 1994, s 106.

[606 Default of administrator, etc]

[(1) This section applies in relation to a retirement benefits scheme if at any time—
(a) there is no administrator of the scheme, or
(b) the person who is, or all of the persons who are, the administrator of the scheme cannot be traced, or
(c) the person who is, or all of the persons who are, the administrator of the scheme is or are in default for the purposes of this section.

(2) If the scheme is a trust scheme, then—
(a) if subsection (1)(b) or (c) above applies and at the time in question the condition mentioned in subsection (3) below is fulfilled, the trustee or trustees shall at that time be responsible for the discharge of all duties imposed on the administrator under this Chapter (whenever arising) and liable for any tax due from the administrator in the administrator's capacity as such (whenever falling due);
(b) if subsection (1)(a) above applies, or subsection (1)(b) or (c) above applies and at the time n question the condition mentioned in subsection (3) below is not fulfilled, the employer shall at that time be so responsible and liable;

and paragraph (b) above shall apply to a person in his capacity as the employer even if he is also the administrator, or a trustee, of the scheme.

(3) The condition is that there is at least one trustee of the scheme who—
(a) can be traced,
(b) is resident in the United Kingdom, and
(c) is not in default for the purposes of this section.

(4) If the scheme is a non-trust scheme, then—
(a) if subsection (1)(b) or (c) above applies and at the time in question the condition mentioned in subsection (5) below is fulfilled, the scheme sponsor or scheme sponsors shall at that time be responsible for the discharge of all duties imposed on the administrator under this Chapter (whenever arising) and liable for any tax due from the administrator in the administrator's capacity as such (whenever falling due);

(b) if subsection (1)(a) above applies, or subsection (1)(b) or (c) above applies and at the time in question the condition mentioned in subsection (5) below is not fulfilled, the employer shall at that time be so responsible and liable;

and paragraph (b) above shall apply to a person in his capacity as the employer even if he is also the administrator of the scheme, or a scheme sponsor.

(5) The condition is that there is at least one scheme sponsor who—
(a) can be traced,
(b) is resident in the United Kingdom, and
(c) is not in default for the purposes of this section.

(6) Where at any time—
(a) paragraph (b) or (c) of subsection (1) above applies in relation to a scheme, and
(b) a person is by virtue of this section responsible for the discharge of any duties, or liable for any tax, in relation to the scheme,

then at that time the person or persons mentioned in paragraph (b) or (as the case may be) paragraph (c) or subsection (1) above shall not, by reason only of being the administrator of the scheme, be responsible for the discharge of those duties or liable for that tax.

(7) Where the scheme is a trust scheme and the employer is not a contributor to the scheme, subsection (2) above shall have effect as if—
(a) for "the employer", in the first place where those words occur, there were substituted "the scheme sponsor or scheme sponsors", and
(b) for "the employer", in the second place where those word occur, there were substituted "scheme sponsor".

(8) Where the scheme is a non-trust scheme and the employer is not a contributor to the scheme, subsection (4) above shall have effect as if paragraph (b) and the words after that paragraph were omitted.

(9) No liability incurred under this Chapter—
(a) by the administrator of a scheme, or
(b) by a person by virtue of this section,

shall be affected by the termination of a scheme or by its ceasing to be an approved scheme or to be an exempt approved scheme.

[(9A) Where by virtue of this section any person is the person, or one of the persons, responsible for the discharge of the duties of the administrator of a scheme, any power or duty by virtue of this Part to serve any notice on, or to do any other thing in relation to, the administrator may be exercised or performed, instead, by the service of that notice on that person or, as the case may be, by the doing of that other thing in relation to that person.]

(10) Where by virtue of this section a person becomes responsible for the discharge of any duties, or liable for any tax, the Board shall, as soon as is reasonably practicable, notify him of that fact; but any failure to give such notification shall not affect that person's being responsible or liable by virtue of this section.

(11) A person is in default for the purposes of this section if—
(a) he has failed to discharge any duty imposed on him under this Chapter, or
(b) he has failed to pay any tax due from him by virtue of this Chapter,
and (in either case) the Board consider the failure to be of a serious nature.

[(11A) In determining for the purposes of this section—
(a) whether all of the persons who are the administrator of a scheme are at any time in default in respect of an amount of tax chargeable by virtue of section 591C, or
(b) whether a trustee of a scheme is in default in respect of any amount of tax so chargeable,

the person who at that time are trustees of the scheme or hold appointments in relation to the scheme under section 611AA(4) to (6) shall be deemed not to include any person who by virtue of section 591D(4) is not liable for that tax.]

(12) References in this section to a trust scheme, a non-trust scheme, trustees and scheme sponsors shall be construed in accordance with section 611AA.

(13) References in this section to the employer include, where the employer is resident outside the United Kingdom, references to any branch or agent of the employer in the United Kingdom, and in this subsection "branch or grant" has the meaning given by section 118(1) of the Management Act.

(14) This section does not apply for the purposes of sections 602 and 603 and Schedule 22.]

NOTES

Derivation

This section as originally enacted derived from the Finance Act 1970, Sch 5, Part II, paras 6–9, and the Finance (No 2) Act 1987, Sch 3, paras 11, 13–15.

Amendment

Substituted, in relation to where the time in question falls on or after 3 May 1994, by the Finance Act 1994, s 104(1), (3).

Sub-s (9A): inserted by the Finance Act 1998, s 92, Sch 15, para 5(1).

Date in force: this amendment is deemed always to have had effect: see the Finance Act 1998, Sch 15, para 5(1).

Sub-s (11A): inserted by the Finance Act 1998, s 92, Sch 15, para 5(2).

Date in force: this amendment has effect for determinations made in relation to any time on or after 17 March 1998: see the Finance Act 1998, Sch 15, para 5(3).

See Further

See further, in relation to judicial pensions: the Judicial Pensions and Retirement Act 1993, s 18.

[606A Recourse to scheme members]

[(1) This section applies where—
(a) an approval of a retirement benefits scheme has ceased to have effect;
(b) a person ("the employer") has become liable by virtue of section 606 to any tax chargeable on the administrator of the scheme under section 591C;
(c) the employer has failed, either in whole or in part, to pay that tax; and
(d) a person falling within subsection (2) below ("the relevant member") was a member of the scheme at that time ("the relevant time") immediately before the date of the cessation of its approval.

(2) A person falls within this subsection in relation to any tax chargeable under section 591C if—

(a) at the relevant time or at any time before that time he was a controlling director of the employer; or

(b) he is a person by or in respect of whom any contributions were made by reference to which the condition in subsection (6A) of that section has been satisfied for the purpose of the charge to that tax.

(3) Subject to subsection (4) below, if in a case where this section applies—

(a) the employer has ceased to exist, or

(b) the Board notify the relevant member that they consider the failure of the employer to pay the unpaid tax to be of a serious nature,

the relevant member shall be treated as included in the persons on whom the unpaid tax was charged and shall be assessable accordingly.

(4) The amount of tax for which the relevant member shall be taken to be assessable by virtue of this section shall not exceed the amount determined by—

(a) taking the amount equal to 40 per cent of his share of the scheme; and

(b) subtracting from that amount his share of any tax charged under section 591C that has already been paid otherwise than by another person on whom it is treated as charged in accordance with this section.

(5) For the purposes of this section the relevant member's share of the scheme is the amount equal to so much of the value of the assets held for the purposes of the scheme at the relevant time (taking the value at that time) as, on a just and reasonable apportionment, would have fallen to be treated as the value at that time of the assets then held for the purposes of the provisions under the scheme of benefits to or in respect of the relevant member.

(6) For the purposes of this section the relevant member's share of an amount of tax already paid is such sum as bears the same proportion to the amount paid as is borne by his share of the scheme to the total value at the relevant time of the assets then held for the purposes of the scheme.

(7) The reference in subsection (5) above to the provision of benefits to or in respect of the relevant member includes a reference to the provision of a benefit to or in respect of a person connected with the relevant member.

(8) For the purposes of this section a person is a controlling director of a company if he is a director of the company and is within section 417(5)(b) in relation to the company.

(9) A notification given to any person for the purposes of subsection (3)(b) above may be included in any assessment on that person of the tax to which he becomes liable by virtue of the notification.

(10) An assessment to tax made by virtue of this section shall not be out of time if it is made within three years after the date on which the employer has failed to pay first became due from him.

(11) Subsections (1) to (3) of section 591D shall apply to the determination of the value at any time of an asset held for the purposes of a scheme as they apply for the purposes of section 591C(2).

(12) Subsections (7) and (8) of section 591D shall apply for the purposes of this section as they apply for the purposes of subsection (1) of section 591C and section 591C, respectively.

(13) Section 839 (connected persons) shall apply for the purposes of this section.]

NOTES

Amendment

Inserted by the Finance Act 1998, s 92, Sch 15, para 6(1).

Date in force: this amendment has effect in relation to any case in which the date of the cessation of the approval is on or after 17 March 1998: see the Finance Act 1998, Sch 15, para 6(2).

607 Pilots' benefit fund

(1) The Board may, if they think fit, and subject to such conditions as they think proper to attach to the approval, approve a pilots' benefit fund for the purposes of this Chapter as if it were a retirement benefits scheme and notwithstanding that it does not satisfy one or more of the conditions set out in section 590(2) and (3).

(2) If a fund is approved by virtue of this section—
- (a) sections 592, 597 to 600 and 604 to 606 shall have effect in relation to the fund with the modifications specified in subsection (3) below;
- (b) pensions paid out of the fund and any sums chargeable to tax in connection with the fund under section 600 shall be treated for the purposes of the Income Tax Acts as earned income; and
- (c) Chapter III of this Part shall have effect as if a member of the fund were the holder of a pensionable office or employment and his earnings as a pilot (estimated in accordance with the provisions of Case II of Schedule D) were remuneration from such an office or employment.

(3) The modifications referred to in subsection (2)(a) above are as follows—
- (a) in section 592, for the references in subsection (7) to an employee and Schedule E there shall be substituted respectively references to a member of the fund and Schedule D, and subsections (4) to (6), and in subsection (7) the words from "incurred" onwards, shall be omitted;
- (b) in sections 597 to 606 (except sections 601 to 603)—
  - (i) for references to an employee there shall be substituted references to a member or former member of the fund;
  - (ii) in section 599(1)(a) for the reference to a year of service there shall be substituted a reference to a year as a pilot licensed by a pilotage authority or authorised by a competent harbour authority;
  - (iii) [section 606(2)(b), (4)(b), (7), (8) and (13)] and so much of any other provision as applies to an employer shall be omitted; and
  - (iv) in section 600, for references to Schedule E there shall be substituted references to Case VI of Schedule D.

(4) In this section "pilots' benefit fund" means a fund established under section 15(1)(i) of the Pilotage Act 1983 or any scheme supplementing or replacing any such fund.

NOTES

Derivation

This section derived from the Finance Act 1980, s 35, the Pilotage Act 1983, Sch 3, and the Pilotage Act 1987, Sch 2, para 4.

Amendment

Sub-s (3): in para (b)(iii) words "section 606(2)(b), (4)(b), (7), (8), and (13)" in square brackets substituted, in relation to where the time in question falls on or after 3 May 1994, by the Finance Act 1994, s 104(2), (3).

See Further

See further, in relation to judicial pensions: the Judicial Pensions and Retirement Act 1993, s 18.

608 Superannuation funds approved before 6th April 1980

(1) This section applies to any fund which immediately before 6th April 1980 was an approved superannuation fund for the purposes of section 208 of the 1970 Act if—

(a) it has not been approved under this Chapter (or under Chapter II of Part II of the Finance Act 1970); and

(b) no sum has been paid to it by way of contribution since 5th April 1980.

(2) Subject to subsection (3) below, exemption from income tax shall, on a claim being made in that behalf, be allowed to a fund to which this section applies in respect of—

(a) income derived from investments or deposits of the fund;

(b) any underwriting commissions which apart from this subsection would be chargeable to tax under Case VI of Schedule D; and

(c) any profits or gains which (apart from this subsection) would be chargeable to tax under Case VI of Schedule D by virtue of section 56(1)(a) and (2);

if, or to such extent as the Board are satisfied that, the income, commissions, profits or gains are applied for the purposes of the fund.

(3) No claim under subsection (2) above shall be allowed unless the Board are satisfied that the terms on which benefits are payable from the fund have not been altered since 5th April 1980.

(4) An annuity paid out of a fund to which this section applies shall be charged to tax under Schedule E and section 203 shall apply accordingly.

NOTES

Derivation

This section derived from the Finance Act 1980, s 36(1), (4), (6).

See Further

See further, in relation to judicial pensions: the Judicial Pensions and Retirement Act 1993, s 18.

609 Schemes approved before 23rd July 1987

Schedule 23 to this Act, which makes provision with respect to retirement benefit schemes approved before 23rd July 1987, shall have effect.

NOTES

See Further

See further, in relation to judicial pensions: the Judicial Pensions and Retirement Act 1993, s 18.

610 Amendments of schemes

(1) This section applies to any amendment of a retirement benefits scheme proposed in connection with an application for the Board's approval for the purposes of this Chapter which is needed in order to ensure that approval is so given, or designed to

enhance the benefits under the scheme up to the limits suitable in a scheme for which approval is sought.

(2) A provision, however expressed, designed to preclude any amendment of a scheme which would have prejudiced its approval under section 208 or 222 of the 1970 Act shall not prevent any amendment to which this section applies.

(3) In the case of a scheme which contains no powers of amendment, the administrator of the scheme may, with the consent of all the members of the scheme, and of the employer (or of each of the employers), make any amendment to which this section applies.

NOTES

Derivation

This section derived from the Finance Act 1971, s 22(1)–(3).

See Further

See further, in relation to judicial pensions: the Judicial Pensions and Retirement Act 1993, s 18.

611 Definition of "retirement benefits scheme"

(1) In this Chapter "retirement benefits scheme" means, subject to the provisions of this section, a scheme for the provision of benefits consisting of or including relevant benefits, but does not include any national scheme providing such benefits.

(2) References in this Chapter to a scheme include references to a deed, agreement, series of agreements, or other arrangements providing for relevant benefits notwithstanding that it relates or they relate only to—
- (a) a small number of employees, or to a single employee, or
- (b) the payment of a pension starting immediately on the making of the arrangements.

(3) The Board may, if they think fit, treat a retirement benefits scheme relating to [scheme members] of two or more different classes or descriptions as being for the purposes of this Chapter two or more separate retirement benefits schemes relating respectively to such one or more of those classes or descriptions of those [scheme members] as the Board think fit.

(4) For the purposes of this section, and of any other provision of this Chapter—
- (a) employees may be regarded as belonging to different classes or descriptions if they are employed by different employers; and
- (b) a particular class or description of [scheme member] may consist of a single [scheme member], or any number of [scheme members], however small.

(5) Without prejudice to subsections (3) and (4) above, the Board may continue to treat as two different schemes, for the purposes of this Chapter, any retirement benefits scheme which, in pursuance of paragraph 5 of Schedule 3 to the Finance Act 1971 (schemes in existence before 5th April 1973), they treated, immediately before the coming into force of this Chapter, as two separate schemes for the purposes of Chapter II of Part II of the Finance Act 1970.

[(6) In this section "scheme member", in relation to a scheme means—
- (a) an employee; or

(b) a person whose rights under the scheme derive from a pension sharing order or provision.]

NOTES

Derivation

Sub-ss (1)–(4) derived from the Finance Act 1970, s 25; sub-s (5) derived from the Finance Act 1971, Sch 3, para 5.

Amendment

Sub-s (3): words "scheme members" in square brackets, in both places they occur, substituted by the Finance Act 1999, s 79, Sch 10, para 9(1).

Date in force: these amendments came into force on 27 July 1999 in the absence of any specific commencement provision.

Sub-s (4): in para (b) words "scheme member" and "scheme members" in square brackets, in each place they occur, substituted by the Finance Act 1999, s 79, Sch 10, para 9(1).

Date in force: these amendments came into force on 27 July 1999 in the absence of any specific commencement provision.

Sub-s (6): inserted by the Finance Act 1999, s 79, Sch 10, para 9(2).

Date in force: this amendment came into force on 27 July 1999 in absence of any specific commencement provision.

See Further

See further, in relation to judicial pensions: the Judicial Pensions and Retirement Act 1993, s 18.

[611AA Definition of the administrator]

[(1) In this Chapter references to the administrator, in relation to a retirement benefits scheme, are to the person who is, or the persons who are, for the time being the administrator of the scheme by virtue of the following provisions of this section.

(2) Subject to subsection (7) below, where—
- (a) the scheme is a trust scheme, and
- (b) at any time the trustee, or any of the trustees, is or are resident in the United Kingdom,

the administrator of the scheme at that time shall be the trustee or trustees of the scheme.

(3) Subject to subsection (7) below, where—
- (a) the scheme is a non-trust scheme, and
- (b) at any time the scheme sponsor, or any of the scheme sponsors, is or are resident in the United Kingdom,

the administrator of the scheme at that time shall be the scheme sponsor or scheme sponsors.

(4) At any time when the trustee of a trust scheme is not resident in the United Kingdom or (if there is more than one trustee) none of the trustees is so resident, the trustee or trustees shall ensure that there is a person, or there are persons—
- (a) resident in the United Kingdom, and
- (b) appointed by the trustee or trustees to be responsible for the discharge of all duties relating to the scheme which are imposed on the administrator under this Chapter.

(5) At any time when the scheme sponsor of a non-trust scheme is not resident in the United Kingdom or (if there is more than one scheme sponsor) none of the scheme sponsors is so resident, the scheme sponsor or scheme sponsors shall ensure that there is a person, or there are persons—

(a) resident in the United Kingdom, and

(b) appointed by the scheme sponsor or scheme sponsors to be responsible for the discharge of all duties relating to the scheme which are imposed on the administrator under this Chapter.

(6) Without prejudice to subsections (4) and (5) above—

(a) the trustee or trustees of a trust scheme, or

(b) the scheme sponsor or scheme sponsors of a non-trust scheme,

may at any time appoint a person who is, or persons who are, resident in the United Kingdom to be responsible for the discharge of all duties relating to the scheme which are imposed on the administrator under this Chapter.

(7) Where at any time there is or are a person or persons—

(a) for the time being appointed under subsection (4), (5) or (6) above as regards a scheme, and

(b) resident in the United Kingdom,

the administrator of the scheme at that time shall be that person or those persons (and no other person).

(8) Any appointment under subsection (4), (5) or (6) above—

(a) must be in writing, and

(b) if made after the time when the scheme is established, shall constitute an alteration of the scheme for the purposes of section 591B(2).

(9) In this section—

(a) references to a trust scheme are to a retirement benefits scheme established under a trust or trusts;

(b) references to the trustee or trustees, in relation to a trust scheme and to a particular time, are to the person who is the trustee, or the person who are the trustees, of the scheme at that time;

(c) references to a non-trust scheme are to a retirement benefits scheme not established under a trust or trusts, and

(d) references to the scheme sponsor or scheme sponsors, in relation to a retirement benefits scheme and to a particular time, are references to any person who established in the scheme and is in existence at that time or, if more than one, all such persons.]

NOTES

Amendment

Inserted by the Finance Act 1994, s 103(1); for effect in so far as it relates to ss 591B, 593, 596A, 598, 599, 599A, 602, 604, 605 hereto see s 103(3) thereof.

[611A Definition of relevant statutory scheme]

[(1) In this Chapter any reference to a relevant statutory scheme is to—

(a) a statutory scheme established before 14th March 1989, or

(b) a statutory scheme established on or after that date and entered in the register maintained by the Board for the purposes of this section, or

(c) a parliamentary pension scheme.]

(2) The Board shall maintain a register for the purposes of this section and shall enter in it the relevant particulars of any statutory scheme established on or after 14th March 1989 which is reported to the Board by the authority responsible for establishing it as a scheme the provisions of which correspond with those of an approved scheme.

(3) The reference in subsection (2) above to the relevant particulars, in relation to a scheme, is a reference to—

- (a) the identity of the scheme,
- (b) the date on which it was established,
- (c) the authority responsible for establishing it, and
- (d) the date on which that authority reported the scheme to the Board.

(4) Where the Board enter the relevant particulars of a scheme in the register maintained by them for the purposes of this section, they shall inform the authority responsible for establishing the scheme of the date of the entry.

[(5) In subsection (1)(c) "parliamentary pension scheme" means—

- (a the Parliamentary pension scheme within the meaning of the Parliamentary and other Pensions Act 1987;
- (b) any pension scheme established for members of the Scottish Parliament under section 81(4) of the Scotland Act 1998;
- (c) any pension scheme established for members of the Welsh Assembly under section 18(2) of the Government of Wales Act 1998;
- (d) any pension scheme established for members of the Northern Ireland Assembly under section 48(2) of the Northern Ireland Act 1998;
- (e) the pension scheme established for members of the European Parliament under section 4 of the European Parliament (Pay and Pensions) Act 1979;
- (f) the pension scheme established under section 3 of the Ministerial Salaries and Members' Pensions Act (Northern Ireland) 1965;
- (g) the pension scheme established under the Assembly Pensions (Northern Ireland) Order 1976.]]

NOTES

Amendment

Inserted by the Finance Act 1989, s 75, Sch 6, paras 15, 18(1).

Sub-s (1): substituted by the Finance Act 1999, s 52(1), Sch 5, para 5(1).

Date in force: this amendment has effect for the year 1999–2000 and subsequent years of assessment: see the Finance Act 1999, s 52(2).

Sub-s (5): inserted by the Finance Act 1999, s 52(1), Sch 5, para 5(2).

Date in force: this amendment has effect for the year 1999–2000 and subsequent years of assessment: see the Finance Act 1999, s 52(2).

See Further

See further, in relation to judicial pensions: the Judicial Pensions and Retirement Act 1993, s 18.

612 Other interpretative provisions, and regulations for purposes of this Chapter

(1) In this Chapter, except where the context otherwise requires—

. . .

"approved scheme" means a retirement benefits scheme for the time being approved by the Board for the purposes of this Chapter;

"director" in relation to a company includes—
- (a) in the case of a company the affairs of which are managed by a board of directors or similar body, a member of that board or body,
- (b) in the case of a company the affairs of which are managed by a single director or similar person, that director or person,
- (c) in the case of a company the affairs of which are managed by the members themselves, a member of that company;

and includes a person who is to be or has been a director;

"employee"—
- (a) in relation to a company, includes any officer of the company, any director of the company and any other person taking part in the management of the affairs of the company, and
- (b) in relation to any employer, includes a person who is to be or has been an employee;

and "employer" and other cognate expressions shall be construed accordingly;

"exempt approved scheme" has the meaning given by section 592(1);

"final remuneration" means the average annual remuneration of the last three years' service;

"pension" includes annuity;

"the permitted maximum" has the meaning given by section 590(3);

"relevant benefits" means any pension, lump sum, gratuity or other like benefit given or to be given on retirement or on death [, or by virtue of a pension sharing order or provision], or in anticipation of retirement, or, in connection with past service, after retirement or death, or to be given on or in anticipation of or in connection with any change in the nature of the service of the employee in question, except that it does not include any benefit which is to be afforded solely by reason of the disablement by accident of a person occurring during his service or of his death by accident so occurring and for no other reason;

"remuneration" does not include—
- (a) anything in respect of which tax is chargeable under Schedule E and which arises from the acquisition or disposal of shares or an interest in shares or from a right to acquire shares; or
- (b) anything in respect of which tax is chargeable by virtue of section 148;

"service" means service as an employee of the employer in question and other expressions, including "retirement", shall be construed accordingly; and

"statutory scheme" means a retirement benefits scheme established by or under any enactment—
- (a) the particulars of which are set out in any enactment, or in any regulations made under any enactment, or
- (b) which has been approved as an appropriate scheme by a Minister or government department (including the head of a Northern Ireland department or a Northern Ireland department).

(2) Any reference in the Chapter [, in relation to a scheme,] to the provision of relevant benefits, or of a pension, for employees [or ex-spouses] includes a reference to the provision of relevant benefits or a pension by means of a contract between the administrator or the employer or the employee [or ex-spouse] and a third person;

and any reference to pensions or contributions paid, or payments made, under a scheme includes a reference to pensions or contributions paid, or payments made, under such a contract entered into for the purposes of the scheme.

[(2A) In subsection (2) above the reference to the employer is a reference to the person who is the employer in relation to the scheme.]

(3) The Board may make regulations generally for the purpose of carrying the preceding provisions of this Chapter into effect.

NOTES

Derivation

Sub-s (1) derived from the Finance Act 1970, s 26(1), the Finance Act 1971, Sch 3, para 12(4), the Northern Ireland Constitution Act 1973, Sch 5, para 8, the Finance Act 1986, Sch 12, para 1(10), and the Finance (No 2) Act 1987, Sch 3, para 7; sub-s (2) derived from the Finance Act 1970, s 26(2), and the Finance (No 2) Act 1987, Sch 3, para 8; sub-s (3) derived from the Finance Act 1970, Sch 5, Part II, para 10, and the Finance Act 1971, Sch 3, para 13(3).

Amendment

Sub-s (1): definition omitted repealed by the Finance Act 1994, ss 103(2), (3), 258, Sch 26, Part V.

Sub-s (1): in definition "relevant benefits" words ", or by virtue of a pension sharing order or provision" in square brackets inserted by the Finance Act 1999, s 79, Sch 10, para 10(1).

Date in force: this amendment came into force on 27 July 1999 in the absence of any specific commencement provision.

Sub-s (2): words ", in relation to a scheme," and "or ex-spouse" in square brackets inserted by the Finance act 1999, s 79, Sch 10, para (2)(a), (c).

Date in force: these amendments came into force on 27 July 1999 in the absence of any specific commencement provision.

Sub-s (2): words "or ex-spouse" in square brackets substituted by the Finance Act 1999, s 79, Sch 10, para 10(2)(b).

Date in force: this amendment came into force on 27 July 1999 in the absence of any specific commencement provision.

Sub-s (2A): inserted by the Finance Act 1999, s 79, Sch 10, para 10(3).

Date in force: this amendment came into force on 27 July 1999 in the absence of any specific commencement provision.

Modification

The Northern Ireland Act 1998 makes new provision for the government of Northern Ireland for the purpose of implementing the Belfast Agreement (the agreement reached at multi-party talks on Northern Ireland and set out in Command Paper 3883). As a consequence of that Act, any reference in this section to the Parliament of Northern Ireland or the Assembly established under the Northern Ireland Assembly Act 1973, s 1, certain office-holders and Ministers, and any legislative act and certain financial dealings thereof, shall, for the period specified, be construed in accordance with Sch 12, paras 1–11 to the 1998 Act.

The Northern Ireland Act 2000 provides for the suspension of the operation of devolved government, and executive responsibility for Northern Ireland is to revert to the Secretary of State. Legislative power of the Assembly shall be exercisable by Order in Council during the suspension period.

See Further

See further, in relation to judicial pensions: the Judicial Pensions and Retirement Act 1993, s 18.

SCHEDULE 15

QUALIFYING POLICIES

SECTION 267

PART I

QUALIFYING CONDITIONS

General rules applicable to whole life and term assurances

1

(1) Subject to the following provisions of this Part of this Schedule, if a policy secures a capital sum which is payable only on death, or one payable either on death or on earlier disability, it is a qualifying policy if—

(a) it satisfies the conditions appropriate to it under sub-paragraphs (2) to (5) below, and

(b) except to the extent permitted by sub-paragraph (7) below, it does not secure any other benefits.

(2) If the capital sum referred to in sub-paragraph (1) above is payable whenever the event in question happens, or if it happens at any time during the life of a specified person—

(a) the premiums under the policy must be payable at yearly or shorter intervals, and either—

(i) until the happening of the event or, as the case may require, until the happening of the event or the earlier death of the specified person, or

(ii) until the time referred to in sub-paragraph (i) above or the earlier expiry of a specified period ending not earlier than ten years after the making of the insurance; and

(b) the total premiums payable in any period of 12 months must not exceed—

(i) twice the amount of the total premiums payable in any other such period, or

(ii) one-eighth of the total premiums which would be payable if the policy were to continue in force for a period of ten years from the making of the insurance, or, in a case falling within sub-paragraph (ii) of paragraph (a) above, until the end of the period referred to in that sub-paragraph.

(3) If the capital sum referred to in sub-paragraph (1) above is payable only if the event in question happens before the expiry of a specified term ending more than ten years after the making of the insurance, or if it happens both before the expiry of such a term and during the life of a specified person—

(a) the premiums under the policy must be payable at yearly or shorter intervals, and either—

(i) until the happening of the event or the earlier expiry of that term or, as the case may require, until the happening of the event or, if earlier, the expiry of the term or the death of the specified person, or

(ii) as in sub-paragraph (i) above, but with the substitution for references to the term of references to a specified shorter period being one ending not earlier than ten years after the making of the insurance or, if sooner, the expiry of three-quarters of that term; and

(b) the total premiums payable in any period of 12 months must not exceed—

(i) twice the amount of the total premiums payable in any other such period, or

(ii) one-eighth of the total premiums which would be payable if the policy were to continue in force for the term referred to in sub-paragraph (i) of paragraph (a) above, or, as the case may require, for the shorter period referred to in sub-paragraph (ii) of that paragraph.

(4) If the capital sum referred to in sub-paragraph (1) above is payable only if the event in question happens before the expiry of a specified term ending not more

than ten years after the making of the insurance, or only if it happens both before the expiry of such a term and during the life of a specified person, the policy must provide that any payment made by reason of its surrender during the period is not to exceed the total premiums previously paid under the policy.

(5) Except where—

(a) the capital sum referred to in sub-paragraph (1) above is payable only in the circumstances mentioned in sub-paragraph (3) or (4) above; and

(b) the policy does not provide for any payment on the surrender in whole or in part of the rights conferred by it; and

(c) the specified term mentioned in sub-paragraph (3) or, as the case may be, (4) above ends at or before the time when the person whose life is insured attains the age of 75 years;

the capital sum, so far as payable on death, must not be less than 75 per cent of the total premiums that would be payable if the death occurred at the age of 75 years, the age being, if the sum is payable on the death of the first to die of two persons, that of the older of them, if on the death of the survivor of them, that of the younger of them, and in any other case, that of the person on whose death it is payable; and if the policy does not secure a capital sum in the event of death occurring before the age of 16 or some lower age, it must not provide for the payment in that event of an amount exceeding the total premiums previously paid under it.

(6) In determining for the purposes of sub-paragraph (5) above whether a capital sum is less than 75 per cent of the total premiums, any amount included in the premiums by reason of their being payable otherwise than annually shall be disregarded, *and if the policy is issued in the course of an industrial assurance business*, [and if the policy provides for payment otherwise than annually without providing for the amount of the premiums if they are paid annually,] 10 per cent of the premiums payable under the policy shall be treated as so included.

(7) Notwithstanding sub-paragraph (1)(b) above, if a policy secures a capital sum payable only on death, it may also secure benefits (including benefits of a capital nature) to be provided in the event of a person's disability; and no policy is to be regarded for the purposes of that provision as securing other benefits by reason only of the fact that—

(a) it confers a right to participate in profits, or

(b) it provides for a payment on the surrender in whole or in part of the rights conferred by the policy, or

(c) it gives an option to receive payments by way of annuity, or

(d) it makes provisions for the waiver of premiums by reason of a person's disability, or for the effecting of a further insurance or insurances without the production of evidence of insurability.

(8) In applying sub-paragraph (2) or (3) above to any policy—

(a) no account shall be taken of any provision for the waiver of premiums by reason of a person's disability, and

(b) if the term of the policy runs from a date earlier, but not more than three months earlier, than the making of the insurance, the insurance shall be treated as having been made on that date, and any premium paid in respect of the period before the making of the insurance, or in respect of that period and a subsequent period, as having been payable on that date.

(9) References in this paragraph to a capital sum payable on any event include references to any capital sum, or series of capital sums, payable by reason of that event but where what is so payable is either an amount consisting of one sum or an amount made up of two or more sums, the 75 per cent mentioned in sub-paragraph (5) above shall be compared with the smaller or smallest amount so payable; and a

policy secures a capital sum payable either on death or on disability notwithstanding that the amount payable may vary with the event.

(10) In relation to any policy issued in respect of an insurance made before 1st April 1976 this paragraph shall have effect—

(a) with the omission of sub-paragraphs (5) and (6) and in sub-paragraph (9) the words "but where what is so payable is either an amount consisting of one sum or an amount made up of two or more sums, the 75 per cent mentioned in sub-paragraph (5) above shall be compared with the smallest amount so payable"; and

(b) with the substitution, for sub-paragraph (7)(b), of—

"(b) it carries a guaranteed surrender value;".

General rules applicable to endowment assurances

2

(1) Subject to the following provisions of this Part of this Schedule, a policy which secures a capital sum payable either on survival for a specified term or on earlier death, or earlier death or disability, including a policy securing the sum on death only if occurring after the attainment of a specified age not exceeding 16, is a qualifying policy if it satisfies the following conditions—

(a) the term must be one ending not earlier than ten years after the making of the insurance;

(b) premiums must be payable under the policy at yearly of shorter intervals, and—

  (i) until the happening of the event in question; or

  (ii) until the happening of that event, or the earlier expiry of a specified period shorter than the term but also ending not earlier than ten years after the making of the insurance; or

  (iii) if the policy is to lapse on the death of a specified person, until one of those times or the policy's earlier lapse;

(c) the total premiums payable under the policy in any period of 12 months must not exceed—

  (i) twice the amount of the total premiums payable in any other such period, or

  (ii) one-eighth of the total premiums which would be payable if the policy were to run for the specified term;

(d) the policy—

  (i) must guarantee that the capital sum payable on death, or on death occurring after the attainment of a specified age not exceeding 16, will, whenever that event may happen, be equal to 75 per cent at least of the total premiums which would be payable if the policy were to run for that term, disregarding any amount s included in those premiums by reason of their being payable otherwise than annually, except that if, at the beginning of that term, the age of the person concerned exceeds 55 years, the capital sum so guaranteed may, for each year of the excess, be less by 2 per cent of that total than 75 per cent thereof, the person concerned being, if the capital sum is payable on the death of the first to die of two persons, the older of them, if on the death of the survivor of them, the younger of them and in any other case the person on whose death it is payable; and

  (ii) if it is a policy which does not secure a capital sum in the event of death before the attainment of a specified age not exceeding 16, must not provide for the payment in that event of an a mount exceeding the total premiums previously paid thereunder; and

(e) the policy must not secure the provision (except by surrender in whole or in part of the rights conferred by the policy) at any time before the happening of the event in question of any benefit of a capital nature there than a payment falling within paragraph (d)(ii) above, or benefits attributable to a right to participate in profits or arising by reason of a person's disability.

(2) For the purposes of sub-paragraph (1)(d)(i) above, 10 per cent of the premiums payable under any policy *issued in the course of industrial assurance business* [that provides for the payment of premiums otherwise than annually without providing for the amount of the premiums if they are paid annually,] shall be treated as attributable to the fact that they are not paid annually.

(3) Sub-paragraphs (8) and (9) of paragraph 1 above shall, with any necessary modifications, have effect for the purposes of this paragraph as they have effect for the purposes of that paragraph.

(4) In relation to any policy issued in respect of an insurance made before 1st April 1976 this paragraph shall have effect with the omission in sub-paragraph (1)(d)(i) of the words from "except that if" to the end, and in sub-paragraph (1)(e) of the words "in whole or in part of the rights conferred by the policy".

Special types of policy

(i) Friendly Society policies

3

(1) Paragraphs 1 and 2 above do not apply to a policy issued by a [friendly society] in the course of tax exempt life or endowment business in respect of an insurance made or varied on or after 19th March 1985, but such a policy shall not be a qualifying policy unless—

(a) in the case of a policy for the assurance of a gross sum or annuity, the conditions in sub-paragraph (2) are fulfilled with respect to it; and
(b) in the case of a policy for the assurance of a gross sum, the conditions in sub-paragraphs (5) to (11) below are fulfilled with respect to it; . . .
(c) . . .

(2) The conditions referred to in sub-paragraph (1) above are as follows—

(a) subject to sub-paragraph (3) below, the period (the "term" of the policy) between—
   (i) the making of the insurance or, where the contract provides for the term to begin on a date not more than three months earlier than the making of the insurance, that date, and
   (ii) the time when the gross sum assured is payable (or, as the case may be, when the first instalment of the annuity is payable),

   shall be not less than ten years, and must not, on any contingency other than the death, or retirement on grounds of ill health, of the person liable to pay the premiums or whose life is insured, become less than ten years;
(b) subject to sub-paragraph (4) below, the premiums payable under the policy shall be premiums of equal or rateable amounts payable at yearly or shorter intervals over the whole term of the policy of assurance, or over the whole term of the policy of assurance apart from any period after the person liable to pay the premiums or whose life is insured attains a specified age, being an age which he will attain at a time not less than ten years after the beginning of the term of the policy of assurance;
(c) . . .

(3) Notwithstanding sub-paragraph (2)(a) above, the policy—

(a) may provide for a payment to a person of an age not exceeding 18 years at any time not less than five years from the beginning of the term of the policy if the premium or premiums payable in any period of 12 months in the term of the policy do not exceed £13;

(b) may provide for a payment at any time not less than five years from the beginning of the term of the policy, if it is one of a series of payments falling due at intervals of not less than five years, and the amount of any payment, other than the final payment, does not exceed four-fifths of the premiums paid in the interval before its payment.

For the purposes of paragraph (a) above, if the term begins on a date earlier than the making of the insurance, any premium paid in respect of a period before the making of the insurance, or in respect of that period and a subsequent period, shall be treated as having been payable on that date.

(4) Notwithstanding sub-paragraph (2)(b) above, the policy—

(a) may allow a payment at any time after the expiration of one-half of the term of the policy of assurance, or of ten years from the beginning of the term, whichever is the earlier, being a payment in commutation of the liability to pay premiums falling due after that time;

(b) may allow the person liable to pay the premiums to commute any liability for premiums where he ceases to reside in the United Kingdom or give satisfactory proof of intention to emigrate;

(c) may allow any liability for premiums to be discharged in consideration of surrendering a sum which has become payable on the maturity of any other policy of assurance issued by the same friendly society [(or any predecessor of it)] to the person liable to pay the premiums, or to his parent, where that other policy of assurance is issued as part of the friendly society's tax exempt life or endowment business; and

(d) may make provision for the waiver of premiums by reason of a person's disability.

[(4A) For the purposes of sub-paragraphs (2) and (4) above—

(a) a friendly society formed on the amalgamation of two or more friendly societies is the successor of each of those societies (and each of those societies was a predecessor of the society so formed), and

(b) an incorporated friendly society that was a registered friendly society before its incorporation is the successor of the registered friendly society (and the registered friendly society was the predecessor of the incorporated friendly society).]

(5) Where the policy secures a capital sum which is payable only on death or only on death occurring after the attainment of a specified age not exceeding 16, that capital sum must be not less than 75 per cent of the total premiums which would be payable if the death of the relevant beneficiary occurred at the age of 75.

(6) Where the policy secures a capital sum which is payable only on survival for a specified term, that capital sum must be not less than 75 per cent of the total premiums which would be payable if the policy were to run for that term.

(7) Where the policy secures a capital sum which is payable on survival for a specified term or on earlier death, or on earlier death or disability (including a policy securing the sum on death only if occurring after the attainment of a specified age not exceeding 16), the capital sum payable on death, whenever that event occurs, must be not less than 75 per cent of the total premiums which would be payable if the policy were to run for that term, except that if, at the beginning of that term, the age of the relevant beneficiary exceeds 55, that capital sum may, for each year of the excess, be less by 2 per cent of that total than 75 per cent thereof.

(8) For the purposes of sub-paragraphs (5) to (7) above—

(a) "the relevant beneficiary" means—

(i) if the capital sum concerned is payable on the death of the first to die of two persons, the older of them;

(ii) if that capital sum is payable on the death of the survivor of two persons, the younger of them; and

(iii) in any other case, the person on whose death that capital sum is payable; and

(b) in determining the total premiums payable in any circumstances—

(i) where those premiums are payable otherwise than annually, and the policy is issued by a new society, there shall be disregarded an amount equal to 10 per cent. of those premiums;

(ii) where the policy is issued by a society other than a new society, there shall be disregarded an amount equal to £10 for each year for which account is taken of those premiums [or, where those premiums are payable otherwise than annually, an amount equal to 10 per cent. of those premiums if that is greater]; and

(iii) so much of any premium as is charged on the ground that an exceptional risk of death is involved shall be disregarded; and

(c) in determining the capital sum payable on any event, there shall be disregarded any provision of the policy under which, on the ground referred to in paragraph (b)(iii) above, any sum may become chargeable as a debt against that capital sum.

(9) If the policy does not secure a capital sum in the event of death occurring before the age of 16 or some lower age, it must not provide for the payment in that event of an amount exceeding the total premiums previously paid under it.

(10) References in this paragraph to a capital sum payable on any event include references to a capital sum or series of capital sums payable by reason of that event, but where what is so payable is either an amount consisting of one sum or an amount made up to two or more sums, any reference in sub-paragraphs (5) to (7) above to 75 per cent. of the total premiums payable in any circumstances shall be compared with the smaller or smallest amount so payable; and for the purposes of those sub-paragraphs a policy secures a capital sum payable either on death or on disability notwithstanding that the amount may vary with the event.

(11) For the purposes of sub-paragraphs (5) to (7) and (10) above, in the case of a policy which provides for any such payments as are referred to in sub-paragraph (3) above ("interim payments"), the amount of the capital sum which is payable on any event shall be taken to be increased—

(a) in the case of a policy which secures such a capital sum as is referred to in sub-paragraph (5) above, by the total of the interim payments which would be payable if the death of the relevant beneficiary (within the meaning of that sub-paragraph) occurred at the age of 75; and

(b) in the case of a policy which secures such a capital sum as is referred to in sub-paragraph (6) or (7) above, by the total of the interim payments which would be payable if the policy were to run for the specified term referred to in that sub-paragraph.

4

(1) The provisions of this paragraph have effect notwithstanding anything in paragraph 3 above.

(2) In determining whether a policy—

(a) which affords provision for sickness or other infirmity (whether bodily or mental), and

(b) which also affords assurance for a gross sum independent of sickness or other infirmity, and

(c) under which not less than 60 per cent of the amount of the premiums is attributable to the provision referred to in paragraph (a) above,

is a qualifying policy, the conditions referred to in paragraph 3(1)(b) above shall be deemed to be fulfilled with respect to it.

(3) A policy shall cease to be a qualifying policy—

(a) if it falls within sub-paragraph (1) of paragraph 3 above and there is such a variation of its terms that any of the conditions referred to in that sub-paragraph ceases to be fulfilled; or

(b) if—

[(i) it was effected in the course of business within class VI of Head A or class I of Head B of Schedule 2 to the Friendly Societies Act 1992,]

(ii) it was issued by a new society, and

(iii) the rights conferred by it are surrendered in whole or in part.

5

Section 466 shall apply for the interpretation of paragraphs 3 and 4 above as it applies for the interpretation of sections 460 to 465.

6

(1) A policy which was issued by [any registered friendly society (as defined in section 466)], or branch of [such a society], in the course of tax exempt life or endowment business (as defined in section 466) in respect of insurances made before 19th March 1985 and which has not been varied on or after that date is a qualifying policy notwithstanding that it does not comply with the conditions specified in paragraph 1 or 2 above.

(2) Notwithstanding paragraphs 3 to 5 or sub-paragraph (1) above, if, on or after 19th March 1985, a person becomes in breach of the limits in section 464, the policy effected by that contract which causes those limits to be exceeded shall not be a qualifying policy; and in any case where—

(a) the limits in that section are exceeded as a result of the aggregation of the sums assured or premiums payable under two or more contracts, and

(b) at a time immediately before on of those contracts was entered into (but not immediately after it was entered into) the sums assured by or, as the case may be, the premiums payable under the contract or contracts which were then in existence did not exceed the limits in that section,

only those policies effected by contracts made after that time shall be treated as causing the limits to be exceeded.

(ii) Industrial assurance policies

7

(1) A policy issued in the course of an industrial assurance business, and not constituting a qualifying policy by virtue of paragraph 1 or 2 above, is nevertheless a qualifying policy if—

(a) the sums guaranteed by the policy, together with those guaranteed at the time the assurance is made by all other policies issued in the course of such a business to the same person and not constituting qualifying policies apart from this paragraph, do not exceed £1,000;

(b) it satisfies the conditions with respect to premiums specified in paragraph 1(2) above;

(c) except by reason of death or surrender, no capital sum other than one falling within paragraph (d) below can become payable under the policy earlier than ten years after the making of the assurance; and

(d) where the policy provides for the making of a series of payments during its term—

(i) the first such payment is due not earlier than five years after the making of the assurance, and the others, except the final payment, at intervals of not less than five years, and

(ii) the amount of any payment, other than the final payment, does not exceed four-fifths of the premiums paid in the interval before its payment; or

(e) the policy was issued before 6th April 1976, or was issued before 6th April 1979 and is in substantially the same form as policies so issued before 6th April 1976.

(2) For the purposes of this paragraph, the sums guaranteed by a policy do not include any bonuses, or in the case of a policy providing for a series of payments during its term, any of those payments except the first, or any sum payable on death during the term by reference to one or more of those payments except so far as that sum is referable to the first such payment.

8

Where a policy issued in respect of an insurance made after 1st April 1976 in the course of an industrial assurance business is not a qualifying policy by virtue of paragraph 1 or 2 above but is a policy with respect to which the conditions in paragraph 7(1)(b) and (c) above as satisfied, it shall be a qualifying policy whether or not the condition in paragraph 7(1)(a) above is satisfied with respect to it; but where that condition is not satisfied, relief under section 266 in respect of premiums paid under the policy shall be given only on such amount (if any) as would have been the amount of those premiums had that condition been satisfied.

(iii) Family income policies and mortgage protection policies

9

(1) The following provisions apply to any policy which is not a qualifying policy apart from those provisions, and the benefits secured by which consist of or include the payment on or after a person's death of—

(a) one capital sum which does not vary according to the date of death, plus a series of capital sums payable if the death occurs during a specified period, or

(b) a capital sum, the amount of which is less if the death occurs in a later part of a specified period than if it occurs in an earlier part of that period.

(2) A policy falling within sub-paragraph (1)(a) above is a qualifying policy if—

(a) it would be one if it did not secure the series of capital sums there referred to, and the premiums payable under the policy were such as would be chargeable if that were in fact the case, and

(b) it would also be if it secured only that series of sums, and the premiums thereunder were the balance of those actually so payable.

(3) A policy falling within sub-paragraph (1)(b) above is a qualifying policy if—

(a) it would be one if the amount of the capital sum there referred to were equal throughout the period to it smallest amount, and the premiums payable under the policy were such as would be chargeable if that were in fact the case, and

(b) it would also be one if it secured only that capital sum so far as it from time to time exceeds its smallest amount, and the premiums payable thereunder were the balance of those actually so payable.

Other special provisions

(i) Short-term assurances

10

A policy which secures a capital sum payable only on death or payable either on death or on earlier disability shall not be a qualifying policy if the capital sum is payable only if the event in question happens before the expiry of a specified term ending less than one year after the making of the insurance.

(ii) Personal accident insurance

11

(1) A policy which evidences a contract of insurance to which sub-paragraph (3) below applies shall not be a qualifying policy unless it also evidences a contract falling within Class I or Class III in Schedule 1 to the Insurance Companies Act 1982.

(2) A policy which evidences a contract of insurance to which sub-paragraph (4) below applies shall not be a qualifying policy unless it also evidences a contract falling within section 83(2)(a) of the Insurance Companies Act 1974.

(3) This sub-paragraph applies to contracts of insurance issued in respect of insurances made on or after 25th March 1982 against risks of persons dying as a result of an accident or an accident of a specified class, not being contracts which—

(a) are expressed to be in effect for a period of not less than five years or without limit of time; and

(b) either are not expressed to be terminable by the insurer before the expiration of five years from their taking effect or are expressed to be so terminable before the expiration of that period only in special circumstances therein mentioned.

(4) This sub-paragraph applies to contracts of insurance issued in respect of insurances made before 25th March 1982 against risks of persons dying as a result of an accident or an accident of a specified class, not being contracts falling within section 83(2)(b) of the Insurance Companies Act 1974.

(iii) Exceptional mortality risk

12

For the purpose of determining whether any policy is a qualifying policy, there shall be disregarded—

(a) so much of any premium thereunder as is charged on the grounds that an exceptional risk of death is involved; and

(b) any provision under which, on those grounds, any sum may become chargeable as a debt against the capital sum guaranteed by the policy on death.

(iv) Connected policies

13

Subject to paragraph 14 below, where the terms of any policy provide that it is to continue in force only so long as another policy does so, neither policy is a qualifying policy unless, if they had constituted together a single policy issued in respect of an insurance made at the time of the insurance in respect of which the first-mentioned policy was issued, that single policy would have been a qualifying policy.

14

(1) A policy shall not be a qualifying policy if the policy is connected with another policy and the terms of either policy provide benefits which are greater than would reasonably be expected if any policy connected with it were disregarded.

(2) For the purposes of this paragraph a policy is connected with another policy if they are at any time simultaneously in force and either of them is issued with reference to the other, or with a view to enabling the other to be issued on particular terms or facilitating its being issued on those terms.

(3) In this paragraph "policy" means a policy effected in the course of long term business, as defined in section 1 of the Insurance Companies Act 1982, and includes any such policy issued outside the United Kingdom.

(4) Where any person issues a policy—
- (a) which by virtue of this paragraph is not a qualifying policy, or
- (b) the issue of which causes another policy to cease by virtue of this paragraph to be a qualifying policy,

he shall within three months of issuing the policy give notice of that fact to the Board.

(5) The Board may, by notice, require any person who is, or appears to them to be, concerned in the issue of any such policy as is mentioned in sub-paragraph (4) above, to furnish them within such time (not being les than 30 days) as may be specified in the notice with such particulars as they think necessary for the purposes of this paragraph and as the person to whom the notice is addressed has or can reasonably obtain; but no solicitor shall be deemed for the purposes of this sub-paragraph to have been concerned in the issue of a policy by reason only that he has given professional advice to a client in connection with that policy.

(6) This paragraph shall apply to policies issued in respect of insurances made before 23rd August 1983 in accordance with sub-paragraphs (7) and (8) below.

(7) Where—
- (a) a policy is issued in respect of an insurance made before 23rd August 1983, and
- (b) a policy is issued in respect of an insurance made on or after that date which is connected with it within the meaning of this paragraph,

sub-paragraphs (1) to (6) above shall apply to the policy issued in respect of an insurance made before that date.

(8) Sub-paragraphs (1) to (7) above shall apply to policies issued in respect of insurances made before 23rd August 1983 (other than policies which, disregarding this paragraph, fall within sub-paragraph (7)) with the substitution—
- (a) in sub-paragraph (1) for the words "and the terms of either policy" of the words "the terms of which";

(b) in sub-paragraph (3) for the words from "long term business" to "1982" of the words "ordinary long-term insurance business within the meaning of section 83(2) of the Insurance Companies Act 1974 (as enacted) or, in relation to a policy made after 25th March 1982, section 96(1) of the Insurance Companies Act 1982"; and

(c) in sub-paragraphs (6) and (7) for the words "23rd August 1983" of the words "26th March 1980".

(9) In any case where payments made—

(a) after 22nd August 1983, and

(b) by way of premium or other consideration in respect of a policy in respect of an insurance made before that date,

exceed £5 in any period of 12 months, the policy shall be treated for the purposes of this paragraph as if it were issued in respect of an insurance made after 22nd August 1983; but nothing in this paragraph shall apply with respect to any premium paid in respect of it before that date.

(10) Sub-paragraphs (8) and (9) above do not apply in relation to policies issued in the course of industrial assurance business.

(v) Premiums paid out of sums due under previous policies

15

(1) Where, in the case of a policy under which a single premium only is payable, liability for the payment of that premium is discharged in accordance with sub-paragraph (2) below, the policy is a qualifying policy notwithstanding anything in paragraph 1(2) or (3) or paragraph 2(1)(b) or (c) above; and where, in the case of any other policy, liability for the payment of the first premium thereunder, or of any part of that premium, is so discharged, the premium or part shall be discharged for the purposes of paragraphs 1(2)(b) and (3)(b) and 2(1)(c) above.

(2) Liability for the payment of a premium is discharged in accordance with this sub-paragraph if it is discharged by the retention by the company with which the insurance is made of the whole part of any sum which has become payable on the maturity of, or on the surrender more than ten years after its issue of the rights conferred by, a policy—

(a) previously issued by the company to the person making the insurance, or, if it is made by trustees, to them or any predecessors in office; or

(b) issued by the company when the person making the insurance was an infant, and securing a capital sum payable either on a specified date falling not more than one month after his attaining 25, or on the anniversary of the policy immediately following his attainment of that age,

being, unless it is a policy falling within paragraph (b) above and the premium in question is a first premium only, a policy which was itself a qualifying policy, or which would have been a qualifying policy had it been issued in respect of an insurance made after 19th March 1968.

(vi) Additional premiums under section 72(9) of the Finance Act 1984

16

In determining whether a policy is a qualifying policy, no account shall be taken of any amount recovered, as if it were an additional premium, in pursuance of section 72(9) of the Finance Act 1984.

(vii) Substitutions and variations

17

(1) Subject to paragraph 19 below, where one policy ("the new policy") is issued in substitution for, or on the maturity of and in consequence of an option conferred by, another policy ("the old policy"), the question whether the new policy is a qualifying policy shall, to the extent provided by the rules in sub-paragraph (2) below, be determined by reference to both policies.

(2) The rules (for the purposes of which, the question whether the old policy was a qualifying policy shall be determined in accordance with this Part of this Schedule, whatever the date of the insurance in respect of which it was issued), are as follows—

- (a) if the new policy would apart from this paragraph be a qualifying policy but the old policy was [not], the new policy is not a qualifying policy unless the person making the insurance in respect of which it is issued was an infant when the old policy was issued, and the old policy was one securing a capital sum payable either on a specified date falling not later than one month after his attaining 25 or on the anniversary of the policy immediately following his attainment of that age;
- (b) if the new policy would apart from this paragraph be a qualifying policy, and the old policy was also a qualifying policy, the new policy is a qualifying policy unless—
  - (i) it takes effect before the expiry of ten years from the making of the insurance in respect of which the old policy was issued, and
  - (ii) subject to sub-paragraph (4) below, the highest total of premiums payable thereunder for any period of 12 months expiring before that time is less than one half of the highest total paid for any period of 12 months under the old policy, or under any related policy issued less than ten years before the issue of the new policy ("related policy" meaning any policy in relation to which the old policy was a new policy within the meaning of this paragraph, any policy in relation to which that policy was such a policy, and so on);
- (c) if the new policy would not apart from this paragraph be a qualifying policy, and would fail to be so by reason only of paragraph 1(2) or (3) or 2(1)(a), (b) or (c) above, it is nevertheless a qualifying policy if the old policy was a qualifying policy and—
  - (i) the old policy was issued in respect of an insurance made more than ten years before the taking effect of the new policy, and, subject to sub-paragraph (4) below, the premiums payable for any period of 12 months under the new policy do not exceed the smallest total paid for any such period under the old policy; or
  - (ii) the old policy was issued outside the United Kingdom, and the circumstances are as specified in sub-paragraph (3) below.

(3) The circumstances are—

- (a) where the new policy referred to in sub-paragraph (2)(c) above is issued after 22nd February 1984, that the policy holder under the new policy became resident in the United Kingdom during the 12 months ending with the date of its issue;
- (b) where paragraph (a) above does not apply, that the person in respect of whom the new insurance is made became resident in the United Kingdom during the 12 months ending with the date of its issue;
- (c) that the issuing company certify that the new policy is in substitution for the old, and that the old was issued either by a branch or agency of theirs outside the United Kingdom or by a company outside the United Kingdom with whom they have arrangements for the issue of policies in substitution for ones held by persons coming to the United Kingdom; and
- (d) that the new policy confers on the holder benefits which are substantially

equivalent to those which he would have enjoyed if the old policy had continued in force.

(4) Where the new policy is one issued on or after 1st April 1976 then, in determining under sub-paragraph (2) above whether that policy would or would not (apart from sub-paragraphs (1) to (3) above) be a qualifying policy, there shall be left out of account so much of the first premium payable thereunder as is accounted for by the value of the old policy.

18

(1) Subject to paragraph 19 below and to the provisions of this paragraph, where the terms of a policy are varied, the question whether the policy after the variation is a qualifying policy shall be determined in accordance with the rules in paragraph 17 above, with references in those rules to the new policy and the old policy construed for that purpose as references respectively to the policy after the variation and the policy before the variation, and with any other necessary modifications.

(2) In applying any of those rules by virtue of this paragraph, the question whether a policy after a variation would be a qualifying policy apart from the rule shall be determined as if any reference in paragraphs [1, 2, 3(5) to (11), 4 to 9], 12 and 13 above to the making of an insurance, or to a policy's term, were a reference to the taking effect of the variation or, as the case may be, to the term of the policy as from the variation.

(3) This paragraph does not apply by reason of—
- (a) any variation which, whether or not of a purely formal character, does not affect the terms of a policy in any significant respect, or
- (b) any variation effected before the end of the year 1968 for the sole purpose of converting into a qualifying policy any policy issued (but not one treated, by virtue of paragraph 8(1) and (2) of Schedule 14, as issued) in respect of an insurance made after 19th March 1968.

19

(1) The following provisions of this paragraph shall have effect for determining for the purposes of this Schedule whether a policy has been varied or whether a policy which confers on the person to whom it is issued an option to have another policy substituted for it or to have any of its terms changed is a qualifying policy.

(2) If the policy is one issued in respect of an insurance made before 1st April 1976—
- (a) any such option shall, until it is exercised, be disregarded in determining whether the policy is a qualifying policy; and
- (b) any change in the terms of the policy which is made in pursuance of such an option shall be deemed to be a variation of the policy.

(3) If the policy is one issued in respect of an insurance made on or after 1st April 1976, the policy shall not be a qualifying policy unless it satisfies the conditions applicable to it under this Schedule before any such option is exercised and—
- (a) each policy that might be substituted for it in pursuance of such an option would satisfy those conditions under the rules of paragraph 17 above; and
- (b) the policy would continue to satisfy those conditions under the rules of that paragraph as applied by paragraph 18 above if each or any of the changes capable of being made in pursuance of such an option had been made and were treated as a variation;

and it shall not be treated as being varied by reason only of any change made in pursuance of such an option.

20

(1) Where, as a result of a variation in the life or lives for the time being assured, a qualifying policy ("the earlier policy") is replaced by a new policy ("the later policy") which in accordance with the rules in paragraph 17 above is also a qualifying policy, then, subject to sub-paragraph (2) below, for the purposes of—

(a) sections 268 to 270 and 540 and 541; and

(b) any second or subsequent application of this paragraph;

the later policy and the earlier policy shall be treated as a single policy issued in respect of an insurance made at the time of the making of the insurance in respect of which the earlier policy was issued; and, accordingly, so long as the later policy continues to be a qualifying policy, the single policy shall also be treated as a qualifying policy for those purposes.

(2) Sub-paragraph (1) above does not apply unless—

(a) any sum which would otherwise become payable by the insurer on or in connection with the coming to an end of the earlier policy is retained by the insurer and applied in the discharge of some or all of the liability for any premium becoming due under the later policy; and

(b) no consideration in money or money's worth (other than the benefits for which provision is made by the later policy) is receivable by any person on or in connection with the coming to an end of the earlier policy or the coming into existence of the later policy.

(3) Any sum which is applied as mentioned in sub-paragraph (2)(a) above—

(a) shall be left out of account in determining, for the purposes of sections 268 to 270 and 540 and 541, the total amount which at any time has been paid by way of premiums under the single policy referred to in sub-paragraph (1) above; and

(b) shall not be regarded, in relation to that single policy, as a relevant capital payment, within the meaning of section 541.

(4) This paragraph applies where the later policy comes into existence on or after 25th March 1982.

NOTES

Derivation

Paras 1, 2 derived from the Income and Corporation Taxes Act 1970, Sch 1, paras 1, 2, and the Finance Act 1975, Sch 2, para 4; paras 3, 4 derived from the Income and Corporation Taxes Act 1970, ss 334(2)–(4), 337(5)(a), Sch 1, paras 3, 3A, the Tax, Consumer Credit and Judicature (Northern Ireland Consequential Amendments) Order 1979, SI 1979/1576, the Finance Act 1984, s 72(a), and the Finance Act 1985, s 41(4), (6), Sch 10, Part I; para 5 derived from the Income and Corporation Taxes Act 1970, s 337(1)(b), and the Finance Act 1985, s 41(7)(a), para 6 derived from the Income and Corporation Taxes Act 1970, Sch 1, para 3, the Friendly Societies Act 1974, s 64(2B), the Finance Act 1985, s 41(1), (4), and the Finance Act 1987, s 30(6); para 7 derived from the Income and Corporation Taxes act 1970, Sch 1, para 4, and the Finance Act 1976, Sch 4, para 12; para 8 derived from the Finance Act 1975, Sch 2, para 7, and the Finance Act 1976, Sch 4, para 19(4); paras 9, 12, 13, 15, 18 derived from the Income and Corporation Taxes Act 1970, Sch 1, paras 5, 6, 7, 8, 10; paras 10, 11 derived from the Finance Act 1976, Sch 4, paras 2, 2A, the Finance Act 1978, Sch 3, para 4, the Insurance Companies Act 1982, Sch 5, para 17, and the Finance Act 1982, s 35(1); para 14 derived from the Finance Act 1980, s 30, the Finance Act 1982, s 35(3), and the Finance

Act 1984, s 74; para 16 derived from the Finance Act 1984, s 72(9)(a); para 17 derived from the Income and Corporation Taxes Act 1970, Sch 1, para 9, the Finance Act 1975, Sch 2, para 5, and the Finance Act 1984, s 76(3), (6); para 19 derived from the Finance Act 1975, Sch 2, para 3; para 20 derived from the Finance Act 1982, s 34.

Amendment

Para 1: in sub-para (6) words "and if the policy is issued in the course of an industrial assurance business," in italics prospectively repealed and subsequent words in square brackets prospectively substituted, in relation to policies issued on or after a day to be appointed by the Board, by the Finance Act 1996, s 167(7)(a), (12).

Para 2: in sub-para (2) words "issued in the course of industrial assurance business" in italics prospectively repealed and subsequent words in square brackets prospectively substituted, in relation to policies issued on or after a day to be appointed by the Board, by the Finance Act 1996, s 167(7)(b), (12).

Para 3: in sub-para (1) words "friendly society" in square brackets substituted by the Finance (No 2) Act 1992, s 56, Sch 9, para 19(2).

Para 3: in sub-para (1)(b) word omitted repealed, in relation to policies issued in pursuance of contracts made on or after 25 July 1991, by the Finance Act 1991, ss 50, 123, Sch 9, para 4, Sch 19, Part V, Note 7.

Para 3: sub-para (1)(c) and the word immediately preceding it repealed, in relation to policies issued in pursuance of contracts made on or after 25 July 1991, by the Finance Act 1991, ss 50, 123, Sch 9, para 4, Sch 19, Part V, Note 7.

Para 3: sub-para (2)(c) repealed by the Finance act 1995, ss 54, 162, Sch 10, para 3, Sch 29, Part VIII.

Para 3: in sub-para (4)(c) words "(or any predecessor of it)" in square brackets inserted by the Finance (No 2) Act 1992, s 56, Sch 9, para 19(4).

Para 3: sub-para (4A) inserted by the Finance (No 2) Act 1992, s 56, Sch 9, para 19(5).

Para 3: in sub-para (8)(b)(ii) words from "or, where" to "is greater" is square brackets inserted by the Finance Act 1990, s 49(5).

Para 4: sub-para (3)(b)(i) substituted by the Finance (No 2) Act 1992, s 56, Sch 9, para 19(6).

Para 6: in sub-para (1) words "any registered friendly society (as defined in section 466)" in square brackets substituted by the Finance (No 2) Act 1992, s 56, Sch 9, para 19(7)(a).

Para 6: in sub-para (1) words "such a society" in square brackets substituted by the Finance (No 2) Act 1992, s 56, Sch 9, para 19(7)(b).

Para 8A: inserted by the Finance Act 1996, s 167(8).

Para 17: in sub-para (2)(a) word "not" in square brackets inserted with retrospective effect by the Finance Act 1988, s 146, Sch 13, Part I, paras 10, 11.

Para 18: in sub-para (2) words "1, 2, 3(5) to (11), 4 to 9" in square brackets inserted with retrospective effect by the Finance Act 1988, s 146, Sch 13, Part I, paras 10, 11.

Modification

Modification: paras 4, 18 modified, in relation to certain policies effected by contracts made aft 31 August 1987 and before 25 July 1991, by the Finance Act 1991, s 50, Sch 9, para 5.

Modification: paras 4, 18 modified, in relation to certain policies effected by contracts made after 31 August 1987 and before 1 May 1995, by the Finance Act 1995, s 54, Sch 10, para 4.

References to solicitors etc modified to include references to bodies recognised under the Administration of Justice Act 1985, s 9, by the Solicitors' Incorporated Practices Order 1991, SI 1991/2684, arts 4, 5, Sch 1.

PART II

CERTIFICATION OF QUALIFYING POLICIES

Policies issued in respect of insurances made on or after 1st April 1976 or varied on or after that date

21

(1) A policy of life insurance issued in respect of an insurance made on or after 1st April 1976 or varied on or after that date (other than one to which paragraph 22(2)(c) below applies) shall not be a qualifying policy unless—

(a) it is certified by the Board as being a qualifying policy; or

(b) it conforms with a form which at the time the policy is issued or varied is either—

(i) a standard form certified by the Board as a standard form of qualifying policy; or

(ii) a form varying from a standard form so certified in no other respect than by making such additions thereto as are, at the time the policy is issued, certified by the Board as compatible with a qualifying policy when made to that standard form and satisfy any conditions subject to which they are so certified;

and any certificate issued in pursuance of paragraph (a) above shall be conclusive evidence that the policy is a qualifying policy.

(2) In issuing a certificate in pursuance of sub-paragraph (1) above the Board may disregard any provision of the policy, standard form or addition which appears to them insignificant.

(3) Where the Board refuse to certify a policy as being a qualifying policy, the person to whom it is issued may appeal to the General Commissioners or, if he so elects, to the Special Commissioners.

(4) Sub-paragraphs (1) to (3) above do not apply in relation to such a policy as is mentioned in paragraphs 3 to 6 above.

22

(1) A body which issues or which, after 5th April 1979, has issued any policy of life insurance (other than one to which sub-paragraph (2)(c) below applies)—

(a) which is certified by the Board as being a qualifying policy; or

(b) which conforms with such a form as is mentioned in paragraph 21(1)(b) above, and is in the opinion of the body issuing it a qualifying policy,

shall, within three months of receipt of a request in writing by the policy holder, give to the policy holder a duly authenticated certificate to that effect, specifying in the certificate the name of the policy holder, the name of the person whose life is assured, the reference number or other means of identification allocated to the policy, the reference number of the relevant Inland Revenue certificate (if any), the capital sum or sums assured and the amounts and dates for payment of the premiums.

(2) Subject to sub-paragraph (3) below, where a policy of life insurance is varied after 5th April 1979, and, after the variation—

(a) it is certified by the Board as a qualifying policy, or

(b it conforms with such a form as is referred to in sub-paragraph (1) above and is in the opinion of the body by whom it was issued a qualifying policy, or

(c) in the case of policy issued in respect of an insurance made before 1st April 1976, it is in the opinion of the body by whom it was issued a qualifying policy,

that body shall, within three months of receipt of a request in writing by the policy holder, give to the policy holder a like certificate with respect to the policy as varied.

(3) Sub-paragraph (2) above shall not apply by reason of—

- *(a) any variation which, whether or not of a purely formal character, does not affect the terms of a policy in any significant respect; or*
- *(b) any variation of a policy issued in respect of an insurance made on or before 19th March 1968, other than a variation by virtue of which the policy falls, under paragraph 8(1) and (2) of Schedule 14, to be treated as issued in respect of an insurance made after that date.*

NOTES

Derivation

Para 21 derived from the Finance Act 1975, Sch 2, para 1, and the Finance Act 1987, Sch 15, para 7; para 22 derived from the Income and Corporation Taxes Act 1970, Sch 1, para 11, the Finance Act 1975, Sch 2, para 2, the Finance Act 1976, s 33, and the Finance Act 1978, Sch 3, para 13(1)(a), (b).

Amendment

Para 21: prospectively repealed with savings by the Finance Act 1995, ss 55(1)(a), 162, Sch 29, Part VIII, in relation to any time on or after a day to be appointed under s 55(9) of that Act, for determining whether a policy is or would be a qualifying policy at that time; for savings see s 55(2) thereof.

Para 22: prospectively repealed by the Finance Act 1995, ss 55(4), 162, Sch 29, Part VIII, in relation to any time on or a day to be appointed under s 55(9) of that Act.

PART III

POLICIES ISSUED BY NON-RESIDENT COMPANIES

23

In this Part—

- (a) any reference to a paragraph is a reference to that paragraph of this Schedule; and
- (b) "the old policy" and "the new policy" have the same meanings as in paragraph 17.

24

(1) This paragraph applies to a policy of life insurance—

- (a) which is issued in respect of an insurance made after 17th November 1983; and
- (b) which is so issued by a company resident outside the United Kingdom;

and in the following provisions of this paragraph such a policy is referred to as "a new non-resident policy" and the company by which it is issued is referred to as "the issuing company".

(2) Notwithstanding anything in paragraph 21—

- *(a) a new non-resident policy shall not be certified under sub-paragraph (1)(a) of that paragraph; and*
- *(b) a new non-resident policy which conforms with such a form as is mentioned in sub-paragraph (1)(b) of that paragraph shall not be a qualifying policy,*

until such time as the conditions in either sub-paragraph (3) or sub-paragraph (4) below are fulfilled with respect to it.

[(2) Subject to section 55(3) of the Finance Act 1995 (transitional provision for the certification of certain policies), a new non-resident policy that falls outside sub-paragraph (2A) below shall not be a qualifying policy until such time as the conditions in sub-paragraph (3) are fulfilled with respect to it.

(2A) A policy falls outside this sub-paragraph unless, at the time immediately before [the appointed date for the purposes of section 55 of the Finance Act 1995 (removal of certification requirements)], it was a qualifying policy by virtue of sub-paragraphs (2)(b) and (4) of this paragraph, as they had effect in relation to that time.]

(3) The conditions *first* referred to in sub-paragraph (2) above are—
- (a) that the issuing company is lawfully carrying on in the United Kingdom life assurance business (as defined in section 431(2)); and
- (b) that the premiums under the policy are payable to a branch in the United Kingdom of the issuing company, being a branch through which the issuing company carries on its life assurance business; and
- (c) the premiums under the policy form part of those business receipts of the issuing company which arise through that branch.

(4) *The conditions secondly referred to in sub-paragraph (2) above are—*
- *(a) that the policy holder is resident in the United Kingdom; and*
- *(b) that the income of the issuing company from the investments of its life assurance fund is, by virtue of section 445, charged to corporation tax under Case III of Schedule D;*

and expressions used in paragraph (b) above have the same meaning as in section 445(1).

25

(1) In the application of paragraph 17 in any case where—
- (a) the old policy was issued in respect of an insurance made after 17th November 1983 and could not be a qualifying policy by virtue of paragraph 24, and
- (b) the new policy is not a new non-resident policy as defined in that paragraph,

the rules for the determination of the question whether the new policy is a qualifying policy shall apply with the modifications in sub-paragraph (2) below.

[(2) The modifications are the following—
- (a) if, apart from paragraph 24, the old policy or any related policy (within the meaning of paragraph 17(2)(b)) of which account falls to be taken would have been a qualifying policy, that policy shall be assumed to have been a qualifying policy for the purposes of paragraph 17(2); and
- (b) if, apart from this paragraph, the new policy would be a qualifying policy, it shall not be such a policy unless the circumstances are as specified in paragraph 17(3); and
- (c) in paragraph 17(3)(c) the words "either by a branch or agency of theirs outside the United Kingdom or" shall be omitted;

and references in this sub-paragraph to being a qualifying policy shall have effect, in relation to any time before [the appointed date for the purposes of section 55 of the Finance Act 1995 (removal of certification requirements)], as including a reference to being capable of being certified as such a policy.]

(3) In the application of paragraph 17 in any case where—
- (a) the old policy is a qualifying policy which was issued in respect of an

insurance made on or before 17th November 1983 but, if the insurance had been made after that date, the policy could not have been a qualifying policy by virtue of paragraph 24, and

(b) the new policy is issued after the date and is not a new non-resident policy, as defined in paragraph 24,

the rules for the determination of the question whether the new policy is a qualifying policy shall apply with the modification in sub-paragraph (2)(c) above.

26

If, in the case of a substitution of policies falling within paragraph 25(1) or (3), the new policy confers such an option as results in the application to it of paragraph 19(3), the new policy shall be treated for the purposes of paragraph 19(3) as having been issued in respect of an insurance made on the same day as that on which was made the insurance in respect of which the old policy was issued.

27

(1) For the purposes of Part I and *paragraphs 21 and* [paragraph] 24, a policy of life insurance which was issued—

(a) in respect of an insurance made on or before 17th November 1983, and

(b) by a company resident outside the United Kingdom,

shall be treated as issued in respect of an insurance made after that date if the policy is varied after that date so as to increase the benefits secured or to extend the term of the insurance.

(2) If a policy of life insurance which was issued as mentioned in sub-paragraph (1)(a) and (b) above confers on the person to whom it is issued an option to have another policy substituted for it or to have any of its terms changed, then for the purposes of that sub-paragraph any change in the terms of the policy which is made in pursuance of the option shall be deemed to be a variation of the policy.

NOTES

Derivation

Paras 23, 25–27 derived from the Finance Act 1984, Sch 15, Part II; para 24 derived from the Finance Act 1975, Sch 2, para 1A, and the Finance At 1984, Sch 15, Part I.

Amendment

Para 24: sub-para (2) prospectively substituted by subsequent sub-paras (2), (2A) in square brackets by the Finance Act 1995, s 55(5)(a), as from a day to be appointed in accordance with s 55 of that Act (as amended by the Finance Act 1996, s 162(1)).

Para 24: In sub-para (2A) words from “the appointed” to “certification requirements)” in square brackets substituted by the Finance Act 1996, s 162(2).

Para 24: in sub-para (3) word “first” in italics prospectively repealed by the Finance Act 1995, ss 55(5)(b), 162, Sch 29, Part VIII, as from a day to be appointed in accordance with s 55 of that Act (as amended by the Finance Act 1996, s 162(1)).

Para 24: sub-para (4) prospectively repealed by the Finance Act 1995, ss 55(5)(b), 162, Sch 29, Part VIII, as from a day to be appointed in accordance with s 55 of that Act (as amended by the Finance act 1996, s 162(1)).

Para 25: sub-para (2) substituted by the Finance Act 1995, s 55(6).

Para 25: in sub-para (2) words from "the appointed" to certification requirements)" in square brackets substituted by the Finance Act 1996, s 162(2).

Para 27: in sub-para (1) words "paragraphs 21 and" in italics repealed and subsequent words in square bracket substituted, except so far as they have effect for the purposes of any case to which paragraph 21 hereto continues to apply, by the Finance Act 1995, s 55(7).

Appendix 5
Main guidance notes, Institute of Actuaries, Nos 1, 2, 7, 8, 15

[15.1]

GN1

ACTUARIES AND LONG-TERM INSURANCE BUSINESS

Classification

Practice Standard

Legislation or Authority

Insurance Companies Act 1982 (1982, c.50)
Friendly Societies Act 1992 (1992, c40)

Application

Appointed Actuaries and other actuaries who are directors or senior employees of insurance companies or friendly societies or companies which control long-term insurance companies. Actuaries responsible for long-term business written by bodies other than those authorised under the relevant Acts are expected to follow the same principles. In particular, Appointed Actuaries advising friendly societies authorised under the Friendly Societies Act 1992 are expected to interpret this Guidance Note with reference to these Acts and associated Regulations; Annex A contains a summary of the principal responsibilities under the 1992 Act for actuaries working with friendly societies. The Guidance Note is also written to help actuaries advising UK supervised long-term insurers and friendly societies on their world-wide business.

Author

Life Board

Status

Approved under Due Process

Version	Effective From
1.0	01.05.75
1.1	[1978-79]
1.2	[1979-80]
1.3	[1983-84]
1.4	01.04.87
1.5	[1985-86]
1.6	01.04.87
2.0	01.12.88
2.1	01.09.90
3.0	01.07.92
4.0	30.12.94
5.0	01.09.96
5.1	01.12.98

A: THE APPOINTED ACTUARY

1 Introduction

1.1 The responsibilities of actuaries who are appointed in terms of Section 19 of the Insurance Companies act 1982 or Section 44 of the Friendly Societies Act 1992 are central to the financial soundness of the long-term insurance business of their companies or societies. The reputation of the profession, therefore, depends in no small measure on the proper discharge of these responsibilities. It is incumbent upon all Appointed Actuaries to ensure, so far as is within their authority, that the long-term business of the company is operated on sound financial lines and with regard to its policyholders' reasonable expectations. Friendly Societies are bound by regulations applicable to them.

2 Considerations Affecting the Position of Appointed Actuaries

2.1 In order to practise as an Appointed Actuary an actuary must possess a Practising Certificate. In addition any actuary, before accepting appointment as an Appointed Actuary, must consider most carefully in the light of individual previous experience and work whether acceptance would be in line with proper professional behaviour and standards. No actuary should act as Appointed Actuary if that individual does not have the appropriate knowledge and practical experience relevant to the company concerned. There may be exceptional circumstances where this need not apply, but in such cases appropriate arrangements must be made for the Appointed Actuary to have recourse on a professional and formal basis to an actuary who has such knowledge and experience.

2.2 A potential Appointed Actuary who has not already worked in close touch with the present Appointed Actuary has a professional duty to consult that individual (if this is possible) to discover whether there are any professional reasons why the appointment should not be accepted. The prospective client should be informed of such consultation and the client's permission sought. If such permission were withheld it would be a material factor which would be relevant to the prospective appointee's decision as to the propriety of accepting the appointment. The Appointed Actuary must have a right of direct access to the board of directors of the company and have access to all relevant information so that the full range of the Appointed Actuary's duties can be carried out satisfactorily. This must be explicit from the inception of the new appointment. It is suggested that Appointed Actuaries who are not employees of the company seek to include these rights in their letter of appointment. Where there is a group structure, the Appointed Actuary should bear in mind the possible implications and ensure a right of direct access to the relevant decision making bodies.

2.3 Where an actuary's financial interests in an insurance company (or related company) by their nature and size are or become such that a material conflict of interest would, in the normal course of events, arise or seem to arise (or where a material conflict arises for some other reason), that individual should not accept the position of Appointed Actuary or continue in it as the case may be. If temporarily in a special situation a material conflict of interest arose, or would seem to arise, the Appointed Actuary before making a report should first ask the company to obtain a report from an actuary who has no conflict of interest.

3 Extent of the Appointed Actuary's Responsibility

3.1 The profession's rules of conduct make it clear that every actuary acting in a professional capacity, whether remunerated by salary or fee, has a duty to the profession and the actuary's responsibility to the client must be consistent with this. The Appointed Actuary is, however, in a special position:

(a) being appointed and remunerated by the company, and at the same time

(b) having responsibilities and obligations to the Supervisory Authority by reason of certain statutory duties, which arise from supervisory functions aimed at the protection of policyholders.

These responsibilities may be in conflict from time to time but it would be seldom that any such conflict could not be resolved by discussions internal to the company.

3.2 Circumstances may arise such that the Appointed Actuary considers that there is a material risk that the long-term fund will be insufficient to cover its liabilities or that the company will fail to meet its obligations under the Act in relation to its long-term business. This may be because:

(a) a particular course of action is being, or is proposed to be, followed by the company, or

(b) the company is failing to take appropriate action in response to a change in circumstances, or

(c) a particular situation has arisen, perhaps outside the control of the company.

In these circumstances the Appointed Actuary must inform the company accordingly. If the company fails to take action to remedy the position and does not advise the Supervisory Authority of the situation then it is the Appointed Actuary's duty to advise the Supervisory Authority after so informing the company.*

* This duty applies, notwithstanding the normal requirement in the Memorandum on Professional Conduct of the Faculty and Institute to maintain the confidentiality of the company's affairs.

3.3 It is part of the Appointed Actuary's continuing responsibility to advise the company of the Appointed Actuary's interpretation of its policyholders' reasonable expectations. In general terms this interpretation should have regard to the broad nature of the company and its approach to the treatment of policyholders both individually and (where appropriate) collectively as a group vis-à-vis shareholders. When a significant change is likely to take place, the Appointed Actuary should take all reasonable steps to ensure that the company appreciates the implications for the reasonable expectations of its policyholders. It is also incumbent upon the Appointed Actuary to take all reasonable steps to ensure that the company's incoming policyholders should not be misled as to their expectations.

3.4 Under the insurance legislation it is a requirement for continuing authorisation that the company should fulfil certain criteria of sound and prudent management. These criteria are set out in the legislation and include the need for insurance business to be conducted with due regard to the interests of policyholders and potential policyholders. In formulating advice to be given to the company, the Appointed Actuary must take account of these interests.

4 The Duties of the Appointed Actuary

4.1 The statutory responsibility of the Appointed Actuary as required under Section 18 of the Insurance Companies Act 1982 is to carry out, from time to time, and to report on an investigation into the financial condition of the company, including a valuation of its long-term liabilities. The Appointed Actuary must certify that, inter alia, GN1 and GN8 have been complied with. This certificate should state the effective dates of these GNs. Although, as a statutory requirement, an investigation is to be made only at specific intervals, the profession regards it as the Appointed Actuary's duty to take all reasonable steps to ensure that the Appointed Actuary is, at all times, satisfied that in any investigation the long-term fund would be sufficient and the company would be able to satisfy any obligation to which it is subject by virtue of the Insurance Companies Act 1982.

4.1.1 More precisely, Section 18 makes it the statutory responsibility of the Appointed Actuary to determine in accordance with any applicable valuation regulations any excess of the assets representing a long-term fund over its liabilities. The Appointed Actuary must also identify separately any excess which relates to a part of such a fund if there are policyholders with a right to participate in profits which also relates to that part. The company is permitted by Section 29 to make transfers of assets representing its long-term fund to the extent that they have been show by a recent Section 18 investigation to exceed the amount of the liabilities, subject to the provisions of Section 30 relating to allocations to any participating policyholders. It is the Appointed Actuary's professional responsibility to advise the company on the extent to which it would be appropriate to distribute any excess to policyholders or transfer it to shareholders and to make recommendations for its specific allocation.

4.1.2 The Appointed Actuary must take all reasonable steps to ensure that the company's constitution or authorised procedures are or will be such that it will not make or undertake to make a specific allocation of profit in a long-term fund (whether to policyholders, shareholders or both) before the directors have obtained from the Appointed Actuary and duly considered a written report containing the Appointed Actuary's observations and recommendations on the subject.

4.2 The Appointed Actuary must have regard to al aspects likely to affect the financial position of the company in respect of its long-term business including the possible effect of any contingent liabilities should they crystallise. Although the following list is not exhaustive the financial position is particularly affected by:

(a) the premium rates on which existing business has been, and current new business is being, written;
(b) the nature of the contracts in force and currently being sold, with particular reference to all options and guarantees;
(c) the existing investments and continuing investment policy including the use of derivative instruments;
(d) the marketing plans, in particular the expected volumes and costs of sales;
(e) the current and likely future level of expenses;
(f) the extent of the company's free assets;
(g) the reinsurance, underwriting and (for health insurances) claims handling arrangements;

(h) the company's policy in regard to the nature and timing of allocations of profits to policyholders and/or shareholders; and
(i) the current and likely future taxation position of the company.

4.3 Information on the above items and any other relevant information should be made available to the Appointed Actuary so that the Appointed Actuary is able to carry out the necessary financial investigations to be satisfied as to the continuing financial state of the company and to sign the relevant certificates. The Appointed Actuary must make sure that the necessity for such information is fully understood by the company, and that suitable arrangements are made to ensure that this information is forthcoming. If sufficient information is not available to ensure compliance with GN1 and GN8, the Appointed Actuary will need to qualify the certificate.

5 Premium Rates and Policy Conditions

5.1 A prime responsibility must lie with the Appointed Actuary to be satisfied that the premium rates being charged for new business are appropriate and consistent with the requirements of Section 35B of the Insurance Companies Act 1982. That is to say in particular they should be sufficient to enable the company in due course to meet its emerging liabilities, having regard to the items listed in Paragraph 4.2 above, not least the extent of the company's free assets. The Appointed Actuary may need to have regard to the provisions of Section 37(2)(a) of the Insurance Companies Act 1982.

5.2 The certification of premium rate adequacy, by the Appointed Actuary, in the company's annual financial returns to the Supervisory Authority, refers to contracts written during the financial year and is thus purely retrospective. Since reserves will have been set up to allow for any anticipated losses the certificate does not in itself make any demands on the Appointed Actuary additional to those required by the Valuation Regulations. However, should premium rates be such that business is expected to be written on terms which require support from the free assets, the Appointed Actuary will need to consider the company's liability to continue to write business on such terms and will need to inform the directors of the ability of the company's financial resources to withstand the writing of business on such terms.

5.3 The statement that a premium rate will be sufficient cannot in fact be an absolute statement – it is inevitably a probability statement because it depends on such future events as mortality, the return on investments, and the expenses. The adequacy or otherwise of premium rates cannot, therefore, be other than a matter of judgement. It is the responsibility of the Appointed Actuary to exercise this judgement.

5.4 The required judgement will, of course, need to be based on the use of sound techniques. Attention is specially drawn to the complex questions of tax relief and allowances for a new company, adequacy of provision for expenses, and contracts involving various options, including guaranteed surrender values, particularly if financial conditions could arise in which the policyholder could gain by surrender and re-entry.

5.5 It may be that a practicable premium basis, whilst commercially justifiable, will involve significant new business strain. The Appointed Actuary must be satisfied that the company will be able to set up the necessary reserve and solvency margin, and must indicate any limits on the volume of business that may prudently be accepted.

5.6 The shareholders' assets in a proprietary office will be taken into account by the Appointed Actuary. However, it cannot automatically be assumed that they are equivalent to free reserves held as part of the long-term fund because they can be used for other than long-term business.

5.7 Some companies may include in their policy contracts a requirement that terms be determined by the Appointed Actuary, or by the company's actuary or by the company on the advice of the Appointed Actuary. For example, policy expense charges and mortality and morbidity charges may be treated in this way, as many market value adjustments to unitise with-profits contracts. In determining such terms, or in providing advice to the company in this area, the Appointed Actuary should have regard to policyholders' reasonable expectations and to existing legislation, including that covering unfair contract terms, where relevant.

5.8 For unit linked business, unit pricing, fund charges, and deductions in respect of taxation are key elements of policyholders' reasonable expectations, to the extent that the company has discretion in applying its policy conditions. The Appointed Actuary must be satisfied that all discretionary elements of unit pricing and fund charges are applied consistently with policyholders' reasonable expectations. In particular, the Appointed Actuary must be satisfied that the procedures for determining:
(a) the prices at which units are allocated to or de-allocated from policies;
(b) the prices at which units are created or cancelled; and
(c) compensation where errors or inequities of a material size in unit pricing have occurred;

are equitable to any policyholders affected both directly and indirectly. For these purposes the Appointed Actuary should have regard to the value of the assets of the unit fund, the tax position of the unit fund, the materiality of amounts involved and any other matters considered relevant.

6 Actuarial Investigations

6.1 The Appointed Actuary must be satisfied in relation to the financial condition of the existing business. To do so the Appointed Actuary must consider the liabilities, the corresponding assets, and their interrelationship, and be satisfied as to the resilience of the financial position of the company in all reasonably foreseeable circumstances which might affect that position.

6.2 The Appointed Actuary should take all reasonable steps to ensure that the data are accurate and if the Appointed Actuary has any doubts management must be asked to provide written assurance as to the correctness and completeness of the data. The Appointed Actuary should be satisfied that the appropriate valuation procedures have been correctly carried out and adequately documented.

6.3 The Appointed Actuary must use liability valuation methods that are appropriate to the contracts in question, taking into account not only the principal benefits but any ancillary benefits such as surrender and paid-up values and any options. When assessing the liabilities f the long-term business of the company the Appointed Actuary must also have regard to policyholders' reasonable expectations.

6.4 Appropriate provision must be made for future expenses of continuing the existing business. This provision must not be less than that which would be required if the company were to be closed to new business one year after the valuation date; it must also have regard, amongst other factors, to the possibility that preferential service agreements might be altered or terminated.

6.5 Subject to any statutory regulations, the responsibility for investment policy rests with the directors of the company, as also does the decision as to the value to be placed on the assets in any balance sheet.

6.6 The Appointed Actuary must decide the rates of interest to be used in the valuation of the liabilities. These are affected by the Appointed Actuary's estimates of the likely future proceeds of the existing assets and of the rate at which future investment will be possible. In relation to the existing assets, the Appointed Actuary must assess the nature of the portfolio and consider what rate of return, capital and income, is likely to be realised over the future period relevant to the liabilities. In addition, due allowance must be made for the current and future taxation position of the company. Any such allowance must be consistent with any allowance made for tax relief on expenses. Judgement on these factors rests with the Appointed Actuary who must decide the basis of the valuation of the liabilities. The Appointed Actuary will need to be aware of the possible effects of derivative instruments used by the company when choosing the valuation basis (including the basis used in the changed investment conditions envisaged under Regulation 75 of the Insurance Companies Regulations 1994). The appropriate valuation interest rates should allow for the return on the assets held as adjusted to reflect economic exposure under futures contracts and contracts for differences. Consideration should be given to the situation with options, particularly when close to an option date.

6.7 The Appointed Actuary must also pay regard to the relationship between the term of the assets and that of the corresponding liabilities. The importance of this will vary widely from one situation to another, but experience suggests that this can be an area of particular danger.

6.7.1 At one extreme, for example, for a company with a large portfolio of long-established with-profits business, and where the company is transacting (and seems likely to continue to transact) a steady volume of new business which is small in relation to the existing business, the possibility of insolvency arising from mismatching of assets and liabilities may be minimal.

6.7.2 At the other extreme, for a company transacting a volume of non-profit new business which is very large in relation to the existing portfolio and which has only low free assets, matching of asset proceeds to liability outgo may be critical to solvency. The dangers are increased if there are alternative guarantees or options which could, in certain circumstances, require a different distribution of assets by term.

6.8 The Appointed Actuary must judge and decide whether the investment policy pursued by the directors is, or could become, inappropriate having regard to the nature and term of the company's liabilities. If this is the case, the Appointed Actuary must advise the company of the constraints on investment policy necessary to protect the position of policyholders.

6.9 The Appointed Actuary must advise the company that appropriate guidelines should be given to the company's investment managers regarding the use of derivative contracts and that appropriate procedures should be in place to monitor the company's exposure to loss through their use. Loss can occurred either through market movements or through failure of a counterparty.

6.10 The nature of the company's reinsurance arrangements including any financing provision implicit therein should be taken into account in the Appointed Actuary's valuation. If the Appointed Actuary considers these arrangement are inappropriate or inadequate the Appointed Actuary should advise the company on the modifications necessary to protect the position of the policyholders. The Appointed Actuary should also have regard to the possibility of failure of a reinsurer or the possibility that reinsurance contracts may lapse or prove unenforceable in certain circumstances.

6.11 The Appointed Actuary must be satisfied that, in each of the assumptions, the margins in any published valuation of the liabilities, including any margins required by statute, are adequate having regard to the Appointed Actuary's own assessment of the risks inherent in the nature and conduct of the company's business.

7 Insolvency

7.1 It is apparent from the foregoing that most of the problems with which the Appointed Actuary is concerned are not capable of precise assessment but are, rather, matters of judgement. In some circumstances, this judgement may appropriately be based on the Appointed Actuary's estimates of the most probable outcome – perhaps, for example, in relation to bonus distribution. If, however, judgement is required in a matter which may affect the solvency of the company, much more rigorous standards must be applied. (Two such contrasting situations are exemplified in Paragraphs 6.7.1 and 6.7.2)

7.2 The possibility of insolvency, or intervention by the Supervisory Authority on the grounds of the company being unable to fulfil the reasonable expectations of its policyholders, may arise from factors, some of which are within the control of the company and some not. To the extent that they are under the control of the company, it is the Appointed Actuary's duty to assess the limits within which the company must act and to advise the company of the necessity for these limits.

7.3 The Appointed Actuary must consider all external factors outside the control of the company which could lead to insolvency and must then take whatever action the Appointed Actuary considers necessary. The profession requires that any Appointed Actuary should pay the most scrupulous regard to prudent judgement in these matters.

8 Written Reports

8.1 The Appointed Actuary is required as part of the Appointed Actuary's statutory duties to report to the Supervisory Authority in a prescribed form on actuarial investigations carried out under Section 18 of the Insurance Companies Act 1982. It is the Appointed Actuary's professional duty first to report in writing to the directors on the results and implications of ay such investigation, whether or not an allocation of profits is involved. In the Section 18 Report to the Supervisory Authority, the Appointed Actuary should use best endeavours to ensure the financial results are presented in a way that demonstrates the true underlying position of the company and that these results are not distorted by any undisclosed valuation methods or assumptions.

8.2 If the Appointed Actuary has reason to believe that the company plans to announce or otherwise undertake to make a specific allocation of profits to policyholders and/or shareholders in anticipation of the results of a Section 18 investigation (notwithstanding that, to comply with Section 29(2), confirmation that the investigation shows a sufficient excess of assets over liabilities must precede an actual transfer of assets out of the long-term fund), the Appointed Actuary must take all reasonable steps to ensure that the directors will be in a position to consider a suitable written actuarial report on the subject before the announcement is due to be made or the undertaking given.

8.3 In reporting on and making recommendations in respect of any proposed allocation of profits the Appointed Actuary must consider the facts listed in Paragraph 4.2 above and any others personally thought to be significant, and must carry out appropriate financial investigations including an appraisal of the relevant experience. The Appointed Actuary must include in the report such information and discussion about each factor, and about the results of any financial investigations, as may be necessary to enable the directors to judge the appropriateness of the allocation and understand its implications for the future conduct of the company's long-term business. In particular, but without prejudice to the generality of this requirement:

8.3.1 If the report anticipates the results of a Section 18 investigation the Appointed Actuary must indicate and discuss how in the context of statutory requirements the allocation will be financed.

8.3.2 The relationship between the proposed allocation and the relevant experience must be discussed and an indication given as to whether in the Appointed Actuary's opinion the continuance of a distribution policy which, in its relationship to relevant experience, was consistent with the allocation now proposed (excluding any component of the allocation that will be declared to be non-recurring) could lead in due course to an unsatisfactory position. If so, the Appointed Actuary must explain how this could appropriately be avoided.

8.3.3 In the case of with-profits business the Appointed Actuary's comments under Paragraph 8.3.2 must cover bonus prospects, with particular reference to the projected development of outgo on and asset cover for unreserved terminal bonus and the like in different investment scenarios.

8.3.4 The Appointed Actuary must justify any recommendations regarding the allocation and its consequences (if any) for the conduct of the company's business by reference as appropriate to the Appointed Actuary's

(a) appraisal of the relevant experience;
(b) understanding of the company's financial and business objectives;
(c) assessment of the company's continuing ability to meet it statutory solvency requirements;
(d) interpretation of the reasonable expectations of the company's policyholders having regard to (a), (b) and (c). Such expectations are clearly influenced by policy literature and other publicly available information such as own charge illustrations. The Appointed Actuary should assumed that among the conditions for the fulfilment of those expectations are:
  (i) that, in the recognition and allocation of profits in accordance with the company's terms of participation and its policy in respect of the matters referred to in Paragraph 4.2(h) above, groups of participating policies are appropriately and equitably distinguished having regard inter alia to the terms of the policies, their duration and their relevant pooled experience; and
  (ii) that the company conducts its affairs, including its new business and investment strategies, with due regard for its financial resources.

8.4 If in the Appointed Actuary's opinion issues required to be covered in a written report to the directors were fully dealt with in a comparable report made within the preceding eleven months and duly discussed by the board, the Appointed Actuary may report in an appropriately abridge form, as for example when interim or terminal bonus rates are being reviewed during the year.

8.5 If a parent of the company reserves the right to approve or vary decisions on matters which are required by this section to be covered in a report by the Appointed Actuary to the company's directors, the Appointed Actuary must take all reasonable steps to ensure that any such report is made available at an appropriate time to the relevant authorities within that parent.

B: THE ACTUARY AS A DIRECTOR OR IN ANY OTHER POSITION OF AUTHORITY IN RELATION TO AN INSURANCE COMPANY

9 Internal

9.1 It is clearly in the public interest that actuaries should be available to act as directors of insurance companies and companies which control insurance companies, particularly those transacting long-term insurance, where by their professional training they are especially fitted to make a useful contribution. Any such actuaries should, however, recognise that the public, and their fellow directors, will assume that they are satisfied as to the way in which the affairs of the insurance company are likely to be conducted whilst they are members of the board. It is appropriate for such actuaries to make suitable enquiries before accepting appointments as directors.

9.2 A common situation is for the Appointed Actuary also to hold a managerial appointment or (whether an employee or not) to be invited to join the board. On occasions the Appointed Actuary will be expressing views as a member of the management or as one director among many; at other times the actuary will be advising the board as the Appointed Actuary. All reasonable steps must be taken to ensure that the other members of the management or the other directors, as the case may be, recognise in what capacity the actuary is expressing these views.

9.3 A professional responsibility is owed to the Appointed Actuary by any other actuary who is a director. Such a director can be of great benefit to the board, and to the Appointed Actuary, in complementing the Appointed Actuary's advice. However that director's presence on the board does not lessen the Appointed Actuary's responsibilities in any way nor reduce the need for the Appointed Actuary to have right of direct access to the board. Such directors should guard against acting as if they were the Appointed Actuary. If providing actuarial advice to the board formally or informally in an area which could encroach on the Appointed Actuary's role, they should ensure that the Appointed Actuary is informed of that advice and given the opportunity to present to the board properly reasoned comments from the Appointed Actuary's perspective. Whilst there is room for differences in opinion in relation to professional advice and judgement, such directors must take care to ensure that, by their actions or absence of action, they do not in any way diminish the status or role of the Appointed Actuary. However, this does not prevent them from making properly reasoned comments on the work of the Appointed Actuary if they feel it is appropriate or necessary to do so.

9.4 A similar responsibility is owed to the Appointed Actuary by any other actuaries who are in a managerial or other position of authority in the company or in a parent company including any Reporting Actuary acting in accordance with GN7. In particular, although their responsibilities may be such as to require them to enter into discussions with the Appointed Actuary on matters which impinge on the latter's professional responsibility, they should at all times take care to respect the status of the Appointed Actuary.

10 External

10.1 There will be circumstances in which a member who is external to a particular insurance company is asked by the company or someone with a legitimate interest in the company to express an opinion on a valuation carried out by the Appointed Actuary or on a report the Appointed Actuary has made to the company in the context of the Appointed Actuary's statutory or professional responsibilities.

10.2 Any members engaged in such assignments should bear in mind that, while there is room for differences of opinion in relation to actuarial advice and judgement, they should at all times take care to respect the status of the Appointed Actuary. However, this does not prevent them from making properly reasoned comments on the work of the Appointed Actuary if they feel it is appropriate or necessary to do so.

GN2

FINANCIAL CONDITION REPORTS

Classification

Recommended practice

Legislation or Authority

Insurance Companies Act 1982 (1982, c.50).
Friendly Societies Act 1992 (1992, c.40).

Application

Appointed Actuaries. Actuaries responsible for long-term insurance business written by bodies other than authorised under the relevant Acts are expected to follow the same principles. The Guidance Note is also written to help actuaries advising UK-supervised long-term insurers and friendly societies (directive and incorporated societies only) on their world-wide business.

Author

Life Board

Status

Approved under Due Process

Version	**Effective from**
1.0	25.3.1996

1 Introduction

1.1 Section 18 of the Insurance Companies Act 1982, and Section 46 of the Friendly Societies Act 1992, require Appointed Actuaries to carry out, and report on the results of, an annual investigation in accordance with associated regulations. As well as meeting this obligation, it is advisable for Appointed Actuaries to provide their Board or Committee of Management with a more extensive written report into the current solvency position of the company or society and its possible future development – a Financial Condition Report.

1.2 The purpose of this Guidance Note is to suggest a possible format and contents for a Financial Condition Report. It also outlines how Dynamic Solvency Testing would normally be used to derive the background information underlying the Financial Condition Report. [This Guidance Note refers to boards/offices/companies for simplicity; Appointed Actuaries for friendly societies should interpret these terms accordingly.]

1.3 The Financial Condition Report should normally be addressed to the Board of the life company concerned. This general intention should be interpreted in the circumstances of the particular organisation. In large and complicated groups the life company Board may not be the most appropriate authority to receive the report. The criterion should be to report to the Board within the group that is responsible for policy formation for the company concerned.

1.4 Within a group of companies it may be appropriate to produce a single report covering more than one company in the group, providing any such combined report is acceptable to all the Appointed Actuaries involved. It is essential that the report is expressed in a form which is accessible to its readers and does not conceal important issues inadvertently by, for example, undue length or complexity. An executive summary or overview drawing attention to important issues would be helpful.

1.5 In the normal course of events this report should be produced annually. It is possible that in a period of financial stability, both externally and within the office, the report could be truncated to avoid undue repetition of information provided in previous years. However, if there are changes either in the company itself or externally the relevant parts of the report may need to be updated as necessary.

1.6 Dynamic Solvency Testing is the principal technique which enables Appointed Actuaries to assess the liability of an office to withstand changes in both the external economic environment and the particular experience of the office. It involves projecting the office's revenue account and balance sheet forward and then changing the important assumptions in turn to establish the sensitivity of the office to changes in that particular assumption or assumptions. The combined effect of a change in two or more related assumptions will in many cases be more important than a change in any one of them in isolation.

1.7 Further, the Appointed Actuary should address the issue of what actions are open to the office for dealing with the particular circumstances and, where appropriate, make suitable recommendations. For the appraisal of many risks, these projections can be on a deterministic basis. However, stochastic techniques can be used to identify additional risks and might be considered depending on the circumstances and nature of the office in question. Stochastic techniques can also be valuable in comparing the relative level of probability of adverse circumstance occurring.

1.8 Appointed Actuaries should use whatever techniques they consider appropriate to the business written by their office.

1.9 It is not essential to have a single report covering all the items in this Guidance Note where the Appointed Actuary has already reported to the Board on some aspects previously.

2 General Points

2.1 The Financial Condition Report should normally include:

2.1.1 The purpose of the report.

2.1.2 The extent, if any, to which the report falls short of its stated purpose.

2.1.3 The conclusions that can be drawn about the financial position of the office at the particular time at which the investigation is carried out.

2.1.4 Relevant historical development of the company and any conclusions that can be drawn from that development which may have implications for the future of the company.

2.1.5 Comments on particular aspects of the historical development of the company, such as any policy conditions, prospectuses, methods of selling etc., which have led to Policyholders' Reasonable Expectations being formed with financial consequences for the company.

2.1.6 A commentary on the business of the company and the environment in which it is expected to operate.

2.1.7 A commentary and opinion on the implications of the Dynamic Solvency Testing or other financial investigations with special reference to any future external factors which present a threat to the company's financial security and the options open to the company to deal with those factors.

2.2 It would be usual for the Appointed Actuary to comment in more detail on:

2.2.1 The methods and assumptions that have been used. The report should distinguish between those assumptions which are important and those which are less so, and also those which are within the company's control and those which are dictated by external circumstances.

2.2.2 Any changes made to the methods or assumptions used in the last similar report.

2.2.3 Any significant restrictions to the scope or detail of the analysis for reasons such as the lack of availability of data, shortcomings in computer systems, or availability of resources to carry out the analysis. The Appointed Actuary should draw attention to any such inadequacies and give an opinion as to their importance and relevance to the company. Thus, for example, attention should be drawn to any blocks of existing or proposed new business that have not been evaluated.

2.2.4 The differing nature of some assumptions as compared with others:

(i) Some assumptions such as mortality (except possibly mortality arising from AIDS) can be relied on as fairly predictable.

(ii) Others, for example policy persistency, may need to be placed in the context of both historical experience and changes anticipated in the light of different operating methods now used by the company.

(iii) Yet others may be highly uncertain and totally outside the control of the office. This is particularly true of investment conditions, the volatility of which may have profound implications for the financial condition of the office.

Where appropriate, the report should state how the assumptions adopted compare with recent experience, and should give explanations where assumptions differ significantly from that experience.

2.2.5 Any particular financial characteristics of existing or current new business that may require special consideration.

2.2.6 The special characteristics of the office in terms of the way in which they may affect its development and future prospects. It is helpful to draw attention to any such characteristics and be clear about the importance of both the absolute position of any particular aspect and, where possible and relevant, the relative position when compared with other companies.

2.3 The report should indicate, where appropriate, how the following issues have been addressed:

2.3.1 Any unusual features of business either on the books, current new business or proposed product development.

2.3.2 Any financially significant reinsurance arrangements and any possible options contained within them.

2.3.3 The effects of any known or planned changes in the company's method of operation, its corporate structure, etc.

2.3.4 Any use made by the company of derivatives, where potentially financially significant, and their purpose.

2.3.5 Post Balance Sheet events – some comment on experience and events since the end of the financial year to which the report relates will almost always be required.

3 Dynamic Solvency Testing

3.1 A distinction should be drawn between testing the effect of a change in individual assumptions in a relatively mechanistic way and testing groups of assumptions which are assumed to change in a related way. This is sometimes described as 'scenario' testing, whereas varying individual assumptions independently is referred to as sensitivity testing. Stochastic modelling will normally incorporate the scenario concept by assuming specific statistical relationships between variables such as inflation and investment returns.

3.2 It may be helpful, as a matter of routine, to test the effect of each assumption separately but in the final report to restrict comment to those which are judged likely to have a material effect. Certain assumptions, in particular those which are a consequence of the economic environment, are best treated as a group. The office's ability to withstand a period of inflation or recession, rising or falling stock markets, increasing market sizes or increasing competitiveness, needs to be investigated using coherent sets of assumptions.

3.3 The choice of the term over which to carry out projections is an important one. Generally a period of five years will be sufficient but there may be some areas of risk where full effects become apparent only over a longer period. Such circumstances might include the effects of bonus smoothing following a period of quickly rising or falling stock market levels, or the impact of a substantial but gradual fall in new business levels.

3.4 It is not thought helpful for guidance to prescribe particular variations in assumptions or even which assumptions need to be tested and reported. Individual Appointed Actuaries will need to judge what is appropriate for a given company in the particular circumstances in which it finds itself. Nevertheless it may be helpful to draw attention to the following:

3.4.1 There would need to be specific reasons for not testing variations in the following assumptions:
(i) future investment conditions;
(ii) levels of new business, where this is being written;
(iii) expenses;
(iv) persistency.

3.4.2 Other assumptions may be of considerable importance in some companies but not others, for example:
(i) allocation of profits and/or special distributions of carried forward surplus to policyholders and/or shareholders;
(ii) mortality and morbidity;
(iii) taxation;
(iv) exercising of options by policyholders;
(v) exercising of options by the company;
(vi) effects of asset-defaults;
(vii) unit pricing bases;
(viii) risk of reinsurer default.

3.4.3 The Appointed Actuary needs to be alert to various factors that might affect a company. For example:
(i) concentrations of assets in particular risk areas;
(ii) derivatives;
(iii) assets containing unusual provisions which may be susceptible to particular risks;
(iv) sources of new business which have unusual characteristics;
(v) impending major claims or litigation that might affect the company;
(vi) operational exposure to accidents, terrorism, or malicious damage;
(vii) unusual contracts or relationships which may have financial implications;
(viii) risks created by deficient product literature or policy documentation;
(ix) loss of a distribution channel;
(x) the effect in different scenarios of options and guarantees in the insurance liabilities.

3.4.4 In each scenario tested, provisions should be made for all elements of the statutory liability including an appropriate level of resilience reserve.

3.5 As well as drawing attention to those potential developments which are of concern, the report should explain the options open to the company and how to deal with those possible developments. Developments which can be dealt with in a straightforward fashion are of relatively little concern. If, however, the Appointed Actuary identifies developments, or sets of developments, which lead to financial difficulty for which no satisfactory remedial action can be found, the Appointed Actuary should ensure that such matters have special prominence in the report and include any recommendations as to what might be done to avoid such circumstances. The very least that it is reasonable for a Board to expect of the advice from the Appointed Actuary is that the company does not unknowingly run foreseeable risks which could jeopardise its financial well-being.

GN7

THE ROLE OF ACTUARIES IN RELATION TO FINANCIAL STATEMENTS OF INSURERS AND INSURANCE GROUPS WRITING LONG-TERM BUSINESS AND THEIR RELATIONSHIP WITH AUDITORS

Classification

Recommended practice

Legislation or Authority

Insurance Companies Act 1982 (1982 c.50)
Companies Act 1985 (1985 c.6). ("Companies Act")
Companies Act (Insurance Companies Accounts) Regulations 1993 ("1993 Regulations")
Auditing Guideline 311 (Life Insurers in the United Kingdom) issued by the Auditing Practices Committee (and subsequently adopted by the Auditing Practice Board) ("Auditing Guideline 311")
ABI Guidance Note – Accounting for Insurance Business (Excluding Accounting for Investments) 1995 ("Modified Statutory Guidance Note")
Insurance Companies (Accounts and Statements) Regulations 1996 ("Supervisory Returns")

Application

This Guidance Note has been issued to give advice to:

- Actuaries calculating the long-term business provision for inclusion in the financial statements of a UK authorised insurance company, a friendly society, or a UK domiciled insurance group;
- Appointed Actuaries;
- Other actuaries involved in the preparation of financial statements under the Companies Act, or equivalent friendly society legislation, for companies, societies, or groups transacting long-term insurance business and domiciled in the United Kingdom;

and includes, in particular, advice regarding their relationship with the Auditor of those statements and the Supervisory Returns.

Author

Life Board.

Status

Approved under Due Process.

Version	Effective from
1.0	01.01.80
1.1	[1983-84]
1.2	[1985-86]
1.3	01.09.90
2.0	01.12.91
3.0	01.11.97

1 Introduction

1.1 Schedule 9A of the Companies Act, introduced by the 1993 Regulations, requires that technical provisions for long-term insurance business be shown explicitly in the annual financial statements and hence they fall within the scope of the audit. This is a significantly different situation from that relating to the Supervisory Returns where the Auditor, when giving an opinion, is permitted to have reliance on the certificate given by the Appointed Actuary.

1.2 This Guidance Note explains the professional duties of the various parties in relation to the financial statements under the 1993 Regulations and the relationships between them. It also refers to the relationship between the Appointed Actuary and the auditors in the preparation of the Supervisory Returns.

1.3 The 1993 Regulations have introduced a new professional role for the actuary. The actuary fulfilling this role is referred to in this Guidance Note as the Reporting Actuary. The introduction of this new role in no way diminishes that of the Appointed Actuary, whose duties remain central to maintaining the soundness of the long-term business of insurance companies.

1.4 The 1993 Regulations require an insurance company writing long-term insurance business to have a Reporting Actuary. In the case of an insurance holding company, however, it may be possible for the company to consolidate the results of its subsidiaries without the involvement of an actuary and hence for holding companies the role of Reporting Actuary may not exist. Any actuary who is in any doubt about whether or not she is fulfilling the role of a Reporting Actuary should seek clarification of his or her status from the company's directors.

1.5 This Guidance Note does not apply to a pension scheme actuary notwithstanding that calculations performed by such an actuary may have implications for the company's financial statements.

1.6 An actuary working for a friendly society is expected to interpret this Guidance Note appropriately, having regard to the relevant legislation for friendly societies. The relevant legislation is not included under Legislation or Authority above.

2 The Directors

2.1 The directors of an insurer writing long-term insurance business or of an insurance holding company are responsible for all statements made and amounts shown in financial statements prepared under the Companies Act. To the extent that these statements contain amounts calculated by an actuary, the directors will be placing reliance on the professional expertise of the actuary to calculate the amounts. Nonetheless the directors remain legally responsible for the preparation of the financial statements and ensuring that they give a true and fair view of the state of affairs, and results of, the company.

2.2 As explained in 3.2 below, it is perfectly proper for the directors to give instructions to the Reporting Actuary on the general approach to be adopted in carrying out his or her work. This contrasts with the situation applicable to the Appointed Actuary's equivalent calculations for the Supervisory Returns.

3 The Reporting Actuary

3.1 The 1993 Regulations state that for the long-term business provision, in the case of an insurance company, the "companies shall be made annually by a Fellow of the Institute or Faculty of Actuaries on the basis of recognised actuarial methods, with due regard to the actuarial principles laid down in Council Directive 92/96/EEC". For group accounts, in the case of a subsidiary having a head office outside the UK the computation shall be made "by an actuary or other specialist in the field on the basis of recognised actuarial methods". The "making of the computation" requires the exercise of professional judgement and hence an individual actuary must provide that judgement. This actuary is referred to as the Reporting Actuary in this Note.

3.2 The Reporting Actuary's principals are the directors of the organisation to whom he or she reports, and as mentioned in 2.2 above it is perfectly proper for the directors to give the Reporting Actuary instructions regarding the broad approach to be followed in the calculation of the long-term business provision. However, the Reporting Actuary should be aware that readers of the financial statements will be placing reliance on the figure shown and in this regard the requirements of the Memorandum of Professional Conduct as regards duties to third parties are relevant.

3.3 In many instances, the Reporting Actuary will be the same person as the Appointed Actuary, but this need not necessarily be the case. Also, in the preparation of holding company accounts, there is no Appointed Actuary to the holding company and a number of individuals may hold the position of Appointed Actuary to various subsidiaries.

3.4 The Reporting Actuary needs to be familiar with accounting principles and current auditing practice as well as the relevant regulations. This is because the computations are being made within a Companies Act framework where a different methodology may be applicable to that appropriate for a solvency test. Moreover, the application of the accounting principles in SSAP 2 is open to interpretation in any particular circumstance. It is recommended that, prior to carrying out the calculations, the Reporting Actuary ensures that the Auditor is aware of the approach which it is proposed to adopt in any situation where there is particular uncertainty regarding the application of these principles.

3.5 The great majority of accounting issues under modified statutory reporting which are relevant to the Reporting Actuary are dealt with in the Modified Statutory Guidance Note. The Reporting Actuary should be familiar with the relevant sections of this Note. On occasion, the Modified Statutory Guidance Note will not cover the situation faced by the Reporting Actuary may need to seek advice on the correct interpretation of accounting principles.

3.6 The Reporting Actuary may choose to base the calculation of the long-term business provision on the equivalent mathematical reserves calculated by the Appointed Actuary but where this is the case the Reporting Actuary retains full responsibility for the calculation of the long-term business provision. In calculating the long-term business provision under the modified statutory approach, the Reporting Actuary will need to modify the reserves calculated by the Appointed Actuary to comply with the Modified Statutory Guidance Note, for example by reducing the level of provision established for contingencies. Modifications may also be necessary if assets are valued on a different basis, for example by using a amortised cost basis for fixed interest securities, and to reflect any explicit asset representing deferred acquisition costs (and associated deferred tax) if the Appointed Actuary has allowed for these in the mathematical reserves.

3.7 The Reporting Actuary may reach different professional judgements from the Appointed Actuary but should defer to the Appointed Actuary on matters regarding policyholders' reasonable expectations. For example, if the Reporting Actuary's advice is sought as to the relative amounts of the long-term business provision, the fund for future appropriations and the reserves for shareholders, the Reporting Actuary should consult with the Appointed Actuary to ensure that policyholders' reasonable expectations are appropriately recognised.

3.8 The Modified Statutory Guidance Note permits the policyholder liabilities of overseas subsidiaries incorporated into group accounts to be computed on a local basis, provided that basis follows the principles of the modified statutory approach. Where it is proposed that the long-term business provision of an overseas subsidiary be consolidated using local GAAP or statutory reserves, the Reporting Actuary should ensure that the accounting conventions used to determine such provisions are not materially different from those of the modified statutory basis. The Reporting Actuary will have to consider the relationship between the long-term business provision and the deferred acquisition cost asset, together with the approach taken to deferred taxation, in forming this judgement.

3.9 It is possible that more than one Reporting Actuary will be required to provide results for an insurer because of the need to report at both company and group level. This could lead to different methods and assumptions being adopted. In these circumstances, the Reporting Actuaries should liaise to ensure that data and realistic assumptions agree, even if the different approaches require different figures to be included in the calculations, for example owing to a different approach being taken to margins.

3.10 There are aspects of work whether the Reporting actuary may be relying on other areas with in the company to produce information on which to base his or her calculation of the long-term business provision. This information will be subject to audit but it may be inappropriate for the Reporting Actuary to place reliance on the Auditor for its accuracy or completeness as the Auditor may have carried out the work to a different level of materiality from that required by the Reporting Actuary. Further, the Auditor may well take the view that it is inappropriate to extend the scope of the Auditor's work to give comfort to the Reporting Actuary. This is on the grounds that the work of the Reporting Actuary may be regarded as being central to the preparation of the financial statements in which case the Auditor is required to be able to express an independent opinion on it.

3.11 The statutory role of the Reporting Actuary is restricted to the calculation of the long-term business provision. It is also likely that actuarial advice will be needed to calculate other elements of the balance sheet and profit and loss account. Examples of where this is likely include the derivation of the technical provisions for linked liabilities and the determination of the deferred acquisition costs asset and its pace of amortisation. Any actuary advising on these other aspects of the financial statements needs to be aware of the accounting conventions adopted throughout the accounts and to ensure that advice given is consistent with them. Experience shows that particular care is needed in the area of deferred taxation, where any test of the recoverability of a deferred acquisition cost asset needs to have regard to the size of any corresponding deferred tax liability.

3.12 When reporting under the modified statutory method a company may be required, or wish, to include an item in its balance sheet representing the present value of part or the whole of its in force business. An actuary may be asked to provide guidance on the calculation of the appropriate amount, and the pace of any future amortisation. As in Paragraph 3.11, the Reporting Actuary needs to be aware of the relevant accounting conventions and the requirement for advice to be consistent with this. Similar obligations rest with any actuary asked to provide guidance on reporting under embedded value or similar methods of reporting.

3.13 An important part of the Reporting Actuary's work is the preparation of a report to the directors setting out the approach taken to computing the long-term business provision and the material assumptions utilised. Under the modified statutory approach, it may be appropriate to describe only those assumptions which differ from those used to calculate the relevant entries in the Supervisory Returns where the directors have received a report from the Appointed Actuary on these latter assumptions. For other reporting regimes and where the long-term business provision under the modified statutory approach is calculated independently of the mathematical reserves to be established in the Supervisory Returns, a report detailing both the method and assumption is appropriate.

3.14 The Reporting Actuary's report should not only address the amounts computed but also recommend suitable disclosure as required by paragraph 46(2) of Schedule 1 of the 1993 Regulations.

4 The Appointed Actuary

4.1 The direct role of the Appointed Actuary is restricted to the Supervisory Returns rather than the financial statements prepared under the Companies Act. The accountancy bodies recognise that the valuation and certification of the liabilities under long-term business for the purposes of the Insurance Companies Act 1982 is solely the professional responsibility of the Appointed Actuary. Hence the Appointed Actuary's certificate and Schedule 4 of the Supervisory Returns are not subject to audit.

4.2 The directors need to confirm to the Supervisory Authority compliance with Prudential Guidance Notes dealing with systems of control and the preparation of the returns and their opinion on this is subject to audit. Although ensuring compliance with these Prudential Guidance Notes is not within the statutory duties of the Appointed Actuary, the Actuary is inevitably closely involved with many aspects covered by these Notes. The Appointed Actuary should therefore be prepared to provide to the directors any relevant evidence concerning compliance (or lack of compliance) with these Guidance Notes and to discuss this with the Auditor.

4.3 There are areas where the work of the Appointed Actuary and the Auditor overlap, most particularly in checking the accuracy of the policy data and the valuation of the assets. It is inappropriate for the Appointed Actuary to place reliance on the work of the Auditor in these areas unless the Auditor has carried out work in accordance with a specifically scoped assignment outlined in a formal engagement letter. This is because, in most instances, the work of the Auditor will be designed to gain comfort at a different level of materiality from that required by the Appointed Actuary. It should be noted that the situation regarding the ability of the Auditor to carry out additional work for the Appointed Actuary is somewhat different from the position described in paragraph 3.10 above.

4.4 For the purpose of the financial statements, the Auditor must form a view as to the ongoing financial progress of the organisation and may wish to discuss with the Appointed Actuary the relevant areas for which the Appointed Actuary is responsible. In particular, the Auditor may wish to see any Financial Condition Report which has been produced, in order to understand the Appointed Actuary's view of the future development of the organisation's finances and the various risks to which the long-term fund is exposed. The Appointed Actuary should be prepared to discuss the issues referred to in the Financial Condition Report with the Auditor but this is not to imply that the Financial Condition Report is itself subject to audit.

4.5 Paragraph 10(1) of Schedule 1 of the 1993 Regulations requires the balance sheet of an insurance company (but not that of an insurance group) to show separately the amount of shareholders' capital and reserves which are required not to be treated as realised profits under section 268 of the Companies Act. This amount will include items which will remain within the long-term fund of the company after the payment of the current year's transfer to shareholders. Decisions taken by the Appointed Actuary directly affect this item of the balance sheet and hence the Auditor may wish to discuss issues relevant to it with the Appointed Actuary.

5 The Auditor and the Actuaries advising the Auditor

5.1 All companies are required by the Companies Act to appoint an Auditor whose responsibility it is to form an independent opinion on the financial statements. Specifically, the Auditor gives an opinion as to whether the financial statements as a whole given a true and fair view, that is that they are consistent with generally accepted accounting principles and show a true and fair view of the state of the company's affairs and of the results for the accounting period.

5.2 In order to form this opinion, the Auditor needs to obtain sufficient, appropriate audit evidence on all material items in the financial statements. The amount of the long term business provision, calculated by the Reporting Actuary will be one such item. Other material items include deferred acquisition costs, technical provisions for linked liabilities, premiums, claims and taxation. The Auditor does not consider any one item as intrinsically more important than any other.

5.3 Auditing guidelines provide help on how auditing standards should be applied to specific industry sectors, and Auditing Guideline 311 deals with long-term insurance. It is recommended that actuaries involved in the preparation of published financial statements should be familiar with Auditing Guideline 311.

5.4 Guidance on the degree to which the Auditor may place reliance on an "expert" in reach an opinion is given in Statement of Auditing Standards (SAS) 520 – Using the Work of an Expert. An expert may be employed by the insurance company, be an independent consultant or be employed by the Auditor. It is recommended that actuaries involved in the preparation of published financial statements should be familiar with SAS 520.

5.5 In order to form an opinion as required by the legislation, the Auditor has to assess, understand and where appropriate challenge the assumptions underlying the work undertaken by the Reporting Actuary. In supporting a reasonable challenge to the work of the Reporting Actuary, an actuary advising the Auditor will not be in breach of the *Memorandum on Professional Conduct*.

GN8

ADDITIONAL GUIDANCE FOR APPOINTED ACTUARIES AND APPROPRIATE ACTUARIES

Classification

Practice Standard

Legislation or Authority

Insurance Companies Regulations 1994. SI 1994/1516
Friendly Societies (Insurance Business) Regulations 1994. SI 1994/1981.

Application

Part I – Appointed Actuaries in Insurance Companies. Part II – Appropriate Actuaries in Friendly Societies which carry on long-term business

Legislation or Authority

This Guidance Note is written to help actuaries advising UK supervised long-term insurers and friendly societies on their world-wide business.

Author

Life Board

Status

Approved under Due Process

Version	Effective from
1.0	01.10.83
1.1	[1984-85]
1.2	[1985-86]
2.0	01.12.88
2.1	01.09.90
3.0	01.07.92
4.0	30.12.94
5.0	01.09.96

PART I: APPOINTED ACTUARIES IN INSURANCE COMPANIES

1 Introduction

1.1 The primary references in this part of the Guidance Note are to Regulations 64 to 75 of the Insurance Companies Regulations 1994 SI No. 1516. Regulation 61 is not the prime responsibility of the Appointed Actuary but that individual should be satisfied as to the reasonableness of the approach adopted. Part IX of the Insurance Companies Regulations 1994 comprises regulations governing the valuation of liabilities of insurance companies for various statutory purposes under the Insurance Companies Act 1982 ('the Act'). In particular these regulations govern the valuations of long-term liabilities for the purposes of an investigation to which Section 18 or Section 42 of the act applies. Such an investigation would normally be for determining:

(a) whether the statutory certificate in respect of long-term business required by Regulation 26(b) of the Insurance Companies (Accounts and Statements) Regulations 1983 (as amended) could be given;

(b) the extent to which assets could be transferred out of the fund in accordance with Section 29(2) of the Act, having regard to Section 30; or

(c) whether a dividend may be declared by the company or a parent, having regard to Section 29(7) of the Act.

These regulations are also relevant to the determination of the margins of solvency required by Section 32 of the Act.

1.2 Such valuations are the responsibility of the Appointed Actuary and this guidance, which is supplementary to that set out in Guidance Not GN1, has been prepared to draw the attention of Appointed Actuaries to certain aspects of their professional responsibilities relevant to these valuations.

1.3 Part IV of the Insurance Companies Regulations 1994 comprises regulations prescribing margins of solvency for insurance companies. The amounts of mathematical reserves and of capital at risk to be used in the calculations required under Regulations 18–20 are required to be assessed by the Appointed Actuary. In addition, in connection with Regulation 23(5), the Department of Trade and Industry has issued guidance notes stating that it requires a certificate (in a prescribed form) from the Appointed Actuary to accompany any application by a company for an order under Section 68 of the Act enabling implicit items as set out in Regulations 24 and 25 to count towards the margin of solvency.

1.4 If for some exceptional reason the Appointed Actuary is unable to comply fully with this guidance the Appointed Actuary has a professional duty to make timely written and reasoned disclosure, both to the company and to the Department of Trade and Industry. In this event the statutory certificate must be qualified accordingly.

2 Regulation 64 – The Actuarial Valuation

2.1 Regulation 64 is paramount. The Appointed Actuary should use prudent bases determined according to actuarial principles, and the professional considerations set out in GN1, particularly Section 6 thereof. The Regulation also refers explicitly to the need to have due regard to policyholders' reasonable expectations and to the inclusion of appropriate margins for adverse deviations of the relevant factors. This means that the valuation basis used should include appropriate margins for adverse deviations of each of the relevant factors having regard to materiality. In deriving the valuation basis it is permissible to group policies by category of contract. The term 'category of contract' is used to mean contracts with similar types of benefit, including options and guarantees, that are considered to be sufficiently homogeneous by the Appointed Actuary. A valuation method which is not in general use in the profession (whether to value a normal type of contract or in other circumstances) is not precluded, but an Appointed Actuary who uses such a method needs to be prepared to justify it by reference to actuarial principles. In relation to an insurance company, the Appointed Actuary should also bear in mind that any excess of assets over liabilities disclosed by the valuation can legally be transferred out of the fund, subject to satisfying, inter alia, the requirements of Section 30 of the Act.

2.2 This regulation also requires that the valuation liability must be determined in accordance with criteria which are set out in Regulations 65 to 75. These criteria require professional interpretation in their application, and guidance on them is therefore given in Section 3 of these notes. However, they should not be regarded as necessarily satisfying the more general actuarial principle set out in Regulation 64(1). They are the basis of a minimum statutory valuation, and the Appointed Actuary should carry out such investigations as considered necessary to be satisfied (and, where required, to satisfy the Department of Trade and industry) that the valuation satisfies the criteria. The criteria apply for each separate category of contract.

2.3 Regulation 64 refers to the valuation having due regard to the reasonable expectations of policyholders. When carrying out the valuation in compliance with Regulations 65 to 75, this should be interpreted as requiring the valuation basis to be sufficiently strong to enable an appropriate level of reversionary bonus to emerge (and similar bonuses which are added periodically over the term of the contract) but not as requiring implicit or explicit provision for any element of terminal bonus or any final payment of additional bonus. The Appointed Actuary would, however, be expected to make other investigations in order to be satisfied that the life fund is liable to support a proper level of future terminal bonus having regard to the bonus smoothing policy followed by the company.

2.4 Regulation 64 refers to the need to provide appropriate margins for adverse deviations of the relevant factors. The Appointed Actuary should consider the resilience of the valuation to changes in circumstances, with special reference to more extreme changes to which the office may be vulnerable, and provide appropriate margins in the valuation basis.

2.5 The Appointed Actuary should take account of any relationship which the company has with another company which is relevant for the purposes of the valuation. For example, where there are service agreements with other companies (whether or not within a group structure) the Appointed Actuary should consider whether any additional provision is appropriate for the contingency that such agreements might cease. This would be particularly relevant where a subsidised or beneficial agreement exists.

3 Regulations 65 to 75 – The Minimum Criteria

3.1 General

3.1.1 As explained in Paragraph 2.2, Regulations 65 to 75 set out minimum criteria against which the valuation basis of an insurance company should be determined for each separate category of contract. However, there are several respects in which these criteria are not precise and the Appointed Actuary has to interpret them in a prudent way, in regard to both the individual criteria and the criteria as a whole. If the Appointed Actuary considers that one of the required provisions or margins for any element of the basis is excessive, then it is not permissible for this purpose to offset part of it against another provision or margin required by the regulations except as set out in Paragraph 3.5.1 below.

3.1.2 The regulations apply equally to both linked and non-linked business, except for Regulations 67 and 68 which do not apply to linked business.

3.2 Regulation 65

3.2.1 Regulation 65 states that liabilities under with-profits policies shall recognises the distribution of profits in an appropriate way over the duration of each policy and have regard to the custom and practice of the company in the manner and timing of the distribution of profits. The Appointed Actuary should ensure that the valuation basis for with-profits business is sufficiently strong to enable an appropriate level of reversionary bonus (or similar bonus which is added periodically over the term of the contract) to emerge in future years on the assumption of anticipated investment returns which themselves are reasonably prudent.

3.2.2 Regulation 65 also refers to the method of calculation and assumptions used in the valuation not being subject to discontinuities from year to year arising from arbitrary changes. This requirement shall not be interpreted to preclude changes to valuation interest rates which arise from changes in market yields, or changes to valuation expense mortality or other assumptions which arise from changes in the company's actual or anticipated experience.

3.3 Regulation 69

3.3.1 Regulation 69(7)(a) requires an adjustment (where relevant) to the yield on assets other than equity shares or land to recognise the possibility of default. This is in addition to the 2½% margin required by 69(2). This Regulation refers to the need to have regard to the yields available on risk-free investments of a similar term in the same currency when assessing this adjustment. It is appropriate to have regard to any differences in yield which arise from differences in marketability of the asset in question as compare with the risk-free alternative when assessing the deduction for the default risk.

3.3.2 Regulation 69(7)(b) requires an adjustment (where relevant) to the yield on equity shares and land to recognise the possibility of a future reduction in aggregate yield on each category of asset. When assessing this adjustment, it is appropriate to allow for market knowledge, degree of marketability and, for land, the covenant of the tenant.

3.3.3 Regulation 69(9) specifies an upper limit for the yield on sterling investments made more than three years after the valuation date and Regulation 69(10) requires a correspondingly prudent approach to be followed where liabilities are denominated in currencies other than sterling. When assessing the maximum reinvestment rate for currencies other than sterling, the Appointed Actuary should seek wherever possible to follow a similar approach to the formula laid down in Regulation 69(9), with a suitable choice of interest parameters (corresponding to the 6% and 7.5% used for sterling) and a benchmark long term rate of interest appropriate to the currency concerned. In a number of countries the 6% and 7.5% may not be appropriate for use, and these rates should be increased or reduced where recent yields on risk free securities and/or inflation prospects for the currency concerned are materially different from the position in the United Kingdom.

3.3.4 Regulation 69(12) allows assets to be notionally apportioned, where appropriate, between different categories of contracts for the purpose of determining the rates of interest to be used in valuing a particular category of contract. Any such apportionment shall have regard to the prudence concept. It would not, for example, be prudent to allocate overseas branch assets to cover United Kingdom policyholders' liabilities where, in practice, local regulations in the territory concerned made such an allocation impractical to achieve. Where derivative contracts are held in connection with particular asses or liabilities in the long-term fund, then it will generally be appropriate to apportion these derivatives together with the corresponding assets and liabilities.

3.4 **Regulation 70**

Regulation 70 requires prudent rates of mortality and disability. Account should be taken of relevant trends in experience within the company or the industry, including appropriate allowance for future improvements in mortality for contracts where the assumption of lighter mortality increases the required reserve. For assurance and sickness business allowance should be made for the incidence of mortality and morbidity arsing from known diseases whose impact may not yet be reflected fully in current mortality or morbidity experience.

3.5 **Regulation 71**

3.5.1 Regulation 71 clearly requires the Appointed Actuary to make provision for the future increases considered likely in expenses for existing business, based, inter alia, on prudent assumptions as to the future rates of increase in prices and earnings. In considering such provision, it would be reasonable for the Appointed Actuary to take into account margins arising from, and restrictions on, interest rate assumptions eg increases in income from existing holding of index-linked stocks, equities and property or the restriction on income created by the limitations of Regulations 69(9), (10) and (11).

3.5.2 In requiring provision to be made for meeting the expenses likely to be incurred in future in fulfilling the existing contracts, it is permissible to take credit to the extent appropriate for the difference between the gross premium and the valuation net premium. Explicit allowance for future expenses will be required for all contracts under which no future premiums are receivable where these are not provided by disclosed margins in the valuation rate of interest.

3.5.3 Whether or not the Appointed Actuary performs the valuation under Regulation 64 on the assumption that the office will continue to transact new business, Regulation 71(1) requires an assessment of the provision for future expenses against the total (net of tax) cost that would be likely to be incurred in fulfilling contracts if the company were to cease to transact new business twelve months after the valuation date. Experience has shown that the transition to a closed fund is likely to be costly and that more than twelve months may elapse from such closure before the lower level of expense appropriate to a closed fund is achieved. In addition, the future tax position of the fund may be affected.

3.5.4 Regulation 71(1) should be interpreted to mean that the Appointed Actuary should provide for any expenses overrun in respect of new business for the following year. The Appointed Actuary should make a prudent assessment of such expense overrun having regard to the amount of new business likely to be written in the twelve months after the valuation date, the terms on which it is to be written and the level of acquisition expenses that will be incurred.

3.5.4.1 In general, no explicit provision would need to be established in respect of an acquisition expense overrun if:

(i) the new business is expected, on a prudent basis, to be self-supporting allowing for the repayment of any valuation strain (together with an appropriate rate of interest); or

(ii) any valuation strain associated with the new business to be issued in the forthcoming twelve months is less than the surplus expected to arise during this period from existing business, using prudent estimates for all relevant assumptions. The surplus anticipated from existing business should exclude any element required to meet the minimum solvency margin by means of an implicit item relating to future profits.

3.5.4.2 Where neither of the above two conditions is met, then an additional provision equal to the lesser of the shortfalls arising, after discontinuing to the valuation date, would be required. For the purpose of calculating mathematical reserves and estimating the cash flow arising from existing business, the estimated expenses in the year following the valuation date should reflect a going concern basis.

3.6 **Regulation 75**

3.6.1 Professional judgement is particularly necessary in applying the requirement in Regulation 75, which applies to the aggregate liability, that the determination of the amount of long-term liabilities shall include prudent provision against the effects of possible future changes in the value of the assets on their adequacy to meet the liabilities. Regulation 75(a) requires actuaries to consider mismatching provisions from the viewpoint of emerging cash flows whilst Regulation 75(b) requires a test of the resilience of the overall reserves to satisfy Regulations 65 to 74 in changed investment conditions. The overall provision established should be at least the greater of the amounts required under these two calculations.

3.6.2 Regulation 75 gives no indication of the range of possible future changes in the value of the assets which is to be allowed for. In determining an appropriate range, the Appointed Actuary must use professional judgement as an experienced financial practitioner. The essential point is that if changes, for example market yield or currency values, would result in a change in the aggregate liability that is not matched by a change in the market value of the corresponding assets, then Regulation 75 requires the appointed Actuary to consider what provision is required as a contingency margin, having regard to the consequences should the provision prove to be insufficient. In particular the Appointed Actuary needs to exercise special care with regard to any investments presenting novel or unorthodox features, derivatives (whether assets or liabilities) and any contracts containing substantial options.

3.6.3 To calculate any provision required under Regulation 75(a) the Appointed Actuary should look at cash flows emerging in from assets and in force policies and where the incidence of these is not identical make a reasonable but prudent assumption that investment markets move against the company. In performing this calculation the Appointed Actuary should comply with the valuation principles set out in Regulation 64 (excluding the reference to Regulations 65 to 74) and have regard to the reinvestment restrictions set out in Regulations 69(8), (9) and (10).

3.6.4 To calculate any provision required under Regulation 75(b) the company's reserves (including any additional reserves required under Regulation 75) should be sufficient to absorb the effect of changes in interest rates and asset values, on a suitably prudent basis, without prejudicing the company's ability to hold reserves which satisfy Regulations 64 to 74 in the changed conditions. Where the life fund has liabilities under derivative contracts, these should be revalued on an estimated market value basis in the changed conditions when assessing any additional reserves required under Regulation 75; there is no requirement to assess a provision for adverse change under Regulation 61 for this purpose.

3.6.5 As referred to in Paragraph 3.3.4 above, Regulation 69(12) allows a notional apportionment of assets for the purposes of determining rates of interest to be used when valuing a particular category of contract. Regulation 75 can, if desired, be applied separately to each differentiated category having regard to the assets notionally apportioned to it. Any assets which are entirely free after such an apportionment do not have to be brought into account in determining the matching position. Furthermore, when applying the valuation regulations to the changed investment conditions postulated, it is appropriate to allow for the revised yields on the relevant assets at their new value and to review any margins in the valuation basis that are not strictly required by the regulations. For with-profits business, however, actuaries must ensure that the liability in the changed investment conditions adequately covers policyholders' (revised) reasonable expectations and (more generally) that the valuation basis satisfies Regulation 64 (excluding the reference to Regulation 75).

4 Solvency Margins etc

4.1 Although it is not a requirement of Part IX of the Insurance Companies Regulations 1994, the Appointed Actuary will need to advise the company as to the action required

(i) to maintain the margins of solvency as prescribed by Part IV of the regulations as the existing business becomes more mature, or

(ii) in view of the requirement under Regulation 28(b) of the Insurance Companies (Accounts and Statements) Regulations 1996 for the Appointed Actuary to continue to give statutory certificates, to protect its position in certain circumstances such as those referred to in Paragraphs 5.5 to 6.10 of GN1, if in the Appointed Actuary's opinion there are reasonably foreseeable circumstances in which the office would be unable to meet its obligations.

4.2.1 The prudent assumptions on which the reserve under Part IX must be calculated will naturally allow for stochastic variations as well as other contingencies. In determining the extent to which the Appointed Actuary would consider it prudent to make provision for the more extreme stochastic variations in valuing particular categories of contract (for example, in relation to morality and morbidity fluctuations, and variations in benefits resulting from the inclusion in a unit-linked contract of a maturity guarantee) the Appointed Actuary may reasonably take into account the basis of the solvency margin that the company is required to hold on account of the liabilities under those contracts (net of the permitted deduction for reinsurance cessions). However, this should only be done if the Appointed Actuary is satisfied that:

(a) the company's available assets can provide explicit cover for the amount of required solvency margin that the Appointed Actuary is taking into account, and

(b) the balance of the solvency margin required in respect of the company's long-term business can be covered by the balance of the available assets and by any allowable implicit items, and that the former are sufficient to satisfy Regulation 22(3).

4.2.2 In exercising professional judgement in the circumstances envisaged under Paragraph 4.2.1 the Appointed Actuary will need to assess the security for the required margin of solvency for the long-term business as a whole, particular caution being required where it is in part covered by assets held outside the long-term fund. Furthermore, the Appointed Actuary will have to certify that the resulting reserves, standing on their own, constitute a proper provision for the long-term liability on actuarial principles and reliance on the margin of solvency must not result in the margins in the valuation basis falling below the level where the Appointed Actuary can give this certificate.

PART II: APPROPRIATE ACTUARIES IN FRIENDLY SOCIETIES WHICH CARRY ON LONG-TERM BUSINESS

1 Introduction

1.1 The primary references in this part of the Guidance Note are to Regulations 38 to 49 of the Friendly Societies (Insurance Business) Regulations 1994 SI No. 1981. Regulation 36 is not the prime responsibility of the Appropriate Actuary but that individual should be satisfied as to the reasonableness of the approach adopted. Part V of the Friendly Societies (Insurance Business) Regulations 1994 comprises regulations governing the valuation of liabilities of Friendly Societies for various statutory purposes under the Friendly Societies Act 1992 ('the Act'). In particular these regulations govern the variations of long-term liabilities for the purposes of an investigation in which Section 46 or section 47 of the Act applies. Such an investigation would normally be for determining whether the statutory certificate in respect of long-term business required by the Friendly Societies Commission could be given. These regulations are also relevant to the determination of the margins of solvency required by Section 48 of the Act.

1.2 Such valuations are the responsibility of the Appropriate Actuary and this guidance, which is supplementary to that set out in Guidance Note GN1, has been prepared to draw the attention to Appropriate Actuaries to certain aspects of their professional responsibilities relevant to these valuations.

1.3 Part II of the Friendly Societies (Insurance Business) Regulations 1994 comprises regulations prescribing margins of solvency for friendly societies to which Section 48 of the act applies. The amounts of mathematical reserves and of capital at risk to be used in the calculations required under Regulation 4 are required to be assessed by the Appropriate Actuary. In addition, in connection with Regulation 8(3), the Friendly Societies Commission requires a certificate from the Appropriate Actuary to accompany any application by a society for implicit items as set out in Regulations 9 and 10 to count towards the margin of solvency.

1.4 If for some exceptional reason the Appropriate Actuary is unable to comply fully with this guidance the Appropriate Actuary has a professional duty to make timely written and reasoned disclosure, both to the society and to the Friendly Societies Commission. In this event the statutory certificate must be qualified accordingly.

2 Regulation 38 – The Actuarial Valuation

2.1 Regulation 38 is paramount. The Appropriate Actuary should use prudent bases determined according to actuarial principles, and the professional considerations set out in GN1, particularly Section 6 thereof. The Regulation also refers explicitly to the need to have due regard to policyholders' reasonable expectations and to the inclusion of appropriate margins for adverse deviations of the relevant factors. This means that the valuation basis used should include appropriate margins for adverse deviations of each of the relevant factors having regard to materiality. In deriving the valuation basis it is permissible to group policies by category of contract. The term 'category of contract' is used to mean contract with similar types of benefit, including options and guarantees, that are considered to be sufficiently homogeneous by the Appropriate Actuary. A valuation method which is not in general use in the profession (whether to value a normal type of contract or in other circumstances) is not precluded, but an appropriate actuary who uses such a method needs to be prepared to justify it by reference to actuarial principles.

2.2 This regulation also requires that the valuation of long-term liabilities must be determined in accordance with criteria which are set out in Regulations

39 to 49. These criteria required professional interpretation in their application, and guidance on them is therefore given in Section 3 of these notes. However, they should not be regarded as necessarily satisfying the more general actuarial principle set out in Regulation 38(1). They are the basis of a minimum statutory valuation, and the Appropriate Actuary should carry out such investigations as considered necessary to be satisfied (and, where required, to satisfy the Friendly Societies Commission) that the valuation satisfies the criteria. The criteria apply for each separate category of contract.

2.3 Regulation 38 refers to the valuation having due regard to the reasonable expectations of policyholders. When carrying out the valuation in compliance with Regulations 39 to 49, this should be interpreted as requiring the valuation basis to be sufficiently strong to enable an appropriate level of reversionary bonus to emerge (and similar bonuses which are added periodically over the term of contract) but not as requiring implicit or explicit provision for any element of terminal bonus or any final payment of additional bonus. The Appropriate Actuary would, however, be expected to make other investigations in order to be satisfied that the long-term benefit funds are able to support a proper level of future terminal bonus having regard to the bonus smoothing policy following by the society.

2.4 Regulation 38 refers to the need to provide appropriate margins for adverse deviations of the relevant factors. The Appropriate Actuary should consider the resilience of the valuation to changes in circumstances, with special reference to more extreme changes to which the office may be vulnerable, and provide appropriate margins in the valuation basis.

2.5 The Appropriate Actuary should take account of any relationship which the society has with another company which is relevant for the purposes of the valuation. For example, where there are service agreements with other companies (whether or not within a group structure) the Appropriate Actuary should consider whether any additional provision is appropriate for the contingency that such agreements might cease. This would be particularly relevant where a subsidised or beneficial agreement exists.

3 Regulations 39 to 49 – The Minimum Criteria

3.1 General

3.1.1 As explained in Paragraph 2.2, Regulations 39 to 49 set out minimum criteria against which the valuation basis of a friendly society should be determined for each separate category of contract. However, there are several respects in which these criteria are not precise and the Appropriate Actuary has to interpret them in a prudent way, in regard to both the individual criteria and the criteria as a whole. If the Appropriate Actuary considers that one of the required provisions or margins for any element of the basis is excessive, then it is not permissible for this purpose to offset part of it against another provision or margin required by the regulations except as set out in Paragraph 3.5.1 below.

3.1.2 The regulations apply equally to both linked and non-linked business, except for Regulations 41 and 42 which do not apply to linked business.

3.2 Regulation 39

3.2.1 Regulation 39 states that liabilities under with-profits policies shall recognise the distribution of profits in an appropriate way over the duration of each policy and have regard to the custom and practice of the society in the manner and timing of the distribution of profits. The Appropriate Actuary should ensure that the valuation basis for with-profits business is sufficiently strong to enable an appropriate level of reversionary bonus (or similar bonus which is added periodically over the term of the contract) to emerge in future years on the assumption of anticipated investment returns which themselves are reasonably prudent.

3.2.2 Regulation 39 also refers to the method of calculation and assumptions used in the valuation not being subject to discontinuities from year to year arising form arbitrary changes. This requirement shall not be interpreted to preclude changes to valuation interest rates which arise from changes in market yields, or changes to valuation expense mortality or other assumptions which arise from changes in the society's actuarial or anticipated experience.

3.3 **Regulation 43**

3.3.1 Regulation 43(7)(a) requires an adjustment (where relevant) to the yield on assets other than equity shares or land to recognise the possibility of default. This is in addition to the 2½% margin required by 43(2). This Regulation refers to the need to have regard to the yields available on risk-free investments of a similar term in the same currency when assessing this adjustment. It is appropriate to have regard to any differences in yield which arise from differences in marketability of the asset in question as compared with the risk-free alternative when assessing the deduction for the default risk.

3.3.2 Regulation 43(7)(b) requires an adjustment (where relevant) to the yield on equity shares and land to recognise the possibility of a future reduction in aggregate yield on each category of asset. When assessing this adjustment, it is appropriate to allow for market knowledge, degree of marketability and, for land, the covenant of the tenant.

3.3.3 Regulation 43(9) specifies an upper limit for the yield on sterling investments made more than three years after the valuation date and Regulation 43(10) requires a correspondingly prudent approach to be followed where liabilities are denominated in currencies other than sterling. When assessing the maximum reinvestment rate for currencies other than sterling, the Appropriate Actuary should seek wherever possible to follow a similar approach to the formula laid down in Regulation 43(9), with a suitable choice of interest parameters (corresponding to the 6% and 7.5% used for sterling) and a benchmark long term rate of interest appropriate to the currency concerned. In a number of countries the 6% and 7.5% may not be appropriate for use, and these rates should be increased or reduced where recent yields on risk free securities and/or inflation prospects for the currency concerned are materially different from the position in the United Kingdom.

3.3.4 Regulation 43(12) allows assets to be notionally apportioned, where appropriate, between different categories of contracts for the purpose of determining the rates of interest to be used in valuing a particular category of contract. Any such apportionment shall have regard to the prudence concept. It would not, for example, be prudent to allocate overseas branch assets to cover United Kingdom policyholders' liabilities where, in practice, local regulations in the territory concerned made such an allocation impractical to achieve. Where derivative contracts are held in connection with particular assets or liabilities in the long-term benefit funds, then it will generally be appropriate to apportion these derivatives together with the corresponding assets and liabilities.

3.4 Regulation 44 requires prudent rates of mortality and disability. Account should be taken of relevant trends in experience within the society or the industry, including appropriate allowance for future improvements in mortality for contracts where the assumption of lighter mortality increases the required reserve. For assurance and sickness business allowance should be made for the incidence of mortality and morbidity arising from known diseases whose impact may not yet be reflected fully in current mortality or morbidity.

3.5 **Regulation 45**

3.5.1 Regulation 45 clearly requires the Appropriate Actuary to make provision for the future increases considerably likely in expenses for existing business, based, inter alia, on prudent assumptions as to the future rates of increase in prices and earnings. In considering such provision, it would be reasonable for the Appropriate Actuary to take into account margins arising from, and restrictions on, interest rate assumptions eg increases in income from existing holdings of index-linked stocks or the restriction on income created by the limitations of Regulations 43(9), (10) and (11).

3.5.2 In requiring provision to be made for meeting the expenses likely to be incurred in future in fulfilling the existing contracts, it is permissible to take credit to the extent appropriate for the difference between the gross premium and the valuation net premium. Explicit allowance for future expenses will be required for all contracts under which no future premiums are receivable where these are not provided by disclosed margins in the valuation rate of interest.

3.5.3 Whether or not the Appropriate Actuary performs the valuation under Regulation 38 on the assumption that the society will continue to transact new business, Regulation 45(1) requires an assessment of the provision for future expenses against the total (net of tax) cost that would be likely to be incurred fulfilling existing contracts if the society were to cease transact new business twelve months after the valuation date. Experience has shown that the transition to a closed fund is likely to be costly and that more than twelve months may elapse from such closure before the lower level of expense appropriate to a closed fund is achieved. In addition, the future tax position of the fund may be affected.

3.6 **Regulation 49**

3.6.1 Professional judgement is particularly necessary in applying the requirement in Regulation 49, which applies to the aggregate liability, that the determination of the amount of long-term liabilities shall include prudent provision against the effects of possible future changes in the value of the assets on their adequacy to meet the liabilities. Regulation 49(a) requires actuaries to consider mismatching provisions from the viewpoint of emerging cash flows whilst Regulation 49(b) requires a test of the resilience of the overall reserves to satisfy Regulations 39 to 48 in changed investment conditions. The overall provision established should be at least the greater of the amounts required under these two calculations. Paragraphs 6.7 and 6.8 of GN1 set out considerations to be taken into account, as does Paragraph 2.4 above.

3.6.2 Regulation 49 gives no indication of the range of possible future changes in the value of the assets which is to be allowed for. In determining an appropriate range, the Appropriate Actuary must use professional judgement as an experienced financial practitioner. The essential point is that if changes, for example in market yield or currency values, would result in a change in the aggregate liability that is not matched by a change in the market value of the corresponding assets, then Regulation 75 requires the Appropriate Actuary to consider what provision is required as a contingency margin, having regard to the consequences should the provision prove to be insufficient. In particular the Appropriate Actuary needs to exercise special care with regard to any investments presenting novel or unorthodox features, derivatives (whether assets or liabilities) and any contracts containing substantial options.

3.6.3 To calculate any provision required under Regulation 49(a) the Appropriate Actuary should look at cash flows emerging from assets and in force policies and where the incidence of these is not identical make a reasonable but prudent assumption that investment markets move against the society. In performing this calculation the Appropriate Actuary should comply with the valuation principles set out in Regulation 64 (excluding the reference to Regulations 39 to 48) and have regard to the reinvestment restrictions set out in Regulations 43(8), (9) and (10).

3.6.4 To calculate any provision required under Regulation 49(b) the society's reserves (including any additional reserves required under Regulation 49) should be sufficient to absorb the effect of changes in interest rates and asset values, on a suitably prudent basis, without prejudicing the society's ability to hold reserves which satisfy Regulations 38 to 48 in the changed conditions. Where the long-term benefit fund has liabilities under derivative contracts, these should be revalued on an estimated market value basis in the changed conditions when assessing any additional reserves required under Regulation 49; there is no requirement to assess a provision for adverse change under Regulation 36 for this purpose.

3.6.5 As referred to in Paragraph 3.3.4 above, Regulation 43(12) allows a notional apportionment of assets for the purposes of determining the rates of interest to be used when valuing a particular category of contract. Regulation 49 can, if desired, be applied separately to each differentiated category having regard to the assets notionally apportioned to it. Any assets which are entirely free after such an apportionment do not have to be brought into account in determining the matching position. Furthermore, when applying the valuation regulations to the changed investment condition postulated, it is appropriate to allow for the revised yields on the relevant assets at their new value and to review any margins in the valuation basis that are not strictly required by the regulations. For with-profits business, however, actuaries must ensure that the liability in the changed investment conditions adequately covers policyholders' (revised) reasonable expectations and (more generally) that the valuation basis satisfies Regulation 38 (excluding the reference to Regulation 49).

4 Solvency Margins etc

4.1 Although it is not a requirement of Part V of the Friendly Societies (Insurance Business) Regulations 1994, the Appropriate Actuary will need to advise the society as to the action required

(i) to maintain the margins of solvency as prescribed by Part II of the regulations as the existing business becomes more mature, or

(ii) to protect its position in certain circumstances such as those referred to in Paragraphs 5.5 to 6.10 of GN1, if in the appropriate actuary's opinion there are reasonably foreseeable circumstances in which the society would be unable to meet its obligations.

4.2.1 The prudent assumptions on which the reserve under Part V must be calculated will naturally allow for stochastic variations as well as other contingencies. In determining the extent to which the Appropriate Actuary would consider it prudent to make provision for the more extreme stochastic variations in valuing particular categories of contract (for example, in relation to mortality and morbidity fluctuations, and variations in benefits resulting from the inclusion in a unit-linked contract of a maturity guarantee) the Appropriate Actuary may reasonably take into account the basis of the solvency margin that the society is required to hold on account of the liabilities under those contracts (net of the permitted deduction for reinsurance cessions). However, this should only be done if the Appropriate Actuary is satisfied that:

(a) the society's available assets can provide explicit cover for the amount of required solvency margin that the Appropriate Actuary is taking into account, and

(b) the balance of the solvency margin required in respect of the society's long-term business can be covered by the balance of the available assets and by any allowable implicit items, and that the former are sufficient to satisfy Regulation 5(3).

4.2.2 In exercising professional judgement in the circumstances envisaged under Paragraph 4.2.1 the Appropriate actuary will need to assess the security for the required margin of solvency for the long-term business as a whole. Furthermore, the Appropriate Actuary will have to certify that the resulting reserves, standing on their own, constitute a proper provision for the long-term liability on actuarial principles and reliance on the margin of solvency must not result in the margins in the valuation basis falling below the level where the Appropriate Actuary can give this certificate.

GN15

TRANSFER OF LONG-TERM BUSINESS OF AN AUTHORISED INSURANCE COMPANY – ROLE OF THE INDEPENDENT ACTUARY

Classification

Recommended Practice.

Legislation or Authority

Insurance Companies Act 1982 (1982, c.50). Schedule 2C, Part I, Paragraph 2(1).
Friendly Societies Act 1992 (1992, c. 40). Section 86.

Application

Actuaries invited to act as the 'Independent Actuary' in a transfer under Part I of Schedule 2C to the Insurance Companies Act 1982. Schedule 2C is given effect by Section 49 and was inserted by the insurance Companies (Third Insurance Directives) Regulations 1994, SI 1994/1696, to replace the previous Sections 49, 49A, 49B, and 50-52. The general principles apply equally to transfers of business by or to friendly societies under the terms of Section 86 of the Friendly Societies Act 1992.

Author

Life Board

Status

Approved under Due Process.

Version	Effective from
1.0	01.06.90
1.1	01.09.90
2.0	01.01.98

1 Introduction

1.1 Under Part I of Schedule 2C of the Insurance Companies Act 1982, any scheme which provides for the whole or part of the long-term business carried on in one or more EU member states by a UK insurance company (or in the UK, in the case of a non-UK insurance company) to be transferred to another body requires the prior sanction of the court. 'UK company' is given a specific meaning in Section 5(4) of the Insurance Companies Act 1982 and a non-UK company accordingly means any company carrying on insurance business which is not a UK company. The court will consider the scheme on the basis of a petition by one of the parties, and the petition must be accompanied by a report on the terms of the scheme by an Independent Actuary.

1.2 The purpose of this Guidance Note is to advise an actuary invited to act as the Independent Actuary in a Schedule 2C transfer of the statutory and professional responsibilities such an appointment entails.

1.3 The Independent Actuary should ascertain whether any business has been written through branches outwith the UK and, if so, whether such business is to remain with the transfer or to be transferor under Schedule 2C or under some similar legislation. In the latter case, a report on similar lines to that required under Schedule 2C may be required.

2 Factors Influencing Acceptance of an Appointment as Independent Actuary

2.1 Before accepting an appointment as the Independent Actuary in any particular case, an actuary must consider whether he or she has relevant practical knowledge and experience. Such experience would necessarily include familiarity with the role and responsibility of an Appointed Actuary and with the types of long-term business transacted by the companies concerned. An actuary must also disclose to all the parties any direct or indirect interest the actuary may have or have had in any of them. Clearly, an actuary cannot act if such interest would, in the opinion of any party or its legal advisers, be likely to prejudice an actuary's status in the eyes of the court. In case of doubt, the situation should be discussed with the supervisory authority and the Secretary to the Professional Affairs Board before the appointment is accepted.

2.2 The Act prescribes that a report on the terms of the scheme by an Independent Actuary accompanies the petition to the court and the Independent Actuary's prime responsibility is, therefore, to the court. The Act does not prescribe who should appoint the Independent Actuary; in practice, the appointment is made by one of the parties to the scheme – usually the party will be petitioning the court. The purpose of the appointment is to secure an independent opinion for the court on the likely effects of the scheme on the long-term policyholders of the companies concerned. It would, therefore, be improper for the Independent Actuary to take instructions from any of the parties on what should be included in or excluded from the report; or to be denied access by any of the parties to persons the Independent actuary may wish to interview, or to information, reports and documents which the Independent Actuary may reasonably consider material to the formulation of an opinion on the likely effects of the scheme on the long-term policyholders of the companies concerned. An actuary should ensure that this is understood by the parties concerned before accepting an appointment.

2.3 If, for any reason other than the abandonment of the scheme, the Independent Actuary's appointment is revoked or the Independent Actuary resigns prior to that individual's report being submitted to the court or being circulated (whether in summary or otherwise) to long-term policyholders, that individual should consider whether the circumstances are such that that individual should make them known to the supervisory authority. Any actuary offered an appointment as an Independent Actuary should enquire if the appointment has previously been accepted and subsequently vacated by another actuary; if so, an actuary should take all reasonable steps to establish the circumstances in which the revocation of the previous actuary's appointment or the resignation of the previous actuary took place.

3 The Extent of the Independent Actuary's Involvement

3.1 Given that the court is unlikely to sanction the scheme if the Independent Actuary indicates serious dissatisfaction with its terms, it is in the interest of all the parties that, once an actuary has been appointed, the Independent Actuary is informed of the draft terms and provisions of the proposed scheme at the various stages of its development. The Independent Actuary should therefore actively seek such information and be prepared to indicate with impartiality any terms or provisions which by their inclusion in or omission from the scheme as drafted, as the case may be, would be likely to cause the Independent Actuary to express reservations about the scheme in the report.

3.2 The Secretary of State for Trade and Industry is entitled to be heard by the court when a petition is being considered. It is therefore advisable for the Independent Actuary to contact the supervisory authority at an early stage, with the knowledge of the petitioner, to establish whether there are any matters pertaining to the scheme which the supervisory authority wishes to draw to the Independent Actuary's attention. The Independent Actuary should maintain this line of communication until he scheme is presented to the court.

3.3 The amount of investigative work that the Independent Actuary will need to do will depend on the circumstances of the case. The Independent Actuary should communicate with the Appointed Actuaries of all affected companies. It is reasonable for the Independent Actuary to expect the Appointed Actuary of the transferor company to provide such valuations of the assets and liabilities as the Independent Actuary may require, and to disclose information on such matters as how bonus rates have been determined in recent years in respect of any with-profit business. If the transferee company already has a long-term business fund of its own, similar information from the Appointed Actuary of that company may be necessary. It has become customary in cases of any complexity for the petition to be accompanied by a report from any Appointed Actuary concerned, although this is not a legal requirement. There may also be private actuarial reports to one or more of the parties, production of which would assist the Independent Actuary in appraising the term of the scheme. The Independent Actuary must, however, from an independent judgement on the quality of the information supplied, the reasonableness of the work of other actuaries, and, therefore, the extent of any investigative or verification work the Independent Actuary needs to do.

3.4 The Independent Actuary might be asked to attend a meeting with the policyholders organised by the management of one of the companies. If so, the Independent Actuary should consider carefully whether to do so would give the impression that the Independent Actuary was not completely independent. If the Independent Actuary should decide to attend the meeting, the Independent Actuary's position should be properly explained, and nothing that the Independent Actuary does or says at the meeting should undermine the perception of independence.

3.5 In the case of a transfer involving a composite company, writing both long-term and general business, the Independent Actuary will need to understand the relevance of the general insurance business to the security of the long-term policyholders, and the Independent Actuary may need to seek independent specialist advice on this.

3.6 Special considerations may also be called for where the transfer forms part of a chain of events including restructure, reinsurance or changes in ownership, and the Independent Actuary should seek explanations regarding corporate plans to the extent necessary for the whole picture to be clear.

3.7 If the Appointed Actuary of any affected company has held that position only for a relatively short period of time, it might be appropriate to the Independent Actuary to seek information from the previous Appointed Actuary.

3.8 Other documents the Independent Actuary will normally wish to examine in relation to each of the companies involved in the transfer will include:

3.8.1 its memorandum and articles of association and, if the company is currently trading, its latest annual report and accounts and supervisory returns;

3.8.2 the latest report submitted by its Appointed Actuary to the directors in accordance with paragraphs 8.1 to 8.5 of GN1, together with any recent reports submitted in accordance with GN2,

3.8.3 with profits guides issued by the company in recent years;

3.8.4 any reports, actuarial or otherwise, dealing specifically with PRE;

3.8.5 the bases used for own-charge illustrations;

3.8.6 sample quotations and policy documents which state or illustrate how policies will participate in profits, qualify for discretionary benefits, or be subject to future variations in charges;

3.8.7 any reports dealing with investment policy of the long-term business fund;

3.8.8 any reports evaluating alternative schemes;

3.8.9 any other relevant documents associated with the transfer.

3.9 In addition, the Independent Actuary should ask about the operational plans of any company which, after the effective date, will have policyholders who fall to be considered in the Independent Actuary's report.

4 The Report

4.1 The Independent Actuary's report on the terms of the scheme is required by Paragraph 2(1) of Schedule 2C to accompany the petition, but the court – unless it has otherwise directed – will not determine the application unless a statement setting out the terms of the scheme and containing a summary of the Independent Actuary's report "sufficient to indicate the opinion of the actuary on the likely effects of the scheme on the long-term policy holders of the companies concerned" has been sent to each of those policyholders and to every member of those companies (Paragraph 2(2)(b) of Schedule 2C). The full report, being a public document, must be available for inspection by any person and therefore by any policyholder or member. The Independent Actuary should therefore bear in mind in preparing the report that policyholders and members may rely on it when considering how to cast their vote in any extraordinary general meeting called to approve the terms of the scheme, and any member of the public may rely on it when considering whether or not to make representations to the court about the likely adverse effect of the scheme on him or her.

4.2 Similar considerations apply to the summary of the Independent Actuary's report which has to be sent to policyholders and members of the companies concerned. It is the Independent Actuary's responsibility to ensure that he contents of the summary are adequate, and that neither it nor any document which will accompany it gives a misleading impression of the findings in the full report. The summary need not contain background factual matter contained in the accompanying documents.

4.3 It follows from 4.1 that the Independent Actuary needs to consider and report as appropriate on the likely effects of the scheme on (a) all transferring long-term policyholders, (b) any long-term policyholders of the transferor company whose polices will remain with that company, and (c) any long-term policyholders of the transferee company. Whilst not directly concerned with the effect of the scheme on those who become policyholders on or after the date when, subject to the approval of the court, it will become effective, the Independent Actuary will need to consider whether the development plans of any of the companies involved may adversely affect policyholders with whom the Independent Actuary is concerned.

4.4 It is a responsibility of the directors and managers of the relevant insurance company to consider alternative arrangements in order that the company may fulfil its obligations to conduct its business with due regard to the interests of policyholders and potential policyholders. The term 'Independent actuary' might be interpreted by members of the public to indicate that the actuary was advising on the relative merits of one scheme of transfer against other possible arrangements, although this is not specifically required by the legislation. Consistent with the nature of the legal requirements, the report must include a comparison of the likely effects on the long-term policyholders of the relevant companies if the scheme of transfer being presented to the court is or is not implemented. In addition, the Independent Actuary should state clearly whether or not reports of alternative arrangements were considered.

4.5 The contents of the Independent Actuary's report will be influenced by the circumstances of each case; the following are, however, some of the matters which the Independent Actuary should, where appropriate, cover in it:

4.5.1 The name of the party which has appointed the Independent Actuary and a statement of who is bearing the costs of that appointment.

4.5.2 A statement of the Independent Actuary's professional qualification.

4.5.3 Whether or not the Independent Actuary has a direct or indirect interest in any of the parties which might be thought to influence the Independent Actuary's independence; if the Independent Actuary has an interest, it should be disclosed.

4.5.4 The scope of the report in accordance with Paragraph 4.4 above.

4.5.5 The purpose of the scheme.

4.5.6 A summary of the terms of the scheme is so far as they are relevant to the contents of the Independent Actuary's report.

4.5.7 What documents and reports the Independent Actuary has considered in relation to each of the companies involved in the transfer and whether there was any additional information which was requested but not provided.

4.5.8 The cost and tax consequences of the scheme, in so far as these will affect policyholders' funds.

4.5.9 The effect of the scheme on the security of policyholders' contractual benefits.

4.5.10 The effect of the scheme on the nature and value of any rights of policyholders to participate in profits. In particular, if any such rights will be diluted by the scheme, how any compensation being offered to those policyholders as a group (which might take the form of an injection of funds, an allocation of shares, or cash payments) compares with the value of that dilution, and whether the extent and method of its proposed division is equitable as between different classes and generations of policyholders.

4.5.11 The likely effect of the scheme on the approach used to determine the amounts of non-guaranteed benefits such as reversionary (or similar bonus which is added periodically over the term of the contract) and terminal bonuses and surrender values, and the levels of discretionary charges, for example under unit-linked policies; and what safeguards are provided by the scheme against a subsequent change of approach that could act to the detriment of existing policyholders of either company and is not due to external circumstances beyond its control.

4.5.12 The likely effects of the scheme on matters such as investment management, new business strategy, administration, expense levels and valuation bases, so far as they may affect the ability of the companies to meet throughout the lifetime of existing policies the reasonable expectations of the holders of those policies.

4.5.13 In the case of any mutual company involved in the scheme, the effect of the scheme on the proprietary rights of members of that company and, in particular, the significance of any loss or dilution of the rights of those members to secure or prevent further constitutional changes which could affect their expectations as policyholders (for example, losing the ability to change the board and therefore control over a board's decision to convert to a closed fund). The Independent Actuary should state whether, and to what extent, members will receive compensation under the scheme for any diminution in their proprietary rights, and comment on its appropriateness. Also, when commenting on the fairness of the scheme, the Independent Actuary should pay particular attention to any differences in treatment between policyholders with voting rights and those without. It will assist the Independent Actuary if the issues involved are adequately explained in the directors' circular to policyholders.

4.5.14 Which matters, if any, the Independent Actuary has not taken into account or evaluated in the report that might nevertheless be relevant to policyholders' consideration of the scheme.

4.5.15 The Independent Actuary's overall assessment of the likely effects of the scheme on the reasonable expectations of long-term policyholders; whether the Independent Actuary is satisfied that for each of the companies concerned the scheme is equitable to all classes and generations of its policyholders; and whether for each relevant company the scheme places obligations on the directors, or provides for future certification by its Appointed Actuary, sufficient in the Independent Actuary's opinion for the protection of those expectations.

4.6 Where the Independent Actuary expresses an opinion in the report, the Independent Actuary should outline the reasons for it.

Appendix 6
Terms for discretionary fund management[1]

[16.1]

CONTENTS

1 Published with the kind permission of the Fund Managers' Association

Private Customers and Occupational Pension Schemes

Terms for Custody Where the Custodian is a Party to the Agreement

Explanatory Notes on the Agreement are available, on request, from the Manager. They do not form part of the Agreement.

PRELIMINARY

1 Definitions

The definitions below are designed for ease of reading. Some are summaries of the full definition which, whether contained in the IMRO Rules (marked*) or in the FSA, shall prevail. References to statutes, IMRO Rules and any other regulations shall be taken to include any amendments made to them from time to time. Any other words or phrases used in the Agreement which are defined in the IMRO Rules shall have the same meanings in the Agreement.

The Terms contain a number of references to the Custodian and paragraphs C1-10 detail the obligations and rights of the Custodian. These references are relevant only where the Custodian is named in and is a party to the Agreement. In all other cases, the Customer should refer to paragraph 28 on page 8 regarding the Outside Custodian.

the Agreement the Terms, the Schedule and any other documents annexed to them, as amended from time to time, which are to be construed as one document together constituting the agreement between the parties.

***Associate**	a company or other person connected to the Manager or, where relevant, the Custodian.
***Best Execution**	the method whereby an investment manager seeks to achieve the best terms for a customer.
Client Money Regulations	the Financial Services (Client Money) Regulations 1991 and the Financial Services (Client Money) (Supplementary) Regulations 1991.
Collective Investment Scheme	an arrangement for assets to be held on a pooled basis on behalf of n behalf of any number of investors, for example a unit trust or open ended investment investment company; a full definition is contained in the FSA s.75
Connected Investment Trust	an investment trust managed by the Manager or an Associate.
***Contingent Liability Transaction**	a Derivatives transaction where a customer may be liable to make further payments.
Contract for Differences	a contract relating to fluctuations in an index, price or other factor. A full definition is contained in the FSA, Schedule 1, paragraph 9.
Custodian	the person (if any) named on the front of the Schedule as custodian charged with providing custody services for the Fund.
Customer	the person named on the front of the Schedule as customer to whom the Manager provides investment services.
***Derivatives**	Options, Futures and Contracts for Differences.
FSA	Financial Services Act 1986.
Fund	the portfolio of assets (including uninvested cash) entrusted from time to time by the Customer to the management of the Manager.
Future	a contract for the sale of a commodity or any other property under which delivery is to be made at a future date at a price agreed upon when the contract is made. A full definition is contained in the FSA, Schedule 1, paragraph 8.
***IMRO**	the Investment Management Regulatory Organisation Limited, the organisation set up pursuant to the FSA to regulate the business of investment management in the United Kingdom.
***IMRO Rules**	the rules established by IMRO.
In-House Funds	Collective Investment Schemes of which the Manager or an Associate is the manager.
***Initial Composition**	respectively the composition and value of the assets

and Initial Value	(collectively and individually) comprising the Fund at the time when the Manager first assumes management of the Fund.
***Investment Business**	those activities of the Manager, defined as investment business in the FSA Schedule 1, which are regulated by IMRO.
***Investment Ombudsman**	the person appointed by IMRO to investigate complaints referred to him directly or via IMRO.
Manager	the person named on the front of the Schedule as manager charged with managing the Fund.
Option	an option to acquire or dispose of investments, currencies or commodities. A full definition is contained in the FSA, Schedule 1, paragraph 7.
Outside Custodian	the person (if any) not being a party to the Agreement nevertheless charged with providing custody services for the Fund.
Schedule	the schedule to the Agreement detailing matters specific to the Customer.
***Soft Commission Agreement**	an agreement between the Manager or an Associate and a broker or counterparty under which the Manager or an Associate benefits from the placing of business on behalf of customers.
Terms	these terms.
***Unit Trust Scheme**	a Collective Investment Scheme where the property is held on trust for the participants, but excluding limited partnerships.

2 Regulation

The Manager is regulated by IMRO in the conduct of its Investment Business and nothing in the Agreement shall exclude any liability of the Manager or, where relevant, the Custodian to the Customer arising under the FSA, or any rules or regulations made under it, the Pensions Act 1995, or the IMRO Rules.

3 Effective Date of Appointment

The Agreement will come into force on the date of receipt by the Manager of a copy of the Agreement signed by the Customer or (where permitted by the IMRO Rules) on such earlier date as may be stated in item 1 of the Schedule.

4 Governing Law

The Agreement will be governed by and construed in accordance with English law. The English courts will have exclusive jurisdiction to settle any disputes or claims which may arise out of or in connection with the Agreement for which purpose all parties agree to submit to such jurisdiction.

PROVISION OF SERVICES

5 Investment Discretion

(a) The Manager will manage the Fund within the investment objectives and any restrictions stated in item 2 of the Schedule and will act in good faith and with due diligence. Subject to such objectives and restrictions, the Manager, normally acting as agent, will have complete discretion for the account of the Customer (and without prior reference to the Customer) to buy, sell, retain, exchange or otherwise deal in investments and other assets, make deposits, subscribe to issues and offers for sale and accept placings, underwritings and sub-underwritings of any investments, effect transactions on any markets, take all day to day decisions and otherwise act as the Manager judges appropriate in relation to the management of the Fund, but always subject to the overriding principles of suitability and Best Execution.
(b) The investment objectives and restrictions stated in item 2 of the Schedule will not be breached as a result of changes in the price or value of assets of the Fund brought about solely through movements in the market.
(c) The Manager will keep such objectives and restrictions under review and may, from time to time, suggest to the Customer such amendments as, in the Manager's opinion, might be made to them.

6 Delegation and Use of Agents

(a) The Manager may delegate any of its functions under the Agreement to an Associate and may provide information about the Customer and the Fund to any such Associate but the Manager's liability to the Customer for all matters so delegated shall not be affected thereby. The Manager will give the Customer written notice of any such delegation of a function which involves the exercise of its discretionary investment management powers and will not, without the written consent of the Customer, delegate the whole or substantially the whole of such powers.
(b) The Manager may, where reasonable, employ agents (including Associates) to perform any administrative, dealing or ancillary services required to enable the Manager to perform its services under the Agreement. The Manager will act in good faith and with due diligence in the selection, use and monitoring of agents.

7 Uninvested Cash

Except where the Customer makes its own banking arrangements, either:
(a) the accounts stated in item 3 of the Schedule will be opened in the name and on behalf of the Customer, and the Manager may give instructions to the relevant bank regarding such accounts; or
(b) cash balances will be held in accounts operated in accordance with the Client Money Regulations whether or not the accounts are within the United Kingdom.

8 Securities Lending, Borrowing and Overdrafts

(a) The Manager may, where stated in item 3 of the Schedule or as separately agreed in writing with the Customer, make arrangements to:

(i) lend to a third party investments or documents of title or certificates evidencing title to investments comprising the Fund or part of it;
(ii) borrow on the Customer's behalf against the security of such investments or other property;
(iii) deposit such investments with a third party by way of collateral.

(b) Any income or fees received (net of charges and expenses) in relation to such loans will be added to the Fund.

(c) Save as stated in items 2 and 3 of the Schedule, the Manager may not, without the written consent of the Customer, commit the Customer to supplement the assets of the Fund by borrowing on the Customer's behalf or by committing the Customer to a contract which may require the Customer to supplement such assets.

(d) The Manager may direct the Custodian to retain a lien or security interest over assets of the Fund to the extent that any costs, losses or claims detailed in the Agreement, for which the Customer is obliged to indemnify the Manager, remain unpaid.

9 Voting

(a) As stated in item 2 of the Schedule, the Manager may procure the exercise of any voting rights attaching to the investments of the Fund, either:
(i) at its discretion, subject always to the Customer's specific instructions (if any); or
(ii) only with the agreement or on the specific instructions of the Customer.

(b) Notwithstanding (a) above, the Manager may not procure the exercise of any voting rights attaching to the Fund's holdings of In-House Funds and Connected Investment Trusts except with the agreement or on the specific instructions of the Customer but may count such holdings for the purpose of constituting a quorum at a general meeting of any In-House Fund or Connected Investment Trust.

10 Advice

Advice may be given by the Manager in such manner as may be agreed with the Customer or as the Manager thinks fit.

11 Valuations and Reports

(a) A valuation showing the Initial Composition and Initial Value is attached (or will be supplied as soon as reasonably practicable) and will (then) constitute part of the Agreement. The basis of all valuations will be as stated in that first valuation unless otherwise notified.

(b) Valuations of the Fund and any other relevant reports will be sent to the Customer at the intervals stated in item 5 of the Schedule.

(c) The Manager will assist the Customer to fulfil any obligations to disclose shareholdings under Part VI of the Companies Act 1985, (or similar overseas legislation), as stated in item 5 of the Schedule.

DEALING AND DERIVATIVES

12 Dealing and Counterparties

(a) The Manager will act in good faith and with due diligence in its choice and use of counterparties.

(b) In effecting transactions for the Fund the Manager shall seek Best Execution at all times and may (subject to item 2 of the Schedule) deal on such markets or exchanges and with such counterparties as it thinks fit. All transactions will be effected in accordance with the rules and regulations of the relevant market or exchange, and the Manager may take all such steps as may be required or permitted by such rules and regulations and/or by appropriate market practice.

(c) If any counterparty should fail to deliver any necessary documents or to complete any transaction, the Manager will take all reasonable steps on behalf of the Customer to rectify such failure or obtain compensation in lieu thereof. All reasonable costs and expenses properly incurred by the Manager shall be paid by the Customer.

(d) The Manager may aggregate transactions for the Fund with those of other customers and of its employees and of Associates and their employees and will allocate such transactions on a fair and reasonable basis in accordance with the requirements of the IMRO Rules.

13 Derivatives

(a) Where item 2 of the Schedule so states, and subject to any restrictions therein and to appropriate risk warnings having been provided to the Customer, the Manager may effect transactions in Derivatives including Contingent Liability Transactions and may settle or close out such transactions without further reference to the Customer.

(b) The Manager may debit the Fund with any sums required to pay or supplement any deposit or margin in support of any such transaction.

MATERIAL INTERESTS

14 Potential Conflicts of Interest and Disclosures

(a) The Manager and any Associate may effect transactions in which the Manager or Associate has, directly or indirectly, a material interest or a relationship of any description with another party, which may involve a potential conflict with the Manager's duty to the Customer. Neither the Manager nor any Associate shall be liable to account to the Customer for any profit, commission or remuneration made or received from or by reason of such transactions or any connected transactions nor will the Manager's fees, unless otherwise provided, be abated.

(b) The Manager will ensure that such transactions are effected on terms which are not materially less favourable to the Customer than if the potential conflict had not existed.

(c) In accordance with the IMRO Rules, the Manager notifies the Customer that such potential conflicting interests or duties may arise because:

  (i) the Manager or an Associate undertakes Investment Business for other customers;

  (ii) a director or employee of the Manager, or of an Associate, is a director of, holds or deals in securities of, or is otherwise interested in any company whose securities are held or dealt in on behalf of the Customer;

  (iii) a transaction is effected in securities issued by an Associate or the customer of an Associate;

  (iv) a transaction is effected in securities in respect of which the Manager or an Associate may benefit from a commission, fee, mark-up or mark-down payable otherwise than by the Customer, and/or the Manager or an Associate may also be remunerated by the counterparty to any such transaction;

(v) the Manager deals on behalf of the Customer with, or in the securities of, an Associate;
(vi) the Manager may act as agent for the Customer in relation to transactions in which it is also acting as agent for the account of other customers and/or Associates;
(vii) the Manager may, acting as principal, sell to or purchase currency from the Customer and may, in exceptional circumstances, deal in securities as principal with the Customer;
(viii) a transaction is effected in units or shares of In-House Funds or Connected Investment Trusts or of any company of which the Manager or an Associate is the manager, operator, banker, adviser, custodian or trustee;
(ix) the Manager may effect transactions involving placings and/or new issues with an Associate who may be acting as principal or receiving agent's commission;
(x) a transaction is effected in securities of a company for which the Manager or an Associate has underwritten, or managed or arranged an issue or offer for sale within the previous 12 months;
(xi) the Manager or an Associate may receive remuneration or other benefits by reason of acting in corporate finance or similar transactions involving a company whose securities are held by the Customer; or
(xii) a transaction is effected in securities in respect of which the Manager or an Associate, or a director or employee of the Manager or an Associate, is contemporaneously trading or has traded on its own account or has either a long or short position.

(d) The Manager will normally act as the agent of the Customer, who will therefore be bound by its actions under the Agreement. Nevertheless, none of the services to be provided hereunder nor any other matter shall give rise to any fiduciary or equitable duties which would prevent or hinder the Manager, or any Associate, in transactions with or for the Customer, acting as both market-maker and broker, principal or agent, dealing with other Associates and other customers, and generally effecting transactions as provided above.

15 Soft Commissions

The Manager's policy on Soft Commission Agreements is, where relevant, stated in item 6 of the Schedule, which also lists any agreements which may be relevant to the Customer.

GENERAL

16 Fees and Charges

(a) The Manager will receive remuneration for its services, and reimbursement of reasonable costs and expenses, as stated in item 4 of the Schedule, which will also state whether or not interest is payable on overdue fees.
(b) The Customer will be liable for any costs properly incurred under the Agreement, including reasonable commissions, transfer and registration fees and for taxes and other fiscal liabilities.

17 Taxation

The Manager shall not take or omit to take any action which to the actual knowledge of the individual taking or omitting to take such action would prejudice the tax position of the Customer stated in item 1 of the Schedule. Subject thereto the Customer and any professional tax adviser of the Customer remain responsible for the management of the Customer's affairs for tax purposes.

18 Liability of Manager

(a) The Manager accepts responsibility for loss to the Customer to the extent that such loss is due to the negligence, wilful default or fraud of itself or any delegates appointed pursuant to paragraph 6(a) above or that of its or their employees. The Manager also accepts liability for any Custodian which is an Associate.
(b) The Manager will not otherwise be liable for any loss to the Customer.
(c) No warranty is given by the Manager as to the performance or profitability of the Fund or any part of it.

19 Customer's Warranties and Liabilities

(a) The Customer warrants that it has full power to employ the Manager and, where relevant, the Custodian on the terms of the Agreement, and that (except as may be stated in item 1 of the Schedule) the Fund is free from all liens and charges, and that no liens or charges will arise from the acts or omissions of the Customer.
(b) The Customer undertakes not to deal, except through the Manager, with any of the assets in the Fund nor to authorise anyone else so to deal.
(c) The Customer warrants that any information which it has provided to the Manager in relation to its status, residence and domicile for taxation purposes is complete and correct, and agrees to provide any further information properly required by any competent authority.
(d) The Customer will provide the Manager with any other relevant information requested in item 1 of the Schedule.
(e) The Customer will notify the Manager promptly if there is any material change in any of the above information.
(f) Except insofar as the same may result from the negligence, wilful default or fraud of the Manager or its employees, or delegates under paragraph 6(a) above or its or their employees, the Customer agrees to indemnify the Manager against all costs, losses, claims and expenses which may be incurred by it or made against it either (i) as a result of any party claiming to be entitled to investments which form part of the Fund at the time when the Manager first assumes management of the Fund, or (ii) in consequence of any breach by the Customer of the Agreement, or (iii) arising out of any action properly taken by the Manager in accordance with the Agreement.
(g) Where the Customer is a trustee, the Customer's liability under the Agreement shall be limited, in the absence of fraud, to the assets of the trust from time to time.

20 Instructions and Communications

(a) Instructions from the Customer (other than instructions to amend the Agreement, to which paragraph 21 below applies) will be acknowledged by the Manager acting upon them unless the Customer is promptly advised that the Manager believes such action may not be practicable or might involve any party in a breach of any law, rule or regulation.
(b) The Manager may rely and act on any instruction or communication which purports to have been given (and which is reasonably accepted as having been given) by or on behalf of any person notified by the Customer from time to time as being authorised to instruct the Manager in respect of the Fund and, subject to item 5 of the Schedule, by whatever means transmitted and, unless the Manager shall have received written notice to the contrary, whether or not the authority of any such person shall have been terminated.
(c) Subject to (b) above, any instruction or communication to be given to the Manager by the Customer under the Agreement must be in writing and sent to the address stated in item 5 of the Schedule or otherwise as notified to the Customer and will take effect upon its actual receipt.

(d) All written communications by the Manager to the Customer shall be sent to the last address notified to the Manager by the Customer.
(e) Communications by electronic methods shall comply with item 5 of the Schedule.
(f) Telephone conversations with the Customer may be recorded by the Manager.

21 Amendments

Any amendment proposed by a party to be made to the Agreement shall be notified in writing to the other party or parties. Any such amendment shall take effect on the date specified (for an amendment proposed by the Customer this shall be not less than 20 business days after receipt of the notice by the Manager, and for an amendment proposed by the Manager not less than 20 business days after the issue of the notice) unless the other party or parties in the meantime give(s) notice to the contrary or request(s) an extension of time.

22 Complaints

All formal complaints should in the first instance be made in writing to the compliance officer of the Manager at the address stated in item 5 of the Schedule. In addition, the Customer has a right to complain direct to the Investment Ombudsman.

23 Compensation

A statement is available from the Manager describing the Customer's rights to compensation, if any, in the event that the Manager is unable to meet its liabilities.

24 Termination of Agreement

(a) The Customer may terminate the Agreement at any time by written notice to the Manager and, where relevant, the Custodian.
(b) The Manager or, where relevant, the Custodian may terminate the Agreement on three months' written notice to the Customer or by immediate notice if so required by any competent regulatory authority.

25 Consequences of Termination

(a) The Manager and, where relevant, the Custodian will complete expeditiously all transactions in progress at termination.
(b) Termination will not affect accrued rights, indemnities, existing commitments or any contractual provision intended to survive termination and will be without penalty or other additional payment. The Customer will pay (i) the fees of the Manager pro rata to the date of termination, and (ii) any additional expenses necessarily incurred by the Manager in terminating the Agreement and will bear any losses necessarily realised in settling or concluding outstanding obligations.
(c) On termination, the Manager may direct the Custodian or, as the case may be, the Outside Custodian, to retain and/or realise such assets as may be required to settle transactions already initiated and to pay any outstanding liabilities of the Customer. If there is a dispute as to the payment of fees to the Manager and/or the Custodian, the Customer may require the disputed amount to be held in an escrow account pending resolution of the dispute.

26 Joint and Sole Accounts

(a) If the Customer is more than one person, their obligations under the Agreement will be joint and several, any notice given to any of them will be deemed to be given to all of them and, subject to item 5 of the Schedule, the Manager may act on the instructions of any of them. On the death of any of the persons constituting the Customer the Agreement will not terminate and the Manager may treat the survivor(s) as the only person(s) entitled to or interested in the Fund.

(b) The Manager's authority under the Agreement is given by the Customer on behalf of its successors in title as well as of itself. Accordingly, on the death of an individual customer (where (a) above does not apply), the Agreement will continue in effect unless and until it is terminated by the Customer's personal representatives in accordance with paragraph 24. The Manager may (but, prior to any grant of representation, is not bound to) act on the instructions of the Customer's personal representatives.

27 Confidentiality and Disclosure

(a) Neither the Manager nor any Associate is obliged to disclose to the Customer or to take into consideration information either:
   (i) the disclosure of which by it to the Customer would or might be a breach of duty or confidence to any other person; or
   (ii) which comes to the notice of an employee, officer or agent of the Manager or of an Associate, but properly does not come to the actual notice of an individual managing the Fund.

(b) The parties to the Agreement shall not disclose information of a confidential nature acquired in consequence of it, except for information which they may be entitled or bound to disclose by law or which is requested by regulatory authorities, or which is disclosed to their advisers where reasonably necessary for the performance of their professional services.

28 Where the Custodian is not a Party to the Agreement (Outside Custodian)

If the Customer appoints an Outside Custodian for the whole or part of the Fund, the provisions of the Agreement relating to services provided by the Custodian in relation to the whole or that part of the Fund shall be of no effect. The Customer will, however, ensure that the Outside Custodian (i) enters into arrangements with regard to the provision of custody services for the whole or relevant part of the Fund which are satisfactory to the Manager, and (ii) is obliged to comply with any instructions of the Manager given in accordance with the Agreement, including directions under paragraph 25. The Manager will not be responsible for supervising an Outside Custodian.

PRIVATE CUSTOMERS AND OCCUPATIONAL PENSION SCHEMES

IMRO requires the following statements and warnings to be given to Private Customers and Occupational Pension Scheme Trustees, which are to be read subject, where relevant, to any provisions in the Schedule:

29 Cold Calling

In the interests of the proper management and administration of the Fund, the Manager, its representatives or employees, may call upon the Customer by telephone, or visit or otherwise communicate with the Customer without express invitation. The Customer's attention is drawn to the fact that the Customer will forfeit any right conferred by the FSA s.56 to treat as unenforceable any investment agreement entered into in the course of or in consequence of such a call.

30 Exchange Rate Risk

A movement of exchange rates may affect, unfavourably as well as favourably, any gain or loss on an investment.

31 Stabilisation

The Manager may effect transactions in investments the prices of which may be being stabilised. The Customer's attention is drawn to the attached Stabilisation Notice.

32 Investments Which are Not Readily Realisable

The Manager may invest in investments which are not readily realisable, which means that there is no recognised market for them. It may therefore be difficult to deal in such investments or to obtain reliable information about their value or the extent of the risks to which they are exposed.

33 Warrants

The Manager may effect transactions in warrants. Warrants often involve a high degree of gearing so that a relatively small movement in the price of the security to which the warrant relates may result in a disproportionately large movement, unfavourable as well as favourable, in the price of the warrant.

34 Fluctuation in Value of Investments

The value of investments and the income from them can go down as well as up and Customers may not get back the amounts originally invested.

Where the Custodian is a Party to the Agreement

These paragraphs apply only where the Custodian is a party to the Agreement or the Manager itself acts as Custodian. The Custodian's appointment shall take effect on the same date as the appointment of the Manager. The arrangements for the Custodian reporting and receiving instructions will be as stated in item 5 of the Schedule and paragraph 20 shall also apply, where relevant, to the Custodian. Details of the Custodian's regulator and any rights to a lien or security interest over the Customer's investments are as stated in item 3 of the Schedule.

C1 Custodian's Responsibilities

(a) The Custodian will be responsible for the safekeeping of any investments forming part of the Fund (including any cash), the settlement of transactions effected by the Manager, the collection of income and the effecting of other administrative actions in relation to the Fund. The Custodian will use reasonable care and diligence in carrying out these services and will at all times act in good faith.

(b) The Custodian may, where reasonable, employ agents (including Associates) to perform any administrative, custodial or ancillary services to assist the Custodian to perform its obligations under the Agreement. The Custodian will act in good faith and with due diligence in the selection, use and monitoring of agents (including sub-custodians).

C2 Registration of Securities

(a) Subject to item 3 of the Schedule, the Custodian will arrange for the Fund's UK securities (other than bearer securities for which the Custodian shall arrange safekeeping) to be registered in the name of a nominee company directly or indirectly as bare trustee for the Customer. The non-UK securities of the Fund will be held by the Custodian or to the order of the Custodian by sub-custodians chosen by it.

(b) The Custodian will keep records which identify each customer's investments separately; details of the Customer's investments held by the Custodian, nominee(s) and sub-custodians will be sent to the Customer at the intervals stated in item 5 of the Schedule. Investments forming part of the Fund may be pooled with those of other customers. Such investments may not be identifiable by separate certificates or other physical documents of title and, should the Custodian default, any shortfall may be shared pro-rata among all Customers whose investments are registered in the same name.

(c) Where any investments are in uncertificated form, or are otherwise transferable by book entry transfer, the Custodian may (where this is good market practice) use the services of any securities depository, clearing or settlement system, account controller or other participant in the relevant system, on such terms as it thinks fit, for the purposes of the holding and transfer of such investments (or entitlements thereto). Such investments or entitlements will be separately identifiable from any investments or entitlements held within the same system for the account of the Manager or Custodian.

(d) If so requested the Customer will promptly arrange for the execution or production of any documents necessary to carry out transactions effected in accordance with the Agreement. Where the Customer envisages a delay or failure in delivering such documents, the Customer shall notify the Custodian forthwith.

C3 Settlement

(a) The Custodian will settle all transactions undertaken by the Manager subject to the Custodian holding or receiving all necessary documents or funds and will do so on such basis as is good market practice for the type of investment and market concerned and normally on the basis of "cash against delivery". Delivery or payment by the other party to any such transaction will be at the Customer's risk, and the Custodian's obligation to account to the Customer for any investment or the proceeds of sale of any investment will be conditional upon receipt by the Custodian of the relevant documents or sale proceeds from the other party.

(b) The Custodian may operate a settlement system under which the Customer is debited with the purchase cost or credited with the proceeds of sale on the usual settlement (or subscription) days for the market concerned, conditionally upon settlement being ultimately effected. This may result in either a benefit or a loss to the Custodian or the Customer where settlement is effected at other times. The Custodian reserves the right to effect the cancellation of any debit or credit so attributed to the Customer if there are unreasonable delays or difficulties in settlement. In this event, the Custodian will promptly notify the Customer and the Manager but, where appropriate, will also continue to seek to effect settlement.

C4 Corporate Actions, Income Collection and Tax Reclaims

(a) The Custodian will attend to the collection of all income due on and the vesting of all other rights and entitlements attaching to investments in the Fund and will inform the Manager accordingly.
(b) Where stated in item 5 of the Schedule, the Manager or the Custodian will make or assist in making any tax repayment claims to which the Fund may be entitled.
(c) Dividends and distributions and any other income will be credited to the Customer not later than the date of receipt of cleared funds by the Custodian. Dividends and distributions on non-UK securities may be credited to the Customer on the date when the Custodian receives notification of receipt by the sub-custodian or after receipt of funds following any necessary currency conversion (which shall be promptly effected).
(d) The Custodian will promptly notify the Manager of all relevant offers, rights issues, investor meetings and other corporate actions of which the Custodian has received notice in its capacity as custodian and will comply promptly with all voting instructions.

C5 Liability

(a) The Custodian accepts responsibility for the acts and omissions of its nominees. The Custodian also accepts responsibility for loss to the Customer which is due to its negligence, wilful default or fraud, or that of any sub-custodian which is an Associate.
(b) Except insofar as the same may result from the negligence, wilful default or fraud of the Custodian, its sub-custodians, nominees or its or their employees, the Customer agrees to indemnify the Custodian against all costs, losses, claims and expenses which may be made against the Custodian either (i) as a result of any party claiming to be entitled to investments which form part of the Fund at the time when the Custodian first assumes custodial responsibility for the Fund or (ii) in consequence of any breach by the Customer of the Agreement or (iii) arising out of any action properly taken by the Custodian in accordance with the Agreement.
(c) Where the Customer is a trustee, the Customer's liability under the Agreement shall be limited, in the absence of fraud, to the assets of the trust from time to time.
(d) If any sub-custodian should fail to deliver any necessary documents or to account for any securities the Custodian will take all reasonable steps on behalf of the Customer to recover such documents or securities, or any sums due, or compensation in lieu thereof, but subject thereto (and to C5(a) above) shall not be liable for any such failure. All reasonable costs incurred by the Custodian shall be paid by the Customer.

C6 Compensation

Item 3 of the Schedule will state whether the Custodian is a member of the Deposit Protection Scheme established under the Banking Act 1987. Payments under the Scheme are limited to 90% of a depositor's total deposits subject to a maximum payment to any one depositor of £18,000 (or ECU 20,000, if greater).

C7 Termination

(a) Where the Custodian resigns or its appointment is terminated in accordance with paragraph 24(a) (but the Agreement continues in force) then, except where the Pensions Act 1995 applies or the Customer informs the Manager within 20 business days that it wishes to make its own arrangements, the Manager may appoint a successor.

(b) On termination, the Custodian will promptly account to the Customer for the assets held by it for the Fund and direct its nominee company and any sub-custodian to do likewise, save that the Manager shall be entitled to direct the Custodian or, as the case may be, the Outside Custodian, to retain and/or realise such assets as may be required to settle transactions already initiated and to pay any outstanding liabilities of the Customer. If a party to the Agreement initiates a change of Custodian that party shall be responsible for any resulting costs.

C8 Foreign Law and Practice

The Custodian draws to the attention of the Customer the fact that, in certain overseas jurisdictions, there may be different settlement, legal and regulatory requirements to those applying in the UK and also different practices for the separate identification and segregation of customers' investments.

C9 Fees

Save where otherwise specified in item 4 of the Schedule and subject to paragraph 16(b), the Custodian's fees and expenses shall be met by the Manager.

C10 Conflicts of Interest

The Custodian notifies the Customer that it may be subject to conflicts of interest in relation to the Fund similar to those identified in paragraph 14(c) above.

Appendix 7
Checklist for service agreement

[17.1]

1. Parties
2. Definitions
3. Description of services to be provided
4. Details of persons within service company who are responsible for the services
5. Documents required by service provider
6. Hardware/software or any other equipment required by service provider which is in the possession of the company outsourcing the services (the company outsourcing the services will have to ensure that licences or maintenance contracts etc with third parties cover or are extended to cover or are assigned to the service provider: the value/cost of the items transferred or assigned should be borne by the service provider)
7. Fees: the amount; whether VAT is payable; when to be paid; interest on late payment
8. Details of information to be contained in reports to be produced by service provider and regularity of reports
9. Timetable if appropriate for delivery of services and any penalty to be imposed for failure to meet timetable
10. Warranty on standards or quality applied to services provided and compliance with relevant legislation[1]
11. Warranty on abilities of companies to enter into agreement
12. Rights of company outsourcing services to access/take possession of files, records and reports relating to the services in possession of service provider and to audit for compliance
13. Copyright of anything produced by the service provider to be property of outsourcing company
14. Standard clauses on assignation, delegation, termination, insurance, liabilities, warranties, confidentiality, exclusion of third party rights, force majeure, non-enticement of personnel, waiver, severability, entire agreement, notices, arbitration, applicable law and jurisdiction.

[1] If the services include services regulated by PIA or IMRO then an undertaking that service company will comply with relevant rules.

Appendix 8
Checklist for standard reassurance agreement

[18.1]

REASSURANCE TREATY

Summary of contents
Scope

Parties: identifies the Reassurer and the Ceding Company
Treaty Type: eg Quota Share, Surplus
Commencement Date
Termination Date: continuous
Policies Covered: eg Group Pensions Plans
Risks Covered: eg Mortality, morbidity
Geographical locations of Reassurer and Ceding company, currency

Limits

Retention
Minimum Cession
Underwriting Limit
Treaty Limit
Claims Approval Limit
Claims Expense Limit

Cover (Amounts Insured and Reinsured)

Total Cover
Cover Reinsured
Cover Calculation Date: Premiums – beginning of year, claims-date of death or disability

Premiums

Reinsurance Premium Rates: usually shown in appendices
Geo-Occupational adjustment
Past Claims Experience Adjustment
Free Cover: formulae for the various benefits covered.
Reinsurance Premium: Product of rate and cover

Accounts and Documentation

Reassurance Premium Mode
Method of Settlement, Account Office and Account Period

Method of Payment of Claims
Account Information Provided (outgoing A/C)
Method of Data Transfer for Account Information
Statistical Information Required, Policy details, Life insured Details, Benefit Details

Special Conditions

Payments on Account

General Terms and Conditions

Basic Agreement
Definitions
Retention
Reinsurance Cession
Reinsurance Premiums
Documentation and Accounts
Alteration, Cancellations, Lapses and Reinstatements
Claims
Information
Notification of Major Business Changes
Set-Off
Interest
Amendments
Termination for New Business
Special Termination
Notices

Appendix 9
Sample wording for financial reassurance clauses

[19.1]
FINANCIAL REASSURANCE

Explanatory note: financial reassurance will normally comprise a standard reassurance agreement covering the reassurance of some part of the policy liabilities plus additional clauses which deal with the repayment. The undernoted clause is from a financing treaty and describes repayment via supplementary reassurance. Each treaty is different and the undernoted clause is simply an example.

PREMIUMS

Supplementary Reinsurance Premiums

Normal Basis

Supplementary Reinsurance Premiums are payable monthly in respect of each product [details of reassured products] and for each year of inception of business [dates]. They are equal to the Appropriate Percentage of the Statutory Profits for the corresponding month included in the projections included in Appendix [ ], minus the Administration Charge for the month.

Supplementary Reinsurance Premiums are payable until the Deficit Account is reduced to zero.

The Appropriate Percentage is defined as 80% for amounts in respect of the period [dates] inclusive and 100% thereafter.

The projections in Appendix [ ] assume volumes and mix of business by product, age, term and risk benefits covered and make various assumptions regarding mortality, morbidity, fund charges to cover risk benefits and expenses, policy fees, lapses, surrenders, commission repayments, expenses, valuation bases and assumptions, investment returns and other matters. Various of these assumptions, including inter alia the volumes and product mix and expense assumptions, are also set out in Appendix [ ].

The Ceding Company warrants that all assumptions used in these projections, with the exception of expenses and volumes and mix of business, are the same as those used in the report [details of actuarial report].

The Ceding Company warrants that the Statutory Profit for [date] and later years calculated on the assumptions underlying the figures included in Appendix [ ], but based on the actual volumes and mix of business in force as at [date], is not, in any three year period, less than 95% of the figures included in Appendix [ ] as attached at the Treaty Commencement Date. If this proves not to be the case, the Reinsurer has the right to vary the terms of the treaty in a manner which is consistent with the degree of shortfall.

Subject to mutual agreement Appendix [ ] may be replaced, from time to time, by a revised Appendix [ ] on revised assumptions which more accurately project future statutory profits.

Net Premium

The Net Premium in respect of each product for each month and each year of inception is equal to the Supplementary Reinsurance Premiums calculated as above but based on Statutory Profits based on the actual mix of business and allowing for actual experience as regards lapses, surrender, expenses, commission repayments, mortality and morbidity in respect of risk retained (replaced by reinsurance premiums for risks reinsured, including risks reinsured under other treaties), fund charges to cover risk benefits and expenses, policy fees and investment returns. With regard to other matters and in particular, but without affecting the generality of the foregoing, with respect to valuation bases and assumptions, the assumptions and models used will be the same as those underlying Appendix [ ] except that increases in expense levels assumed are allowed provided they are covered by increases in policy fees and fund charges for expenses.

Appendix 10
Checklist for tied agency agreement

[20.1]

1. Appointment
2. Term of agreement
3. Responsibilities of agent
   - Due diligence
   - Proper facilities
   - Market intelligence – enquiries
   - Compliance with law and PIA rules and co-operation with regulatory bodies
   - Polorisation: activities restricted to Principal's products and services
   - Confidentiality
   - No authority to bind principal – extent of agents authority
   - Sales levels
   - Financial: separate bank account, Client Money Rules, commission, expenses
   - Monthly/Annual reports
4. Responsibilities of the Principal
   - Marketing literature, advertisements, information
   - Payment of commission, expenses
   - Setting sales targets
   - Authorisation under FSA 1986, rights to audit and monitor compliance, access to files, records, databases etc
   - Responsibility for agents acts in relation to giving advice on investments under agreement
5. Territorial or other restrictions (this should be drafted so as not to breach competition law)
6. Termination of agreement and consequences – commercial agents (Council Directive) Regulations 1993
7. No joint venture or partnership
8. IT, trademarks
9. Standard clauses on assignation, delegation, notices, applicable law, third party rights exclusion, definitions, interpretation

Appendix 11
Checklist for scheme under Insurance Companies Act 1982, Schedule 2C

[21.1]

1. Definitions.
2. Descriptions of transferor/ee companies.
3. That business (description/definition to include assets and liabilities of long-term business) will be transferred in accordance with the Scheme.
4. That the transferor/transferee companies will be bound by the Scheme.
5. Description of mechanics of how business to be transferred: date business vests in transferee company and that it will form part of the long-term business of that company
   (i) if assets being transferred need consent or some other formality before they vest in the transferee company after the Scheme has been sanctioned by the court then provision has to be made for this – ie that there will be subsequent vesting dates and that the transferor company will hold any assets in trust for the transferee company until that date;
   (ii) indemnity given by the transferee company to the transferor company in respect of transferred liabilities;
   (iii) both companies undertake to execute any relevant documents and take such other acts necessary to perfect the transfer of any assets;
   (iv) if any payment or right is given to the transferor company after the business has been transferred then the transferor company undertakes to pay the amount or transfer the right to the transferor company.
6. Description of the internal sub-funds of long-term business fund of transferee company and how the transferred business is to be divided amongst these and that transferee company has the right to restructure the sub-funds subject to the auditors of the transferor company certifying that the correct funds have been transferred and the appointed actuary certifying that any changes to the fund structure are equitable as between the policyholders (will not need this if transferee company is new company).
7. Principles by which the distribution of surplus and bonus levels determined in respect of with profits business.
8. That any premiums and other sums payable to the transferor company to become automatically payable to the transferee company and any mandates in force construed accordingly.
9. That any annuities or other sums payable by the transferor company to become automatically payable by the transferee company.
10. List of consents and/or waivers required before the Scheme can take effect (eg from HMT, IR, Pensions Schemes Office, OPRA, IMRO etc).

Index